Early Childhood Special Education Programs and Practices

Series Editor
Dee Berlinghoff, PhD

Early Childhood Special Education Programs and Practices

Editors

Karin M. Fisher, PhD, CDE
Georgia Southern University
Statesboro, Georgia

Kate E. Zimmer, PhD
Branch Alliance for Educator Diversity
Austin, Texas

SLACK
INCORPORATED

SLACK Incorporated
6900 Grove Road
Thorofare, NJ 08086 USA
856-848-1000   Fax: 856-848-6091
www.slackbooks.com
ISBN: 978-1-63091-702-9
© 2023 by SLACK Incorporated

Vice President, Editorial: Jennifer Kilpatrick
Vice President, Marketing: Mary Sasso
Vice President, Acquisitions: Tony Schiavo
Director of Editorial Operations: Jennifer Cahill
Vice President/Creative Director: Thomas Cavallaro
Cover Artist: Lori Shields

Instructors: *Early Childhood Special Education Programs and Practices* includes ancillary materials specifically available for faculty use. Included are an *Instructor's Manual* and PowerPoint slides. Please visit www.efacultylounge.com to obtain access.

The procedures and practices described in this publication should be implemented in a manner consistent with the professional standards set for the circumstances that apply in each specific situation. Every effort has been made to confirm the accuracy of the information presented and to correctly relate generally accepted practices. The authors, editors, and publisher cannot accept responsibility for errors or exclusions or for the outcome of the material presented herein. There is no expressed or implied warranty of this book or information imparted by it. Care has been taken to ensure that drug selection and dosages are in accordance with currently accepted/recommended practice. Off-label uses of drugs may be discussed. Due to continuing research, changes in government policy and regulations, and various effects of drug reactions and interactions, it is recommended that the reader carefully review all materials and literature provided for each drug, especially those that are new or not frequently used. Some drugs or devices in this publication have clearance for use in a restricted research setting by the Food and Drug and Administration or FDA. Each professional should determine the FDA status of any drug or device prior to use in their practice.

Any review or mention of specific companies or products is not intended as an endorsement by the author or publisher.

SLACK Incorporated uses a review process to evaluate submitted material. Prior to publication, educators or clinicians provide important feedback on the content that we publish. We welcome feedback on this work.

Library of Congress Control Number: 2022941839

For permission to reprint material in another publication, contact SLACK Incorporated. Authorization to photocopy items for internal, personal, or academic use is granted by SLACK Incorporated provided that the appropriate fee is paid directly to Copyright Clearance Center. Prior to photocopying items, please contact the Copyright Clearance Center at 222 Rosewood Drive, Danvers, MA 01923 USA; phone: 978-750-8400; website: www.copyright.com; email: info@copyright.com

Printed in the United States of America.

Last digit is print number: 10   9   8   7   6   5   4   3   2   1

CONTENTS

Acknowledgments...vii

About the Editors...ix

Contributing Authors...xi

Introduction...xiii

Chapter 1   Overview of Early Childhood and Development (Ages 4 to 8) 1
            Karin M. Fisher, PhD, CDE and Kate E. Zimmer, PhD

Chapter 2   Using Culturally Relevant Pedagogy With All Children and Families 23
            Nai-Cheng Kuo, PhD, BCBA

Chapter 3   Early Childhood Assessments (Ages 4 to 8) 41
            Melissa K. Driver, PhD and Christie H. Ingram, MEd

Chapter 4   Positive Behavioral Supports and Strategies for Young Children 69
            Kathy Ralabate Doody, PhD and Gliset Colón, PhD

Chapter 5   Planning for Success 99
            Marla J. Lohmann, PhD; Ariane N. Gauvreau, PhD, BCBA-D;
            and Katrina A. Hovey, PhD

Chapter 6   Language Development (Prekindergarten to Second Grade)................ 117
            Sherri K. Prosser, PhD; Kate E. Zimmer, PhD; Zachary T. Barnes, PhD;
            and Karin M. Fisher, PhD, CDE

Chapter 7   Early Childhood Reading... 139
            Dena D. Slanda, PhD and Marisa Macy, PhD

Chapter 8   Emergent Writing in the Early Childhood Years.......................... 161
            Marisa Macy, PhD and Dena D. Slanda, PhD

Chapter 9   Early Childhood Mathematics (Ages 4 to 8)............................. 179
            Lisa A. Finnegan, PhD

Chapter 10 Teaching Science to Students With Disabilities in........................207
            Early Childhood Classrooms
            Karin M. Fisher, PhD, CDE and Kania A. Greer, EdD

Chapter 11   Social Studies in Prekindergarten to Second-Grade Classrooms 233
Stacy Delacruz, EdD and Raynice Jean-Sigur, PhD

Chapter 12   Social-Emotional Learning for Young Children 257
Marla J. Lohmann, PhD; Kania A. Greer, EdD; and Marisa Macy, PhD

Conclusion by Kate E. Zimmer, PhD and Karin M. Fisher, PhD, CDE 269

Glossary 271

Financial Disclosures 279

Index 281

Instructors: *Early Childhood Special Education Programs and Practices* includes ancillary materials specifically available for faculty use. Included are an *Instructor's Manual* and PowerPoint slides. Please visit www.efacultylounge.com to obtain access.

ACKNOWLEDGMENTS

We want to thank the following for their support:

To my students, I am grateful to have known each one of you. You taught me more than you will ever know.

To my sons, Jacob, Kyle, and Scott, for their ongoing support and encouragement and especially to my husband, Steve, for his unwavering faith in me.

To my youngest son with autism, thank you for teaching me patience, to focus on what is important, and to let the rest go.

To Kahli Crews, undergraduate research assistant at Georgia Southern University in the Department of Elementary and Special Education. We will forever be grateful for your support and eye for detail. The undergraduate perspective of each chapter is what will set this textbook apart.

I also want to thank the Georgia Southern College of Education for their continued support of scholarly pursuits and accomplishments.

—*Karin M. Fisher, PhD, CDE*

To educators, you have one of the hardest and most rewarding jobs on the planet. There are not enough words to express the gratitude I feel for my own children's teachers, my friends and colleagues, and all teachers across the country. I see you, hear you, and I value the work that you do. Thank you for making a difference each and every day. I hope this textbook helps create more inclusive and welcoming classrooms for all students.

To my husband, Jeff, thank you for your support, patience, and humor; you make life entertaining and a better place.

To my boys, Evan, Wes, and Logan, thank you for making each day brighter, fun, and a bit crazier; I love you to the moon and back.

Karin, it has been a fun ride! I appreciate your work ethic and friendship. Thank you for leading such a great team.

—*Kate E. Zimmer, PhD*

ABOUT THE EDITORS

Karin M. Fisher, PhD, CDE started her career in education when she earned her master's of art in teaching special education from the University of Central Florida in Orlando, Florida. She taught students with moderate intellectual disabilities and autism as a self-contained, resource, and inclusion teacher for 8 years. She was also the co–department chair for her school's large special education department. In 2013, she was accepted into a grant program at the University of Central Florida to start her career in academia, earning her PhD in 2016. Her dissertation compared standardized science scores with participation in extracurricular science, technology, engineering, and mathematics activities.

Currently, Dr. Fisher teaches undergraduate and graduate courses at Georgia Southern University in the Department of Elementary and Special Education in Statesboro, Georgia. Her courses include special education procedures, methods, leadership, curriculum and instruction, language development, and collaboration. She also has extensive experience supervising special education internships.

Dr. Fisher was nominated for and accepted the position of vice president, president elect, and eventually will be president of the Georgia Council for Exceptional Children. She co-chairs the Early Career Faculty Special Interest Group of the Teacher Education Division of the Council for Exceptional Children and is a member of the Division for Early Childhood. She also was selected to co-chair the Georgia State Special Education Advisory Panel where she represents parents of students with disabilities in her district as well as institutes in higher education across the state. As the parent of a son with an autism spectrum disorder, she is in a unique position to view special education from the educator and parent lens.

Dr. Fisher's work reflects her expertise in early childhood special education. She has extensive experience using and teaching evidence-based strategies and high-leverage practices in special education. Her education and experience working with her son, academic peers, students, their families, school personnel, and administrators contribute to her qualifications to edit and contribute to this text.

Kate E. Zimmer, PhD received a bachelor's degree in elementary education from Saint Leo University, St. Leo, Florida, and a master's degree in curriculum and instruction from the University of Central Florida in Orlando, Florida. Dr. Zimmer taught at the elementary level for 7 years in a multi-age classroom serving students with a variety of special needs. She was also involved in pediatric research on attention-deficit/hyperactivity disorder, childhood anxiety, and childhood depression. In 2013, she graduated with her PhD in special education from the University of Florida, Gainesville, Florida, where she examined the effects of a storybook reading intervention on the initiation of joint attention in young children with autism.

Dr. Zimmer is currently Branch Alliance for Educator Diversity's Director of the BIRCH Professional Learning Center in Austin, Texas. In this role, Dr. Zimmer collaborates with the BIRCH professional learning and development team to create goals and design trainings for in-person and virtual programs, resources, and learning communities. In addition, Dr. Zimmer leads Branch Alliance for Educator Diversity's mixed-reality simulation laboratory where she provides leadership by coordinating and directing activities to ensure the successful operation of the laboratory. These activities include technical direction, simulation design, strategic planning, fundraising, outreach, partnerships, and working closely with simulation specialists to ensure quality control. In recent years, her research focus has been on teacher preparation, high-leverage practices, and mixed-reality simulation. Dr. Zimmer works with numerous faculty members and external partners to purposefully embed mixed-reality simulation within courses and professional development so that pre- and in-service teachers are able to engage in a powerful, interactive learning experience that prepares them for the real world and hones in on specific teaching strategies that impact student outcomes.

Dr. Zimmer has taught both graduate and undergraduate courses that focused on autism, behavior, curriculum and instruction, and instructional practices. She developed an online graduate endorsement in autism spectrum disorders and works closely with the Early Childhood Faculty Special Interest Group in the Teacher Education Division of the Council for Exceptional Children. Her numerous peer-reviewed presentations, articles, and grants along with her passion for teacher education make her an excellent co-author and editor for this textbook.

CONTRIBUTING AUTHORS

Zachary T. Barnes, PhD (Chapter 6)
Austin Peay State University
Clarksville, Tennessee

Gliset Colón, PhD (Chapter 4)
SUNY Buffalo State College
Buffalo, New York

Stacy Delacruz, EdD (Chapter 11)
Kennesaw State University
Kennesaw, Georgia

Kathy Ralabate Doody, PhD (Chapter 4)
Exceptional Education
SUNY Buffalo State College
Buffalo, New York

Melissa K. Driver, PhD (Chapter 3)
Kennesaw State University
Kennesaw, Georgia

Lisa A. Finnegan, PhD (Chapter 9)
Florida Atlantic University
Boca Raton, Florida

Ariane N. Gauvreau, PhD, BCBA-D (Chapter 5)
University of Washington
Seattle, Washington

Kania A. Greer, EdD (Chapters 10 and 12)
Georgia Southern University
Statesboro, Georgia

Katrina A. Hovey, PhD (Chapter 5)
Western Oregon University
Monmouth, Oregon

Christie H. Ingram, MEd (Chapter 3)
Kennesaw State University
Kennesaw, Georgia

Raynice Jean-Sigur, PhD (Chapter 11)
Kennesaw State University
Kennesaw, Georgia

Nai-Cheng Kuo, PhD, BCBA (Chapter 2)
Augusta University
Augusta, Georgia

Marla J. Lohmann, PhD (Chapters 5 and 12)
Colorado Christian University
Lakewood, Colorado

Marisa Macy, PhD (Chapters 7, 8, and 12)
University of Nebraska at Kearney
Kearney, Nebraska

Sherri K. Prosser, PhD (Chapter 6)
Austin Peay State University
Clarksville, Tennessee

Dena D. Slanda, PhD (Chapters 7 and 8)
University of Central Florida
Orlando, Florida

INTRODUCTION

Welcome! You are about to embark on a learning experience based on multiple experts in early childhood special education. This book aims to prepare pre- and in-service teachers to develop the knowledge, skills, and dispositions to deliver evidence-based instruction that promotes positive academic and behavioral outcomes for young children with disabilities. This methods book emphasizes high-leverage practices (HLPs), evidence-based practices, and culturally sustaining pedagogy in alignment with the Division for Early Childhood (DEC) Recommended Practices, skills, and competencies. It will provide you with the skills and techniques you need to serve young children, their families, and their communities. Pre- and in-service early childhood special education teachers, general early childhood education teachers, administrators of early childhood special education and early childhood education programs, and families will find this book useful.

This text provides examples of educational, social, independent, and other various learning activities within the specialized curriculum while keeping the requirements of the Individuals with Disabilities Education Act (IDEA) in mind. We emphasize pedagogy that provides HLPs and guides young students to learn in different content areas while gaining foundational skills.

Organization of This Text

This book begins with an overview of early childhood and development and the seminal theories that guide teaching young children. It focuses on cognitive, behavioral, and social-emotional learning. We also include a detailed discussion of culturally relevant pedagogy and building relationships with students, families, communities, and school personnel. Experts provide an understanding of the functions of behavior and an overview of positive behavior intervention and supports and help pre- and in-service teachers develop skills to implement proactive strategies to create a caring and positive classroom. We cover eligibility, standardization, issues, and vocabulary used in early childhood assessment, emphasizing data-based planning and progress monitoring. We include differentiation, Universal Design for Learning, writing standards-based lesson plans, explicit instruction, and Individualized Education Program goals and objectives. Experts provide information on early literacy and language behaviors that precede and later grow into conventional literacy skills.

This text explains explicit, evidence-based literacy instruction for students with disabilities within the content areas with a focus on phonological awareness, word study, fluency, vocabulary, comprehension, and writing strategies. This text includes evidence-based instruction on teaching mathematics. We also provide information on evidence-based pedagogy, including the 5E model of instruction, HLPs, interventions, and learning supports in science and social studies.

Chapter 1: Overview of Early Childhood and Development (Ages 4 to 8)

This chapter provides an overview of early childhood and development for ages 4 through 8, focusing on developmental domains in cognitive, motor, social-emotional, and language skills. The content includes early child development in physical, intellectual, social, and emotional skills. We provide seminal theories of child development, including those by Freud, Piaget, Erikson, Pavlov, Skinner, Watson, Bandura, and Vygotsky. Next, we examine how the developmental domains were formed from the theories to determine school readiness and the need for interventions or special education services when children struggle in one or more developmental stages. Lastly, we introduce the DEC Recommended Practices and the HLPs in special education.

Chapter 2: Using Culturally Relevant Pedagogy With All Children and Families

This chapter discusses cultural awareness and how it is vital to reduce the misdiagnosis of students with disabilities. The author provides information on how teachers need to know students' diverse cultural and linguistic backgrounds that affect their learning. The chapter provides the reader with the knowledge to respond to these students' unique needs, adjust instructional activities, and collaborate with others. The term *culturally relevant pedagogy* is used as an umbrella term in this chapter to embrace different cultural theories. This chapter aims to help teachers understand cultural theories and align them with HLPs in special education.

Chapter 3: Early Childhood Assessments (Ages 4 to 8)

This chapter explores the purpose of evaluations, cultural and linguistic considerations, collaboration in assessment, the evaluation's role in the eligibility process, guidelines for early childhood assessment, forms of evaluation, data-based individualization, and progress monitoring. Readers are exposed to numerous ways to assess students and how to use valid and reliable data with fidelity to make educational decisions. This chapter describes how teachers use summative assessments to determine what students currently know and can do. The reader will learn that teachers use formative assessments to assess instruction design and intervention programs to best support learning through data-based individualization. The chapter focuses on assessment as a collaborative process involving numerous key stakeholders, including family members and other school personnel.

Chapter 4: Positive Behavioral Supports and Strategies for Young Children

Research shows that thousands of preschool children are subjected to disciplinary action each year, resulting in school suspensions or expulsions; this chapter focuses on behavior. Readers will learn how we can and should reverse the troubling trend of high preschool removal rates, particularly because early childhood programs establish a critical foundation for years of subsequent education. The authors stress the importance of high-quality early childhood programs. They also provide an overview of Early Head Start and the U.S. Departments of Education and Health and Human Services. The chapter exposes the reader to well-designed research studies that have shown us how to create early childhood settings that are linguistically and culturally sensitive, to use evidence-based practices as part of the instructional model, and to develop the academic and social-emotional skills of children. This chapter discusses the components of effective, culturally and linguistically strong early childhood practices in behavior management using the tenets of evidence-based practice while maintaining a learning environment that fosters a child's academic and social development.

Chapter 5: Planning for Success

This chapter focuses on teachers using evidence-based teaching strategies that align with the DEC Recommended Practices and the Council for Exceptional Children's HLPs. This chapter offers a brief overview of practices that meet this criterion. First, the authors present information about differentiated instruction and the use of the Universal Design for Learning framework to ensure teachers meet all students' learning needs. Second, the authors discuss standards-based lesson planning. The third topic the chapter presents is explicit instruction. Finally, the authors discuss the development of SMART (Specific, Measurable, Action oriented, Relevant and realistic, and Time limited) Individualized Education Program goals for young children.

Chapter 6: Language Development (Prekindergarten to Second Grade)

Chapter 6 covers the development of language, especially as it relates to children ages 4 through 8. Additionally, the authors explain and show connections between evidence-based practices, the Council for Exceptional Children's HLPs in special education, and the DEC's Recommended Practices that contribute to language acquisition. Lastly, readers will learn the role of phonological awareness, pragmatics, semantics, and syntax in promoting language development. Suggestions for teaching include adult–child interactions, play-based activities, peer interventions, and assistive technology devices.

Chapter 7: Early Childhood Reading

This chapter covers emergent reading. The reader will learn how oral language acquisition develops over time to include reading text with accuracy, fluency, and making meaning of the words on a page. This chapter (a) introduces the learning theories that have guided teacher approaches to reading instruction; (b) provides the elements of building literacy knowledge (e.g., print-rich environments, activating background knowledge, and selecting appropriate texts); and (c) establishes the five components of reading (i.e., phonemic awareness, phonics, fluency, vocabulary, and reading comprehension) that have guided reading instruction since 2000. Furthermore, this chapter shares each of the models of reading instruction that drive today's reading programs. Finally, this chapter highlights the need for collaboration between teachers, families, and professionals.

Chapter 8: Emergent Writing in the Early Childhood Years

In this chapter, the reader will learn that writing is a skill that develops in early childhood slowly and over time. This chapter covers other writing domains, such as fine motor and cognitive development. The reader will learn how professionals identify instructional targets and high-impact practices for creating opportunities for young children to develop their writing skills. This chapter examines high-impact practices designed to address young children's emergent writing with and without disabilities.

Chapter 9: Early Childhood Mathematics (Ages 4 to 8)

This chapter focuses on providing teacher candidates with an understanding of mathematical methods for children ages 4 through 8. The reader will connect student learning to mathematical standards and foundational organizations and pedagogical theorists. This chapter's contents provide a practical approach for assessing students' understanding and knowledge of mathematical concepts and an engaging process for instruction that fosters a lifelong curiosity and interest in mathematical concepts. The reader will explore both formal and informal assessments and both direct instruction and incidental learning opportunities in mathematical activities. Additionally, the reader will identify the importance of structuring their mathematics instruction with a continuous learning mindset by extending learning into the home environment through collaboration with students' families.

Chapter 10: Teaching Science to Students With Disabilities in Early Childhood Classrooms

This chapter covers the development of scientific practices that allow for the joy of play while inspiring a child to develop critical thinking skills. Using two well-established, evidence-based pedagogical practices, the 5E model and play-debrief-replay, this chapter provides early childhood educators with a foundation for taking learning beyond play and into discovery while encouraging a child's development in asking critical questions. The reader will learn that purposeful planning of experiences for early childhood learners requires educators to think beyond a science lesson or activity and consider all learning opportunities. This chapter provides educators with two different lesson plan examples and the Next Generation Science Standards for educators to implement into their lesson plans. The text also provides strategies for educators to differentiate science instruction to meet the needs of all learners. The authors also present ideas for specially designed science instruction for students with disabilities. Lastly, this chapter covers HLPs for students with disabilities and DEC Recommended Practices to equip the reader with evidence-based approaches to meet all students' needs.

Chapter 11: Social Studies in Prekindergarten to Second-Grade Classrooms

This chapter introduces the foundation of an early childhood classroom and the importance of forming relationships with others, building community, engaging with others, and contributing to the group. The authors discuss a developmental approach to teaching social studies in early childhood classrooms. This discussion highlights evidence-based instruction in special education within social studies. The chapter introduces social studies strands from K–5, along with suggestions for teachers to consider when developing lesson plans and preparing to teach social studies. The author aligns the recommendations with evidence-based practices and HLPs.

Chapter 12: Social-Emotional Learning for Young Children

This chapter provides teachers with practical strategies for supporting social-emotional development in the early childhood classroom. The authors begin by explaining the prevalence and importance of understanding childhood trauma. Next, they describe how social-emotional learning integrates with HLPs and the DEC Recommended Practices as well as with positive behavior intervention and supports mentioned in Chapter 4. The authors provide suggestions for storybooks to read and the steps to creating evidence-based direct instruction lessons. Lastly, the authors describe how to partner with families to create planned and routine learning opportunities.

Supplemental Materials

Supplemental materials include an *Instructor's Manual* and PowerPoint slides. The *Instructor's Manual* contains chapter review questions and answers and resources. The PowerPoint presentations reinforce the topics covered in each chapter. Instructors should visit efacultylounge.com to obtain access.

Overview of Early Childhood and Development (Ages 4 to 8)

Karin M. Fisher, PhD, CDE and Kate E. Zimmer, PhD

INTRODUCTION

Early childhood is a critical time in child development. Children vary in how they develop physical, intellectual, social, and emotional skills. As a result of these variabilities, developmental psychologists suggested theories on early childhood development stages and when children should reach different levels. Seminal theories include those by Freud, Piaget, Erikson, Pavlov, Skinner, Watson, Bandura, and Vygotsky. From these theories, scientists created developmental domains (cognitive, socioemotional, motor, and language skills) to determine children's school readiness in early childhood. When children struggle in one or more developmental domains, they need interventions and may be eligible for special education services. When teaching young children, educators need to consider the Division for Early Childhood Recommended Practices and the high-leverage practices in special education.

Fisher, K. M., & Zimmer, K. E. (Eds.).
Early Childhood Special Education Programs and Practices (pp. 1-22).
© 2023 SLACK Incorporated.

CHAPTER OBJECTIVES

→ Compare and contrast the different theories of child development.
→ Describe the developmental domains of child development.
→ Determine when teachers should refer students for a special education evaluation.
→ Provide at least one strategy for each of the developmental domains.

KEY TERMS

- **Applied Behavioral Analysis:** A type of therapy that focuses on improving specific behaviors, such as social skills, communication, reading, and academics, as well as adaptive learning skills, such as fine motor dexterity, hygiene, grooming, domestic capabilities, punctuality, and job competence.
- **Behaviorism:** The theory or doctrine that scientists can accurately study human or animal psychology only by examining and analyzing objectively observable and quantifiable behavioral events, contrasting with subjective mental states.
- **Classical Conditioning:** A learning process that occurs when two stimuli are repeatedly paired; a response that is first elicited by the second stimulus is eventually elicited by the first stimulus alone.
- **Cognitive Development:** Attempts to understand, explain, organize, manipulate, construct, and predict the world around them.
- **Dexterity:** Skill or adroitness in using the hands or body; agility.
- **Egocentric Speech:** The act of a child talking to themself, usually through an event or activity.
- **Emergent Writing:** The first attempts at the writing process, imitating writing by creating drawings and symbolic markings representing their thoughts and ideas.
- **Erogenous Zone:** An area of the body that is sensitive to stimulation, such as touch.
- **Fine Motor Skills:** The small movements of the hands, wrists, fingers, feet, toes, lips, and tongue.
- **Gross Motor Skills:** Physical skills that require whole-body movement and involve core-stabilizing muscles of the body to perform everyday functions.
- **Literacy Development:** The ongoing development of skills needed to communicate through written communication successfully.
- **Metacognitive Strategies:** Methods used to help students understand how they learn; in other words, it means processes designed for students to "think" about their "thinking."
- **Operant Conditioning:** A type of associative learning process through which scientists modify the strength of behavior by reinforcement or punishment.
- **Oral Comprehension:** The ability to listen to a text, interpret the vocabulary, derive sentences using that vocabulary, and discuss the interpretation of the text.
- **Positive Behavior Interventions and Supports:** A proactive approach that schools use to improve school safety and promote positive behavior.
- **Print Awareness:** The ability to understand the general rules and functions of written language.
- **Proximal Development:** The distance between the actual developmental level as determined by independent problem-solving and the level of potential development determined through problem-solving under adult guidance or collaboration with more capable peers.
- **Psychoanalytic:** A systematic structure of theories concerning the relation of conscious and unconscious psychological processes.
- **Punishments:** A change in a human's or animal's surroundings, which occurs after a given behavior or response, that reduces the likelihood of that behavior occurring again in the future.

- **Reinforcement:** The process of encouraging or establishing a belief or pattern of behavior, especially by encouragement or reward.
- **Representational Thinking:** The intellectual ability of a child to picture something in their mind.
- **Reward:** An appetitive stimulus given to a human or some other animal to alter its behavior.
- **Scaffolding Instruction:** A process through which a teacher adds support for students to enhance learning and aid in the mastery of tasks.
- **School Readiness:** School readiness is foundational across early childhood systems and programs. It means children are ready for school, families are prepared to support their children's learning, and schools are prepared for children.
- **Social Learning Theory:** Explains human behavior in terms of continuous reciprocal interaction between cognitive, behavioral, and environmental influences.
- **Socioemotional:** How children start to understand who they are, what they are feeling, and what to expect when interacting with others.
- **Stimuli:** Any object or event that elicits a sensory or behavioral response in an organism.
- **Theory of Mind:** The ability to distinguish between their point of view and the point of view of others.

> *"When you are born into a world where you don't fit in,*
> *it's because you were born to help create a new one."*
> —*Anonymous*

Early childhood is a stage in human development and is defined by psychologists as the time between birth and 8 years of age. This text focuses on the latter part of early childhood, which covers the more formal school years (i.e., ages 4 to 8). Children in this age range typically are in prekindergarten through second grade.

As children grow, they develop in several different ways. Physical, intellectual, social, and emotional changes take place. It is often difficult to determine "typical development" because children grow and mature at different rates, and the child's development is influenced by genetic makeup, environment, and cognitive skills. In the pages that follow, the reader will learn about the theories and domains of child development and special education roles. We provide an overview of the high-leverage practices (HLPs) in special education and the Division for Early Childhood (DEC) Recommended Practices.

THEORIES OF CHILD DEVELOPMENT

Child development theories provide a foundation for early childhood education because they explain how children change and grow. Understanding child development is essential because it allows educators to better understand children's cognitive, emotional, physical, social, and educational growth. A few of the major child development theories are summarized in the following paragraphs.

Psychoanalytic Theory

Sigmund Freud's psychosexual development theory, also known as the *psychoanalytic theory*, states child development occurs in five stages: oral, anal, phallic, latency, and genital. Table 1-1 provides an overview of the five stages. Freud (1961) believed libido (i.e., sexual drive or instincts) impacts the body and plays a significant role in human development. Freud believed that as a child develops, they seek pleasure through different erogenous zones. The theory states that as individuals grow physically, certain parts of their body become sources of potential joy or frustration.

TABLE 1-1. PSYCHOSEXUAL STAGES OF DEVELOPMENT		
STAGE	**AGE RANGE**	**EROGENOUS ZONE AND BEHAVIORS**
Oral	Birth to 1 year	Mouth: Sucking, swallowing, chewing
Anal	1 to 3 years	Anus: Bowel and bladder control
Phallic	3 to 6 years	Genitals: Masturbation, realizes differences between sexes, sexual curiosity
Latent	6 years to puberty	Little or no sexual motivations (libido inactive)
Genital	Puberty to death	Genitals: Sexual interest and development of intimate relationships

Data source: Lantz, S. E., & Ray, S. (2021, February). *Freud developmental theory*. StatPearls Publishing. https://www.ncbi.nlm.nih.gov/books/NBK557526/

Freud's theory emphasized that the first 5 years of life greatly influence one's personality. Furthermore, Freud theorized that an individual's failure to complete a stage resulted in fixation at that stage in development and would affect a person's behavior as an adult. Although Freud's psychosexual theory is not considered very accurate (Robinson, 1993) and does not consider individuals with special needs, it influenced early childhood education. It provided a starting point for theorists who came after him.

Psychosocial Development Theory

The next major theory is Erikson's theory of psychosocial development (1950). Rather than focusing on sexual interest, Erikson believed social interaction and experience played a more prominent role in child development. The eight-stage theory describes the process from birth to death, and during each stage, individuals are faced with a conflict that impacts later functioning and growth. According to this theory, successful management of these challenges at each step leads to the emergence of a lifelong psychological virtue. Table 1-2 describes each stage in more detail.

Teachers can see the influence of Erikson's theory in preschool when children exert their independence. Early childhood education aims to help children find their independence from their parents; they begin to discover themselves and their abilities. Preschool teachers must provide supervision without interfering with the newly developed independent skills.

Behaviorism

Scientists introduced behavioral child development theories, also known as *behaviorism,* in the first half of the 20th century. Theorists such as Watson, Pavlov, and Skinner believed learning occurs purely through association and reinforcement processes. Behavioral theories focus on how environmental interactions influence behavior and are found in observable and measurable behaviors. Behavioral child development theories believe that an individual's action (also known as their *behaviors*) responds to rewards, punishments, stimuli, and reinforcement. Two types of learning emerged from behaviorist theories: classical and operant conditioning. Classical conditioning (Figure 1-1) involves pairing a naturally occurring stimulus with a neutral stimulus, whereas operant conditioning uses reinforcement and punishment to modify behaviors (Skinner, 1963). The difference between the two conditions can be seen in the following video: https://youtu.be/H6LEcM0E0io_. These theories provide the foundation of applied behavioral analysis therapy for children with significant behavioral needs, individuals with autism, and Positive Behavior Interventions and Support initiatives, which are explained in detail in Chapter 4.

TABLE 1-2. ERIKSON'S STAGES OF PSYCHOSOCIAL DEVELOPMENT

STAGES	AGE RANGE	IMPORTANT EVENTS	VIRTUE	EXPLANATION
Trust vs. mistrust	Birth to 18 months	Feeding	Hope	Safe environment with regular access to nutrition and affection
Autonomy vs. shame	18 months to 3 years	Toilet training	Will	Safe environment while encouraging self-sufficiency
Initiative vs. guilt	3 to 5 years	Exploration	Purpose	Child's interests are encouraged and supported
Industry vs. inferiority	5 to 13 years	School	Competency	Expectations provided at school and home; positive feedback provided
Identity vs. role confusion	13 to 21 years	Social relationships	Fidelity	Adolescents begin to set their own values and "find themselves"
Intimacy vs. isolation	21 to 39 years	Relationship	Love	Long-term partnerships and close friendships
Generativity vs. stagnation	40 to 65 years	Work and parenthood	Care	Parenting, coaching, teaching next generation
Ego integrity vs. despair	65 and older	Reflection on life	Wisdom	Personal life accomplishments acknowledged

Data source: Orenstein, G. A., & Lewis, L. (2020, November). *Erikson's stages of psychosocial development*. StatPearls Publishing. https://www.ncbi.nlm.nih.gov/books/NBK556096/

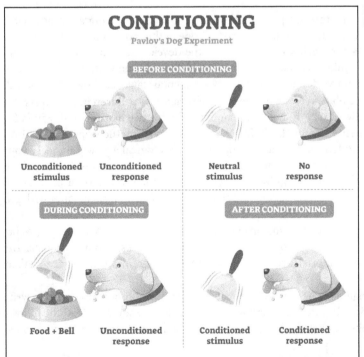

Figure 1-1. Classical conditioning. (VectorMine/Shutterstock.com)

TABLE 1-3. PIAGET'S STAGES OF COGNITIVE DEVELOPMENT		
STAGE	**AGE RANGE**	**EXPLANATION**
The sensorimotor stage	Birth to 2 years	An infant's knowledge is limited to their sensory perceptions and motor activities. Behavior is limited to motor responses caused by sensory stimuli.
The preoperational stage	2 to 6 years	The child learns to use language. Children do not understand concrete logic and cannot take other people's perspective, also known as *theory of mind*.
The concrete operational stage	7 to 11 years	Children gain a better understanding of mental operations. Children begin to think logically about concrete events but have difficulty with abstract concepts. According to Hattie (2012), children with autism are typically at this stage, which accounts for their problems with abstract concepts.
The formal operational stage	12 years to adult	Children develop the ability to think about abstract concepts. Skills such as logical thought, deductive reasoning, and systematic planning emerge during this stage. Additionally, students' knowledge to make inferences or determine the point of view, common standards in language arts classes, begin at the formal operational stage.

Data source: Malik, F. (2021, July). *Cognitive development*. StatPearls Publishing. https://www.ncbi.nlm.nih.gov/books/NBK537095/

Cognitive Development Theory

The development of a person's thought process through their life is the foundation of Piaget's cognitive development theory (Piaget, 1971). It is considered one of the most influential theories of cognitive development. Piaget's approach seeks to describe the development of mental states and thought processes and how they influence our understanding and interaction with the environment around us. Piaget's theory of cognitive development has developmental stages, as shown in Table 1-3.

Piaget believed teachers are observers whose job is to help facilitate children in their quest for knowledge. According to Hattie (2012), to become a highly effective teacher, the first step is for teachers to understand how their students think. In other words, knowing the stages of cognitive development and where your students are, regardless of their chronological age, will increase your effectiveness as an educator. Once a student's level is determined, the next step is to teach them how to get to the next stage using metacognitive strategies. Students at the formal operational stage are more likely to successfully master lessons at the highest level of Bloom's taxonomy/depth of knowledge.

Throughout this book, you will see Bloom's taxonomy (1956) and depth of knowledge (Webb, 2002) to help create and evaluate learning objectives, lesson plans, activities, and assessments. The following YouTube video provides a brief overview of how these two frameworks work together: https://youtu.be/P_0kJcxJxI8.

In 1956, Bloom and colleagues created an educational framework commonly used to help write learning objectives; it was revised by Anderson and Krathwohl in 2001. They described the following six learning levels: remember, understand, apply, analyze, evaluate, and create. Bloom intended

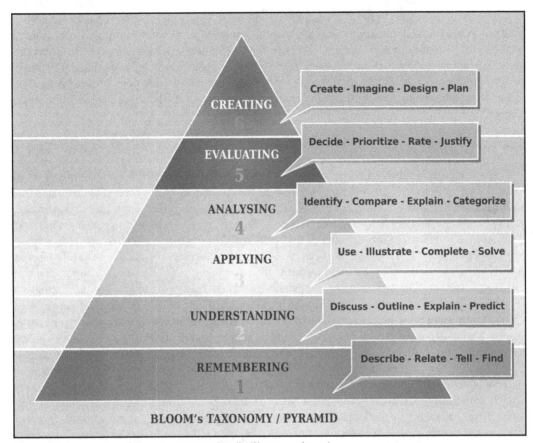

Figure 1-2. An overview of Bloom's taxonomy. (artellia/Shutterstock.com)

for this framework to be hierarchical, which implies that one must understand the previous level's knowledge to move to the next level. Furthermore, Bloom's framework uses verbs that are associated with the six groups. Figure 1-2 provides an overview of Bloom's taxonomy.

Depth of knowledge is a framework created by Dr. Norman Webb (2002) that consists of four levels: acquired knowledge, knowledge application, analysis, and augmentation. Depth of knowledge focuses on what teachers expect students to do during learning and is typically used to measure assessments. Both frameworks play an important role in instruction and evaluation and are integrated throughout this textbook.

Social Learning Theory

Bandura's social learning theory (1977) states people are proactive agents in their learning and change. In 1986, Bandura wrote people are self-organized, self-directing, and self-regulating. In other words, people react to more than the external forces in their lives. Components of Bandura's theory are observational learning and modeling, self-efficacy, and self-regulation in which children can learn behaviors through observation and modeling. As a result of observation and modeling, children develop new skills and acquire unique information. The theory suggests that viewing live models, fictional characters, and listening to verbal instructions influence learning behaviors. An example of Bandura's seminal experiments with a Bobo doll resulted in the power of violence as portrayed by the media on aggression. An example of this experiment can be seen in the following video: https://youtu.be/dmBqwWlJg8U.

According to Bandura (1971), a student is more likely to engage in observed behaviors when they see a positive consequence for another student. An example of social learning theory is when a student is praised for positive actions because another student is exhibiting problem behaviors. Indeed, Bandura emphasized that children learn by their social experiences, goals, and development of knowledge and skills. Bandura's theory is the basis of teachers' explanations (direct instruction) linked to demonstration (modeling) that significantly enhance students' conceptual learning (independent practice). This is discussed further in Chapter 5.

Sociocultural Theory

Vygotsky's sociocultural theory proposed that children learn actively through hands-on experiences. Learning is a social process, and, by interacting with others, learning becomes integrated into the understanding of the environment. Vygotsky (1978) also stressed the importance of play in education because through playing and imagination children can stretch their conceptual abilities and knowledge. As you will see throughout this text, early childhood educators need to provide many opportunities for play. The term *play* can be seen in various ways, such as imaginary play, role-playing, games, and re-enactments of real events, which will foster the growth of abstract thought. Teachers also use sociocultural theory when they use ability grouping, direct instruction, and prompting.

An important concept to come out of this theory is called the *zone of proximal development* (ZPD). Specifically, Vygotsky (1978) defined the ZPD as "the distance between the actual developmental level as determined by independent problem solving and the level of potential development as determined through problem-solving under adult guidance or in collaboration with more capable peers" (p. 86). The ZPD can typically be determined with assessments and can help determine an individual's current skill level. Once teachers obtain this information, they can offer instruction to stretch the limit of each child's capabilities based on their ZPD. At first, the student may need assistance from a teacher or scaffolded instruction, but, eventually, the child's skill level will increase. Thus, the zone will expand. The practice of scaffolding instruction and gradual release (e.g., direct instruction, modeling, guided practice, and independent practice) is based on Vygotsky's work and is discussed throughout this textbook.

In summary, the foundation for early childhood education is based on the theories described previously. Early childhood educators must understand how these theories have impacted education and the strategies depicted throughout this text. In the next section, the developmental domains of early childhood are described.

DEVELOPMENTAL DOMAINS

Child development usually includes when children reach typical milestones. Researchers organized these milestones into domains. These domains consist of cognitive, socioemotional, motor, and language skills (Black et al., 2017; Mwaura et al., 2008; Rao et al., 2014). These skills impact how children learn in school and are known as *school readiness*. The U.S. Department of Education (2020) defined the essential domains of school readiness as follows:

- Language and literacy development
- Cognition and general knowledge
  ○ Early mathematics
  ○ Early scientific development
- Approaches toward learning
- Physical well-being and motor development
- Social and emotional development

Figure 1-3. A family reading. (Unsplash)

Teachers must have an understanding of the five essential developmental domains because they are indicators of a child's ability to succeed in school. These skills typically develop simultaneously and serve as a guide for developmentally appropriate practices integrated into early childhood education programs. A child struggling in one or more domains will need careful monitoring and intervention. If the child continues to struggle, teachers should consider a referral for an evaluation for specially designed instruction available through special education.

Language and Literacy

Language is an extension of a child's ability to use symbols. As their brains develop, children begin to use representational thinking. *Representational thinking* is when a child thinks about their environment using images or language. Brown (1973) stated that language develops in stages from utterances, phrases with inflections, and simple sentences to complex sentences. He further asserted that children who use more sentences have a more complex language. In Chapter 6, you will learn more about the development of language in young children.

Some young children are bilingual and can speak more than one language. They typically grow up with bilingual parents who speak both languages at home. Some children may talk fluently in both languages by the age of 4. Diverse children may communicate with a dialect or a variation of English. Examples of dialects are Black English and Spanish English.

Children acquire language through social and cultural contexts. They acquire language through shared reading, as shown in Figure 1-3. They demonstrate their knowledge of vocabulary receptively and expressively. *Receptive knowledge* is what children know or can mentally retrieve, and *expressive vocabulary* is what they can communicate. Babies should produce their first words by 15 months of age and first word combinations by 24 months (Hagan et al., 2008). Vocabulary development progresses at the fastest rate between 2 and 3 years of age.

Vocabulary is developed by imitating parents, siblings, peers, teachers, and the media during daily routines, familiar situations, songs, stories, and play (Bochner & Jones, 2003). The quality of language development from birth to age 3 predicts the child's social growth and academic success (Fillmore & Snow, 2000; Hart & Risley, 1995). In 2003, Hart and Risley found that 3-year-old children from families on welfare were exposed to 30 million fewer words than their peers. The lack of exposure to vocabulary is a reason many children from low-income homes struggle in school. Children who lag in developing vocabulary struggle with literacy development. Children with limited vocabulary have difficulty sounding out words while reading. They also have trouble spelling, comprehending text, and predicting what will happen next (Dickinson & Porche, 2011). Vocabulary knowledge is needed to activate prior learning for children to be more engaged in their lessons (Figure 1-4).

Figure 1-4. A teacher reading to her class. (Monkey Business Images/Shutterstock. com)

Literacy also includes emergent writing. Emergent writing uses tracing, writing names, spelling single words, and scribbling or drawing to convey meaning (Rowe & Neitzel, 2010). Emergent writing is a strong predictor of children's later reading and writing success (Puranik & Lonigan, 2012). By the time a child reaches kindergarten, they should be able to use letter-like forms, symbols, or recognizable letters; use writing tools with adult guidance; and show an emerging awareness that they can use writing for various purposes. For more information on the development of writing in young children, see Chapter 8.

Oral comprehension was defined by Hoover and Gough (1990) as the ability to listen to a text, interpret the vocabulary, derive sentences using that vocabulary, and discuss the interpretation of the text. Oral or listening comprehension precedes reading comprehension. Children can listen to and talk about more complex ideas before they can read or write them. Through prelistening activities, listening exercises, and postlistening reflection, students can increase their oral comprehension.

Listening activities give students background knowledge and prompts them to focus their attention on keywords or concepts. Teachers should also provide an image that depicts the keyword, model their thought processes, and use kid-friendly definitions. Teachers can also use guided notes and graphic organizers to scaffold instruction for young children with and without disabilities. Guided notes are evidence-based practices in which the teacher provides students with a handout containing an outline with critical information left blank (Haydon et al., 2011). Graphic organizers are also an evidence-based practice that provide a visual display of relationships between facts, ideas, and/ or terms (Smith & Okolo, 2010). Often, teachers can create such activities into a game-like exercise. For example, they can use a bingo card with a square for each vocabulary word; the students place a marker on the square when they hear the target item. Questioning or call-and-response exercises promote the social aspect of listening and ask students to choral answer or repeat in unison the target word or idea when read by the speaker. Throughout the listening activity, teachers should ask questions to check for understanding. Students can write or draw in journals to summarize what they heard. Teachers can use the journals as a record of student progress.

Print awareness is the ability to understand the general rules and functions of written language (Altinkaynak, 2019). Up to the preschool period, educators do not expect children to read but rather learn the concepts of and awareness about writing (Justice & Ezell, 2004). Print awareness skills include book and print order and the meaning of the writing, letters, and words (Justice & Sofka, 2010). An example of print awareness is shared reading (Figure 1-5) and allowing the child to turn the book's pages. If the child turns the page the right way, they are demonstrating print awareness.

Teachers can promote print awareness by making sure students know how authors organize books. For instance, early educators can teach that books are read from left to right and top to bottom, books may include pictures or graphics, and the pages are numbered. Teachers can facilitate

Figure 1-5. Reading to a child. (Unsplash)

discussions about the author's purpose for writing the story. When selecting books, early childhood teachers should choose books that are age appropriate, have large fonts and colorful pictures, and use predictable text (e.g., books by Dr. Seuss). Big books help children notice and learn to recognize frequently occurring sight words (e.g., a, you, was, is, and the). Print awareness can also be encouraged by labeling objects in your classroom, thus helping children understand the relationship between spoken and written language. Encouraging children to incorporate print in play is another way to strengthen a child's print awareness. For example, children can pretend to construct a stop sign, make a birthday card, or write a shopping list.

Cognitive and General Knowledge

The cognitive development of young children includes their attempts to understand, explain, organize, manipulate, construct, and predict the world around them. However, young children also have difficulty controlling their attention and memory. Many young children confuse fiction with reality and focus on a single aspect of an experience.

Cognitive development includes the ability to memorize. Memory is the ability to encode, retain, and recall information. Young children must encode people, places, and things and later recall them from their long-term memory. Preschoolers do not remember as much as older children and adults because of immature brain development, the lack of background knowledge, and poor attention skills.

According to Piaget's preoperational stage, children between the ages of 2 and 7 years increase their use of language and imitate adult behaviors when they play. Children play using their imagination. Piaget also stated that children at this stage could not distinguish between their point of view and the point of view of others, also known as *theory of mind*. Although most children eventually overcome deficits in theory of mind, some children with autism have difficulty understanding perspective well into adulthood. Piaget (1971) also wrote that when children and even adults are stressed and overwhelmed, they tend to regress to an egocentric speech during times of frustration.

Early Mathematics Skills

Scientists included early mathematics skills in the cognitive development of young children. Piaget (1971) indicated children at the preoperational stage will have difficulty with classification or the ability to group according to specific features (Figure 1-6). Counting is hard, and children between the ages of 2 and 6 years may tell you that a handful of nickels is more money than a single 10-dollar bill.

Figure 1-6. A child sorting.

Foundation numeracy skills are needed to develop more complex math skills. When starting kindergarten, the average child can count to 10; however, 5% of those students will not recognize numbers (Zill & West, 2001). An example of an emergent numeracy skill is the ability to classify and sort objects. Organizing and sorting involve finding items that are the same or alike and grouping them by specific traits or attributes. Children can organize anything, including blocks, leaves, plates, and shapes. Once items are classified, they can compare items for similarities and differences both within and between matched groups (Raney, 2015).

Another example is counting a small number of objects and making numerical comparisons. Children can represent the number of items with a symbol by 5 years old (Kolkman et al., 2013). Scientists link the understanding of symbolic numbers to the development of counting. To count, children need to recite the number words in the established order, match each object in the set to one and only one number word per item, and identify the last number word representing the numerosity of the collection (Gelman & Gallistel, 1978). Teachers can incorporate activities to improve children's symbolic mathematical skills. Activities include playing board games, reading stories involving quantities, and reciting nursery rhymes (e.g., One, two, buckle my shoe, etc.).

Numerical comparison means to view something in relation to another. To compare is to examine the difference between numbers, quantities, or values to decide if it is greater than, smaller than, or equal to another amount. To compare numbers, children need to place numbers or digits on a horizontal number line reliably. Knowledge of the spatial arrangement of digits on a number line is a powerful source of information. The size of an integer can be determined by its location in relation to other digits.

Teachers use number and shape identification to determine early numeracy skills along with simple arithmetic. Learning about shapes is a precursor to understanding geometry. This involves recognizing and naming shapes and their attributes. At the age of 4, children are building their shape vocabulary of the square, circle, triangle, pentagon, and hexagon (Figure 1-7). Teachers can help students understand the differences between shapes by counting sides and corners. In kindergarten, students can copy or draw symmetrical shapes. By second grade, students should know the names and differences between two- and three-dimensional shapes (e.g., cubes, cones, and cylinders).

Figure 1-7. Shapes.

Figure 1-8. Science.

Without these foundational skills, children will enter school behind their peers, and educators are more likely to refer them for special education. More information on early mathematics skills is presented in Chapter 9.

Early Scientific Skills

Teachers can draw preschool children toward science with their sense of creativity, curiosity, and persistence (Banko et al., 2013). The ability to observe, explore, and discover their world should be encouraged and lay the foundation for science learning throughout their lives. Children can construct conceptual learning and use reasoning and inquiry (National Research Council [NRC], 2012). Children learn to organize and communicate what they learn and know the difference between concrete and abstract ideas (Carey et al., 2017). Teachers should engage children in scientific inquiry (Figure 1-8) by asking questions, investigating, and constructing explanations in developmentally appropriate environments (NRC, 2007; National Science Teacher Association [NSTA], 2014). Playing with blocks, water, and sand is related to science and should be encouraged.

Teachers can play a central and vital role in helping children learn science when they prepare the environment for science exploration, focus children's observations, and provide time to talk about what happened (NSTA, 2014). Teachers should support children's play and direct attention, structure experiences, support learning attempts, and regulate science information's complexity and difficulty (NRC, 2007). Furthermore, teachers need to support children's curiosity, learning, and understanding of the world around them.

Teachers need to provide multiple and varied opportunities to engage in science exploration, discovery, and inquiry (NSTA, 2014). The experiences should provide a basis for seeing patterns, forming theories, building knowledge, and considering alternative explanations. Teachers can provide opportunities to explore outdoors to examine and duplicate the habitats of animals and insects, explore how things move, investigate the flow of water, recognize different textures, make predictions, and test their knowledge.

Children can explore science in both formal and informal settings. Formal settings include intentional lessons planned by teachers. In addition to traditional instruction, children need to have opportunities to engage in science learning in informal settings after school, on field trips, or during outdoor play. Children develop science skills and knowledge over time. They need opportunities for sustained engagement with materials and lessons that focus on the same set of ideas over weeks, months, and years (NRC, 2007). Teachers should provide interdisciplinary topics by providing a science lesson about a story they are reading in language arts. For example, a book about a dolphin can be made interdisciplinary by having the students research (science), create a habitat for a dolphin (science, art, and math if measurements are needed), and then tell or write a story about the dolphin in its habitat (language arts).

In summary, teachers should provide learning environments that encourage children to ask questions, plan investigations, and record and discuss findings. Educators should determine, guide, and focus on children's natural interests and abilities through carefully planned open-ended inquiry-based explorations. Teachers can emphasize the learning of science, mathematics, and engineering practices including developing and using models; planning and carrying out investigations; constructing explanations and designing solutions; engaging in argument from evidence; and obtaining, evaluating, and communicating information (NRC, 2012, 2015). More information on early science education is presented in Chapter 10.

Approaches Toward Learning

Approaches toward learning focus on the foundational behaviors, dispositions, and attitudes children bring to learning experiences and social interactions. These include curiosity, initiative, and motivation to participate in new and varied experiences and challenges. These behaviors are needed to take advantage of learning opportunities. Within this domain is the level of attention, engagement, and persistence to complete various tasks and predict academic success (Duncan et al., 2007). Lastly, children need creativity and flexibility of thought to use materials in unconventional ways and express themselves in various media.

To show readiness for school, children need to show initiative and curiosity. Examples of initiative and curiosity at the preschool level are as follows:

- Puts materials together in new ways to test results
- Takes risks (i.e., climbs to the top of the climber to ring the playground bell)
- Approaches new material in a classroom with interest
- Joins a peer-created game or activity

Children who can take the initiative and show curiosity are also ready to learn. Examples include the following:

- Follows classroom routines and anticipates what happens next independently or with the use of picture prompts
- Puts away books or other material when they finish
- Self-selects a variety of activities during free choice
- Asks questions to seek explanations about phenomena of interest

Children also participate in planning, action, and reflection when they are ready to learn. They develop, initiate, and carry out simple plans to obtain a goal. For example, the child considers the needed material, gets the material, and creates an art project. Children will also use prior knowledge and information to assess, inform, and plan future actions and learning. Examples of this are as follows:

- After sending a variety of shaped toys down a ramp, the child begins to select round objects more frequently, noting that round objects roll more easily.
- The child expresses intention and interests.
- The child describes several solutions to reach a goal and weighs the pros and cons of each option.

To be ready to learn, children also need attention to focus on an activity with deliberate concentration despite distractions (e.g., continues with a high-interest activity when children are playing nearby; chooses to play with a friend later while continuing to engage in an activity; continues to build with blocks when other children play with cars; and focuses on their book, retelling the story while turning the pages despite distractions). Persistence is needed to learn and carry out tasks, activities, projects, or experiences from beginning to end. Examples include returning to a task and continuing it after lunch and maintaining an interest in a project or activity over time. Children also need to focus on the task at hand, even when frustrated or challenged. Examples include the following:

- Completes a puzzle even though the pieces are challenging to fit together (Figure 1-9)
- Continues to work on a clay cow, trying to figure out why the legs do not hold up the body
- Dresses independently and continues to attempt proper use of zippers, gloves, belts, and shoelaces

To be able to learn, students must show innovation and inventions. To do this, they must use imagination and creativity to interact. Examples may include using blankets and boxes to create a fort and directing friends in imaginary games. Additionally, students ready for school should use creative and flexible thinking to problem solve. The child will use alternatives and varied resources to approach tasks with flexibility and originality. For example, the child will develop a different yet realistic idea about getting a Frisbee out of a tree branch. Children who engage in inventive social play are ready to learn. Examples include playing restaurant and defining players' roles and making up a new way of playing the memory game and explaining the new rules to peers.

The last approach to learning needed by children is expressing ideas and feelings through the arts. Children should express individuality, life experiences, and what they know and can do through various media. Examples are as follows:

- Uses their own body to demonstrate how a flower grows
- Watches a TikTok video and demonstrates favorite dance moves
- Represents family members through painting, collage, and sculpture

Additionally, children express an interest in and show appreciation for the creative work of others. Examples include the following:

- Offers opinions to friends about their artwork (e.g., "I like the unicorn you made." or "When you draw a body, the hands go here.")
- Communicates praise to a peer (e.g., "I like it because the shapes are cool.")
- Looks at the Play-Doh (Hasbro) object (Figure 1-10) and asks "How did you make it so bumpy?"

Figure 1-9. A child with a puzzle. (Unsplash)

Figure 1-10. A child playing with Play-Doh.

Figure 1-11. Jumping. (Unsplash)

Children between the ages of 4 and 8 are interested in learning and often take the initiative to learn. They are curious about the world and often become frustrated when knowledge does not come quickly or they fail to remember what they learned. When teachers create structured learning by setting reasonably attainable goals and provide guidance and support, children can process information and learn at their rate.

In summary, approaches toward learning are as critical to child development as language development. A child may be precocious in language and yet struggle with their attention span and not be motivated to sit still long enough to learn their numbers and shapes. The children who struggle need to be monitored and provided with interventions. If they continue to labor, educators should evaluate them for specially designed instruction and services through special education. More information on the behavior of children is provided in Chapter 4.

Physical Well-Being and Motor Development

Physical well-being and motor development are essential skills for healthy growth and development and success in school. Physical well-being includes good health, which encompasses nutrition, sleep, and regular checkups. When caregivers do not provide proper food, sleep, and/or medical care, their children are at risk for learning problems. As a result, educators need to know how to identify when a child has not had enough to eat or sleep. Sleep-deprived and/or hungry children cannot learn until their needs are met, and teachers should provide the child with nutrition and/or a nap. If a pattern develops, the teacher needs to communicate with the caregivers.

Motor skills are the physical abilities of people. Children develop and refine these skills during early childhood. Early childhood researchers noted delayed motor skill development might be a determinant of school readiness (McClelland & Cameron, 2019). Experts categorize motor skills as locomotor skills (e.g., run, hop, jump, and slide; Figure 1-11) and object control skills (e.g., throw, catch, kick, and dribble). These skills allow children to function independently and provide a foundation for cognitive, social, and physical growth (Logan et al., 2012). McClelland and Cameron (2019) also found that children with insufficient motor skills are likely to be cognitively unprepared for academic demands.

According to Bandura's theory of observational learning, children must be biologically capable of learning motor skills. To develop these skills, Bandura asserted children need to observe the dexterity in others, form a mental image, imitate, and practice the skill. Lastly, the child needs to be motivated to repeat the behavior. Indeed, children need to be ready, have opportunities, and be interested in developing motor skills to become competent.

Within the motor domain are gross and fine motor skills. *Gross motor skills* are physical skills that require whole-body movement and involve core-stabilizing muscles of the body to perform everyday functions. These functions include standing, walking, running, jumping, and sitting upright at a table. Fine motor skills develop more slowly than gross motor skills. They involve the coordination between small muscles (e.g., hands, fingers, and eyes) of the body and include strength and dexterity. Examples of using fine motor skills are writing, grasping small objects, and fastening objects. Gross and fine motor skills within the motor domain include the following:

- Copying a shape
- Drawing a person
- Folding paper
- Hopping on one foot

Early childhood teachers need to monitor children's physical well-being and motor development. If a child is not meeting motor skill milestones and interventions are not successful, the teacher may need to refer the child for an evaluation by a physical (gross motor) and/or occupational therapist (fine motor).

Socioemotional

There is growing evidence that socioemotional development plays a vital role in children's academic outcomes (Dobbs et al., 2006). Socioemotional behaviors that have the most significant impact on academics are prosocial behaviors, conduct problems, hyperactivity, peer problems, and emotional problems (Ponitz et al., 2009; Trentacosta & Shaw, 2009).

Parents, siblings, peers, teachers, and the media provide opportunities for children to learn how to socialize in which they see how to think and act in a socially acceptable manner. Parents and others demonstrate society's formal and informal rules of proper behavior along with values and norms. *Socioemotional development* is a child's ability to understand other people's feelings, control their emotions and actions, and get along with peers. Necessary skills include cooperation, following directions, paying attention, and demonstrating self-control. Additionally, feelings of affection, confidence, trust, friendship, pride, and humor are part of socioemotional development. The set of skills children need include the ability to read and comprehend emotional states in others, identify and understand one's feelings, regulate one's behavior, develop empathy, manage strong emotions, and establish and maintain relationships.

Socioemotional behaviors can predict later academic achievement. A child who has difficulty with prosocial behaviors, conduct problems, hyperactivity, peers, and emotional problems (Figure 1-12) is more likely to have poor academic performance (Ponitz et al., 2009; Trentacosta & Shaw, 2009). Children who have positive peer relationships have better literacy and math outcomes (Malecki & Elliot, 2002). Indeed, a child's ability to self-regulate their behaviors in early life is related to continued academic success in high school and beyond (Bernier et al., 2010). As a result, early childhood educators need to monitor their students' socioemotional skills and provide interventions for children who have difficulty regulating themselves. Students who continue to struggle may need to be evaluated for specially designed instruction through special education. Chapter 12 provides the reader with strategies to assist students who struggle.

DIVISION FOR EARLY CHILDHOOD RECOMMENDED PRACTICES AND HIGH-LEVERAGE PRACTICES IN SPECIAL EDUCATION

The DEC Recommended Practices are an initiative from the Council for Exceptional Children that offer guidance to parents and professionals who have or are at risk for developmental delays or disabilities. These practices are based on research and have been shown to provide better outcomes

Figure 1-12. An angry child. (Unsplash)

for young children between the ages of birth through 5 years. The recommended practices have eight domains: leadership, assessment, environment, family, instruction, interaction, teaming and collaboration, and transition. Throughout the chapters in this textbook, the reader will be introduced to the DEC Recommended Practices and gain more understanding of what these practices look like in the classroom. For further information on standards and alignment, we encourage you to visit the DEC website (https://www.dec-sped.org/ppc-standards-alignment).

McLeskey and colleagues (2017) created a set of 22 essential practices called *high-leverage practices* that all teachers and teacher candidates in special education should know and practice that provide central support to student learning and fundamentals for educators to develop more complex practices. The HLPs are organized into four categories: collaboration, assessment, social-emotional-behavioral practices, and instruction. Like the DEC Recommended Practices, the reader will be introduced to and asked to purposefully practice HLPs throughout this textbook.

SUMMARY

Children grow and develop at different rates, and it can be challenging to determine typical development. Children may need special education services when they do not meet the developmental domains required to succeed in school. Child development theorists like Freud, Piaget, Erikson, Pavlov, Skinner, Watson, Bandura, and Vygotsky influenced the creation of these domains. This chapter provided a basic overview of the developmental theories and disciplines and is a foundation for the rest of this textbook. It is important for you as the reader to have an understanding of major theories and domains of child development and the DEC Recommended Practices and to be able to purposefully practice HLPs so that you have the tools to create an engaging, effective, and successful early childhood classroom.

CHAPTER REVIEW

1. According to Sigmund Freud's psychosexual development theory (psychoanalytic theory), what are the five stages of child development?
2. Who believed learning occurs purely through processes of association and reinforcement?
3. What are the two types of learning that emerged from the behaviorist theories?
4. What are the six levels of learning according to Bloom's taxonomy?
5. What does the social learning theory by Bandura state?
6. What are the five developmental domains?
7. What does cognitive development of young children include?
8. What should lay the foundation for science learning throughout children's lives?
9. Compare and contrast the different theories of child development.
10. List and explain the domains of child development.
11. Provide an example of when teachers should refer a child for an evaluation for special education.
12. List and describe at least one strategy for each developmental domain.

RESOURCES

- Bloom's Taxonomy Verb Chart: https://tips.uark.edu/blooms-taxonomy-verb-chart/
- DEC Recommended Practices: https://www.dec-sped.org/dec-recommended-practices
- Depth of Knowledge: https://www.windham-schools.org/docs/DOK%20Wheel%20Slide%20for%20Teachers-0.pdf
- Evidence Based Practices for Autism: https://autismpdc.fpg.unc.edu/evidence-based-practices
- HLPs: https://highleveragepractices.org/

REFERENCES

Altinkaynak, S. O. (2019). The effect of interactive book reading activities on children's print and phonemic awareness skills. *International Journal of Progressive Education, 15*(1), 88-99.

Anderson, L. W., & Krathwohl, D. R. (2001). *A taxonomy of teaching, learning, and assessing: A revision of Bloom's taxonomy of educational objectives.* Longman.

Bandura, A. (1971). *Physiological modeling: Conflicting theories.* Aldine-Atherton.

Bandura, A. (1977). *Social learning theory.* Prentice-Hall.

Bandura, A. (1986). *Social foundations of thought and action: A social cognitive theory.* Prentice Hall.

Banko, W., Grant, M. L., Jabot, M. E., McCormack, A. J., & O'Brien, T. (2013). *Science for the next generation: Preparing for the new standards.* National Science Teachers Association Press.

Bernier, A., Carlson, S. M., & Whipple, N. (2010). From external regulation to self-regulation: Early parenting precursors of young children's executive functioning. *Child Development, 81*(1), 326-339.

Black, M. M., Walker, S. P., Fernald, L. C., Andersen, C. T., DiGirolamo, A. M., Lu, C., McCoy, D. C., Fink, G., Shawar, Y. R., Shiffman, J., Devercelli, A. E., Wodon, Q. T., Varag-Baron, E., & Grantham-McGregor, S. (2017). Early childhood development coming of age: Science through the life course. *The Lancet, 389*, 77-90. https://doi.org/10.1016/S0140-6736(16)31389-7

Bloom, B. S. (1956). *Taxonomy of educational objectives, handbook I: The cognitive domain* (pp. 20-24). David McKay Co. Inc.

Bochner, S., & Jones, J. (2003). *Child language development: Learning to talk* (2nd ed.). Whurr.

Brown, K. (1973). *A first language: The early stages.* Harvard University Press.

Carey, S., Shusterman, A., Haward, P., & Distefano, R. (2017). Do analog number representations underlie the meanings of young children's verbal numerals? *Cognition, 168*, 243-255.

Dickinson, D. K., & Porche, M. V. (2011). Relation between language experiences in preschool classrooms and children's kindergarten and fourth grade language and reading abilities. *Child Development, 82*(3), 870-886. https://doi.org/10.1111/j.1467-8624.2011.01576.x

Dobbs, J., Doctoroff, G. L., Fisher, P. H., & Arnold, D. H. (2006). The association between preschool children's socioemotional functioning and their mathematical skills. *Journal of Applied Developmental Psychology, 27*, 97-108. https://doi.org/10.1016/j.appdev.2005.12.008

Duncan, G. J., Dowsett, C. J., Claessens, A., Magnuson, K., Huston, A. C., Klebanov, P., Pagani, L. S., Feinstein, L., Engel, M., Brooks-Gunn, J., Sexton, H., Duckworth, K., & Japel, C. (2007). School readiness and later achievement. *Developmental Psychology, 43*(6), 1428-1446. https://doi.org/10.1037%2F0012-1649.43.6.1428

Erikson, E. H. (1950). *Childhood and society.* Norton.

Fillmore, L. W., & Snow, C. E. (2000). *What teachers need to know about language.* Center for Applied Linguistics.

Freud, S. (1961). *The ego and the id.* W.W. Norton & Co.

Gelman, R., & Gallistel, C. R. (1978). *The child's understanding of number.* Harvard University Press.

Hagan, J., Shaw, J. S., & Duncan, P. M. (Eds.). (2008). *Bright futures: Guidelines for health supervision of infants, children, and adolescents* (3rd ed.). American Academy of Pediatrics.

Hart, B., & Risley, T. R. (1995). *Meaningful differences in the everyday experience of young American children.* Paul H. Brookes.

Hart, B., & Risley, T. R. (2003). The early catastrophe: The 30 million word gap by age 3. *American Educator, 27*(1), 4-9.

Hattie, J. (2012). *Visible learning for teachers.* Routledge.

Haydon, T., Mancil, G. R., Kroeger, S. D., McLeskey, J., & Lin, W. J. (2011). A review of the effectiveness of guided notes for students who struggle learning academic content. *Preventing School Failure, 55*(4), 226-231.

Hoover, W. A., & Gough, P. B. (1990). The simple view of reading. *Reading and Writing, 2*(2), 127-160.

Justice, L., & Ezell, H. (2004). Print referencing: An emergent literacy enhancement strategy and its clinical applications. *Language, Speech and Hearing Services in School, 35*, 185-193.

Justice, L., & Sofka, A. E. (2010). *Engaging children with print: Building early literacy skills through quality read-alouds.* The Guilford Press.

Kolkman, M. E., Kroesbergen, E. H., & Leseman, P. P. M. (2013). Early numerical development and the role of non-symbolic and symbolic skills. *Learning and Instruction, 25*, 95-103. https://doi.org/10.1016/j.learninstruc.2012.12.001

Logan, S. W., Robinson, L. E., Wilson, A. E., & Lucas, W. A. (2012). Getting the fundamentals of movement: A meta-analysis of the effectiveness of motor skill interventions in children. *Child: Care, Health and Development, 38*(3), 305-315.

Malecki, C. K., & Elliot, S. N. (2002). Children's social behaviors as predictors of academic achievement: A longitudinal analysis. *School Psychology Quarterly, 17*(1), 1.

McClelland, M. M., & Cameron, C. E. (2019). Developing together: The role of executive function and motor skills in children's early academic lives. *Early Childhood Research Quarterly, 46*, 142-151.

McLeskey, J., Council for Exceptional Children, & Collaboration for Effective Educator Development, Accountability and Reform. (2017). *High-leverage practices in special education.* Council for Exceptional Children.

Mwaura, P. A., Sylva, K., & Malmberg, L. E. (2008). Evaluating the Madrasa preschool programme in East Africa: A quasi-experimental study. *International Journal of Early Years Education, 16*, 237-255. https://doi.org/10.1080/09669760802357121

National Research Council. (2007). *Taking science to school: Learning and teaching science in grades K-8.* National Academies Press.

National Research Council. (2012). *Education for life and work: Developing transferable knowledge and skills in the 21st century.* The National Academies Press.

National Research Council. (2015). *Guide to implementing the next generation of science standards.* National Academies Press.

National Science Teacher Association. (2014). *NSTA position statement: Early childhood science education.* https://www.naeyc.org/sites/default/files/globally-shared/downloads/PDFs/resources/position-statements/Early%20Childhood%20FINAL%20FINAL%201-30-14%20%281%29%20%281%29.pdf

Piaget, J. (1971). The theory of stages in cognitive development. In D. R. Green, M. P. Ford, & G. B. Flamer (Eds.), *Measurement and Piaget.* McGraw-Hill.

Ponitz, C. C., McClelland, M. M., Matthews, J. S., & Morrison, F. J. (2009). A structured observation of behavioral self-regulation and its contribution to kindergarten outcomes. *Developmental Psychology, 45*(3), 605-619. https://doi.org/10.1037/a0015365

Puranik, C. S., & Lonigan, C. J. (2012). Early writing deficits in preschoolers with oral language difficulties. *Journal of Learning Disabilities, 45*(2), 179-190.

Raney, L. E. (2015). Integrating primary care and behavioral health: The role of the psychiatrist in the collaborative care model. *American Journal of Psychiatry, 172*(8), 721-728.

Rao, N., Sun, J., Ng, M., Becher, Y., Lee, D., Ip, P., & Bacon-Shone, J. (2014). *Validation, finalization and adoption of the East Asia-Pacific Early Child Development Scales* (EAP-ECDS). United Nations Children's Fund.

Robinson, P. (1993). *Freud and his critics.* University California Press.

Rowe, D. W., & Neitzel, C. (2010). Interest and agency in 2- and 3-year-old's participation in emergent writing. *Reading Research Quarterly, 45*(2), 169-195.

Skinner, B. F. (1963). Operant behavior. *American Psychologist, 18*(8), 503-515. https://doi.org/10.1037/h0045185

Smith, S. J., & Okolo, C. (2010). Response to intervention and evidence based practices: Where does technology fit? *Learning Disability Quarterly, 33*(4), 257-272.

Trentacosta, C. J., & Shaw, D. S. (2009). Emotional self-regulation, peer rejection, and antisocial behavior: Developmental associations from early childhood to early adolescence. *Journal of Applied Developmental Psychology, 30,* 356-365. https://doi.org/10.1016/j.appdev.2008.12.016

U.S. Department of Education. (2020). *Definitions.* https://www.ed.gov/early-learning/elc-draft-summary/definitions

Webb, N. L. (2002, March 28). *Depth-of-knowledge levels for four content areas.* https://www.maine.gov/doe/sites/maine.gov.doe/files/inline-files/dok.pdf

Vygotsky, L. S. (1978). *Mind in society.* Harvard University Press.

Zill, N., & West, J. (2001). *Entering kindergarten: A portrait of American children when they begin schools. Findings from the condition of education* (NCES 2001-035). U.S. Department of Education, Office of Educational Research & Improvement.

Using Culturally Relevant Pedagogy With All Children and Families

Nai-Cheng Kuo, PhD, BCBA

INTRODUCTION

Cultural awareness is vital to reduce the misdiagnosis of students with disabilities and to prevent inappropriate referrals of these students to special education (Aronson & Laughter, 2016; Klingner et al., 2016; Linn & Hemmer, 2011; Samson & Lesaux, 2009; U.S. Department of Education, 2016). Teachers need to know how students' diverse cultural and linguistic backgrounds affect their learning. They then need to take action to respond to these students' unique needs by adjusting instructional activities and collaborating with others. The term *culturally relevant pedagogy* is used as an umbrella term in this chapter to embrace different cultural theories, such as culturally relevant pedagogy (Ladson-Billings, 1995), culturally responsive teaching (Gay, 2000, 2002), culturally sustaining pedagogy (Paris, 2012), critical culturally sustaining/revitalizing pedagogy (McCarty & Lee, 2014), and culturally relevant pedagogy 2.0 (Ladson-Billings, 2015). This chapter aims to help teachers understand the cultural theories and how to align these theories with high-leverage practices in special education.

Fisher, K. M., & Zimmer, K. E. (Eds.).
Early Childhood Special Education Programs and Practices (pp. 23-39).

CHAPTER OBJECTIVES

→ Understand the development of culturally responsive pedagogy and five high-leverage practices in special education that focus on culturally and linguistically diverse students.

→ Analyze the connections between cultural theories and high-leverage practices.

→ Create a framework to facilitate special educators' work with culturally and linguistically diverse students with disabilities.

KEY TERMS

- **Critical Culturally Sustaining/Revitalizing Pedagogy (CSRP):** McCarty and Lee (2014) highlighted the importance of maintaining and reviving Native American students' unique traditions, including their language, history, culture, and distinct living styles. This pedagogy is named CSRP.

- **Culturally Relevant Pedagogy (CRP):** Ladson-Billings (1995) is the first scholar who systematically explored CRP with a focus on academic success, cultural competence, and sociopolitical consciousness of African American/Black students.

- **Culturally Relevant Pedagogy 2.0 (CRP 2.0):** CRP 2.0 is an update of CRP by Ladson-Billings (2015), who extended the scope and meaning of her initial CRP to remix the latest innovations of current cultural theories, research, and practices.

- **Culturally Responsive Teaching (CRT):** Gay (2000/2002) proposed CRT to include five essential components for preparing teachers who work with culturally and linguistically diverse students: (a) a cultural diversity knowledge base, (b) culturally relevant curricula, (c) cultural caring and a learning community, (d) cross-cultural communications, and (e) multiculturalism and cultural congruity.

- **Culturally Sustaining Pedagogy (CSP):** Paris (2012) emphasized education must help foster and support linguistic, literature, and cultural pluralism of students who have been marginalized by systemic inequalities. He named this approach CSP.

- **High-Leverage Practices (HLPs):** Grounded in theory and research, the Council for Exceptional Children and the Collaboration for Effective Educator Development, Accountability, and Reform Center compiled 22 effective practices that have been shown to make a positive impact on students with disabilities. Five of the HLPs have a strong focus on working with culturally and linguistically diverse students and their families (McLeskey et al., 2017).

CASE STUDY 1

Tam, a 3-year-old girl with autism, recently moved to the United States from Vietnam with her parents. Tam lacks verbal and nonverbal communication skills so she often screams or cries to get what she wants. She has several incidents of elopement in school. Tam's early childhood special education classroom teacher, Mrs. Brandon, is worried about Tam's safety. Tam's mother does not understand English and neither does Tam. Tam has a younger brother who is 16 months old. Tam's father, who speaks English, is busy with his new job and rarely has a chance to get involved in Tam's school activities. Due to the lack of effective communication with Tam's parents, Mrs. Brandon is worried whether her instructional activities meet Tam's academic and behavioral needs.

Case Study 2

Jose, a transfer student, is currently a second grader in Mrs. Perdue's general education classroom. Jose's parents originally come from Mexico. Jose is a sweet, well-disciplined boy. He and his family speak Spanish at home, and he is learning English in school. Mrs. Perdue notices that Jose sometimes mixes the use of Spanish and English in school. Jose's benchmark assessments indicate that his reading level is below the kindergarten level. With 25 students in her class, Mrs. Perdue feels that she cannot dedicate sufficient time to help Jose individually. Therefore, in February, she refers Jose to the Response to Intervention Tier 2 reading intervention program offered by a group of special education teacher candidates from a nearby university. This program is provided to struggling students twice a week for 30 minutes each time. The interventionist-to-student ratio is 1:2. Although the Tier 2 reading program is tied to the state standards, Mrs. Perdue is unsure what skills Jose has learned in the reading intervention program and how she can reinforce the skills that Jose has learned in a different setting. She is nervous about Jose's upcoming benchmark assessments at the end of the semester, which will determine if Jose can move up to the next grade level.

"If a curriculum doesn't respond to a culture, the culture won't respond to the curriculum."
—Author unknown

The diversity of families in the United States is ever growing. According to the U.S. Census Bureau (2019), among the 328.2 million people living in the United States, 60.4% are White alone, 18.3% are Hispanic or Latino alone, 13.4% are Black or African American alone, 5.9% are Asian alone, 2.7% are two or more races, 1.3% are American Indian and Alaska Native alone, and 0.2% are Native Hawaiian and Other Pacific Islander alone. About 21.5% of the U.S. population (age 5 years+) speaks a language or languages other than English at home. Furthermore, 19.6% of U.S. households do not have the internet, 10% of the people (under age 65) do not have health insurance, and 11.8% of the U.S. population lives in urban areas.

Despite today's diverse families in the United States (about 40% of the total population), there is a lack of diversity across sex, class, linguistic and cultural diversity, and ethnicities in the early childhood education workforce (Center for the Study of Child Care Employment, 2018). Although many factors (e.g., political, economic, cultural, social, or personal) may contribute to this workforce's inequality, every teacher must understand how students' diverse cultural and linguistic backgrounds influence their learning. This chapter helps teachers understand cultural theories and how these theories align with high-leverage practices (HLPs) in special education.

Culturally Relevant Pedagogy

In 1995, Ladson-Billings used the term *culturally relevant pedagogy* (CRP) to address the strategies and dispositions that positively impacted African American/Black students' success in the K-12 classroom. Ladson-Billings spoke to eight teachers she found to be inspiring. She studied these teachers' practices and identified three significant domains: (a) academic success, (b) cultural competence, and (c) sociopolitical consciousness. *Academic success* refers to helping students grow intellectually through high-quality instruction and activities. *Cultural competence* is the ability to guide students to appreciate and understand their own cultures and the cultures of others, whereas *sociopolitical consciousness* aims to cultivate students' critical thinking and encourage them to view social issues with a critical eye and a solution-oriented mindset (Ladson-Billings, 1995).

Culturally Responsive Teaching

In 2000, Gay published a book entitled *Culturally Responsive Teaching: Theory, Research, and Practice*. This book explored why African, Asian, Latino, and Native American students are underachieving in school. Gay (2002) expressed that teachers must be prepared to teach culturally and linguistically diverse students to close the achievement gaps that many of these students face. She named this practice *culturally responsive teaching* (CRT), which has five essential components: (a) developing a cultural diversity knowledge base, (b) designing culturally relevant curricula, (c) demonstrating cultural caring and building a learning community, (d) preparing for cross-cultural communications, and (e) promoting multiculturalism and cultural congruity in classroom instruction. Gay urged teachers to learn about their students' different cultures and embed them throughout their daily curriculum.

Moreover, they should promote multiculturalism (i.e., cultural diversity) in the educational system and be prepared to engage in dialogue across cultures. The second edition of Gay's book was published in 2010, and the third edition was published in 2018. Gay extends her discussions in the new editions of her book to a broader range of diverse populations with more examples to validate CRP.

Culturally Sustaining Pedagogy

In 2012, Paris questioned the terms *relevant* and *responsive*. He argued that "relevance and responsiveness do not guarantee in stance or meaning that one goal of an educational program is to maintain heritage ways and to value cultural and linguistic sharing across difference" (p. 95). He believed the two terms are descriptive and do not explicitly teach how to sustain and support multilingualism and multiculturalism. To maintain "linguistic, literature, and cultural pluralism as part of the democratic project of schooling," he called for culturally sustaining pedagogy (CSP) to prevent diverse students from losing their cultural heritage when receiving American schooling (Paris, 2012, p. 93). Under CSP, diverse students not only develop cultural competence but also have access to the dominant cultures. Paris suggested that incorporating learning projects on cultural and social justice across languages, literacy, and community activities is one way to sustain and create a more equitable education in society.

Critical Culturally Sustaining/Revitalizing Pedagogy

In 2014, McCarty and Lee created the term *critical culturally sustaining/revitalizing pedagogy* (CSRP). They extended Paris's CSP to focus on the unique cultures of Native American students. McCarty and Lee (2014) argued that in addition to languages, literacies, and all forms of differences, Native American's tribal sovereignty, including the rights of their self-government, self-education, and self-determination, must be sustained and revitalized in education. They encouraged educators to understand CSP from the lens of revitalizing and to know that cultural revitalization is a challenging process that involves possibilities, tensions, and constraints. McCarty and Lee (2014) also argued that cultural revitalization is to awaken people to appreciate their heritage language, history, and culture.

TABLE 2-1. THE DEVELOPMENT OF CULTURALLY RELEVANT PEDAGOGY

PEDAGOGY	DEFINITION
1995 Gloria Ladson-Billings Culturally relevant pedagogy (CRP)	Prepare teachers to help K-12 African American students with academic success, cultural competence, and sociopolitical consciousness
2000, 2002 Geneva Gay Culturally responsive teaching (CRT)	Include a cultural diversity knowledge base, culturally relevant curriculum, cultural caring and a learning community, cross-cultural communications, multiculturalism, and congruity
2012 Django Paris Culturally sustaining pedagogy (CSP)	Foster and sustain linguistic, literature, and cultural pluralism of those who are marginalized by systemic inequalities
2014 Teresa L. McCarty and Tiffany S. Lee Critical culturally sustaining/revitalizing pedagogy (CSRP)	Focus on Native American students, advocate the uniqueness of Native American cultures, and recognize community-based accountability
2015 Gloria Ladson-Billings Culturally relevant pedagogy 2.0 (CRP 2.0)	Extend the initial culturally relevant pedagogy to remix the innovation across art, science, and pedagogy; adopt a dynamic view of cultural diversity

CULTURALLY RELEVANT PEDAGOGY 2.0

In 2015, Ladson-Billings proposed culturally relevant pedagogy 2.0 (CRP 2.0) to recognize many scholars' efforts in cultural diversity, particularly Paris's CSP. Ladson-Billings (2015) argued culture is dynamic and ever changing; thus, it is time to remix the latest innovations of cultural diversity with her original idea of CRP. She cautioned, "the academic death of students is made evident in the disengagement, academic failure, dropout, suspension, and expulsion in urban schools" (Ladson-Billings, 2015, p. 77). CRP 2.0 views diverse students as "subjects" who can actively contribute to society rather than "objects" being studied as a topic. Like Paris (2012), she encouraged teachers to incorporate activities and projects that will motivate students to think critically about the issues impacting their lives and communities. A summary of the development of CRP is provided in Table 2-1.

HIGH-LEVERAGE PRACTICES

To support special education teachers in working with students who have disabilities in the K-12 school setting, the Council for Exceptional Children, in collaboration with the Collaboration for Effective Educator Development, Accountability, and Reform Center, compiled 22 HLPs. These HLPs are divided into four groups: collaboration, assessment, social/emotional/behavioral, and instruction (McLeskey et al., 2017). In particular, HLPs 3, 4, 5, 7, and 18 focus on culturally and linguistically diverse students and their families. Table 2-2 shows an overview of the 22 HLPs.

TABLE 2-2. AN OVERVIEW OF THE 22 HIGH-LEVERAGE PRACTICES (HLPs)

COLLABORATION HLPs

HLP 1	Collaborate with professionals to increase student success.
HLP 2	Organize and facilitate effective meetings with professionals and families.
HLP 3[a]	Collaborate with families to support student learning and secure needed services.

ASSESSMENT HLPs

HLP 4[a]	Use multiple sources of information to develop a comprehensive understanding of a student's strengths and needs.
HLP 5[a]	Interpret and communicate assessment information with stakeholders to collaboratively design and implement educational programs.
HLP 6	Use student assessment data, analyze instructional practices, and make necessary adjustments that improve student outcomes.

SOCIAL/EMOTIONAL/BEHAVIORAL HLPs

HLP 7[a]	Establish a consistent, organized, and respectful learning environment.
HLP 8	Provide positive and constructive feedback to guide students' learning and behavior.
HLP 9	Teach social behaviors.
HLP 10	Conduct functional behavioral assessments to develop individual student behavior support plans.

INSTRUCTION HLPs

HLP 11	Identify and prioritize long- and short-term learning goals.
HLP 12	Systematically design instruction toward a specific learning goal.
HLP 13	Adapt curriculum tasks and materials for specific learning goals.
HLP 14	Teach cognitive and metacognitive strategies to support learning and independence.
HLP 15	Provide scaffolded supports.
HLP 16	Use explicit instruction.
HLP 17	Use flexible grouping.
HLP 18[a]	Use strategies to promote active student engagement.
HLP 19	Use assistive and instructional technologies.
HLP 20	Provide intensive instruction.
HLP 21	Teach students to maintain and generalize new learning across time and settings.
HLP 22	Provide positive and constructive feedback to guide students' learning and behavior.

[a]HLPs 3, 4, 5, 7, and 18 focus on culturally and linguistically diverse students and families.

Data source: McLeskey, J., et al. (2017). *High-leverage practices in special education.* Council for Exceptional Children & CEEDAR Center.

HLP 3 (teachers should respectfully and effectively communicate considering the background, socioeconomic status, language, culture, and priorities of the family) focuses on the fact that teachers need to understand and respect cultural diversity and know how to collaborate with families coming from diverse cultures (McLeskey et al., 2017, p. 32). Professional development on cultural diversity should be made available to both teachers and parents to enhance their communication skills and promote mutual understanding.

HLP 4, which focuses on assessment, indicates that to identify students' strengths and weakness, special education teachers need to "compile a comprehensive learner profile through the use of a variety of assessment measures and other sources (e.g., information from parents, general educators, other stakeholders) that are sensitive to language and culture" (McLeskey et al., 2017, p. 42). By finding ways to engage parents in students' learning process, teachers will know how students' cultural and linguistic differences contribute to their academic and behavioral performance.

HLP 5 further highlights that "special educators must understand each assessment's purpose, help key stakeholders understand how culture and language influence the interpretation of data generated, and use data to collaboratively develop and implement individualized education and transition plans" (McLeskey et al., 2017, p. 45). One way to achieve this goal is to collaboratively design assessments with stakeholders and implement adequate accommodations to maximize students' achievements. Every assessment has its strengths and limitations. To reduce the number of students with disabilities being misdiagnosed, the Individuals with Disabilities Education Act mandates that teachers take students' culture and language into account when assessing and interpreting their assessment data.

In terms of social, emotional, and behavioral practices, HLP 7 emphasizes that "teachers should establish age-appropriate and culturally responsive expectations, routines, and procedures within their classrooms that are positively stated and explicitly taught and practiced across the school year" to build a positive relationship with culturally and linguistically diverse students (McLeskey et al., 2017, p. 56). When using social stories to teach social and behavior skills, both stories and instruction need to be tailored to meet the needs of students and their classrooms. Teachers engage students by respecting and valuing their different perspectives, cultures, and languages. When teachers are willing to learn with their students and incorporate their cultural and linguistic assets into the teaching of rules, expectations, and activities, it will foster mutual respect and student engagement.

Regarding instruction, HLP 18 indicates that teachers can promote engagement by "connecting learning to students' lives (e.g., knowing students' academic and cultural backgrounds) and using a variety of teacher-led . . . peer-assisted . . . student-regulated . . . and technology supported strategies shown empirically to increase student engagement" (McLeskey et al., 2017, p. 84). There is no one single approach that can reach all students. Thus, it is necessary for teachers to incorporate a variety of high-quality activities in their instruction. Activities tied to students' interests and the relevance of their real-life situations are more likely to generate meaningful learning moments. Take Tam as an example (Case Study 1); although Tam's father cannot attend Tam's school activities due to his hectic schedule, the school can still communicate with him to see if he can fill out a 5-minute survey to help teachers know what types of activities Tam is engaged in at home. This will help Tam's teachers tailor school activities around her interests and ability.

ALIGNMENT OF CULTURALLY RELEVANT PEDAGOGY AND HIGH-LEVERAGE PRACTICES

To align CRP and HLPs, this chapter offers the following suggestions: (a) practicing cultural sensitivity, (b) establishing trust, (c) demonstrating respect, (d) sustaining high expectations, (e) creating an inclusive setting, and (f) reflecting on one's use of CRP.

Practicing Cultural Sensitivity

Teachers should engage themselves in conversations and activities to get to know diverse students and their families to implement CRP. Without knowledge about students and their families, it will be difficult for teachers to be culturally responsive. In addition to responding to students' unique needs, teachers should create cultural activities to help students sustain and revitalize their own cultures. Examples of activities that can be used to align cultural pedagogy with HLPs are described in the following sections.

Collaboration High-Leverage Practices

By collaborating with parents, teachers learn different cultural norms and values, parents' preferred ways to communicate, and any past or current life circumstances that could impact interactions. Quarterly activities with families to enhance teachers' cultural sensitivity may include report cards and progress reports; monthly activities could consist of telephone calls, in-person communications, and tool kits; weekly activities can be newsletters; and daily activities include learning journals and attendance calls (Staples & Diliberto, 2010).

Assessment High-Leverage Practices

Teachers need to examine if cultural diversity plays a role in students' performance and how future assessments can be improved. Multiple data sources must be collected and analyzed to understand students' strengths and needs on a deeper level.

Social/Emotional/Behavioral High-Leverage Practices

For adolescent students, dialogue is an excellent way to understand why students act the way they do and what improvements they hope to see in their school that would enable them to be successful. Restorative justice dialogue (Umbreit et al., 2007) helps students discuss social issues with a critical eye. It allows them to repair their communities of care as well as sustain and revitalize their own cultures.

Instruction High-Leverage Practices

Teachers should be aware that culturally and linguistically diverse students may not understand specific terms translated in English and what they mean in the U.S. context. Lacking such knowledge can easily lead students to misunderstand the school's intentions, policies, or practices. Adding a high-quality, short video to the verbal and written explanations can greatly benefit diverse students. Sometimes teachers need to take time to meet and talk with students individually.

Establishing Trust

Teachers can build trustful relationships with culturally and linguistically diverse students and their families by (a) keeping an open-door policy and open communication lines for all students and parents to share their concerns, (b) acting responsively to the needs of diverse students, and (c) providing community-based resources in individually identified areas of concern or need.

Collaboration High-Leverage Practices

Teachers who are positive, proactive, and solution oriented are likely to gain families' trust (Edwards & Fonte, 2012). They monitor how students are doing in school and use simple, natural, and effective ways to communicate with parents about their children's performance. Being mindful of the language used with parents and ensuring that parents are being provided with clear and accurate responses are ways to establish trust with parents. How can you collaborate with students to build trust?

Assessment High-Leverage Practices

When communicating students' high-stake assessments, teachers may consider the RISC steps (Blackwell & Stockall, 2019)—Review the report, Interpret the results, Streamline the report with the interpretation, and Communicate the next step to the students. These steps take time to practice and require teachers to engage in reflective practice.

Social/Emotional/Behavioral High-Leverage Practices

Teachers can establish trust with students by collaborating to develop meaningful and practical behavioral plans. Keeping the procedures of any plans transparent, treating students fairly, and respecting their privacy are essential ways to gain students' trust.

Instruction High-Leverage Practices

Sharing tips and detailing homework plans that allow parents to support their children's progress will build trusting relationships (Hampshire et al., 2014; Nagro, 2015). Family message journals (Valerie & Foss-Swanson, 2012) are useful ways to help parents know what students have learned in school. When using family message journals, it is essential to educate parents not to overcorrect their children's spelling and grammar. Prioritizing skills to teach and only focusing on one or two errors each time will motivate students to continue writing. If parents cannot read their children's journals, teachers can assign school personnel to help.

Demonstrating Respect

It is vital to affirm students' and their families' identities, the values they bring, and their opinions. Teachers must intervene in situations that threaten the dignity of students or their families. Other strategies to demonstrate teachers' respect include listening to parents patiently, incorporating activities that align with students' interests and priorities, and engaging parents and students in the decision-making process. Teaching students multicultural content in an unbiased and authentic manner will positively help students view the diverse world and their own cultures. The various circumstances of each family can serve as a barrier or facilitator to engagement. Thus, teachers need to use information acquired about students and families in a way that shows respect.

Collaboration High-Leverage Practices

Teachers may check if their school districts have English as a second language teachers or multicultural liaisons fluent in English and different languages. Some state laws require certified interpreters. Despite the help from multicultural liaisons or interpreters, teachers still need to do their very best to communicate with parents. One way is to consider Nagro's (2015) PROSE checklist to enhance written communication with parents—Print (e.g., font, size, and highlighting), Readability (e.g., word limits, fifth-grade level, simple words, and short sentences), Organization (e.g., diagrams), Structure (e.g., one page, space, and image quality), and Ease (e.g., active voice, easy and relevant examples, and terms written out). Also, adopting a family partnership model (deFur, 2012) that centers on students will foster respect between families and school collaborators. This model requires teachers to examine their attitude and value toward diverse students and their families.

Assessment High-Leverage Practices

Teachers need to carefully select or develop assessment questions to avoid conflicts or discrimination among students with different cultural backgrounds. Teachers need to be patient when parents and students do not understand the assessment or disagree with assessment results. When communicating progress monitoring data and setting learning goals, teachers can adopt an Individualized Education Program (IEP) checklist (Lo, 2012) to prepare for effective meetings before, during, and after the IEP meeting. When parents feel that they are respected in the entire process, it will enhance communication and collaboration.

Social/Emotional/Behavioral High-Leverage Practices

When students know that their teachers welcome cultural diversity, it will promote mutual respect. Teachers can use multicultural content that enables students to compare and contrast social behaviors in different cultures. This will help all students understand and respect different cultural perspectives. Teachers are encouraged to work with students to identify the areas that can be further improved. All stakeholders (students, parents, and school personnel) can initiate communication if they need help.

Instruction High-Leverage Practices

Teachers can demonstrate that they respect students as people by merely being on time, giving fair comments, and providing timely and constructive feedback. Respecting students' voices and incorporating their ideas into instructional activities will demonstrate that teachers value students' suggestions. This creates empowering and engaging learning environments for students. Moreover, integrating multicultural content helps students know that what they learn in school will help them outside the classroom. When examples are relevant, it increases students' comprehension and application. Teachers can work with English as a second language teachers and multicultural liaisons on developing instructional activities for diverse students. Can you provide an example of a multicultural activity?

Sustaining High Expectations

Sustaining high expectations for diverse students and their families educates all students that everyone, regardless of their background, can contribute to the community. To achieve this, teachers can encourage culturally and linguistically diverse students to share their knowledge with others. They can also strengthen family members' capacities to engage in leadership opportunities with other community members.

Collaboration High-Leverage Practices

Parents need to feel that their children's teachers hold appropriately high expectations for their children and that they offer support to help their children succeed. Parents and students are encouraged to advocate for their needs so that their teachers know what expectations parents and students have. Teachers should communicate with parents and students to ensure that every stakeholder has a shared vision and is ready to move toward the same goal.

Assessment High-Leverage Practices

Different cultures have different expectations for students' academic performance. Thus, it is essential to involve parents in the decision-making process as early as possible to help teachers understand parents' expectations. This will also give parents a holistic view of their children's performance. What does this have to do with assessment?

Social/Emotional/Behavioral High-Leverage Practices

Like academic performance, different cultures have different social norms. For example, in some Asian cultures, students are expected to wait for their teachers to call their names before responding to teachers' questions. If teachers are not aware of cultural diversity, they may think that their diverse students are less prepared or motivated. To prevent misunderstanding, teachers should communicate clearly with students and their parents about what the classroom rules are and how they will lead to high expectations for all students.

Instruction High-Leverage Practices

Instead of holding deficit views that lead to lower academic expectations for students with disabilities, teachers should treat students as a whole person. They can consider adopting a 3E planning process (Espiner & Guild, 2012) to capture what matters most for students and their families and engage them in educational planning. The first E stands for Engage. Teachers discuss with students and learn about their dreams, strengths, and interests and ideas for getting there. The second E is Envisage (i.e., teachers collaborate with students to develop learning objectives and provide the needed support to help students achieve their goals). The third E stands for Enact. It is necessary to have an effective progress monitoring system to continually evaluate the effectiveness of instructional activities.

Creating an Inclusive Setting

An inclusive setting nurtures mutual understanding among all members of the community. Communication is key. Creating an inclusive environment requires using a language that situates the classroom as a community and fairly acknowledges students' and their families' contributions. Teachers must be capable of facilitating positive interactions among all individuals and preventing any situations that will make students and their families feel less valued. Assisting students and families in navigating conflicts in such a way that each member's position is affirmed and that an acceptable resolution is reached will create positive learning opportunities for all members of the community.

Collaboration High-Leverage Practices

The steps of Sawyer's (2015) BRIDGES may help teachers build an inclusive relationship with families. These steps are as follows: Build a relationship, Recruit input, Individualize support, Dialogue frequently, Generate ideas, Empower parents, and Strengthen partnerships. Teachers can flexibly adjust these steps to meet families' different needs.

Assessment High-Leverage Practices

In an inclusive setting, teachers need to make sure that culturally and linguistically diverse students have received sufficient time to practice skills before taking a formal, summative assessment. They should monitor if these students can generalize new skills in different settings. Modeling and guided practices should be made available to give a quick reteach for struggling students.

Social/Emotional/Behavioral High-Leverage Practices

Students do not develop good behavior simply by observing others or watching a video that models such behavior, especially those who have disabilities and come from different cultural backgrounds. Some students need their teachers to explicitly and systematically teach them how to develop new skills. What does this have to do with an inclusive classroom?

Instruction High-Leverage Practices

When having culturally and linguistically diverse students with disabilities in the inclusive setting, teachers need to create a learning environment that is structured and predictable so that students can easily follow along. For example, establishing classroom routines and procedures will make it easier for students to learn.

Reflecting on One's Use of Cultural Pedagogy

Reflecting on the patterns of how teachers engage their students and families will help teachers learn and relearn cultural diversity. Different forms of reflection include engaging in critical conversations with experts and colleagues, self-examination of personal biases, and dialoguing with students and their families.

Collaboration High-Leverage Practices

Rossetti and colleagues (2017) developed a series of guiding questions and action plans to help teachers build a collaborative partnership with diverse families. These questions include the following: "How culturally responsive am I?" "Who is the family?" and "Have we developed a collaborative partnership?" (p. 174). Their recommended action plans include reflecting on one's cultural beliefs and experiences, identifying areas to improve culturally responsive practices, gaining knowledge about different cultures and languages, showing a willingness to get to know students and their families, assessing current relationships with parents and the quality of IEP meetings, and enacting collaborative partnerships during the IEP process.

Assessment High-Leverage Practices

When teachers reflect on their practices, they may notice things that they did not consider previously for diverse families. If any unexpected issues arise, teachers should handle them promptly. Additionally, teachers need to demonstrate that they are willing to listen and adjust to meet the students' best interests. Sometimes teachers need to find creative ways to solve problems, which may differ from what they do with typical learners. Teachers' sincerity and positive attitude will foster a better outcome.

Social/Emotional/Behavioral High-Leverage Practices

Teachers need to continually reflect on how their cultural backgrounds affect how they view students' behavior. They can work with students to develop a reflective questionnaire (e.g., Do I respect people's differences?) to help teachers and students grow their knowledge about different cultures.

Instruction High-Leverage Practices

Students with disabilities from diverse families may not make adequate progress as quickly as typical learners. Teachers need to reflect on these students' efforts and celebrate their progression. They should follow up with parents regarding their satisfaction with their children's learning and modify their instructional activities based on parents' suggestions.

A FRAMEWORK OF ALIGNING CULTURALLY RELEVANT PEDAGOGY AND HIGH-LEVERAGE PRACTICES

To align CRP and HLPs, teachers should equip themselves with the fundamental knowledge of cultural theories. Then, they need to put the theories into practice by intentionally applying the collaboration, assessment, social/emotional/behavioral, and instruction HLPs. IRIS modules created by Vanderbilt University (IRIS Center, 2020) serve as an excellent resource to help teachers become familiar with HLPs (Appendix). Because no two students are identical, teachers still have to use their practical wisdom (Shulman, 2004) to adjust the HLPs for individual students. Figure 2-1 shows the framework. The included case studies are examples of this.

For Tam, who is nonverbal, has autism, and whose mother does not speak English, Mrs. Brandon can ask the school district to see if there is a multicultural liaison who helps Vietnamese families. If not, she may create visual aids to assist her communication with Tam's parents. Mrs. Brandon can also videotape Tam's classroom performance to help Tam's mother understand what she has learned in school. In this way, Tam's mother knows what skills need to be reinforced at home. Mrs. Brandon can incorporate applied behavior analysis techniques to teach Tam communication skills and use engaging activities to help Tam interact with peers. Ongoing progress monitoring can help Mrs. Brandon see if Tam is on the right trajectory.

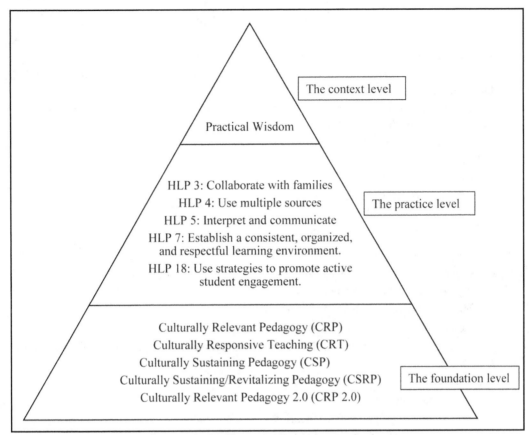

The context level

Practical Wisdom

HLP 3: Collaborate with families
HLP 4: Use multiple sources
HLP 5: Interpret and communicate
HLP 7: Establish a consistent, organized,
and respectful learning environment.
HLP 18: Use strategies to promote active
student engagement.

The practice level

Culturally Relevant Pedagogy (CRP)
Culturally Responsive Teaching (CRT)
Culturally Sustaining Pedagogy (CSP)
Culturally Sustaining/Revitalizing Pedagogy (CSRP)
Culturally Relevant Pedagogy 2.0 (CRP 2.0)

The foundation level

Figure 2-1. Aligning CRP and HLPs across the foundation, practice, and context levels.

For Jose, because most essential documents in U.S. public schools are translated in Spanish, Mrs. Perdue needs to check with his parents to make sure that they have the school's messages and if they have any questions for her. Compared with Tam, Jose's parents feel more pressured about Jose's academic performance due to his age and grade level. In this situation, early intervention with explicit and intensive instruction is needed to help Jose catch up. Although Jose is receiving a Response to Intervention Tier 2 intervention provided by a group of special education teacher candidates from a nearby university, Mrs. Perdue should work collaboratively with Jose's interventionist to continue reinforcing the skills. Creating a form to monitor Jose's academic and behavioral performance in both Tier 1 and Tier 2 settings will help Mrs. Perdue know if Jose is making adequate progress.

SUMMARY

Over 25 years, it has been abundantly clear that CRP stands out as one of the most significant predictors to engage culturally and linguistically diverse students and their families. Although HLPs in special education provide concrete directions and strategies about what teachers can do across collaboration, assessment, social/emotional/behavioral, and instruction domains, teachers still need to base their application of the HLPs on their practical wisdom (i.e., teachers should determine individual students' needs and real-life contexts and use them to adjust their application of the HLPs).

CHAPTER REVIEW

1. Describe the major differences among CRP, CRT, CSP, CSRP, and CRP 2.0.

2. Discuss the HLPs that have a focus on culturally and linguistically diverse students and their families.

3. In addition to the foundation level of cultural theories and the practice level of HLPs, what plays a crucial role in putting the cultural theories into practice?

4. There are several major theories on cultural diversity. Please put them in order from the oldest to the most recent.
    a. CRP, CRP 2.0, CRT, CSP, and CSRP
    b. CRT, CSP, CSRP, CRP, and CRP 2.0
    c. CRP, CRT, CSP, CSRP, and CRP 2.0
    d. CRP, CRP 2.0, CSP, CRT, and CSRP

5. HLPs are divided into which of the following groups:
    a. Collaboration, assessment, social/emotional/behavioral, and instruction
    b. Academic, behavioral, social, and emotional
    c. Microsystem, mesosystem, exosystem, and macrosystem
    d. Home, school, society, and cross-contexts

6. To work with diverse students and their families, teachers need to possess different levels of knowledge EXCEPT:
    a. The context level of practical wisdom
    b. The practice level of HLPs
    c. The foundational level of CRP theories
    d. The proficiency level of a second language

7. What are the five essential components of CRT?

8. True or False: Teachers should learn about their students' different cultures and embed them throughout their daily curriculum.

9. Incorporating learning projects on cultural and social justice across _____, _____, and _____ activities is one way to sustain and create a more equitable education.

10. Cultural revitalization is a challenging process that involves:
    a. Possibilities
    b. Tensions
    c. Constraints
    d. All of the above

APPENDIX. IRIS RESOURCES ON HIGH-LEVERAGE PRACTICES (HLPs) WITH A FOCUS ON CULTURAL DIVERSITY

COLLABORATION

HLP 3	*Collaborate with families to support student learning and secure needed services.*
Classroom Diversity: An Introduction to Student Differences	https://iris.peabody.vanderbilt.edu/module/div/
Cultural and Linguistic Differences: What Teachers Should Know	https://iris.peabody.vanderbilt.edu/module/clde/
Dual Language Learners with Disabilities: Supporting Young Children in the Classroom	https://iris.peabody.vanderbilt.edu/module/dll/
Serving Students with Visual Impairments: The Importance of Collaboration	https://iris.peabody.vanderbilt.edu/module/v03-focusplay/
Family Engagement: Collaborating with Families of Students with Disabilities	https://iris.peabody.vanderbilt.edu/module/fam/

ASSESSMENT

HLP 4	*Use multiple sources of information to develop a comprehensive understanding of a student's strengths and needs.*
Functional Behavioral Assessment: Identifying the Reasons for Problem Behavior and Developing a Behavior Plan	https://iris.peabody.vanderbilt.edu/module/fba/
The Pre-Referral Process: Procedures for Supporting Students with Academic and Behavioral Concerns	https://iris.peabody.vanderbilt.edu/module/preref/
HLP 5	*Interpret and communicate assessment information with stakeholders to collaboratively design and implement educational programs.*
RTI: Data-Based Decision Making	https://iris.peabody.vanderbilt.edu/wp-content/uploads/pdf_case_studies/ics_rtidm.pdf
RTI: Progress Monitoring	https://iris.peabody.vanderbilt.edu/wp-content/uploads/pdf_case_studies/ics_rtipm.pdf
Secondary Transition: Student-Centered Transition Planning	https://iris.peabody.vanderbilt.edu/module/tran-scp/#content

SOCIAL/EMOTIONAL/BEHAVIORAL

HLP 7	*Establish a consistent, organized, and respectful learning environment.*
Accommodations to the Physical Environment: Setting Up a Classroom for Students with Visual Disabilities	https://iris.peabody.vanderbilt.edu/module/v01-clearview/
Cultural and Linguistic Differences: What Teachers Should Know	https://iris.peabody.vanderbilt.edu/module/clde/
Dual Language Learners with Disabilities: Supporting Young Children in the Classroom	https://iris.peabody.vanderbilt.edu/module/dll/#content

(continued)

APPENDIX (CONTINUED). IRIS RESOURCES ON HIGH-LEVERAGE PRACTICES (HLPS) WITH A FOCUS ON CULTURAL DIVERSITY

Effective Room Arrangement: Elementary	https://iris.peabody.vanderbilt.edu/wp-content/uploads/pdf_case_studies/ics_effrmarr_elementary.pdf
Instructional Accommodations: Making the Learning Environment Accessible to Students with Visual Disabilities	https://iris.peabody.vanderbilt.edu/module/v02-successsight/#content
Autism Spectrum Disorder (Part 2): Evidence-Based Practices	https://iris.peabody.vanderbilt.edu/module/asd2/#content
Early Childhood Environments: Designing Effective Classrooms	https://iris.peabody.vanderbilt.edu/module/env/
Classroom Management (Part 1): Learning the Components of a Comprehensive Behavior Management Plan	https://iris.peabody.vanderbilt.edu/module/beh1/
Classroom Management (Part 2): Developing Your Own Comprehensive Behavior Management Plan	https://iris.peabody.vanderbilt.edu/module/beh2/
Early Childhood Behavior Management	https://iris.peabody.vanderbilt.edu/wp-content/uploads/pdf_case_studies/ics_ec_behavior_mgmt.pdf
Early Childhood Behavior Management: Developing and Teaching Rules	https://iris.peabody.vanderbilt.edu/module/ecbm/
Establishing Classroom Norms and Expectations	https://iris.peabody.vanderbilt.edu/wp-content/uploads/pdf_case_studies/ics_norms.pdf
INSTRUCTION	
HLP 18	***Use strategies to promote active student engagement.***
Classroom Diversity: An Introduction to Student Differences	https://iris.peabody.vanderbilt.edu/module/div/
SOS: Helping Students Become Independent Learners	https://iris.peabody.vanderbilt.edu/module/sr/
CSR: A Reading Comprehension Strategy	https://iris.peabody.vanderbilt.edu/module/csr/
PALS: A Reading Strategy for Grades 2–6	https://iris.peabody.vanderbilt.edu/module/pals26/
PALS: A Reading Strategy for Grades K–1	https://iris.peabody.vanderbilt.edu/module/palsk1/
PALS: A Reading Strategy for High School	https://iris.peabody.vanderbilt.edu/module/palshs/
Universal Design for Learning: Creating a Learning Environment that Challenges and Engages All Students	https://iris.peabody.vanderbilt.edu/module/udl/
Data source: IRIS Center. (2020). High-leverage practices. https://iris.peabody.vanderbilt.edu/resources/high-leverage-practices/	

REFERENCES

Aronson, B., & Laughter, J. (2016). The theory and practice of culturally relevant education: A synthesis of research across content areas. *Review of Educational Research, 86*, 163-205. https://doi.org/10.3102/0034654315582066

Blackwell, W. H., & Stockall, N. (2019). RISC: Four steps for interpreting and communicating high-stakes assessment results. *Teaching Exceptional Children, 51*(4), 265-275.

Center for the Study of Child Care Employment. (2018). *Early childhood workforce index.* Institute for Research on Labor and Employment University of California, Berkeley. https://cscce.berkeley.edu/files/2018/06/2-About-the-Workforce.pdf

deFur, S. (2012). Parents as collaborators: Building partnerships with school and community-based providers. *Teaching Exceptional Children, 44*(3), 58-67.

Edwards, C. C., & Fonte, A. D. (2012). The 5-point plan: Fostering successful partnerships with families of students with disabilities. *Teaching Exceptional Children, 44*(3), 6-13.

Espiner, D., & Guild, D. (2012). Capturing what matters most: Engaging students and their families in educational planning. *Teaching Exceptional Children, 44*(5), 56-67.

Gay, G. (2000). *Culturally responsive teaching: Theory, research and practice.* Teachers College Press.

Gay, G. (2002). Preparing for culturally responsive teaching. *Journal of Teacher Education, 53*(2), 106-116.

Hampshire, P. K., Butera, G. D., & Hourcade, J. J. (2014). Homework plans: A tool for promoting independence. *Teaching Exceptional Children, 46*(6), 158-168.

IRIS Center. (2020). *High-leverage practices.* https://iris.peabody.vanderbilt.edu/resources/high-leverage-practices/

Klingner, J. K., Brownell, M. T., Mason, L. H., Sindelar, P. T., Benedict, A. E., Griffin, G. G., Lane, K., Israel, M., Oakes, W. P., Menzies, H. M., Germer, K., & Park, Y. (2016). Teaching students with special needs in the new millennium. In D. Gitomer & C. Bell (Eds.), *Handbook of research on teaching* (5th ed., pp. 639-717). American Educational Research Association.

Ladson-Billings, G. (1995). Toward a theory of culturally relevant pedagogy. *American Educational Research Journal, 32*(3), 465-491.

Ladson-Billings, G. (2015). Culturally relevant pedagogy 2.0: A.k.a. the remix. *Harvard Educational Review, 84*(1), 74-84.

Linn, D., & Hemmer, L. (2011). English language learner disproportionality in special education: Implications for the scholar-practitioner. *Journal of Educational Research and Practice, 1*, 70-80. https://doi.org/10.5590/JERAP.2011.01.1.06

Lo, L. (2012). Demystifying the IEP process for diverse parents of children with disabilities. *Teaching Exceptional Children, 44*(3), 14-20.

McCarty, T. L., & Lee, T. S. (2014). Critical culturally sustaining/revitalizing pedagogy and Indigenous education sovereignty. *Harvard Educational Review, 84*(1), 101-124.

McLeskey, J., Barringer, M-D., Billingsley, B., Brownell, M., Jackson, D., Kennedy, M., Lewis, T., Maheady, L., Rodriguez, J., Scheeler, M. C., Winn, J., & Ziegler, D. (2017). *High-leverage practices in special education.* Council for Exceptional Children & CEEDAR Center.

Nagro, S. A. (2015). PROSE checklist: Strategies for improving school-to-home written communication. *Teaching Exceptional Children, 47*(5), 256-263.

Paris, D. (2012). Culturally sustaining pedagogy: A needed change in stance, terminology, and practice. *Educational Researcher, 41*(3), 93-97.

Rossetti, Z., Sauer, J. S., Bui, O., & Ou, S. (2017). Developing collaborative partnerships with culturally and linguistically diverse families during the IEP process. *Teaching Exceptional Children, 49*(5), 328-338.

Samson, J. F., & Lesaux, N. K. (2009). Language-minority learners in special education: Rates and predictors of identification for services. *Journal of Learning Disabilities, 42*, 148-162. https://doi.org/10.1177/0022219408326221

Sawyer, M. (2015). BRIDGES: Connecting with families to facilitate and enhance involvement. *Teaching Exceptional Children, 47*(3), 172-179.

Shulman, L. S. (2004). *The wisdom of practice: Essays on teaching, learning and learning to teach.* Jossey-Bass.

Staples, K. E., & Diliberto, J. A. (2010). Guidelines for successful parent involvement: Working with parents of students with disabilities. *Teaching Exceptional Children, 42*(6), 58-63.

Umbreit, M. S., Coates, R. B., & Vos, B. (2007). Restorative justice dialogue: A multi-dimensional, evidence-based practice theory. *Contemporary Justice Review, 10*(1), 23-41.

U.S. Census Bureau. (2019). *United States quick facts.* https://www.census.gov/quickfacts/fact/table/US/PST045218

U.S. Department of Education. (2016). *Racial and ethnic disparities in special education.* Office of Special Education and Rehabilitation. http://www2.ed.gov/programs/osepidea/618-data/LEA-racial-ethnic-disparities-tables/index.html

Valerie, L. M., & Foss-Swanson, S. (2012). Using family message journals to improve student writing and strengthen the school-home partnership. *Teaching Exceptional Children, Jan/Feb,* 40-48.

Early Childhood Assessments (Ages 4 to 8)

Melissa K. Driver, PhD and Christie H. Ingram, MEd

INTRODUCTION

Assessment is central to early childhood instruction, including the eligibility process and ongoing progress monitoring. Teachers must understand the numerous ways to assess students and use valid and reliable data with fidelity to make educational decisions. Educators use assessment data to determine what students know and can do for summative purposes. Educators should also use assessment data formatively to determine how to design instruction and intervention programs to best support learning through data-based individualization. Early childhood assessment is a collaborative process involving numerous key stakeholders, including family members and other school personnel. As with all aspects of instruction, the examination must be nondiscriminatory and consider the unique linguistic and cultural assets each child brings to the classroom. This chapter explores the purpose of evaluations, cultural and linguistic considerations, collaboration in assessment, the evaluation's role in the eligibility process, guidelines for early childhood assessment, forms of assessment, data-based individualization, and progress monitoring.

Fisher, K. M., & Zimmer, K. E. (Eds.).
Early Childhood Special Education Programs and Practices (pp. 41-68).

CHAPTER OBJECTIVES

→ Formulate connections between special education law and assessments required in the eligibility process.

→ Discover the purpose of assessments.

→ Examine the guidelines for early childhood assessments.

→ Outline the different forms of early childhood assessments.

→ Use progress monitoring to identify learning targets and monitor progress.

→ Select evidence-based teaching strategies and interventions that align with the Division for Early Childhood Recommended Practices and the Council for Exceptional Children's high-leverage practices.

KEY TERMS

- **Accommodations:** Services or supports that allow a student to access the general education curriculum without changing the content or reducing the expectations/requirements.

- **Curriculum-Based Measurement:** An assessment used to assess and monitor a student's academic skills directly.

- **Data-Based Individualization:** A research-based approach to help teachers plan instructional programs that accelerate students' growth with and without disabilities.

- **Eligibility:** The comprehensive evaluation process once a child is referred for special education to qualify for Individuals with Disabilities Education Act services.

- **Formative Assessment:** Used during a lesson or unit to provide a teacher with information about students' understanding of the instructional concepts and guide future instruction within the lesson or unit (Klute et al., 2017).

- **Individualized Education Program (IEP):** The educational program identifies an individual's strengths and areas of need, specific disability, present levels of performance, accommodations and modifications, assessment considerations, a continuum of service delivery, least restrictive environment, behavior intervention plans, and transition plans (as appropriate). Assessment is an integral part to all aspects of IEP development and implementation.

- **Modifications:** Adaptations that alter the level of difficulty and/or actual content as a part of specially designed instruction and assessment.

- **Norm-Referenced Assessment:** An assessment that compares a specific student's ability with that of same-age students in a national sample.

- **Progress Monitoring:** Involves administering assessment measures frequently, graphing and analyzing data over a set period of time, and using these data to inform instruction and intervention assessment measures. Progress monitoring data provide an indicator of a student's performance in relation to an intervention or instruction. These data help provide feedback on the current intervention to adjust various components, such as dosage or rate of reinforcement.

- **Standardized Assessment:** This assessment follows standard administration procedures for all children using the same sequence, testing and scoring methods, and materials.

- **Summative Assessment:** This is given at the conclusion of the lesson or unit and provides data that can be delivered to educational stakeholders and inform educators of class-wide learning.

Figure 3-1. A student presenting a project to her class. (adriaticfoto/Shutterstock.com)

CASE STUDY

Five-year-old Mia is in Ms. Smith's co-taught kindergarten classroom. Since October, she has been in the Response to Intervention process due to concerns with her reading and math skills. Her preschool teacher from the previous year had concerns based on progress reports and conference notes provided by Mia's parents. The kindergarten team agreed to closely monitor Mia during the first quarter of kindergarten and use multiple forms of data and assessment to determine if further testing for special education would be warranted.

"The quality of assessors is critical to the quality of the assessment result."
—*Pearl Zhu*

One of the most critical aspects of a child's education involves the role of assessment. Because of its importance, identified high-leverage practices (HLPs) in special education include evaluation as one of the four core areas of expertise essential for special educators (McLeskey et al., 2017). Assessment is central to the federal law protecting children with documented disabilities and also to the process of identifying children with disabilities. Assessment should reveal what students have learned, indicate what still needs to be taught, and inform future instruction. This is often referred to as *assessment of and for learning.*

This chapter introduces a range of formal and informal assessment procedures. Often, the term *assessment* invokes images of students sitting in desks taking high-stakes tests. You might hear, or personally believe, that students are tested too much or perhaps that testing has taken the place of learning in today's classrooms. Although this chapter neither confirms nor denies this common sentiment, it will broaden and/or reinforce your understanding of assessment and why it is critical for all learners' success. Asking a question midlesson, observing a student's behavior during lunch, and conversing with a family member are all assessment examples. The following sections of this chapter explore the purpose of evaluations, cultural and linguistic considerations, collaboration in evaluation, the evaluation's role in the eligibility process, guidelines for early childhood assessment, forms of evaluation, data-based individualization, and progress monitoring. Figure 3-1 depicts a student presenting a project to her class. This is an example of a formative assessment performed through project-based learning.

Figure 3-2. An example of students working in a collaborative group. (Ground Picture/Shutterstock.com)

PURPOSE OF EARLY CHILDHOOD ASSESSMENT

The purpose of assessment in early childhood is to develop a comprehensive understanding of a child's strengths, preferences, interests, and academic and social-emotional areas of need and support. This understanding should serve as the foundation of eligibility and instructional decisions and inform the next steps to provide the child's best educational services. Educators assess all areas of development and behavior to develop this comprehensive understanding (Division for Early Childhood [DEC] Recommended Practice A4 and HLP 4) and ensure students are accurately identified and served under the Individuals with Disabilities Education Act (IDEA, 2004).

Educators assess young children for many reasons, including to establish an instructional baseline before beginning instruction, to plan for teaching, to understand what they have learned after instruction, to understand what they can generalize and maintain, to determine their coping and social-emotional skills, to know how they are progressing in the curriculum over time, and to determine if they qualify for a disability and are eligible to receive special education services. Assessment plays a central role in many, if not all, of the instructional decisions educators make for young children. Many of these decisions can have a life-altering impact on a child for better and, unfortunately, worse if a child is inaccurately diagnosed. All teachers have an ethical obligation to ensure that assessments are administered, analyzed, and used in equitable and fair ways for all children. Figure 3-2 depicts an example of students working in a collaborative group. Teacher observation during collaborative group activities is an example of an informal assessment.

CULTURAL AND LINGUISTIC CONSIDERATIONS IN ASSESSMENT

A key consideration for assessment is a young child's and family members' native language. This is important in both the formal eligibility process as well as informal daily classroom assessment. The intersection of language, assessment, and instruction presents a risk of misidentifying young children who are English-language learners (ELLs) for special education during the eligibility process (McMaster et al., 2008; Sullivan, 2011). This intersection is especially salient for young children because students who are not proficient in their native language or English are at an increased risk for special education identification (Artiles et al., 2005). Research shows disturbing trends for students who are ELLs. For example, longitudinal data analyses indicate ELLs are often under-represented in special education at kindergarten and first grade and over-represented in late elementary and

Figure 3-3. A teacher using a whole-group lesson as a formative assessment strategy. (Unsplash)

secondary levels (Artiles et al., 2005; Samson & Lesaux, 2009). Teachers must conduct assessments in the child's dominant language and in additional languages if they are learning more than one language (DEC Recommended Practice A5). This is not just best practice but also falls under federal law. The national IDEA (2004) mandates nondiscriminatory assessment for children with disabilities, including evaluation throughout the eligibility process.

The eligibility process for young children under IDEA (2004) relies on educator judgment of eligibility criteria, the validity and reliability of the assessment measures, and the process's cultural appropriateness (Artiles et al., 2010). Assessments used in the identification process are often designed for and normed with the English language, which can be especially problematic for ELLs (Basterra et al., 2011; Sanchez et al., 2013). The following sections further detail the eligibility process and the importance of ongoing progress monitoring. The essence of effective collaboration is central throughout all aspects of assessment.

COLLABORATION IN ASSESSMENT

Collaboration with key stakeholders is integral to the assessment process. For young children, stakeholders might include co-teachers, teaching assistants, school administration and/or directors, family members, and other service providers (i.e., speech-language pathologists, occupational therapists, and applied behavior analysts). Together, a team of stakeholders collaboratively work to collect data and make educated decisions in the child's best interest (e.g., teaching assistants might assist in observational data collection on a child's behavior). An occupational therapist might analyze the child's fine motor skills. Classroom teachers might complete numerous surveys and data collection forms on the child's learning and behavior throughout multiple time points in the day. Family members contribute invaluable insights into how the classroom observations align with the child's interactions at home and provide unique insights into learning and behavior patterns. Before moving on, it is essential to note that numerous individuals might care for and make educational decisions for a child. There is a range of primary and secondary caregivers; thus, caregivers, parents, and/or guardians will be referred to as family or family members for this chapter. This terminology intends to emphasize an inclusive approach toward all caregivers, parents, and/or guardians throughout the educational process as mandated in the IDEA. Figure 3-3 depicts how a teacher can use a whole-group lesson as a formative assessment strategy. This is an informal assessment strategy in which the teacher can assess comprehension by asking questions before, during, and after the read aloud.

Figure 3-4. A group of educators and additional stakeholders collaborating together to make educational decisions for students. (Unsplash)

Teachers should work as a team with a child's family to gather assessment information and identify family preferences (DEC Recommended Practices A1 and A2). Collaboration is essential in all aspects of instruction and assessment. Although this is important for students with disabilities of all ages, it is imperative for young children. Working collaboratively allows teachers to balance the scientific assessment process and procedures with family preferences and requests and the educational expertise of other service providers and school leaders (Friend & Cook, 2017).

Special education teachers increasingly spend less time in self-contained classrooms and more time co-teaching in general education settings (Eisenman et al., 2010). A collaborative classroom in which two teachers work together can benefit all the students in the classroom (Simmons et al., 2012). This is particularly relevant for classroom assessment. As you will learn in this chapter, assessing young children often requires observational data and individualized attention to performance-based tasks. One teacher might lead whole- or small-group instruction in a co-taught classroom while another teacher assesses students individually.

Research on effective collaboration emphasizes the ability to communicate effectively, clearly, and consistently (Pellegrino et al., 2014). Communication is a critical aspect of effective collaboration (Mattessich et al., 1992). Family members of children with disabilities advocate for teachers who will openly communicate, share resources, partner, and demonstrate respect and understanding (West & Pirtle, 2014). It is also essential to consider how language and cultural perspectives and differences can impact communication, both in terms of style and approach. Teachers should seek to learn about their students' families, prior school experiences (both positive and negative), and linguistic preferences for communication. A translator may be needed to communicate effectively with family members, and teachers can work with their district to build an ongoing relationship between the school, translator, and family. Conversations about assessment can often be sensitive topics, particularly if a child struggles in a specific area or the eligibility process. The stronger the relationship with a child's family, the more equipped a teacher will be to navigate these sensitive conversations (HLP 5 and DEC Recommended Practice A11). Figure 3-4 depicts a group of educators and additional stakeholders collaborating together to make educational decisions for students.

Conversations about young children should remain asset based and include the numerous strengths and cultural wealth (i.e., funds of knowledge and identity; Esteban-Guitart & Moll, 2014; Moll et al., 1992) each child brings to the classroom, in addition to areas of concern. Strong collaboration and communication can take commitment and intentionality to establish, but the benefits are worthwhile and essential for student success. Collaboration between family members and other school professionals allows teachers to obtain information about a child's skills throughout daily activities both in and outside of the classroom (DEC Recommended Practice A7).

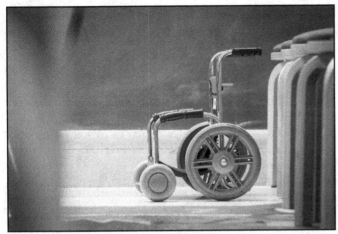

Figure 3-5. A reminder that we also serve students in education with disabilities, and specific considerations must be made when assessing these students. (Unsplash)

Ms. Smith collaborates with her paraprofessional, the special education teacher with whom she co-teaches, and Mia's parents to discuss ongoing concerns despite the interventions already put into place. Based on weekly progress, monitoring data, and classroom observation notes, Mia's progress is minimal. The assessments show that she struggles with phonemic awareness and number sense. She has difficulty with rhyming and segmenting sounds. In math, she has difficulty identifying numbers and discriminating between quantities. Baseline assessments administered during the first weeks of school show that Mia falls significantly below the benchmark compared with her peers. Ms. Smith met with her co-teacher to develop appropriate intervention strategies to help Mia progress toward these skills. They used curriculum-based measurements weekly to gather data during the period of progress monitoring. It is now the end of the first semester of kindergarten, and Mia continues to fall below the benchmark in phonemic awareness and number sense. Both teachers schedule a meeting with Mia's parents to discuss their continued concerns and a plan moving forward. Mia's parents are reluctant to discuss the possibility of moving forward with a special education evaluation. Although they were honest that Mia struggled in preschool, they were hopeful that a more structured environment with more elementary school support would be the answer. Ms. Smith is aware of the parents' feelings and knows that she needs to positively and supportively present her plan. She knows it is vital not only to discuss the area where Mia is struggling but also to discuss the positives, including Mia's creativity and cooperative nature in the classroom. Mia's parents also must be made to feel that they are part of Mia's team and that their opinions and input matter.

Assessment and Special Education Eligibility

The IDEA (2004) was initially enacted in 1975 to ensure free and appropriate public education, special education, and related services to students with disabilities throughout the country. The IDEA regulates how states and public agencies provide early intervention and special education services to infants, toddlers, children, and youth with disabilities deemed eligible. There are four parts to the IDEA, but we focus on Part B, Assistance for Education of All Children with Disabilities, in this chapter. Part B is the foundation for how school-age children with disabilities (ages 3-22 years) will receive special education and related services (Center for Parent Information and Resources, 2018). Figure 3-5 serves as a reminder that we also serve students in education with disabilities, and specific considerations must be made when assessing these students.

Before being considered for special education services, a team evaluation must be completed individually with the child to determine if the child has a disability that impacts their ability to participate in the school setting without interventions and supports. There are three primary purposes for conducting a special education evaluation:

1. To determine if the young child is a "child with a disability" as defined by the IDEA
2. To gather comprehensive data to determine if the child's deficits are impacting them educationally
3. To determine the child's needs and make decisions on appropriate educational programs to help the child be successful

It is important to note that all children with disabilities are not automatically eligible for special education services. For special education, the child's disability must have an educational impact. Children with disabilities who do not require individualized assistance may be eligible for supports under Section 504 of the Rehabilitation Act of 1973 instead of under the IDEA. To initiate a special education evaluation under the IDEA, one of the following may occur:

- Parents may request an evaluation due to concerns regarding their child. Federal law requires the evaluation is performed at no cost to the parent.
- The school system may recommend an evaluation for the child. This recommendation can originate from a teacher recommendation, results from standardized tests, and/or classroom observations.
- Young children who receive early intervention services will transition to the school system before their third birthday. A team meeting to determine eligibility must occur before the child's third birthday.

The Child Find mandate is one component of the IDEA. It is a legal requirement for schools to identify children who may have a disability and require services through the school system (Lee, n.d.). Identifying these students early is an essential step in making sure they have the support needed to be successful in an educational environment. This mandate covers all children from birth to age 21; however, for assessment in early childhood educational settings, the district's Child Find team starts at age 3. School districts are mandated to have a process to identify and evaluate any child with suspected delays. Children do not have to be enrolled in a school in order for the Child Find team to conduct an evaluation. Many systems have a developmental screening several times a year. This process is an efficient tool to determine if a child does present with deficits and should be referred for a full evaluation. A developmental screening typically takes 1 hour, and the child is screened by a school audiologist, speech pathologist, special education teacher, occupational therapist, and physical therapist. The most beneficial piece of this process is to use a screening tool that will provide accurate and specific information on what the child is able or not able to do (SRI Education, 2016). The information gathered from the screening can be used to determine if the child should be referred for a comprehensive evaluation with the school system.

The Ages and Stages Questionnaires is a widely used tool for screening children from birth through age 6. It can also be combined with the Ages and Stages Questionnaires: Social Emotional to give parents and practitioners a complete look at the child's development. This assessment is broken down by the child's age, and the child is assessed through parent interviews and interactions with the practitioners. The assessment takes minutes to score, and the child's score is compared with the cutoff points provided on the scoring sheet (How ASQ Works, n.d.). The cutoff scores provide information to determine if the child is developing on-target skills for their age as well as areas that may need to be monitored. The team may recommend the child return for a team evaluation if they fall below the cutoff score for one or more of the developmental areas. If the child is close to falling below the cutoff score, the school team may recommend multitiered systems of support in the child's preschool setting for 6 weeks of monitoring. In this instance, educators will collect and analyze data. At the end of the multitiered systems of support period, the team may refer the child for a comprehensive evaluation if they do not show progress with evidence-based strategies.

Informed parent consent is required before an evaluation can take place per the IDEA. Informed parent consent is defined as "the parent has been fully informed regarding the action of the school system for which parental consent is being requested" (Center for Parent Information and Resources, 2017, para. 1). Parent communication must also be in their native language. This includes all activity

Figure 3-6. A father and a young child. (Unsplash)

and personnel involved in the evaluation process. Once the parent signs consent, the evaluation team has 60 days to complete the evaluation. This provides the team time to gather additional data from parents, medical professionals, private therapists, and/or classroom teachers. If a state establishes a shorter timeline, the team must follow the timeline set forth by their state government. The state cannot establish a longer timeline from what the federal law requires (Center for Parent Information and Resources, 2017). Figure 3-6 depicts a father and a young child. It demonstrates an example of early intervention, reminding the reader that not just school-age children are eligible for evaluations through the school system.

After meeting with Mia's teachers, the counselor, and a school administrator, her parents decided that it was time to have Mia evaluated to determine if she would be eligible for special education services. During the meeting, Mia's teachers shared work samples from a cumulative portfolio, progress monitoring graphs, observation notes, and the instructional strategies implemented during the progress monitoring phase. Mia's parents felt supported by the school team, and they thought that the team communicated Mia's needs effectively. They appreciated seeing Mia's work samples and progress monitoring graphs collected throughout the first semester. This visual representation of Mia's performance gave them a clear picture of Mia's classroom needs. The accommodations implemented were shared with the team, including individualized interventions, one-on-one assessment, and reteaching the concepts with which Mia struggles. Because Mia is already in a co-taught classroom, Ms. Smith collaborated with her paraprofessional and the school special education teacher to devise a plan to support Mia. The paraprofessional and special education teacher were able to teach small groups while Mia worked one on one with Ms. Smith on reteaching and assessments. Also, Mia was able to work in differentiated small groups with the special education teacher as she used specific interventions with other students who struggled with similar skills. Both teachers took anecdotal notes while working with Mia and communicated their findings throughout each evaluation step. They helped Mia's parents understand that additional support would be available if Mia were found eligible for special education services. Mia's parents had the misconception that Mia would be removed from her kindergarten classroom if she needed additional support. Because of the school team's collaboration and effective communication with Mia's parents, the team addressed this misconception, and the parents' concerns were eased. Mia's parents signed consent for an evaluation. The team will now have 60 days to complete a comprehensive evaluation on Mia to determine if she will be eligible for special education services.

Once parental consent occurs, the evaluation process can begin. Examiners will use clinical reasoning in addition to assessment results to identify the child's current levels of functioning and to determine the child's eligibility and plan for instruction (DEC Recommended Practice A8). To establish eligibility, the evaluation consists of more than a child sitting with examiners to complete the requested tasks. The IDEA mandates that the evaluation be comprehensive to gather sufficient data of the child's functional, educational, and developmental strengths and needs. A thorough evaluation includes information regarding the child's overall health, both past and present; hearing/vision; social and emotional functioning; cognitive functioning; communication and language; adaptive skills; fine and gross motor skills; preacademic or academic functioning; sensory (if applicable); and parent input and family history.

Examiners must gather information in a variety of ways for eligibility. Direct assessments, observations, parent and teacher rating scales, work samples, and interviews provide a comprehensive picture of the child. These data must also come from various sources, including parents, teachers, therapists, diagnosticians, psychologists, and so on. The IDEA also mandates that the evaluation team uses assessments that are found through research to be valid, reliable, and standardized. Validity ensures that the assessment measures what it is supposed to measure. This includes both the validity of the actual assessment instrument and the validity of use (Overton, 2016). This is especially important to consider for young children because not all testing formats are developmentally appropriate for young learners. *Reliability* refers to the degree that the assessment will produce consistent results (i.e., its dependability). According to Overton (2016), reliability relates to the likelihood that an assessment instrument will "yield the same score for the same student if the test were administered more than once and to the degree with which a skill or trait is measured consistently across items of a test" (p. 75). Figure 3-7 provides an illustration of validity and reliability. If an assessment is reliable, the scores should consistently land in a close, similar range. If an assessment is valid, it should measure the intended target. In other words, the assessment consistently hits the bull's-eye. Both reliability and validity are critical to ensure educators make sound instructional decisions using assessment data.

Norm-referenced assessments compare the child's performance with others in their age group. This is a standard method used in special education assessments to provide the examiners with reliable data to determine special education eligibility. Examiners must also be sure to administer assessments with fidelity. In an educational context, *fidelity* refers to the degree to which examiners follow the directions outlined in the assessment manual (National Center on Response to Intervention, 2013). Implementation and scoring fidelity are critical components in assessment, especially when using the assessment data to determine if a child will qualify under an eligibility category. The lack of adherence can lead to an inaccurate representation of the child's performance and skills. Examples may include an examiner giving incorrect instructions, arranging materials differently than outlined in the manual, providing assistance, and/or making modifications. Likewise, examiners must follow the scoring procedures outlined in the testing manual so that scoring bias does not interfere with providing accurate results. Table 3-1 provides examples of standardized assessments that can be used with young children when trying to determine special education eligibility.

It is also essential for the evaluation team to consider that the assessments used do not discriminate against race or culture. The team must select materials and implement procedures to ensure appropriate evaluation for a child whose native language is not English and that the assessment accurately measures educational needs rather than measuring English-language skills. Suppose the examiner deviates from the standard protocol outlined in the assessment manual, such as a parent translating in the native language, or the method of test administration is changed. The team documents any changes or variations in the eligibility report, which educators consider during the evaluation process.

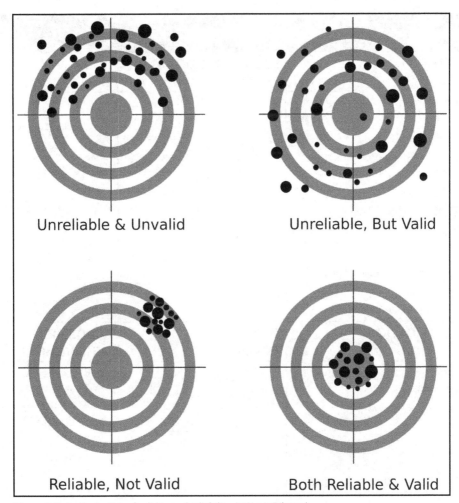

Figure 3-7. An illustration of validity and reliability. (© Nevit Dilmen.)

Examiners must use various methods for collecting data to gather information about the child being assessed to determine eligibility. Table 3-2 lists several forms of informal and formal assessment in early childhood. Each of these forms is useful to include in the process of determining a child's eligibility for special education under the IDEA.

Once all of the information is collected, the team writes the eligibility report. The evaluation team will have a meeting with the parents to determine if the child qualifies for a disability category under the IDEA. The team will discuss assessment findings, analyze strengths and needs, and consider any possible exclusionary factors that could influence a child's performance. Exclusionary factors include a lack of appropriate instruction in reading, writing, or math; a vision or hearing impairment; limited English proficiency; or an environmental and economic disadvantage, just to name a few. Suppose no exclusionary factors are present and the evaluation results meet the criteria for one or more eligibility requirements under the IDEA, the team will decide on eligibility and will go on to develop an Individualized Education Program (IEP) to support the child's educational needs. Figure 3-8 is a picture of colorful sidewalk chalk. It represents using age-appropriate and hands-on activities with young children to determine the skills the child can perform.

TABLE 3-1. STANDARDIZED ASSESSMENTS FOR ELIGIBILITY

COGNITIVE SKILLS	SOCIAL/EMOTIONAL SKILLS	ADAPTIVE SKILLS
• Developmental Assessment of Young Children-Second Edition (DAY-C) • Kaufman Brief Intelligence Test-Second Edition (KBIT-2) • Differential Ability Scales-Second Edition (DAS-II) • Cognitive Assessment of Young Children (CAYC) • Woodcock-Johnson IV (WJ IV) • Wechsler Preschool and Primary Scale of Intelligence (WPPSI)	• Adaptive Behavior Assessment Scales (ABAS) • Behavior Assessment Scales for Children (BASC) • Preschool and Kindergarten Behavior Scales (PKBS) • DAY-C	• ABAS • Vineland Adaptive Behavior • DAY-C

COMMUNICATION SKILLS	MOTOR SKILLS	ACADEMIC ACHIEVEMENT
• Expressive One-Word Picture Vocabulary Test (EOWPVT) • Receptive One-Word Picture Vocabulary Test (ROWPVT) • Comprehensive Receptive & Expressive Vocabulary Test Clinical Evaluation of Language Fundamentals (CELF) • Preschool Language Scale (PLS) • DAY-C	• DAY-C • Peabody Developmental Motor Scales-Second Edition (PDMS-2)	• Bracken School Readiness Assessment-Third Edition (BSRA-3) • Brigance Early Childhood

DEVELOPMENTAL ASSESSMENTS	AUTISM RATING SCALES	SENSORY PROCESSING
• Developmental Profile-Third Edition (DP-3) • Battelle Developmental Inventory-Third Edition (BDI-3) • Preschool Evaluation Scales-Second Edition (PES-2)	• Autism Diagnostic Observation Schedule (ADOS) • Childhood Autism Rating Scale (CARS) • Autism Spectrum Rating Scales (ASRS) • Gilliam Autism Rating Scale (GARS)	• Sensory Processing Measure (SPM): ages 5 to 12 • Sensory Processing Measure-Preschool (SPM-P): ages 2 to 5 • Sensory Profile-Second Edition (SP-2)

TABLE 3-2. FORMS OF ASSESSMENT

FORM OF ASSESSMENT	DESCRIPTION
Observations	Observing the child in their natural environment (i.e., school classroom) can provide the team with valuable information on the child's overall ability to function and cope in the classroom setting. Observers can take notes on the child's ability to make transitions, attend to group activities, follow teacher-directed activities, and how well the child does with social interactions. Often, a young child may do well in a one-to-one testing situation; however, their functionality in a classroom may look very different. In addition to classroom observations, anecdotal observation notes from the testing session should be included in the eligibility report. For example, did the child make eye contact with examiners? Did the child follow directions? Was the child socially connected?
Parent rating scales/interviews	Parents know their child best, and their input is vital to the assessment process. There are several standardized rating scales for parents to rate their children in the five areas of development, including social, cognitive, adaptive, motor, and communication skills. Sensory processing, attention-deficit/hyperactivity disorder, and autism rating scales may also be provided to parents. In addition to the parent rating scales, examiners should interview the parents about the child's past medical history, developmental milestones, strengths and weaknesses, and concerns parents have regarding their child's development.
Teacher rating scales	Teacher rating scales are instrumental because they provide a picture of how well the child functions within the classroom. Teachers can be given the same rating scales as the parent; however, the questions differ based on the home vs. school environment. These rating scales are compared with the parent rating scales to determine if the child is functioning consistently between home and school or if the child is struggling more in the school environment vs. the home environment.
Portfolios/work samples	Portfolios are a collection of a child's work samples over time to show progress. Portfolios can also include pictures of the young child participating in group activities and assignments. Other sources of information used in a portfolio include videos, interviews with parents and other teachers, and skill checklists. Some examples of student work samples are included in Figures 3-11 through 3-14.
Standardized assessments	These formal assessments follow standard administration procedures, meaning that the assessment is given to all children following the same sequence, methods, and materials (Slentz et al., 2008). Best practices for standardized assessment in young children include opportunities for authentic content and hands-on manipulatives when possible. As Guddemi and Case (2004) stated, "Because standardized assessments are not as accurate, valid, and reliable for young children as they are for older children, they should not be used solely to make high stakes decisions until grade 3 and preferably not until grade 4" (p. 7). This is why it is crucial to incorporate the assessment methods listed earlier in combination with standardized assessments.

Figure 3-8. A picture of colorful sidewalk chalk. (Unsplash)

GUIDELINES FOR EARLY CHILDHOOD ASSESSMENT

Practitioners should use assessment materials and strategies appropriate for the child's age and level of development and accommodate the child's sensory, physical, communication, cultural, linguistic, social, and emotional characteristics (DEC Recommended Practice A3). The assessment of young children should focus on the child's overall development and skills, including social/emotional, adaptive, fine and gross motor, cognitive, and language. Young children do not fully comprehend the purpose of testing, so it is crucial that the evaluating team understands early childhood development and how to present assessment tasks in an age-appropriate and engaging way. When possible, hands-on activities are helpful to determine the skills a child can perform. Paper-and-pencil assessments are not developmentally appropriate, especially for very young children. Examples of suitable materials and strategies for assessing young children may include the following:

- Asking a young preschool child to sort colored bears or rings on a post by color
- Watching a child play on age-appropriate playground equipment to assess gross motor skills
- Using items that pertain to the child's interest when assessing skills, such as counting or naming colors
- Using colorful and engaging pictures when considering language
- Observing the child in their natural environment to assess social and adaptive skills

In addition to using materials and developmentally appropriate strategies, examiners must also consider a child's sensory needs. Before an initial assessment, examiners should consult with parents and review background information to accommodate a child's sensory needs during the evaluation. Likewise, teachers should be familiar with their students' sensory needs and provide accommodations for classroom assessments to meet these needs. Characteristics to consider may include the following:

- Does the child need frequent movement breaks?
- Does the lighting need to be reduced in the classroom or testing room?
- Does the child need a fidget or a weighted vest/lap pad?
- Do materials need to be out of the child's reach and presented one at a time?
- Does the child have noise sensitivity and need a quiet area to test?

Figure 3-9 depicts a child filling a toy dump truck in a sandbox. This serves as another example of how to use age-appropriate and hands-on activities in the child's natural environment to determine the child's strengths and weaknesses. Observation on a playground is a great way to informally assess a child's social skills.

Figure 3-9. A child filling a toy dump truck in a sandbox. (Unsplash)

Cultural and linguistic considerations also must be made. Examiners should be sure that the materials they are using are culturally sensitive and are not biased against families of different cultural backgrounds. They should administer testing items and parent rating scales in the child's native language. Examiners should also be familiar with the cultural gestures of the child they are evaluating. For example, it is disrespectful for a child to make eye contact with an adult in some cultures. An examiner could misinterpret this behavior as a social deficit if not aware of cultural norms. The National Research Council (2001) states, "One of the greatest dangers in assessing young children is to associate developmental status with the norms of the dominant middle-class culture. This will lead to misunderstanding of children's functional abilities and misjudging pedagogical strategies" (p. 238).

For all assessment purposes, examiners should use assessment tools with sufficient sensitivity to detect child progress, especially for the child with significant support needs (DEC Recommended Practice A10). In the early childhood setting, teachers should use formal and informal assessment strategies through observations and age-appropriate, hands-on activities to measure what their students know and understand and what skills or concepts may need further instruction. In addition to assessing the students, teachers use assessments to gauge the effectiveness of their teaching and classroom management skills. Educators may need to use more specialized or individualized methods for children who have more significant needs. One example of this is to modify their assessment practices so that all children can participate regardless of their disability. Figure 3-10 depicts colored pencils used in an early childhood classroom. This picture provides another example of using age-appropriate materials in an early childhood classroom. Children may use these materials to create work samples to be used in portfolios.

Accommodations and modifications are two critical aspects of specially designed instruction for children with disabilities. Accommodations and/or modifications should be formally listed in the IEP to ensure consistent and fair administration. An accommodation is a service or support that

Figure 3-10. Colored pencils used in an early childhood classroom. (Unsplash)

allows students to access the general education curriculum without changing the content or reducing the expectations/requirements. For example, a child might receive extended time or frequent breaks during an assessment period, have the text read aloud, have the opportunity to respond orally instead of through written response, or be able to use a calculator or manipulatives to solve mathematics problems. The actual content is not different, but how the child interacts with the content might differ from their peers.

In contrast, modifications do alter the level of difficulty and/or actual content. One example is providing a fourth-grade child with a second-grade–level reading passage to assess comprehension. The accommodations and modifications selected should align directly with the child's disability, educational needs, and learning goals. It is important to remember that expectations will not be less; the expectations will be different. Accommodations and modifications are allowable education adaptations to help students overcome barriers associated with their disability.

Teachers may need to (a) use an alternative measure that is appropriate for the child, (b) modify how they ask a child to demonstrate a skill, (c) assess the child's background knowledge or prerequisite skills needed to participate in the assessment, and (d) reduce the number of test/progress monitoring items (DEC of the Council for Exceptional Children, 2007). It is important to remember that educators must not modify standardized assessments. When examiners do not follow the standardized procedures set forth by the assessment, the reliability of the results is jeopardized. It is important to remember that ongoing assessment is critical for helping teachers implement appropriate teaching strategies, measure each student's progress, make adjustments to teaching as needed, and determine if students with disabilities would benefit from accommodations and/or modifications in the classroom. Without ongoing assessment, teachers do not have the data required to help them make informed decisions nor do they have the data to measure student progress toward identified goals. Figures 3-11 through 3-14 are examples of student work that can be used in a student portfolio used for assessment.

The team involved in Mia's evaluation includes her teachers who know her and a school psychologist. Her teachers continue with the progress monitoring data, collecting work samples, making observation notes, and giving formative and summative assessments. The psychologist schedules two mornings to come and administer standardized achievement tests. She will use the Woodcock-Johnson IV and the Wechsler Preschool and Primary Scale of Intelligence because these assessments are appropriate for young children. The psychologist needs to schedule two sessions so that Mia does not fatigue or become frustrated during the evaluation. They will research a quiet room for them to work together to avoid distractions during the assessment. The speech-language pathologist will also schedule a time to complete a language screening using the Clinical Evaluation of Language Fundamentals–Fifth Edition

Figure 3-11. An example of student work that can be used in a student portfolio for assessment.

Figure 3-12. An example of student work that can be used in a student portfolio for assessment.

Figure 3-13. An example of student work that can be used in a student portfolio for assessment.

Figure 3-14. An example of student work that can be used in a student portfolio for assessment.

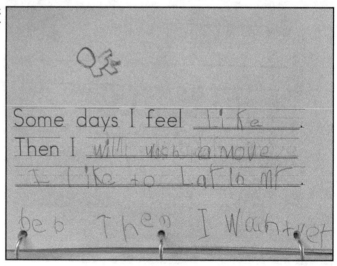

screening test. If Mia does not pass the language screening, the evaluator will complete a full language evaluation. Her parents will be provided with developmental questionnaires to provide the team with information regarding when Mia reached her developmental milestones, health history, strengths, and areas of need her parents see at home. Once the evaluator scores all of the assessments, they will write an eligibility report to document all scores from standardized assessments, work samples, and progress monitoring graphs. In addition, the school psychologist will include the information provided by her parents. Educators will involve her parents in the eligibility meeting and include them in the decision-making process.

Using Assessment to Inform Instruction in Early Childhood

Not only is an assessment used to determine if a child is eligible for special education services, but also it should be used to inform instruction in the early childhood classroom. Assessments help teachers identify the strengths and needs of their students and help parents better understand the needs of their children. To develop a deep understanding of a student's learning needs, special educators and examiners alike can put together a comprehensive profile of the child through the use of a variety of assessment measures and other sources (e.g., parent interview, general educators, and other stakeholders in the child's life). These assessments should be sensitive to language and culture to (a) analyze and describe students' strengths and needs and (b) analyze the school-based learning environments to determine potential supports and barriers to students' academic progress (HLP 4). Instruction and assessment are intricately linked throughout the entire educational process. Table 3-3 outlines the alignment of instructional practices with the DEC Recommended Practices and HLPs.

Examples of assessments that teachers can use include curriculum-based measures; informal classroom assessments; observations of student academic performance and behavior; and discussions with key stakeholders, including students, families, and other professionals (McLeskey et al., 2017). It may also be helpful for a teacher to complete a self-assessment and reflection when completing a lesson to improve instructional practices. When special educators consistently use data to inform and adjust instruction, they increase the frequency and appropriateness of instructional decision making and improve student achievement (Lembke et al., 2019). Summative and formative assessments are two examples of assessments teachers can integrate into the early childhood classroom.

1. Summative assessments indicate what a child has learned over time. In the early childhood classroom, this may be a portfolio of the child's work over time, individual or group projects to demonstrate learning, and hands-on performance tasks. For older students, examples of summative assessments are end-of-chapter tests, book reports, and final examinations. Summative assessments are given after the lesson or unit and provide data that can be delivered to educational stakeholders and inform educators of class-wide learning.

2. Formative assessments are informal types of assessments that measure ongoing progress. In the early childhood classroom, formative assessments may look like gathering data from a group game, participation during circle time, and frequent monitoring and observations. For older students, examples of formative assessments are tickets out the door, contests, and polls. Formative assessments are used during a lesson or unit to provide a teacher with information about students' understanding of the instructional concepts and guide future instruction within the lesson or unit (Klute et al., 2017).

Research has shown that high-quality assessment systems in the early childhood environment can significantly impact the quality of teaching and learning and improve outcomes for young children (King, 2019). Instruction for young children with disabilities should consist of evidence-based, specially designed instruction implemented with fidelity. Throughout instruction, assessment should occur regularly through progress monitoring. The process of using progress monitoring data to improve outcomes for children is well illustrated through data-based individualization (DBI). The IRIS Center Progress Monitoring: Reading is a useful case study to help practice administering, scoring, and analyzing progress monitoring assessments. Figure 3-15 depicts an additional example of using age-appropriate materials and hands-on activities in the assessment of young children.

TABLE 3-3. ALIGNMENT OF INSTRUCTIONAL PRACTICES WITH ASSESSMENT STANDARDS

INSTRUCTIONAL PRACTICE	ALIGNED DEC RECOMMENDED PRACTICES	ALIGNED HLPs
Collaboration	A1: Practitioners work with the family to identify family preferences for assessment purposes. A2: Practitioners work as a team with the family and other professionals to gather assessment information. A6: Practitioners use a variety of methods, including observation and interviews, to gather assessment information from multiple sources, including the child's family and other significant individuals in the child's life. A7: Practitioners obtain information about the child's skills in daily activities, routines, and environments such as home, center, and community.	HLP 1: Collaborate with professionals to increase student success. HLP 4: Use multiple sources of information to develop a comprehensive understanding of a student's strengths and needs. HLP 5: Interpret and communicate assessment information with stakeholders to collaboratively design and implement educational programs.
Specially designed instruction	A9: Practitioners implement systematic ongoing assessments to identify learning targets, plan activities, and monitor the child's progress to revise instruction as needed. A10: Practitioners use assessment tools with sufficient sensitivity to detect child progress, especially for the child with significant support needs.	HLP 5: Interpret and communicate assessment information with stakeholders to collaboratively design and implement educational programs. HLP 6: Use student assessment data, analyze instructional practices, and make necessary adjustments that improve student outcomes.
Progress monitoring	A9: Practitioners implement systematic, ongoing assessments to identify learning targets, plan activities, and monitor the child's progress to revise instruction as needed. A10: Practitioners use assessment tools with sufficient sensitivity to detect child progress, especially for the child with significant support needs.	HLP 6: Use student assessment data, analyze instructional practices, and make necessary adjustments that improve student outcomes.

(continued)

TABLE 3-3 (CONTINUED). ALIGNMENT OF INSTRUCTIONAL PRACTICES WITH ASSESSMENT STANDARDS

INSTRUCTIONAL PRACTICE	ALIGNED DEC RECOMMENDED PRACTICES	ALIGNED HLPs
Formative and summative assessment	A3: Practitioners use assessment materials and strategies that are appropriate for the child's age and level of development and accommodate the child's sensory, physical, communication, cultural, linguistic, social, and emotional characteristics. A4: Practitioners conduct assessments that include all areas of development and behavior to learn about the child's strengths, needs, preferences, and interests. A5: Practitioners conduct assessments in the child's dominant language and in additional languages if the child is learning more than one language. A8: Practitioners use clinical reasoning in addition to assessment results to identify the child's current levels of functioning and to determine the child's eligibility and plan for instruction. A9: Practitioners implement systematic ongoing assessment to identify learning targets, plan activities, and monitor the child's progress to revise instruction as needed. A10: Practitioners use assessment tools with sufficient sensitivity to detect child progress, especially for a child with significant support needs.	HLP 4: Use multiple sources of information to develop a comprehensive understanding of a student's strengths and needs. HLP 6: Use student assessment data, analyze instructional practices, and make necessary adjustments that improve student outcomes.
Use of SMART IEP goals	A7: Practitioners obtain information about the child's skills in daily activities, routines, and environments such as home, center, and community. A10: Practitioners use assessment tools with sufficient sensitivity to detect child progress, especially for the child with significant support needs. A11: Practitioners report assessment results so that they are understandable and useful to families.	HLP 1: Collaborate with professionals to increase student success. HLP 4: Use multiple sources of information to develop a comprehensive understanding of a student's strengths and needs. HLP 5: Interpret and communicate assessment information with stakeholders to collaboratively design and implement educational programs.

DEC = Division for Early Childhood; HLPs = high-leverage practices; IEP = Individualized Education Program; SMART = Specific, Measurable, Action oriented, Relevant and realistic, and Time limited.

Data sources: Division for Early Childhood. (2014). DEC recommended practices in early intervention/early childhood special education. 2014. http://www.dec-sped.org/recommendedpractices and McLeskey, J., et al. (2017). *High-leverage practices in special education.* Council for Exceptional Children & CEEDAR Center.

Figure 3-15. An additional example of using age-appropriate materials and hands-on activities in the assessment of young children. (Unsplash)

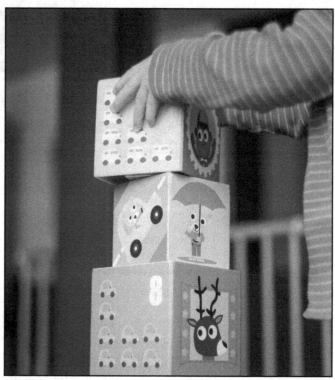

DATA-BASED INDIVIDUALIZATION AND PROGRESS MONITORING

DBI is a research-based approach to help teachers plan instructional programs that accelerate students' growth with and without disabilities (Fuchs et al., 2014). It is an ongoing process that links instruction, intervention, and assessment to improve student academic and/or behavior outcomes (Danielson & Rosenquist, 2014). DBI can be used as a framework to intensify interventions in academic areas such as reading (Lemons et al., 2014), mathematics (Powell & Stecker, 2014), and writing (McMaster et al., 2020) and to support student behavior (Kern & Wehby, 2014). There are five steps of the DBI process. A link to a helpful visual of the DBI process is provided in the Resources section included in this chapter.

Analyzing student progress monitoring data to inform decision making for when and how to intensify instruction is central to the DBI process. To effectively monitor progress, teachers should first select an appropriate, valid, and reliable assessment measure and collect at least three baseline data points. The median score of the baseline data is the student's "starting" point. Teachers should then set a goal for the intervention period that considers the length of intervention time, the starting point, and an appropriate growth rate. A line graph represents the baseline data, numerical goal, and goal/aim line drawn from the median score to the numerical goal. Teachers then implement an intervention and collect weekly data on the same progress monitoring measure throughout the intervention period. Teachers graph and analyze data to determine if the goal line should increase (i.e., the intervention is working and data points are above the goal line), if the intervention needs an adjustment (i.e., the intervention does not seem to be working and data points are below the goal line), or if the intervention should continue as is (i.e., data points are right around the goal line; Fuchs et al., 2014). Figure 3-16 provides a basic example of a progress monitoring graph. A helpful video of the process is linked in the Resources section (Curriculum-Based Measurement in Reading: Oral Reading Fluency).

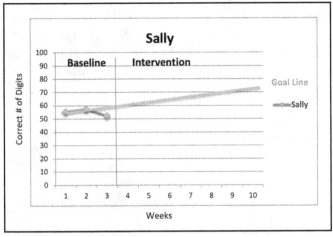

Figure 3-16. A basic example of a progress monitoring graph.

The Academic Screening Tools Chart (link provided in the Resources section) provides examples of early childhood progress monitoring measures. Progress monitoring data indicate a student's performance in response to an intervention or instructional practice toward a learning goal. Educators frequently collect progress monitoring data to give feedback on the current intervention. Progress monitoring helps teachers make instructional decisions rather than merely measuring academic performance (e.g., Stecker et al., 2005). Graphed over time, progress monitoring data provide invaluable insight into adjusting various components such as frequency, length, intensity, or instructional approach (HLP 6 and DEC Recommended Practice A9).

Throughout the evaluation process, assessment data helped inform the best educational course for Mia. The formal and informal data points created a common ground for educators and family members to center high-stakes conversations around; the assessment process allowed numerous voices to provide critical input throughout the evaluation process. Regardless of the outcome for Mia's evaluation, the assessment will continue to play an integral role in her education, as it should for all students. Ms. Smith will continue to collaborate with her paraprofessional, special education teacher, and Mia's family as she provides individualized data-based instruction. She will continue to set goals with Mia, provide targeted instruction, collect and graph data to monitor progress, analyze ongoing data, adjust instruction to ensure alignment, and intensify intervention as needed. The information gained throughout the evaluation process is invaluable. If the process ends with a disability diagnosis, the team will formally secure all of this information and effective supports for Mia in an IEP.

SUMMARY

Assessment is central to all aspects of early childhood instruction. Special education teachers must intimately understand the numerous ways to assess students and use valid and reliable data to make educational decisions. Assessment helps determine what students currently know and can do and informs how to design instruction and intervention programs to support learning through DBI. In the eligibility process and ongoing progress monitoring, educators must administer assessment measures with fidelity and analyze results holistically. Early childhood assessment is a collaborative process involving numerous key stakeholders, including family members and other school personnel. As with all aspects of instruction, the assessment must be nondiscriminatory and consider the unique linguistic and cultural assets each child brings to the classroom.

Figure 3-17. A student using a computer to facilitate online instruction; many students have had to make this shift due to the pandemic. (Unsplash)

As the school experience increasingly shifts to online and remote learning, educators can apply the assessment principles described in this chapter for online and remote education. Educators can administer progress monitoring measures virtually through individual interviews with children using videoconferencing technology. For example, to assess reading fluency, a teacher might share a brief passage on their computer screen, timing the student while they read. Teachers can record the assessment videoconference for later analysis and compare growth with parental and school permission. For assessments that may require materials such as manipulatives, educators should consider using everyday household items or working with their school/district to obtain a set to provide for family members. Family members may need to take an active role in assisting during the assessment period for very young children. Although remote learning can present challenges for young learners, it also allows for additional opportunities to build collaborative relationships with family members and to have intentional one-on-one time with each student. Figure 3-17 depicts a student using a computer to facilitate online instruction; many students have had to make this shift due to the pandemic.

CHAPTER REVIEW

1. Which law refers to how school-age children with disabilities (ages 3 to 22) will receive special education and related services?

   a. LRE (least restrictive environment)

   b. FAPE (free and appropriate public education)

   c. IDEA, Part B

   d. Due process

2. How can young children be referred for a special education evaluation?
    a. Parents may request an evaluation due to concerns regarding their child. Educators must conduct this evaluation at no cost to the parent.
    b. The school system may recommend for the child to be evaluated. This can be based on a teacher's recommendation, results from standardized tests, and observations in the classroom.
    c. Young children who receive early intervention services will transition to the school system before their third birthday. A team will conduct the evaluation, and they must hold the meeting before the child's third birthday.
    d. All of the above
3. Ongoing and informal assessment in the classroom is called:
    a. Summative assessment
    b. Formative assessment
    c. Standardized assessment
    d. High-stakes assessment
4. The following considerations must be made during assessment:
    a. Cultural/linguistic considerations
    b. Parents must provide informed consent
    c. Child's age and developmental level
    d. All of the above
5. What is the general timeline set forth by the IDEA that the assessment team has to complete the evaluation and hold the eligibility meeting?
    a. 60 days
    b. 30 days
    c. 6 months
    d. 2 weeks
6. A comprehensive evaluation of a child may include the following:
    a. Parent/teacher information
    b. Observations
    c. Direct testing
    d. All of the above
7. This assessment compares a specific student's ability with that of same-age students in a national sample:
    a. Criterion-referenced tests
    b. Norm-referenced tests
    c. Standardized tests
    d. Dynamic assessment
8. A step of the DBI process is to:
    a. Implement the current validated intervention program (Tier 2, secondary intervention, or standard protocol intervention) with increased intensity (e.g., smaller group size or more time).
    b. Use the diagnostic data along with educator expertise to modify or adapt the intervention to better meet the student's individual need.
    c. If the student continues to struggle, collect diagnostic information to identify specific skill deficits or behavior concerns.
    d. Collect frequent progress monitoring data to determine whether the student is responding to the intervention.

9. The purpose of graphing progress monitoring data is to:
   a. Analyze consecutive data points to determine if the goal line should be increased (i.e., data points are above the goal line).
   b. Analyze consecutive data points to determine if you should adjust the intervention (i.e., data points are below the goal line).
   c. Analyze consecutive data points to determine if the goal line of the intervention should continue as is.
   d. All of the above

10. In a hypothetical data set, imagine a child's progress monitoring data show consistent upward progress that remains below the goal line. This child's teacher should:
    a. Make no instructional changes and reduce the frequency of progress monitoring.
    b. Make no instructional changes but continue weekly progress monitoring.
    c. Continue the intervention but increase the frequency or intensity of the intervention.
    d. Implement a new intervention to increase student progress.

11. Discuss the three main purposes for conducting a special education evaluation.

12. List the steps included in a comprehensive evaluation. Provide examples of information gathered during the evaluation process.

13. Discuss the difference between formal and informal assessments. Give examples of each.

14. Discuss the guidelines that should be followed for early childhood assessment.

RESOURCES

- Academic Screening Tools Chart: https://charts.intensiveintervention.org/chart/academic-screening
- CEEDAR Center Practice-Based Learning Opportunities: https://ceedar.education.ufl.edu/plos/
- Curriculum-Based Measurement in Reading: Oral Reading Fluency: https://vimeo.com/channels/550360/58381922
- DBI Visual Flowchart: https://intensiveintervention.org/sites/default/files/DBI_One-Pager_508.pdf
- Division for Early Childhood of the Council for Exceptional Children, DEC Recommended Practices (with examples): https://fpg.unc.edu/sites/fpg.unc.edu/files/resources/presentations-and-webinars/Recommended%20Practices%20with%20Examples_0.pdf
- Intensive Intervention: www.intensiveintervention.org
- IRIS Module–Accommodations: https://iris.peabody.vanderbilt.edu/module/acc/
- IRIS Module–Early Childhood Assessment: Children's Classroom Environment: https://iris.peabody.vanderbilt.edu/wp-content/uploads/pdf_activities/independent/IA_Assessment_Childrens_Environments.pdf
- IRIS Module–Early Childhood Assessment: Cognitive Skills: https://iris.peabody.vanderbilt.edu/wp-content/uploads/pdf_activities/independent/IA_Cognitive_Skills.pdf
- IRIS Module–Early Childhood Assessment: Play Skills: https://iris.peabody.vanderbilt.edu/wp-content/uploads/pdf_activities/independent/IA_Assessment_of_Play_Skills.pdf
- IRIS Module–Early Childhood Assessment: Preschool Classroom Observation: https://iris.peabody.vanderbilt.edu/wp-content/uploads/pdf_activities/independent/IA_Preschool_Classroom_Observation.pdf
- IRIS Module–Early Childhood Assessment: Social Skills: https://iris.peabody.vanderbilt.edu/wp-content/uploads/pdf_activities/independent/IA_Assessment_of_Social_Skills.pdf

- IRIS Module–Intensive Intervention (Part 1): Using Data-Based Individualization to Intensify Instruction: https://iris.peabody.vanderbilt.edu/module/dbi1/
- IRIS Module–Intensive Intervention (Part 2): Collecting and Analyzing Data for Data-Based Individualization: https://iris.peabody.vanderbilt.edu/module/dbi2/
- IRIS Module–Progress Monitoring: Reading: https://iris.peabody.vanderbilt.edu/module/pmr/#content
- Resource for Early Learning–Early Childhood Assessments: http://resourcesforearlylearning.org/fm/early-childhood-assessment/

REFERENCES

Artiles, A. J., Kozleski, E. B., Trent, S. C., Osher, D., & Ortiz, A. (2010). Justifying and explaining disproportionality, 1968–2008: A critique of underlying views of culture. *Exceptional Children, 76,* 279-299.

Artiles, A. J., Rueda, R., Salazer, J., & Higareda, I. (2005). Within-group diversity in minority disproportionate representation: English language learners in urban school districts. *Exceptional Children, 71,* 283-300. https://doi.org/10.1177/001440290507100305

Basterra, M. D. R., Trumbull, E., & Solano-Flores, G. (2011). *Cultural validity in assessment: Addressing linguistic and cultural diversity.* Routledge.

Center for Parent Information and Resources. (2017, October 6). *Parental consent.* https://www.parentcenterhub.org/consent/

Center for Parent Information and Resources. (2018, September 24). *Part B of IDEA: Services for school-aged children.* https://www.parentcenterhub.org/partb/

Danielson, L., & Rosenquist, C. (2014). Introduction to the TEC special issue on data-based individualization. *Teaching Exceptional Children, 46,* 6-12. https://doi.org/10.1177/0040059914522966

Dilmen, N. (2012). Reliability and validity [Electronic image]. *Wikipedia Commons.* https://commons.wikimedia.org/wiki/File:Reliability_and_validity.svg

Division for Early Childhood of the Council for Exceptional Children. (2007). *Promoting positive outcomes for children with disabilities: recommendations for curriculum, assessment, and program evaluation.* https://www.naeyc.org/sites/default/files/globally-shared/downloads/PDFs/resources/position-statements/PrmtgPositiveOutcomes.pdf

Eisenman, L. T., Pleet, A. M., Wandry, D., & McGinley, V. (2010). Voices of special education teacher in an inclusive high school: Redefining responsibilities. *Remedial and Special Education, 32,* 91-104. https://doi.org/10.1177/0741932510361248

Esteban-Guitart, M., & Moll, L. C. (2014). Funds of identity: A new concept based on the funds of knowledge approach. *Culture & Psychology, 20,* 31-48. https://doi.org/10.1177/13540 67X13515934

Friend, M., & Cook, L. (2017). *Interactions: Collaboration skills for school professionals* (8th ed.). Longman Publishing Group.

Fuchs, D., Fuchs, L. S., & Vaughn, S. (2014). What is intensive instruction and why is it important? *Teaching Exceptional Children, 46,* 13-18. https://doi.org/10.1177/0040059914522966

Guddemi, M., & Case, B. J. (2004). *Assessing young children.* Pearson Education. images.pearsonassessments.com/images/tmrs/tmrs_rg/AssessingYoungChildren.pdf

How ASQ Works. (n.d.). https://agesandstages.com/about-asq/how-asq-works/

Individuals with Disabilities Education Act, 20 U.S. Code § 1400 et seq. (2004).

Kern, L., & Wehby, J. H. (2014). Using data to intensify behavioral interventions for individual students. *Teaching Exceptional Children, 46,* 45-53. https://doi.org/10.1177/0040059914522970

King, H. (2019). *Early childhood assessment.* https://source.cognia.org/issue-article/early-childhood-assessment2/

Klute, M., Apthorp, H., Harlacher, J., & Reale, M. (2017). *Formative assessment and elementary school student academic achievement: A review of the evidence* (REL 2017–259). Washington, DC: U.S. Department of Education, Institute of Education Sciences, National Center for Education Evaluation and Regional Assistance, Regional Educational Laboratory Central. http://ies.ed.gov/ncee/edlabs

Lee, A. J. (n.d.). *Child Find: What it is and how it works.* https://www.understood.org/en/school-learning/your-childs-rights/basics-about-childs-rights/child-find-what-it-is-and-how-it-works

Lembke, E. S., Hwang, J., & Thomas, E. (2019, November). *Integrating assessment high-leverage practice 6 in special education teacher learning* (Issue Brief No. 7). https://tedcec.org/sites/default/files/2020-12/TED-Brief-7-Assessment-PDF.pdf

Lemons, C. J., Kearns, D. M., & Davidson, K. A. (2014). Data-based individualization in reading: Intensifying interventions for students with significant reading disabilities. *Teaching Exceptional Children, 46,* 20-29. https://doi.org/10.1177/0040059914522978

Mattessich, P. W., Monsey, B. R., & Amherst H. Wilder Foundation. (1992). *Collaboration: What makes it work. A review of research literature on factors influencing successful collaboration.* Fieldstone Alliance.

McLeskey, J., Barringer, M-D., Billingsley, B., Brownell, M., Jackson, D., Kennedy, M., Lewis, T., Maheady, L., Rodriguez, J., Scheeler, M. C., Winn, J., & Ziegler, D. (2017, January). *High-leverage practices in special education.* Council for Exceptional Children & CEEDAR Center.

McMaster, K. L., Kung, S., Han, I., & Cao, M. (2008). Peer-assisted learning strategies: A "Tier 1" approach to promoting English learners' response to intervention. *Exceptional Children, 74,* 194-214. https://doi.org/10.1177/001440290807400204

McMaster, K. L., Lembke, E. S., Shin, J., Poch, A. L., Smith, R. A., Jung, P.-G., Allen, A. A., & Wagner, K. (2020). Supporting teachers' use of data-based instruction to improve students' early writing skills. *Journal of Educational Psychology, 112*(1), 1-21. https://doi.org/10.1037/edu0000358

Moll, L. C., Amanti, C., Neff, D., & González, N. (1992). Funds of knowledge for teaching: Using a qualitative approach to connect homes and classrooms. *Theory Into Practice, 31,* 132-141. https://doi.org/10.1080/00405849209543534

National Center on Response to Intervention. (2013, January). *Ensuring fidelity of assessment and data entry procedures* (Issue Brief No. 4). https://intensiveintervention.org/sites/default/files/DataFidelity_Final508.pdf

National Research Council. (2001, January). *Eager to learn: Educating our preschoolers.* National Academy Press. https://www.nap.edu/read/9745/chapter/8

Overton, T. (2016). *Assessing learners with special needs: An applied approach* (8th ed.). Pearson.

Pellegrino, A., Weiss, M. P., Regan, K., & Mann, L. (2014). Learning to collaborate: Exploring collective and individual outcomes of special and general educators. *Journal of Social Studies Research,* 96-104.

Powell, S. R., & Stecker, P. M. (2014). Using data-based individualization to intensify mathematics intervention for students with disabilities. *Teaching Exceptional Children, 46,* 31-37. https://doi.org/10.1177/0040059914523735

Samson, J. F., & Lesaux, N. K. (2009). Language-minority learners in special education: Rates and predictors of identification for services. *Journal of Learning Disabilities, 42,* 148-162. https://doi.org/10.1177/0022219408326221

Sanchez, S. V., Rodriguez, B. J., Soto-Huerta, M. E., Villarreal, F. C., Guerra, N. S., & Flores, B. B. (2013). A case for multidimensional bilingual assessment. *Language Assessment Quarterly, 10,* 160-177.

Simmons, K. D., Carpenter, L. B., Dyal, A., Austin, S., & Shumack, K. (2012). Preparing secondary special educators: Four collaborative initiatives. *Education, 132,* 754-763.

Slentz, K. L., Early, D. M., McKenna, M. (2008). *A guide to assessment in early childhood infancy to age eight.* Washington State Office of Superintendent of Public Instruction. https://wvde.state.wv.us/oel/docs/Washington%20Assessment%20Guide.pdf

SRI Education. (2016). *Preventing suspensions and expulsions in early childhood settings: A program leader's guide to supporting all children's success.* Retrieved April 3, 2021. https://preventexpulsion.org/1c-integrate-developmental-screening-and-assessment-into-the-programschool/

Stecker, P. M., Fuchs, L. S., & Fuchs, D. (2005). Using curriculum-based measurement to improve student achievement: Review of research. *Psychology in the Schools, 42*(8), 795-819.

Sullivan, A. L. (2011). Disproportionality in special education identification and placement of English Language Learners. *Exceptional Children, 77,* 317-334. https://doi.org/10.1177/001440291107700304

West, E. A., & Pirtle, J. M. (2014). Mothers' and fathers' perspectives on quality special educators and the attributes that influence effective inclusive practices. *Education & Training In Autism & Developmental Disabilities, 49*(2), 290-300.

Positive Behavioral Supports and Strategies for Young Children

Kathy Ralabate Doody, PhD and Gliset Colón, PhD

INTRODUCTION

Although we often view the early childhood years as carefree, it is estimated that thousands of preschool children are subjected to disciplinary action each year, resulting in school suspensions or expulsions. The National Association for the Education of Young Children estimated that nearly 9000 children were removed from preschool settings due to behavioral concerns. If unchecked, it is merely a matter of time before this trend becomes more problematic. We can and should reverse the troubling trend of high preschool removal rates, particularly because early childhood programs establish a critical foundation for years of subsequent education. It is critical not to overstate the importance of high-quality early childhood programs. The benefits of strong early childhood programs have long been researched and documented by programs such as the federally funded Early Head Start and the U.S. Department of Education and Health and Human Services. Years of clinical practice and well-designed research studies have shown us how to create early childhood settings that are linguistically and culturally sensitive, to use evidence-based practices as part of the instructional model, and to develop academic and social-emotional skills of children. This chapter discusses the components of effective, culturally, and linguistically strong early childhood practices in behavior management using the tenets of evidence-based practice while maintaining a learning environment that fosters a child's academic and social development.

Fisher, K. M., & Zimmer, K. E. (Eds.).
Early Childhood Special Education Programs and Practices (pp. 69-98).
© 2023 SLACK Incorporated.

CHAPTER OBJECTIVES

→ Examine the principles of culturally responsive positive behavior and classroom management in early childhood education.

→ Design a hypothesis to determine the function of inappropriate behavior.

→ Select a socially appropriate replacement behavior instead of inappropriate behavior.

→ Analyze how culture impacts behavior and classroom management.

→ List effective strategies to promote positive social and emotional learning.

→ Select evidence-based teaching strategies and interventions that align with the Division for Early Childhood Recommended Practices and the Council for Exceptional Children's high-leverage practices.

KEY TERMS

- **Anecdotal Observations:** A narrative description of an observed event or incident.
- **Fidelity:** Strict observance of a procedure or intervention with adherence to a predetermined, specified process.
- **Inappropriate Behavior:** Behavior that does not provide adequate or appropriate adjustment to the environment or situation.
- **Interwoven:** To intermingle or combine as if by weaving.
- **Planned Ignoring:** A consequence used to decrease inappropriate behavior whereby the child's targeted behavior is deliberately and intentionally ignored.
- **Preverbal Child:** A child who has not yet acquired or demonstrated verbal language.
- **Proprioceptive Sense:** Controls the self-awareness of our body's position and degree of movement.
- **Schedule of Reinforcement:** A predetermined schedule of reinforcement with a set duration or a number of correct responses occurring between reinforcement.
- **Sociocultural Theory:** Ties different language frameworks together by allowing the students to learn via their social interactions.
- **Vestibular Sense:** Our sense of balance.

CASE STUDY 1

Danny (Figure 4-1) is a 4-year-old boy who was diagnosed with autism spectrum disorder at age 3. He resides in an apartment with his mother, father, and older sister. Danny's mother works two jobs; his father is home and out of work due to an injury 7 years ago on a job site. The family lives in a rental apartment and has been warned that if Danny is loud or disruptive again, the landlord will evict them. Consequently, his parents quickly give in to his demands for toys or television shows and allow him to refuse to brush his teeth, eat the food served to him, and so on.

When frustrated, Danny will bite his arm and cry loudly. Danny can become agitated when asked to do work or engage in a nonpreferred activity. When he is particularly distraught, he will use his thumbs to exert significant pressure on his closed eyelids, potentially damaging his eyes by pressing them into their sockets. Aside from periods of disruptive behavior, Danny presents as a quiet, passive child. He will often stare off into the distance or out of his classroom window. It is challenging to engage Danny in a task because his attention span is limited to about 2 to 4 minutes.

Figure 4-1. A 4-year-old boy named Danny who was diagnosed with autism spectrum disorder at age 3.

CASE STUDY 2

Heriberto (Figure 4-2) recently moved to the United States due to his family's relocation from Puerto Rico after Hurricane Maria. Hurricane Maria (Figure 4-3) was a Category 5 hurricane that devastated Dominica, the U.S. Virgin Islands, and Puerto Rico. Heriberto lives with his mother, grandmother, and two older siblings who only speak Spanish. Heriberto understands little English. He can communicate in English using basic social prompts (i.e., hello, go to the bathroom, hungry, etc.). Mrs. Roberts is a first-year teacher at Bengal Elementary School. She is Irish American and grew up in the Northeastern United States. She is struggling to manage Heriberto's behavior. Heriberto loses his temper frequently and is easily frustrated. He yells and screams in Spanish and is often out of his seat during academic time.

"It is easier to build strong children than to repair broken adults."
—Frederick Douglass

The Institute for Child Success has estimated that thousands of preschool children are subjected to disciplinary action each year, resulting in school suspensions or expulsions. In 2017, the National Association for the Education of Young Children estimated that nearly 9000 children were removed from preschool settings due to behavioral concerns. If unchecked, it is merely a matter of time before this trend becomes more problematic. The benefits of strong early childhood programs have long been researched and documented by programs such as the federally funded Early Head Start and the U.S. Department of Education and Health and Human Services. Within early childhood, the development of social-emotional behavior is often a focal point of our instruction. *Social* refers to the individual's ability to interact appropriately with others, whereas *emotional* refers to the

Figure 4-2. A boy named Heriberto who recently moved to the United States due to his family's relocation from Puerto Rico after Hurricane Maria. (Unsplash)

Figure 4-3. A satellite picture of Hurricane Maria passing over the island of Puerto Rico. (Unsplash)

individual's ability to recognize and manage their behavior. The effectiveness of social-emotional learning (SEL) programs demonstrates that front-loading behavioral supports decrease the need for disciplinary actions as children age. Although this observation might be evident to some, young children must attend early childhood programs to realize the social-emotional, academic, recreational, and behavioral benefits. Suspended or expelled children denied participation in early childhood structured programs are at risk for developing more significant behavioral concerns down the road because they do not benefit from the support that early childhood programs can provide (Stegelin, 2018). This is an issue that has become increasingly problematic for young children across all demographics, including young children from diverse backgrounds, both with and without disabilities. For example, African American children are expelled twice as often as Latino and White children and five times more often than children who are Asian American (National Center on Early Childhood Health and Wellness, 2020). However, suspensions and expulsions can be reduced by implementing some basic behavioral principles (e.g., clearly stated behavioral expectations) in the classroom environment.

Positive Behavior Intervention and Supports

When providing support to young children attempting to regulate their own behaviors, educators often teach children skills that fall within the adaptive domain. Adaptive skills include the ability to appropriately respond to the changing demands of an environment or situation, particularly when the child is struggling to cope with challenges, stressors, or increased stimulation. When faced with stressful situations, children must filter out distractions, maintain a state of emotional regulation, and control impulses. This set of skills is called *executive functioning*. Because these skills are primarily developed between the ages of 3 and 5 years, early childhood educators are often responsible for the teaching, reinforcing, and practicing of these skills as part of a behavior management system (Center on the Developing Child at Harvard University, 2016).

Teaching executive functioning skills is just one of the many items found in a teacher's bag of tricks with regard to their approach to behavior management. Years of research have demonstrated effective classroom and behavior management begins when teachers view the classroom as a systematic, organized, and consistent setting. Positive Behavior Interventions and Supports (PBIS) is a multitiered system of support that creates and maintains positive school climates. This evidence-based framework emphasizes the prevention of behavioral difficulties. PBIS provides ideas to support the modeling and teaching of appropriate behavior in educational settings. It also identifies systems for systematically responding to class-wide and individual student challenges. By reducing behavioral difficulties, PBIS creates and maintains safe learning environments where learning can ultimately occur.

In addition to the focus on executive function skills, PBIS at the early childhood level should promote the SEL of young children. One PBIS framework that can be used in early childhood settings is the Pyramid Model for Promoting Social-Emotional Competence in Infants and Young Children (Fox et al., 2003). The Pyramid Model includes elements of PBIS such as universal practices to support the active social-emotional competence of young learners, secondary supports to address the needs of children who may be at risk, and tertiary or individualized practices for children who demonstrate the most challenging behavior (Hemmeter et al., 2016). At the universal level or Tier 1, teachers focus on fostering nurturing relationships and supportive environments with their students and families (e.g., joining in play, engaging in supportive conversations, providing encouraging feedback, teaching clear rules and expectations, and structuring transition times). At the secondary level or Tier 2, teachers focus on skill acquisition, fluency, generalization, and maintenance of social-emotional competence using evidence-based practices. At the tertiary level or Tier 3, teachers address persistent challenging behavior using individualized behavior support plans (Hemmeter et al., 2016). In summary, the Pyramid Model provides a framework for implementing PBIS in early childhood settings. Recent research also suggests the implementation of the Pyramid Model and culturally responsive practices may address implicit bias and prevent suspensions, expulsions, and other issues of equity in disciplinary practices (Allen & Steed, 2016; Fox et al., 2021).

The Importance of Behavioral Expectations (Rules) in Early Childhood Settings

Although we often view childhood as a carefree time and without imposed limitations, the reality is that we all benefit from clearly defined expectations, including young children. Enter any well-designed early childhood classroom, and you will see a series of rules (behavioral expectations) posted in a central location, typically next to the circle time rug. Next to each written rule, there will most likely be some type of graphic or photograph visually representing the stated rule. Visual prompts allow all children to access the rules regardless of language, literacy level, or communication mode. For example, Heriberto's classroom may have a posted rule encouraging students to "use a quiet voice" with an accompanying graphic to demonstrate a quiet voice visually.

What Do Rules Look Like?

Effective rules, or classroom expectations, have several attributes in common. They should be written in a grammatically correct format to model appropriate conventions of the spoken language. Therefore, rules are worded in a consistent form, following the same rules of syntax. For example, all rules should contain a verb, and it is required that all verbs are in the same tense (i.e., present, past, or infinitive). Rules should be stated in the positive, thereby clearly stating the behavior the child should demonstrate instead of telling the child merely what not to do. Another commonly used rule, "use a quiet voice," informs a student of the socially appropriate expected behavior vs. "don't yell," which only states what not to do but provides no guidance in what to do. Well-stated rules are concise and easily generalizable. Hence, rules should state expectations that can be applied in any situation, environment, or context. "Use a quiet voice" can be applied in the cafeteria while waiting in line or while in a reading group. Rules provide proactive measures that set the stage in environments that encourage appropriate behavior. Instead of reactively responding to inappropriate behavior with punishing consequences, we can reinforce it by demonstrating proper behaviors, colloquially called *catching them being good*. Commonly used and positively worded behavioral expectations for early childhood settings are listed later in this chapter. Child-friendly and engaging photographs or graphics could easily be added to each rule for added visual support, as shown in Figures 4-4 through 4-7.

Using graphics or visual supports as an accompaniment for classroom or home rules allows accessibility to all students, including those who are culturally and linguistically diverse (CLD). For example, Danny's parents could consider implementing a set of rules at home to instruct him visually to use a quiet voice. When Danny becomes upset or agitated and his parents fear that his voice volume is becoming problematic, they would merely point to the picture depicting "use a quiet voice" to cue him to speak softly.

CULTURAL RELEVANCE IN BEHAVIOR MANAGEMENT

Students who are CLD and students with disabilities have historically been affected by poor student outcomes (U.S. Department of Education, Institute of Education Sciences, National Center for Education Statistics, 2019). These adverse outcomes include high levels of grade retention and school dropout rates (Calderón et al., 2011; Sullivan, 2011). These students are perceived to underperform on both academic and behavioral measures (Brown et al., 2019). This misperception is due to the mismatch between the students' cultures and the classroom teachers' norms. The mismatch in communication, instruction, teacher preparation, and culture adversely affects CLD students because it results in a disproportionate representation of CLD students in special education (Sullivan, 2011). This is detrimental because research suggests students who are inappropriately placed in special education regress even further academically (Huang et al., 2011), and the adverse effects can be long term (e.g., low graduation rates, high dropout rates, lower wages, etc.; Brown et al., 2019).

Moreover, a body of research confirms disparities in the discipline of students with disabilities and students of color, particularly males. Students who intersect across both categories (i.e., CLD students with disabilities) are in triple jeopardy. Our young students have the daunting task of learning how to decode classroom behavioral norms, which may be in a language other than their own, all while navigating the challenges imposed by their disabilities. CLD students who also have a disability are affected by higher detention rates, suspension rates, and expulsion. This directly correlates with the school-to-prison pipeline (Artiles et al., 2010; McIntosh et al., 2018). Many school districts in the United States will consist of a majority of CLD students, particularly in urban settings. Classroom teachers must recognize the importance of making sound decisions regarding behavior management and must ensure that referrals align with their students' cultural,

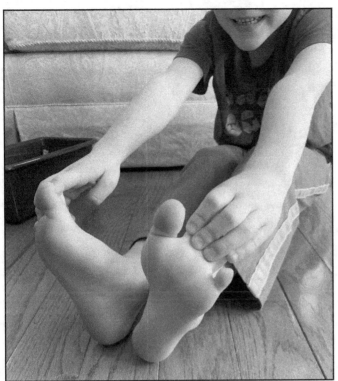

Figure 4-4. Keep your hands and feet to yourself.

Figure 4-5. Use a quiet voice.

Figure 4-6. Follow directions.

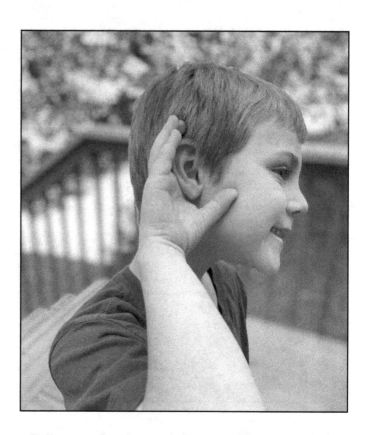

Figure 4-7. Stay in your area. (Monkey Business Images/Shutterstock.com)

linguistic, and ability backgrounds. It is even more critical for teachers to have these skills during the foundational years. Early childhood education is crucial as children acquire fundamental motor, cognitive, and social skills (Melekoğlu et al., 2017). Research corroborates that early identification, early intervention, and proper teacher preparation are paramount in preventing and managing problematic behaviors.

SOCIOCULTURAL THEORY

Sociocultural theory (SCT) ties different language frameworks together by allowing them to learn via their social interactions. SCT was developed from the work of Vygotsky (1978). Vygotsky suggested children learn via their social interactions with others. From a sociocultural perspective, early language learning is dependent on the process of meaning making in cooperative activities with other members of a given culture (Aimin, 2013). The classroom culture is one of the primary environments in which language development occurs. One form of language children learn from an early stage is the language of the classroom or classroom norms and expectations. Social interaction and cooperative learning via the lens of SCT are vital in constructing meaning and, subsequently, effective behavior and classroom management.

THEORIES OF BEHAVIOR AND CLASSROOM MANAGEMENT

All behavior serves a function or purpose. Individuals, including young children, display behaviors for a reason, whether they realize it or not. Therefore, we demonstrate behaviors that we learn through repetition and reinforcement. Young children, in particular, often exhibit learned behavior that was previously reinforced. Simply, this means that from an early age we know that certain behaviors elicit specific responses or consequences. We learn most willful or deliberate behaviors, and, therefore, we can unlearn them. An example of a willful behavior is Danny crying loudly in an attempt to request nacho-flavored tortilla chips for breakfast. We have become conditioned to conduct ourselves in ways that elicit desired responses to those around us and our environment. Danny has learned to cry loudly for his preferred foods during breakfast, especially when his parents are rushing to get out the door on time during their busy morning routine. Hence, even young children realize that they can outlast their teachers or parents by engaging in a behavior that the adult finds unpleasant, such as screaming. Danny has learned that he can eventually wear down his parents and receive his desired breakfast. Through our experiences as humans, we know what we need to do to elicit and receive our desired response. We may not be able to fully articulate why we do what we do, particularly if we are very young or have communicative challenges. However, it is imperative for adults and other educators to identify the "why we do" reasons, functions, or motivators for behavior to then attempt to manage that behavior.

DETERMINATION OF FUNCTION OF BEHAVIOR AND INSTRUCTIONAL STRATEGIES

So, why do we as humans behave the way we do? In order to answer that question, a functional behavioral assessment (FBA) should be conducted to determine the function, cause, or reason for the behavior. FBAs help us to formulate a hypothesis, which guides us to possible reasons for the child's behavior. In other words, what is the payoff to the child as a result of engaging in said behavior? Individuals demonstrate behavior for a reason, and an FBA helps us to determine, or at least hypothesize, as to what that reason might be. An FBA helps us to determine the function of a behavior (Lloyd et al., 2017). The functions of behavior are often listed as five main categories and remembered by the acronym MEATS (Medical, Escape/avoidance, Attention seeking, Tangible, Sensory; Table 4-1).

TABLE 4-1. MEATS ACRONYM WITH EXAMPLES		
FUNCTION	**POTENTIALLY CAUSED BY**	**WHAT IT MIGHT LOOK LIKE**
Medical	Events that are biological or physical in nature	Prolonged crying Pulling on ears, pressing of eyes, grinding of teeth
Escape/avoidance	Desire to circumvent what is aversive	Elopement Noncompliance
Attention seeking	Desire to draw attention	Disruptive vocalizations Aggression
Tangible	Desire to obtain or pursue the palpable item	Perseveration or fixation on item Anger
Sensory	Under- or over-reactivity to sensory stimuli	Covering ears with hands Spinning of body or objects

There are several user-friendly and free tools available to hypothesize the function of or motivation behind behavior. One such tool, the Durand Motivational Assessment Scale (MAS), is a simple, Likert scale survey posing 16 questions. Responses to the survey questions assist in the determination of a reasonable hypothesis for the behavior's motivation. The MAS is user friendly and provides clear directions for implementation (Ray-Subramanian, 2013). Although it does not definitely point to the function of an inappropriate behavior, it does provide a starting point to formulate a hypothesis, which can then be tested.

As we have done throughout this chapter, let's revisit Danny's story and consider the possible underlying reasons for his behavior. To determine the function of one of his target behaviors (i.e., pressing his eyes), we could follow the step-by-step methodology described in the following section. Each of these motivators or functions of behavior is discussed individually.

MEATS as an Acronym to Formulate a Hypothesis

It is important to note that when formulating a hypothesis about the function of a behavior, we address each function individually so that each is considered discretely. As such, Medical (the M in MEATS) is often the first function of behavior that we explore as adults seeking to manage a child's behavior, quite simply because it might involve a health, medical, or biological concern. For example, if a preverbal child, like Danny, is pressing his eyes by pushing with his thumbs and we cannot ask him what is bothering him, our first hypothesis might be that he is experiencing some type of pain due to a headache. To test this hypothesis, we might have him evaluated by the school nurse or suggest to his parents that his pediatrician see him. If Danny's primary physician suggests giving him a children's pain reliever and the behavior ceases, our initial hypothesis was most likely correct. If the behavior persists, we might suggest that his parents have his eyesight evaluated to determine if he requires corrective lenses. If the behavior continues, then eyestrain is most likely not the underlying cause of the behavior. Next, we suggest that his parents have him evaluated by an allergist or empirically using an allergy medication to determine if Danny is experiencing itching or burning eyes. Once we confidently feel we have exhausted all possibilities related to biological factors or health-related issues, we would move on to our next hypothesis in this example—the E in MEATS (Escape/avoidance).

Further expanding on eye pressing's target behavior, we would examine the antecedent or preceding trigger for his eye-gouging behavior. What was asked of Danny immediately before the initiation of this behavior? Was he asked to complete a difficult or nonpreferred task? Did we expect him to demonstrate an action that is not currently in his repertoire of mastered skills? Perhaps his environment was loud, chaotic, or overly stimulating, causing him agitation.

Consequently, we might see him "escape" into his own world and engage in a self-directed behavior of eye pressing. At this time, most likely any demands placed on him would be removed while an adult attended to his safety. Similarly, Danny might be led out of the classroom and into a quiet section of the hallway to decrease the self-injurious behavior. If the behavior persists after all these environmental changes, we would move on to our next hypothesis—(obtaining) Attention.

It is conceivable that Danny is pressing at his eyes to obtain the Attention (the A in MEATS) of another peer or adult. Behaviors as intensive as this one will typically garner quite a bit of attention because adults may fuss over Danny, trying to distract him from his current behavior or shower him with attention. Adults may try to coax him into lowering his hands or attempt to engage him in some type of conversation or competing activity to shift his focus away from his self-injurious behavior by attending to him. Danny may be trying to catch the attention of nearby peers, playing adjacently but exclusively of him. If we attend to the child and the behavior endures, the function is most likely not to seek attention, and we would test another hypothesis—(obtaining) a Tangible item.

Is Danny currently being denied access to a toy, food, privilege, or another item he desires? Does he want to eat circus peanuts instead of his sandwich for lunch? Does a classmate have an iPad (Apple) that he wants to try? Has he spotted a box of crayons on a shelf out of his reach that he wants to obtain? Quite simply, a *Tangible* (the T in MEATS) is an item that can be touched, held, consumed, or manipulated. Restricted access to the actual thing could be the motivation for inappropriate behavior. If not, the final hypothesis we would consider as a function of the inappropriate behavior would be Sensory (the S in MEATS).

Sensory stimulation generally triggers inappropriate behavior in two ways: children typically seek more stimulation or attempt to escape or avoid stimulation. Children's tolerance for sensory stimulation could be under- or overdeveloped. Hence, we classify children who are under-reactive as sensory seekers, and children who are over-reactive as sensory avoiders. It is important to note that many young children, particularly those on the autism spectrum, may be sensory seekers and avoiders. Regardless, the implication of either can result in the demonstration of inappropriate behavior.

Sensory Inputs

When we consider sensory inputs, we often think of merely the five senses we were all taught as children: sight (visual), hearing (auditory), taste (gustatory), smell (olfactory), and touch (tactile). Additionally, we also consider input from two more senses: vestibular (our response to motion and balance) and proprioceptive (self-awareness of the body's position and degree of movement). Danny may be pressing his thumbs into his eyes to stimulate his proprioceptive sense, thereby seeking more input, indicating he is under-reactive, or he may enjoy the sensation of touching his eyelids with the skin receptors on his fingers, again suggesting that he is a sensory seeker. Conversely, he may be overstimulated by the amount of light his pupils are taking in and may close his eyes tightly to avoid/escape the brightness around him. Further elaboration of the seven senses is provided in Table 4-2.

BEHAVIOR AS A FORM OF COMMUNICATION

It is important to note that there is an underlying theme to each of the scenarios previously discussed—communication. In each instance related previously, Danny attempts to express a want or need regardless of whether his terminal goal is to obtain or escape. Although the behaviors described are attributed to a preverbal child in this particular scenario, any child can and will resort

TABLE 4-2. THE SEVEN SENSES WITH UNDER-/OVER-REACTIVITY EXAMPLES		
SENSE	EXAMPLE OF UNDER-REACTIVITY	EXAMPLE OF OVER-REACTIVITY
Auditory	Loudly vocalizing or turning up the volume on the television	Covering ears with hands
Gustatory	Preferring foods sprinkled with hot sauce, cayenne, or black pepper	Preferring room temperature, bland, nonseasoned foods
Olfactory	Smelling materials or hair of a peer	Gagging or plugging the nose
Proprioceptive	Shedding of clothing or refusal to wear hat/glasses	Throwing oneself against walls or floor mats, seeking "bear hugs" from others
Tactile	Shying away from an embrace or refusing to engage in messy play	Stroking the hair of another, holding a stuffed animal during circle time
Vestibular	Feeling nauseous during periods of movement, such as swinging or driving in a car	Spinning oneself or objects, shaking head vigorously to/from
Visual	Dangling beads in front of eyes	Burying head in pillow or shoulder of an adult

to demonstrating inappropriate behavior when not "heard," acknowledged, or understood. The action must be viewed as the most rudimentary form of communication regardless of the presence or absence of verbal speech in a child. Studied in totality, these five functions or motivators may be why a child is demonstrating an inappropriate behavior while each hypothesis is individually considered and tested. Once we determine the function of a behavior, we can teach a socially appropriate replacement behavior, which is discussed later. First, how do we teach this new skill? We have a powerful tool or evidence-based practice at our disposal, namely two types of consequences: reinforcing and punishing.

REINFORCING CONSEQUENCES

Using reinforcing consequences is an evidence-based practice that we often use to increase desired or appropriate behaviors. By definition, a punishment must increase the likelihood that the action will occur again; therefore, we intend to increase the occurrence of appropriate behaviors. There are two types of reinforcement: positive and negative. We tend to associate good connotations with the word "positive" and harmful connotations with the word "negative." However, within the realm of behavior, please remember that positive merely means "to add" and negative "to take away."

There are several types of positive reinforcement, including behavior-specific social praise ("Thank you for using your quietest voice, Danny!"), preferred tangible items (edibles, toys, books, and manipulatives), privileges (engaging in fingerplays, songs, storybook read alouds, and one-on-one time with a preferred adult or peer), and movement activities (running, jumping, climbing, and swinging). All of these types of reinforcement are stimuli that we add as a rewarding consequence for appropriate behaviors, so they fall under the classification of positive reinforcement.

Negative reinforcement is nevertheless reinforcement, which means that its purpose is still to increase a behavior but by taking away a stimulus to increase the likelihood that a behavior will occur again. When implementing negative reinforcement, we remove the stimulus to increase a behavior, so it would stand to reason that we are removing unwanted or nondesired stimuli. We often use several classic examples when describing negative reinforcement. For example, when a baby has a soiled diaper, she cries. Presumably, an adult hears the baby's cry and removes the dirty diaper or unwanted stimulus. Hence, we have reinforced the baby's behavior by attending to it. The next time the baby has a dirty diaper, we have increased the likelihood that she will cry until an adult removes the soiled diaper.

Another example is that annoying "beep beep" heard in our cars before fastening our seat belt. We quickly buckle up to remove the unwanted stimulus (i.e., the annoying beeping that we find so aversive). The next time we hear the displeasing "beep beep," the likelihood that we fasten our seat belt increases by the use of negative reinforcement.

Punishing Consequences

In conjunction with the reinforcement strategies described earlier, we often use punishing consequences when reinforcement by itself is not sufficient. It is important to note that we always attempt to manage behavior by using reinforcement alone. If that is not sufficient, we carefully formulate a plan to implement punishing consequences. Although the word "punisher" seems harsh, punishment can be relatively mild. However, by definition, a punishment must decrease the likelihood that the behavior will occur again. Let's think about Danny again. Telling Danny "No, you cannot have chocolate for breakfast" is a form of punishment because we deny him access to something he desires. When he cries loudly because he cannot have candy, we would first try to reinforce his appropriate behavior. For example, we might praise him during the quiet intervals between vocalizations. However, if the use of reinforcement was ineffective, we would next try a punishing consequence.

Punishment can be broken down into two categories: positive punishment and negative punishment. Positive punishment would involve adding an unwanted or aversive stimulus. Again, the use of the term *positive* in behaviorism does not indicate "good" but rather "added." When Danny cries loudly at the breakfast table, we could use positive punishment, requiring him to do something he disliked. Therefore, we might present him with a nonpreferred task, such as washing his breakfast dishes. This is considered positive punishment because we are adding a consequence that is nonpreferred or aversive. If we implemented negative punishment, we would take away something he liked. In this case, we might remove his favorite blue juice cup and crazy straw. This is considered negative punishment because we would deny Danny access to an object he prefers or wants. We would accomplish this by removing an item or privilege that Danny desires. Again, the definition of the term *negative* here does not connote "bad" but rather "to remove."

To summarize, we have discussed two types of consequences: reinforcement and punishment. We define consequences as positive or negative. Remember, when applied in terms of behavior, the words positive and negative take on meanings that differ slightly from what we often use in everyday language. Specifically, positive means to add, and negative means to remove or take away. Table 4-3 clearly illustrates the two types of consequences and the distinction between positive and negative.

Planned Ignoring

Punishment can be implemented in other forms as well. If Danny attempted to gain a peer's attention by pulling on his friend's shirt, we would train the friend to use planned ignoring. *Planned ignoring* is a punishing consequence whereby the child's inappropriate behavior is deliberately and intentionally ignored. Obviously, planned ignoring would not come easily to a same-aged peer and would initially prove challenging to carry out. However, with some preteaching and a careful selection

TABLE 4-3. REINFORCING AND PUNISHING CONSEQUENCES		
	DECREASES LIKELIHOOD BEHAVIOR WILL OCCUR AGAIN	**INCREASES LIKELIHOOD BEHAVIOR WILL OCCUR AGAIN**
ADD STIMULUS	Positive punishment	Positive reinforcement
REMOVE STIMULUS	Negative punishment	Negative reinforcement

process of a peer, planned ignoring can be successful and the results significant. If Danny is seeking the attention of a friend by pulling on her shirt and the friend is careful to refrain from bestowing any attention on Danny at all, the inappropriate behavior is subsequently punished. If implemented with fidelity or consistency, the use of punishment (planned ignoring) should yield favorable results, and the problematic behaviors should diminish. However, decreasing inappropriate behavior is just one piece of the solution. We have successfully used consequences to teach Danny what not to do, but now we must teach him what to do instead. Our next step is to teach him a replacement behavior that will continue to meet his needs but in a socially appropriate way. The function of the replacement behavior should match the function of the inappropriate behavior. Therefore, if the function of tugging on a friend's shirt is to obtain attention, the replacement behavior should also receive attention but in a socially appropriate way. One such example would be to present the peer with a laminated card asking her in words and pictures if she wants to play.

HOW DO WE USE CONSEQUENCES TO TEACH REPLACEMENT BEHAVIORS?

How are replacement behaviors taught? The answer is relatively straightforward—explicitly, systematically, and by using consequences. Using Danny as an example, we would first introduce the "Do you want to play?" picture card to Danny. We might begin by presenting him with a laminated card displaying the question and an accompanying picture of one of his preferred toys. Danny would first be asked "Where is your play card?" and prompted to point to it or touch it. Large quantities of reinforcement would ensue. We would tell Danny "Great job finding your play card!" and present him with a small, preferred edible, such as a small fragment of chocolate or cookie. The child is asked a question, responds to the question, and then receives a consequence or reinforcement.

Use of Discrete Trial Training

The series of events, described previously, is called a *discrete trial*, which is an evidence-based practice, or an *ABC*, where the A stands for Antecedent (the question posed), the B is the child's Behavior, and the C is the resulting Consequence. This discrete trial is repeated until Danny demonstrates mastery (80% accuracy or higher). Next, we would introduce a "distracter" card presented alongside our target "play" card. The distracter card could say "Do you want to sleep?" and have a photo of a sleeping child. Once Danny could repeatedly identify the target card (basically by not attending to the distracter card), we would increase the field size of distracters and present three cards simultaneously, one target play card and two distracters.

The next logical step in this process would be to use the same strategies to teach Danny to hand his play card to a trained peer. Again, upon successful completion of the task, Danny would be given positive reinforcement. Ultimately, by using these behavioral strategies, Danny would be rewarded or reinforced for his ability to identify and appropriately use his play card with a peer.

SOCIALLY APPROPRIATE REPLACEMENT BEHAVIORS

As we discussed earlier, once we have determined the function of a target behavior, we can then attempt to supplant the action with a more socially acceptable, replacement behavior that serves the same function for the child. This is an essential feature of any behavioral intervention. We may determine that Danny is exerting pressure on his eyes because he is visually under-reactive. This means that Danny is a sensory seeker in terms of visual stimulus. If there is not enough visual stimulation in his environment, he will seek or create more to meet his sensory needs. Hence, he may enjoy the added stimulation of seeing a display of lights and color in his closed lids. Therefore, we would attempt to replace that behavior by teaching him to ask for a toy kaleidoscope or light-up LED toy. If Danny is pressing on his eyes to entice a nearby peer to notice him or gain the attention of another, we will teach him to initiate an appropriate overture for seeking attention, such as tapping a friend on the shoulder or handing her a "Do you want to play?" picture card.

Some Cautions

Identifying and teaching a socially appropriate replacement behavior is a critical step in decreasing young children's inappropriate behavior. Suppose this step is overlooked, and the child is merely reinforced for the absence of the actual inappropriate behavior and punished for the presence of the same. In this case, the result is that the child will replace one inappropriate or challenging behavior for another. In all likelihood, the second inappropriate behavior will be just as undesired as the first, if not more. For example, if the function of Danny's eye pressing is to obtain his aide's attention and we do not teach him a more socially acceptable means to draw notice upon himself, even if he suppresses his eye-pressing behavior, another action could very likely develop in its place. Perhaps Danny would resort to pinching his aide on the arm or spitting at her. These behaviors will undoubtedly garner attention, so, in Danny's mind, he has achieved his intended outcome—attention from others. However, if we teach Danny to approach his paraprofessional and demonstrate the manual sign for "help, please" (Figure 4-8), he will be successful in gaining his paraprofessional's attention but in an appropriate manner.

MODELING

In addition to the use of discrete trial training as described previously to teach Danny how to use his play card, we could also employ the practice of modeling. Modeling is an evidence-based practice that is quite simple to implement. *Modeling* is a visual demonstration of the desired target behavior. In this case, the use of modeling would include showing Danny repeatedly how to hand his play card to a peer. Danny could observe a friend giving the play card to a peer and, in turn, see the friend respond positively and begin to play. Danny could also be videotaped or photographed appropriately handing his play card to a peer. The videotape could be used to show Danny an example of appropriately playing with a peer. This is an evidence-based practice called *video modeling*, and it is quite effective in increasing appropriate behavior. Photographs of Danny using his play card with a peer could be included in book form and presented to him in a laminated hard copy in the form of

Figure 4-8. The manual sign for "help, please."

a social narrative. *Social narratives* are stories created to demonstrate the positive impact appropriate behaviors have for ourselves and those around us. Social narratives are an evidence-based practice. Viewing the video and reading the social narrative are examples of modeling because they include appropriate demonstrations of the target behavior in a visual format.

MONITORING STUDENT PROGRESS THROUGH DATA COLLECTION

To reiterate, so far we have discussed how to formulate a hypothesis and how to identify the function of the inappropriate behavior. We have discussed using reinforcement and punishment as consequences to increase appropriate behaviors and decrease inappropriate behaviors. Additionally, we have discussed selecting a socially appropriate replacement behavior and then explicitly teaching that replacement behavior. We have also discussed several evidence-based practices that enhance our instruction. Given all this information, how do we know if our interventions have been effective? How do we determine if Danny has made progress? Specifically, how do we know if the inappropriate behavior has subsided as a result of our efforts? Although many teachers, especially early childhood educators, consider "data" to be a four-letter word, data are our friend.

First, as we formulate our hypothesis, we can collect preliminary data, which is called *baseline data collection*. This means that we are using some reliable means to measure the behavior or quantify it by tabulating the frequency of the behavior's occurrence or keeping track of the duration of the action before we have deliberately done anything to change the behavior in any way. Baseline data collection is behavior in its most natural state, untouched and free from intervention. We simply want to ascertain how problematic the behavior is or is not before we attempt to change it. Baseline data collection is valuable for the following reasons: it provides us with a starting point, it paints an objective picture of how intensive the behavior is, and it allows us to monitor student progress toward behavioral objectives.

Once baseline data collection shows some degree of stability (similar results over three to five data collection sessions), we begin teaching our socially appropriate replacement behavior, along with our reinforcing/punishing consequences and modeling techniques. During each of these phases, we will continue to observe the behavior directly, collect data, and jot down any field notes or anecdotal observations that we feel are noteworthy. Collecting behavioral data essentially takes the guesswork out of attempting to reduce problematic behavior and provides accountability. We can assess if our behavioral intervention efforts have yielded the desired results. If so, then we can continue our efforts to maintain the presence of our desired replacement behavior. If not, we will add additional prompts, introduce novel reinforcement to avoid satiation, increase our schedule of reinforcement, or vary the form of punishment we are implementing. It is important to note that we would introduce these changes one at a time to identify which factors led to an increase in our desired behavior.

Instructional Strategies:
Social-Emotional Learning in Early Childhood

SEL develops positive self-awareness, self-control, and interpersonal skills (Collaborative for Academic, Social, and Emotional Learning [CASEL], 2013). Early childhood is a critical period in social and emotional development. Children learn how to identify a continuum of emotions and to regulate their own feelings. Students who are at risk or diagnosed with a disability may struggle to develop these skills. Therefore, it is imperative that we explicitly teach SEL skills to young students with disabilities. Students who have not yet developed SEL skills may struggle both academically and behaviorally. A body of research suggests that social and emotional deficits during the early years often persist into the later years (Kramer et al., 2010). SEL instruction should begin in preschool and continue throughout students' academic years (CASEL, 2013). There are five SEL categories: self-awareness, self-management, social awareness, relationship skills, and responsible decision making. Table 4-4 provides a description of each type and examples of each.

The explicit instruction of these skills is particularly important for students who have experienced trauma. Early childhood teachers are very likely to teach young children who have experienced some sort of trauma. These traumas may include early loss or lack of consistent caregivers; emotional, physical, or sexual abuse; domestic violence; various forms of neglect; natural disasters; medical and surgical procedures; and serious accidents (National Child Traumatic Stress Network Schools Committee, 2008).

Mrs. Roberts has tried several behavior management techniques to decrease Heriberto's outbursts. She has tried redirecting him to his seat, asking him to count to 10 while deep breathing, and sending him to the principal's office on numerous occasions. She has had little success with these strategies. Mrs. Roberts is concerned about instructional time loss because Heriberto is performing below grade level in all subjects. To support Heriberto in the classroom, Mrs. Roberts needs to recognize he has been affected by trauma. Heriberto witnessed an extreme natural disaster. Heriberto may have faced the danger of death or physical injury and/or seen the injury or death of a loved one. Subsequently, the hurricane's aftermath resulted in the loss of his home, possessions, and community because he and his family had to emigrate to the mainland. These stressors place him at risk for social and emotional difficulties. Heriberto may continue to experience stressors in his new city as he and his family learn to adapt to a new culture and language while mitigating any economic stressors such as the loss of a job and finances.

To support Heriberto, Mrs. Roberts should carefully select and effectively implement an evidence-based SEL program. CASEL (2013) outlines three fundamental principles (engaging diverse stakeholders, implementing evidence-based SEL programs in the context of systemic district programming, and considering local contextual factors) to support the effective selection, implementation, impact, and sustainability of evidence-based SEL programs. Following these principles will ensure Heriberto benefits socially, emotionally, and academically.

Schools and districts should engage diverse stakeholders in the program adoption process. Stakeholders should include district-level personnel along with teachers, parents, students, and community members. First, Mrs. Roberts should be part of her school-based team that participates in the decision-making process when selecting an evidence-based SEL program. Mrs. Roberts should consult with Heriberto, his family, and local Hispanic/Latinx community leaders to better understand

TABLE 4-4. SOCIAL-EMOTIONAL LEARNING CATEGORIES AND EXAMPLES

CATEGORY	DESCRIPTION	EXAMPLES
Self-awareness	The ability to accurately recognize one's own emotions, thoughts, and values and how they influence behavior. The ability to accurately assess one's strengths and limitations, with a well-grounded sense of confidence, optimism, and a "growth mindset."	Identifying emotions, accurate self-perception, recognizing strengths, self-confidence, self-efficacy
Self-management	The ability to regulate one's emotions, thoughts, and behaviors in different situations; effectively manages stress; controls impulses; and motivates oneself. The ability to set and work toward personal and academic goals.	Impulse control, stress management, self-discipline, self-motivation, goal setting, organizational skills
Social awareness	The ability to take the perspective of and empathize with others, including those from diverse backgrounds and cultures. Understanding social and ethical norms for behavior and recognizing family, school, and community resources and supports.	Perspective taking, empathy, appreciating diversity, respect for others
Relationship skills	The ability to establish and maintain healthy and rewarding relationships with diverse individuals and groups. The ability to communicate clearly, listen well, cooperate with others, resist inappropriate social pressure, negotiate conflict constructively, and seek and offer help when needed.	Communication, social engagement, relationship building, teamwork
Responsible decision making	The ability to make constructive choices about personal behavior and social interactions based on ethical standards, safety concerns, and social norms. The realistic evaluation of the consequences of various actions and a consideration of oneself and others' well-being.	Identifying problems, analyzing situations, solving problems, evaluating, reflecting, ethical responsibility

Data source: https://casel.org/core-competencies/

the impact of Hurricane Maria on the island and the aftermath. Ultimately, Mrs. Roberts should consider an SEL program that addresses trauma, specifically trauma experienced from natural disasters and forced migration. Table 4-5 describes several SEL programs that have a focus on early childhood settings.

Next, Mrs. Roberts must implement an evidence-based SEL program within the systemic, ongoing district and school planning, programming, and evaluation. This will lead to better practice and more positive outcomes for Heriberto (CASEL, 2013). With support from her administrator, Mrs. Roberts should evaluate the quality of her school's SEL programs and policies. Mrs. Roberts should participate in ongoing professional development in SEL. When planning instruction, Mrs.

TABLE 4-5. SOCIAL-EMOTIONAL LEARNING PROGRAM CANDIDATES

SOCIAL-EMOTIONAL LEARNING PROGRAM	AVAILABLE RESOURCES IN SPANISH
Sanford Harmony: https://online.sanfordharmony.org/	Yes
Al's Pals: www.wingspanworks.com	Yes
Incredible Years: www.incredibleyears.com	Yes
Good Behavior Game: www.interventioncentral.org/behavioral-interventions/schoolwide-classroommgmt/good-behavior-game	No
Responsive Classroom: www.responsiveclassroom.org	No
PATHs: www.pathsprogram.com/	Yes
Second Step: www.secondstep.org	Yes
Open Circle: www.open-circle.org	Yes
Michigan Model for Health: www.michiganmodelforhealth.org	No
HighScope Educational Approach for Preschool: www.highscope.org	No
4Rs (Reading, Writing, Respect, Resolution): www.morningsidecenter.org	Yes
Tools of the Mind: www.toolsofthemind.org	Yes
Peaceworks: http://www.peace-ed.org/earlychildhood.html	Yes
MindUP: https://mindup.org/	No
Competent Kids, Caring Communities: http://www.competentkids.org/	Yes
Positive Action: https://www.positiveaction.net/	Yes
Character First: http://characterfirsteducation.com/c/curriculum.php	No
I Can Problem Solve: https://www.researchpress.com/books/590/icps-i-can-problem-solve	No
Social Thinking: https://www.socialthinking.com/	Yes
Lions Quest: https://www.lions-quest.org/explore-our-sel-curriculum/	Yes
Toolbox: https://www.berkeleyschools.net/teaching-and-learning/toolbox/	Yes

Roberts should link the chosen SEL program with her student-centered instruction, curriculum, and assessments (CASEL, 2013). Mrs. Roberts should then use data on SEL program implementation, including Heriberto's social-emotional competence, school and classroom climate, and school performance, to inform her administrator of needed resources to support Heriberto's social and emotional needs.

Additionally, Mrs. Roberts should consider other contextual factors when implementing an SEL program in her classroom. Mrs. Roberts should have an understanding of Heriberto and his family's needs as well as her own. With support from her administrator, Mrs. Roberts should assess her capacity and her school's capacity to take on SEL programming and decide whether to address Heriberto's needs systematically or start small and build a program. More specifically, Heriberto's classification is as an English-language learner. To provide Heriberto with SEL instruction, he may need home language support. Mrs. Roberts must assess her capacity to provide SEL instruction to Heriberto with the necessary scaffolds for English-language support and/or the strategic use of the Spanish language. Mrs. Roberts could give Heriberto Spanish-language support in the feeling figures activity by giving him student materials printed in Spanish.

FAMILY INVOLVEMENT

Family involvement results in improved academic outcomes for all students regardless of cultural and linguistic background, ability level, and socioeconomic class (Baker et al., 2016). Family involvement leads to improved student attendance and behavioral outcomes (Baker et al., 2016). Despite this proof, parental involvement among CLD families is continually limited for a plethora of reasons. To address this issue, the concept of family involvement must be redefined to better align with the cultural and linguistic norms of diverse students with disabilities.

The Division for Early Childhood (DEC) of the Council for Exceptional Children highlights best practices for facilitating parental involvement. "The DEC Recommended Practices were developed to provide guidance to practitioners and families about the most effective ways to improve the learning outcomes and promote the development of young children, birth through five years of age, who have or are at-risk for developmental delays or disabilities" (DEC, 2014). The recommended family practices encompass three themes: family-centered practices, family capacity–building practices, and family and professional collaboration.

A DEC-recommended family practice includes practitioners building trusting and respectful partnerships with the family through sensitive and responsive interactions to cultural, linguistic, and socioeconomic diversity (DEC Recommended Practice F1). In both case studies, the students will benefit from parent–teacher collaboration via a communication journal to share information with the family about how their child is progressing. In turn, the family can share information about how their child is doing at home. For Heriberto, the teacher should make attempts to translate all written communication to Spanish to ensure the family understands and allows the family to write in Spanish. See Table 4-6 for a full list of the family-centered recommendations and their alignment with the high-leverage practices in special education.

SUMMARY

With deliberate planning and student success perpetually in mind, we can remediate the current trajectory of suspension and expulsion in early childhood programs. We can turn the tide with an underlying understanding of cultural competence and the employment of evidence-based behavioral strategies by early childhood educators. With systematic and evidence-based supports in place, students can be set up for success and placed on a path of social-emotional growth and competence. Early childhood settings should be places of learning, wonder, exploration, and development. Punishment, reprimands, and program dismissal should be remnants of our past. By using established behavior management principles and culturally responsive instructional practices, even our youngest and most vulnerable students are in a position to experience success. When our youngest generations of children develop into culturally acclimated and well-adjusted teens and adults, we have all done our jobs. We can reap the benefits of our labors as a society.

TABLE 4-6. ALIGNMENT OF INSTRUCTIONAL PRACTICES WITH RECOMMENDED PRACTICES AND HIGH-LEVERAGE PRACTICES (HLPs)

INSTRUCTIONAL, EVIDENCE-BASED PRACTICE	ALIGNED DEC RECOMMENDED PRACTICES	ALIGNED CEC HLPs
Data collection	A9: Practitioners implement systematic ongoing assessment to identify learning targets, plan activities, and monitor the child's progress to revise instruction as needed. INS3: Practitioners gather and use data to inform decisions about individualized instruction. INS10: Practitioners implement the frequency, intensity, and duration of instruction needed to address the child's phase and pace of learning or the level of support needed by the family to achieve the child's outcomes or goals. L12: Leaders collaborate with stakeholders to collect and use data for program management and continuous program improvement and to examine the effectiveness of services and supports in improving child and family outcomes.	HLP 4: Use multiple sources of information to develop a comprehensive understanding of a student's strengths and needs. HLP 5: Interpret and communicate assessment information with stakeholders to collaboratively design and implement educational programs. HLP 6: Use student assessment data, analyze instructional practices, and make necessary adjustments that improve student outcomes.

(continued)

TABLE 4-6 (CONTINUED). ALIGNMENT OF INSTRUCTIONAL PRACTICES WITH RECOMMENDED PRACTICES AND HIGH-LEVERAGE PRACTICES (HLPs)

INSTRUCTIONAL, EVIDENCE-BASED PRACTICE	ALIGNED DEC RECOMMENDED PRACTICES	ALIGNED CEC HLPs
Discrete trial training	A8: Practitioners use clinical reasoning in addition to assessment results to identify the child's current levels of functioning and to determine the child's eligibility and plan for instruction. A9: Practitioners implement systematic ongoing assessment to identify learning targets, plan activities, and monitor the child's progress to revise instruction as needed. NS3: Practitioners gather and use data to inform decisions about individualized instruction. INS7: Practitioners use explicit feedback and consequences to increase child engagement, play, and skills. INT2: Practitioners promote the child's social development by encouraging the child to initiate or sustain positive interactions with other children and adults during routines and activities through modeling, teaching, feedback, or other types of guided support.	HLP 6: Use student assessment data, analyze instructional practices, and make necessary adjustments that improve student outcomes. HLP 8: Provide positive and constructive feedback to guide students' learning and behavior. HLP 9: Teach social behaviors. HLP 12: Systematically design instruction toward a specific learning goal. HLP 13: Adapt curriculum tasks and materials for specific learning goals. HLP 15: Provide scaffolded supports. HLP 16: Use explicit instruction. HLP 20: Provide intensive instruction. HLP 21: Teach students to maintain and generalize new learning across time and settings. HLP 22: Provide positive and constructive feedback to guide students' learning and behavior.
Modeling	INS8: Practitioners use peer-mediated intervention to teach skills and to promote child engagement and learning. INT2: Practitioners promote the child's social development by encouraging the child to initiate or sustain positive interactions with other children and adults during routines and activities through modeling, teaching, feedback, or other types of guided support.	HLP 8: Provide positive and constructive feedback to guide students' learning and behavior. HLP 9: Teach social behaviors. HLP 15: Provide scaffolded supports. HLP 16: Use explicit instruction. HLP 18: Use strategies to promote active student engagement.

(continued)

TABLE 4-6 (CONTINUED). ALIGNMENT OF INSTRUCTIONAL PRACTICES WITH RECOMMENDED PRACTICES AND HIGH-LEVERAGE PRACTICES (HLPs)		
INSTRUCTIONAL, EVIDENCE-BASED PRACTICE	**ALIGNED DEC RECOMMENDED PRACTICES**	**ALIGNED CEC HLPs**
Planned ignoring	INS4: Practitioners plan for and provide the level of support, accommodations, and adaptations needed for the child to access, participate, and learn within and across activities and routines. INS7: Practitioners use explicit feedback and consequences to increase child engagement, play, and skills. INS9: Practitioners use functional assessment and related prevention, promotion, and intervention strategies across environments to prevent and address challenging behavior.	HLP 9: Teach social behaviors.
Punishment (positive/negative)	INS4: Practitioners plan for and provide the level of support, accommodations, and adaptations needed for the child to access, participate, and learn within and across activities and routines. INS7: Practitioners use explicit feedback and consequences to increase child engagement, play, and skills. INS9: Practitioners use functional assessment and related prevention, promotion, and intervention strategies across environments to prevent and address challenging behavior.	HLP 8: Provide positive and constructive feedback to guide students' learning and behavior. HLP 9: Teach social behaviors. HLP 10: Conduct functional behavioral assessments to develop individual student behavior support plans.

(continued)

TABLE 4-6 (CONTINUED). ALIGNMENT OF INSTRUCTIONAL PRACTICES WITH RECOMMENDED PRACTICES AND HIGH-LEVERAGE PRACTICES (HLPs)

INSTRUCTIONAL, EVIDENCE-BASED PRACTICE	ALIGNED DEC RECOMMENDED PRACTICES	ALIGNED CEC HLPs
Reinforcement (positive/negative)	INS4: Practitioners plan for and provide the level of support, accommodations, and adaptations needed for the child to access, participate, and learn within and across activities and routines. INS7: Practitioners use explicit feedback and consequences to increase child engagement, play, and skills. INS9: Practitioners use functional assessment and related prevention, promotion, and intervention strategies across environments to prevent and address challenging behavior. INT4: Practitioners promote the child's cognitive development by observing, interpreting, and responding intentionally to the child's exploration, play, and social activity by joining in and expanding on the child's focus, actions, and intent.	HLP 4: Use multiple sources of information to develop a comprehensive understanding of a student's strengths and needs. HLP 8: Provide positive and constructive feedback to guide students' learning and behavior. HLP 9: Teach social behaviors. HLP 10: Conduct functional behavioral assessments to develop individual student behavior support plans.
Rules (behavioral expectations)	F5: Practitioners support family functioning, promote family confidence and competence, and strengthen family–child relationships by acting in ways that recognize and build on family strengths and capacities. F6: Practitioners engage the family in opportunities that support and strengthen parenting knowledge and skills and parenting competence and confidence in ways that are flexible, individualized, and tailored to the family's preferences.	HLP 7: Establish a consistent, organized, and respectful learning environment. HLP 8: Provide positive and constructive feedback to guide students' learning and behavior. HLP 9: Teach social behaviors. HLP 22: Provide positive and constructive feedback to guide students' learning and behavior.

(continued)

TABLE 4-6 (CONTINUED). ALIGNMENT OF INSTRUCTIONAL PRACTICES WITH RECOMMENDED PRACTICES AND HIGH-LEVERAGE PRACTICES (HLPS)		
INSTRUCTIONAL, EVIDENCE-BASED PRACTICE	**ALIGNED DEC RECOMMENDED PRACTICES**	**ALIGNED CEC HLPs**
Social narrative	INS8: Practitioners use peer-mediated intervention to teach skills and to promote child engagement and learning. INT1: Practitioners promote the child's social-emotional development by observing, interpreting, and responding contingently to the range of the child's emotional expressions. INT2: Practitioners promote the child's social development by encouraging the child to initiate or sustain positive interactions with other children and adults during routines and activities through modeling, teaching, feedback, or other types of guided support.	HLP 8: Provide positive and constructive feedback to guide students' learning and behavior. HLP 9: Teach social behaviors. HLP 13: Adapt curriculum tasks and materials for specific learning goals. HLP 16: Use explicit instruction. HLP 19: Use assistive and instructional technologies. HLP 21: Teach students to maintain and generalize new learning across time and settings. HLP 22: Provide positive and constructive feedback to guide students' learning and behavior.
Video modeling	INS8: Practitioners use peer-mediated intervention to teach skills and to promote child engagement and learning. INT1: Practitioners promote the child's social-emotional development by observing, interpreting, and responding contingently to the range of the child's emotional expressions. INT2: Practitioners promote the child's social development by encouraging the child to initiate or sustain positive interactions with other children and adults during routines and activities through modeling, teaching, feedback, or other types of guided support.	HLP 8: Provide positive and constructive feedback to guide students' learning and behavior. HLP 9: Teach social behaviors. HLP 12: Systematically design instruction toward a specific learning goal. HLP 13: Adapt curriculum tasks and materials for specific learning goals. HLP 15: Provide scaffolded supports. HLP 16: Use explicit instruction. HLP 19: Use assistive and instructional technologies. HLP 20: Provide intensive instruction. HLP 21: Teach students to maintain and generalize new learning across time and settings. HLP 22: Provide positive and constructive feedback to guide students' learning and behavior.

(continued)

INSTRUCTIONAL, EVIDENCE-BASED PRACTICE	ALIGNED DEC RECOMMENDED PRACTICES	ALIGNED CEC HLPs
Visual supports	INS2: Practitioners, with the family, identify skills to target for instruction that help a child become adaptive, competent, socially connected, and engaged and that promote learning in natural and inclusive environments.	HLP 8: Provide positive and constructive feedback to guide students' learning and behavior. HLP 9: Teach social behaviors. HLP 13: Adapt curriculum tasks and materials for specific learning goals. HLP 15: Provide scaffolded supports. HLP 16: Use explicit instruction. HLP 19: Use assistive and instructional technologies. HLP 20: Provide intensive instruction. HLP 21: Teach students to maintain and generalize new learning across time and settings. HLP 22: Provide positive and constructive feedback to guide students' learning and behavior.

TABLE 4-6 (CONTINUED). ALIGNMENT OF INSTRUCTIONAL PRACTICES WITH RECOMMENDED PRACTICES AND HIGH-LEVERAGE PRACTICES (HLPs)

(continued)

CHAPTER REVIEW

1. How can we use culturally responsive instruction to encourage socially appropriate behavior in early childhood settings?

2. How can the Durand MAS be used by all stakeholders (parents, related service providers, and educators) in hypothesizing the function of inappropriate behavior?

3. Consider the evidence-based practices discussed in this chapter. How could you use these interventions in your early childhood classroom to foster social-emotional development, provide individual and systematic instruction through discrete trial training, and increase socially appropriate behavior?

4. Reflect on your own early childhood experiences as a young child at home and school. How did your culture impact those experiences behaviorally, socially, and academically? How could an understanding of these personal experiences provide you with the tools necessary to implement culturally responsive teaching practices in your classroom?

5. Review the content presented in this chapter. How can you use this knowledge when selecting evidence-based teaching strategies and interventions that align with the DEC Recommended Practices and the Council for Exceptional Children high-leverage practices?

6. Which of the following is NOT a function of behavior, as discussed in this chapter?
   a. Attention-seeking
   b. Escape-avoidance
   c. Stimulus overselectivity
   d. Tangible

TABLE 4-6 (CONTINUED). ALIGNMENT OF INSTRUCTIONAL PRACTICES WITH RECOMMENDED PRACTICES AND HIGH-LEVERAGE PRACTICES (HLPS)

INSTRUCTIONAL, EVIDENCE-BASED PRACTICE	ALIGNED DEC RECOMMENDED PRACTICES	ALIGNED CEC HLPs
Social-emotional learning	A3: Practitioners use assessment materials and strategies that are appropriate for the child's age and level of development and accommodate the child's sensory, physical, communication, cultural, linguistic, social, and emotional characteristics. INS2: Practitioners, with the family, identify skills to target for instruction that help a child become adaptive, competent, socially connected, and engaged and that promote learning in natural and inclusive environments.	HLP 3: Collaborate with families to support student learning and secure needed services. HLP 4: Use multiple sources of information to develop a comprehensive understanding of a student's strengths and needs. HLP 5: Interpret and communicate assessment information with stakeholders to collaboratively design and implement educational programs. HLP 6: Use student assessment data, analyze instructional practices, and make necessary adjustments that improve student outcomes. HLP 7: Establish a consistent, organized, and respectful learning environment. HLP 8: Provide positive and constructive feedback to guide students' learning and behavior. HLP 9: Teach social behaviors. HLP 10: Conduct functional behavioral assessments to develop individual student behavior support plans. HLP 21: Teach students to maintain and generalize new learning across time and settings. HLP 22: Provide positive and constructive feedback to guide students' learning and behavior.

CEC = Council for Exceptional Children; DEC = Division for Early Childhood.

Data sources: Division for Early Childhood. (2014). DEC recommended practices in early intervention/early childhood special education. 2014. http://www.dec-sped.org/recommendedpractices and McLeskey, J., et al. (2017). *High-leverage practices in special education*. Council for Exceptional Children & CEEDAR Center.

7. Your new microwave chimes once the designated time has expired. It continues to chime, every 5 seconds, increasing in volume, until you open the microwave door. You open the door as you find the chiming annoying. This is an example of:

    a. Positive reinforcement
    b. Negative reinforcement
    c. Positive punishment
    d. Negative punishment

8. Which is a well-stated rule?

    a. Remember, I'm watching you!
    b. Do the right thing!
    c. Don't run!
    d. Use a quiet voice.

9. Which of the following is an example of a willful behavior?

    a. Spitting
    b. Drooling
    c. Shivering
    d. Perspiring

10. Maggie douses her favorite foods in cayenne hot sauce, including breakfast items like waffles and fresh watermelon. What is a reasonable hypothesis to explain Maggie's food preferences?

    a. She has an under-reactive sense of taste
    b. She has an over-reactive sense of taste
    c. She is overstimulated when eating breakfast
    d. She prefers bland foods

11. Amanda and Kristoff are playing together at the sand table. When Kristoff pulls Amanda's hair, she does not respond to him. When he asks her if he can use her funnel and measuring cups, she smiles, says yes, and hands him his desired objects. This is an example of:

    a. Children who have not yet learned to share
    b. Planned ignoring
    c. Over-reactivity
    d. Under-reactivity

12. True or False: A mismatch in the culture and language of the classroom when compared to the culture and language of a student may result in an inappropriate special education classification.

13. The classroom culture is one of the primary environments in which language development occurs. One form of language, vital to classroom management, children learn from an early stage is the language of the classroom, which consists of:

    a. Classroom celebrations
    b. Classroom norms and expectations
    c. The English alphabet
    d. Academic language

RESOURCES

- Autism Internet Modules (Discrete Trial Training, Punishment, Reinforcement, Rules, Visual Supports, etc.): https://autisminternetmodules.org/
- CASEL: https://casel.org/
- Center for Social and Emotional Foundations for Early Learning: http://csefel.vanderbilt.edu/resources/wwb/wwb9.html
- Center for Social and Emotional Foundations for Early Learning Training Modules (3A, 3B, and 4 focus on behavior): http://csefel.vanderbilt.edu/resources/training_preschool.html
- CONNECT Modules: https://www.connectmodules.dec-sped.org/
- Early Childhood Knowledge and Resource Center Culture and Language: https://eclkc.ohs.acf.hhs.gov/culture-language
- Early Childhood Knowledge and Resource Center Dual Language Learners Resources: https://childcareta.acf.hhs.gov/resource/dual-language-learners-resources
- IRIS Early Childhood Behavior Management: http://www.iris.peabody.vanderbilt.edu/wp-content/uploads/pdf_case_studies/ics_behaviormgmt.pdf
- National Association for the Education of Young Children: https://www.naeyc.org/standing-together-against-suspension-expulsion-early-childhood-resources
- National Association for the Education of Young Children Building Environments That Encourage Positive Behavior: https://www.naeyc.org/resources/pubs/yc/mar2016/building-environments-encourage-positive-behavior-preschool
- Sanford Harmony: https://online.sanfordharmony.org/
- Sanford Inspire: https://www.inspireteaching.org/

REFERENCES

Aimin, L. (2013). The study of second language acquisition under socio-cultural theory. *American Journal of Educational Research, 1*(5), 162-167. https://doi.org/10.12691/education-1-5-3

Allen, R., & Steed, E. A. (2016). Culturally responsive pyramid model practices: Program-wide positive behavioral support for young children. *Topics in Early Childhood Special Education, 36,* 1-11.

Artiles, A., Kozleski, E. B., Trent, S. Osher, D., & Ortiz, A. (2010). Justifying and explaining disproportionality, 1968-2008: A critique of underlying views of culture. *Exceptional Children, 76*(3), 279-299. https://doi.org/10.1177/001440291007600303

Baker, T. L., Wise, J., Kelley, G., & Skiba, R. J. (2016). Identifying barriers: Creating solutions to improve family engagement. *School Community Journal, 26*(2), 161-184.

Brown, M. R., Dennis, J. P., & Matute-Chavarria, M. (2019). Cultural relevance in special education: Current status and future directions. *Intervention in School and Clinic, 54*(5), 304-310. https://doi.org/10.1177/1053451218819252

Calderón, M., Slavin, R., & Sánchez, M. (2011). Effective instruction for English learners. *The Future of Children, 21*(1), 103-127.

Center on the Developing Child at Harvard University. (2016). *From best practices to breakthrough impacts: A science-based approach to building a more promising future for young children and families.* www.developingchild.harvard.edu

Collaborative for Academic, Social, and Emotional Learning. (2013). *Effective social and emotional learning programs: preschool and elementary school edition.* https://files.eric.ed.gov/fulltext/ED581699.pdf

Division for Early Childhood. (2014). DEC recommended practices in early intervention/early childhood special education 2014. https://www.dec-sped.org/dec-recommended-practices

Fox, L., Dunlap, G., Hemmeter, M. L., Joseph, G. E., & Strain, P. S. (2003). The teaching pyramid: A model for supporting social competence and preventing challenging behavior in young children. *Young Children, 58,* 48-52.

Fox, L., Strain, P. S., & Dunlap, G. (2021). Preventing the use of preschool suspension and expulsion: Implementing the pyramid model. *Preventing School Failure, 65*(4), 312-322. https://doi.org/10.1080/1045988X.2021.1937026

Hemmeter, M. L., Snyder, P. A., Fox, L., & Algina, J. (2016). Evaluating the implementation of the Pyramid Model for promoting social emotional competence in early childhood classrooms. *Topics in Early Childhood Special Education, 36*, 133-146.

Huang, J., Clarke, K., Milczarski, E., & Raby, C. (2011). The assessment of English language learners with learning disabilities: Issues, concerns, and implications. *Education, 131*(4), 732-739.

Kramer, T. J., Caldarella, P., Christensen, L., & Shatzer, R. H. (2010). Social and emotional learning in the kindergarten classroom: Evaluation of the strong start curriculum. *Early Childhood Education, 37*(4), 303-309. https://doi.org/10.1007/s10643-009-0354-8

Lloyd, B., Weaver, E., & Staubitz, J. (2017). Classroom-based strategies to incorporate hypothesis testing in functional behavior assessments. *Beyond Behavior, 26*(2), 48-56. https://doi.org/10.1177/1074295617711145

McIntosh, K., Ellwood, K., McCall, L., & Girvan, E. J. (2018). Using discipline data to enhance equity in school discipline. *Intervention in School and Clinic, 53*(3), 146-152.

Melekoğlu, M., Bal, A., & Diken, I. H. (2017). Implementing school-wide positive behavior intervention and supports (SWPBIS) for early identification and prevention of problem behaviors in Turkey. *International Journal of Early Childhood Special Education, 9*(2), 98-110.

National Center on Early Childhood Health and Wellness. (2020). *Understanding and eliminating expulsion in early childhood programs.* https://eclkc.ohs.acf.hhs.gov/sites/default/files/pdf/understanding-eliminating-expulsion-early-childhood-factsheet.pdf

National Child Traumatic Stress Network Schools Committee. (2008). *Child trauma toolkit for educators.* https://www.nctsn.org/sites/default/files/resources/child_trauma_toolkit_educators/pdf

Ray-Subramanian, C. (2013). Motivation Assessment Scale. In: F. R. Volkmar (Ed.), *Encyclopedia of Autism Spectrum Disorders.* Springer.

Stegelin, D. A. (2018). *Preschool suspension and expulsion: Defining the issues* (pp. 1-18). Institute for Child Success.

Sullivan, A. (2011). Disproportionality in special education identification and placement of ELLs. *Exceptional Children, 77*(3), 317-334.

U.S. Department of Education, Institute of Education Sciences, National Center for Education Statistics. (2019). *The condition of education.* Authors.

Vygotsky, L. (1978). *Mind in society: The development of higher psychological processes.* MIT Press.

Planning for Success

Marla J. Lohmann, PhD; Ariane N. Gauvreau, PhD, BCBA-D;
and Katrina A. Hovey, PhD

INTRODUCTION

Planning for success in the early childhood classroom requires teachers to use evidence-based teaching strategies that align with the Division for Early Childhood Recommended Practices and the Council for Exceptional Children's high-leverage practices. This chapter offers a brief overview of practices that meet this criterion. First, information about differentiated instruction and the use of the Universal Design for Learning framework to ensure that teachers meet the learning needs of all young children is presented. Second, standards-based lesson planning is discussed. The third topic presented is explicit instruction. Finally, the authors discuss the development of SMART (Specific, Measurable, Action oriented, Relevant and realistic, and Time limited) Individualized Education Program goals for young children.

Fisher, K. M., & Zimmer, K. E. (Eds.).
Early Childhood Special Education Programs and Practices (pp. 99-115).
© 2023 SLACK Incorporated.

CHAPTER OBJECTIVES

→ Identify appropriate differentiation strategies to ensure student success in the early elementary school classroom.

→ Select evidence-based teaching strategies and interventions that align with the Division for Early Childhood Recommended Practices and the Council for Exceptional Children's high-leverage practices.

→ Design unit and lesson objectives that align with state academic standards.

→ Create SMART (Specific, Measurable, Action oriented, Relevant and realistic, and Time limited) Individualized Education Program goals for students with disabilities.

KEY TERMS

- **Common Core State Standards:** A set of academic standards adopted in most U.S. states that outlines the learning goals in language arts and mathematics for students at each grade level, from kindergarten through 12th grade, to ensure that all students throughout the country achieve the same learning standards.

- **Differentiated Instruction:** Occurs when teachers individualize instruction and support for specific students, provide extra help or information, or change the environment to help them learn or participate independently.

- **Explicit Instruction:** A group of evidence-based teaching strategies that collectively support student learning; strategies include modeling and think alouds, supports and prompts that are systematically removed over time, specific feedback on student responses, and opportunities for students to practice the skill.

- **SMART (Specific, Measurable, Action oriented, Relevant and realistic, and Time limited) Individualized Education Program (IEP) Goals:** SMART IEP goals that specifically state what is expected of the student so that all stakeholders have the same understanding of necessary instruction and know what skills to target for instruction and assessment.

- **Universal Design for Learning:** A systematic framework for supporting the learning needs of all children in the classroom through the use of multiple means of (a) engagement, (b) representation, and (c) action and expression.

CASE STUDY

Mr. Ruiz is the lead teacher in an inclusive kindergarten classroom. The children in his classroom come from various backgrounds, including five children with an Individualized Education Program (IEP) and four children who have been identified as needing English-language learner support. Mr. Ruiz firmly believes that all children can learn and wants to ensure that he uses best practices in early childhood instruction. To ensure that all of his students are successful, Mr. Ruiz uses differentiated and explicit instruction for the class as a whole. He supports the school special education teacher in designing high-quality IEP goals for each student receiving special education services.

"If a child can't learn the way we teach,
maybe we should teach the way they learn."
—Ignacio Estrada

When planning for success in the inclusive early elementary school and the early childhood special education classroom, teachers must use best practices in classroom instruction and instructional planning. Best practices in teaching are supported by research and are considered evidence based. In special education, evidence-based teaching practices have been outlined through both the Division for Early Childhood (DEC) Recommended Practices and the Collaboration for Effective Educator Development, Accountability, and Reform Center and Council for Exceptional Children's high-leverage practices (HLPs). This chapter provides a brief overview of practices elementary special educators should use to plan for student success in their classrooms. These teaching practices and their alignment with both the DEC Recommended Practices and the HLPs are outlined in Table 5-1.

DIFFERENTIATED INSTRUCTION

Today's classrooms include learners from a wide variety of backgrounds with varying learning strengths and needs. Differentiated instruction is necessary to meet each child's unique needs. Differentiated instruction occurs when teachers individualize instruction and support for specific students, provide extra help or information, or change the environment in a way that will help the student learn or participate independently (Tomlinson, 2000). Through the differentiation of learning, teachers can support students with disabilities in both the inclusive classroom and in the special education classroom (Gartin et al., 2016). Furthermore, the use of differentiated instruction meets the legal mandates for instruction as outlined in the Individuals with Disabilities Education Act Section 300.39. Table 5-2 shows the specific phrasing that discusses this requirement for differentiated instruction.

Teachers can differentiate classroom instruction in four ways: (a) content, (b) process, (c) products, and (d) learning environment (Tomlinson, 2017). The *content* refers to the material being taught and how a student might access that information. The *process* is how the student engages with the learning, and the *products* are the assignments the student may complete. Finally, the *learning environment* is the classroom itself (Tomlinson, 2000, 2017). Research indicates that differentiated instruction leads to academic gains for students (Valiandes, 2015). Table 5-3 provides examples of common ways to provide differentiated instruction in each of these four areas.

UNIVERSAL DESIGN FOR LEARNING

One way to provide differentiated instruction and ensure success for all students in the classroom is Universal Design for Learning (UDL). UDL is a systematic framework for supporting the learning needs of all children in the classroom through the use of multiple means of (a) engagement, (b) representation, and (c) action and expression (Center for Applied Special Technologies, 2018). When teachers use UDL in their classrooms, they proactively plan for potential student needs through the use of a flexible curriculum designed to ensure that all children can access the learning (Hitchcock et al., 2002; Rose et al., 2010; Rose & Strangman, 2007).

Teachers can use multiple means of engagement to enhance children's motivation for learning and keep students engaged in the classroom (Glass et al., 2013; Rose & Strangman, 2007). Teachers may use a variety of potential strategies to increase student engagement including (a) offering choice, (b) providing and using classroom materials that are reflective of the cultures represented in the classroom, (c) using classroom materials that align with students' interests, and (d) intentionally building relationships with students (Lohmann et al., 2018). Table 5-4 offers a list of specific actions elementary teachers may take to increase student engagement.

TABLE 5-1. ALIGNMENT OF INSTRUCTIONAL PRACTICES WITH RECOMMENDED PRACTICES AND HIGH-LEVERAGE PRACTICES (HLPs)

INSTRUCTIONAL PRACTICE	ALIGNED DEC RECOMMENDED PRACTICES	ALIGNED HLPs
Differentiated instruction, including Universal Design for Learning	E2: Practitioners consider Universal Design for Learning principles to create accessible environments. INS4: Practitioners plan for and provide the level of support, accommodations, and adaptations needed for the child to access, participate, and learn within and across activities and routines. INS10: Practitioners implement the frequency, intensity, and duration of instruction needed to address the child's phase and pace of learning or the level of support needed by the family to achieve the child's outcomes or goals. INT5: Practitioners promote the child's problem-solving behavior by observing, interpreting, and scaffolding in response to the child's growing level of autonomy and self-regulation.	HLP 6: Use student assessment data, analyze instructional practices, and make necessary adjustments that improve student outcomes. HLP 13: Adapt curriculum tasks and materials for specific learning goals. HLP 15: Provide scaffolded supports. HLP 18: Use strategies to promote active student engagement. HLP 21: Teach students to maintain and generalize new learning across time and settings. HLP 22: Provide positive and constructive feedback to guide students' learning and behavior.
Standards-based lesson planning	INS1: Practitioners, with the family, identify each child's strengths, preferences, and interests to engage the child in active learning. INS2: Practitioners, with the family, identify skills to target for instruction that help a child become adaptive, competent, socially connected, and engaged and that promote learning in natural and inclusive environments.	HLP 12: Systematically design instruction toward a specific learning goal. HLP 13: Adapt curriculum tasks and materials for specific learning goals.
Explicit instruction	INS6: Practitioners use systematic instructional strategies with fidelity to teach skills and to promote child engagement and learning. INS7: Practitioners use explicit feedback and consequences to increase child engagement, play, and skills.	HLP 8: Provide positive and constructive feedback to guide students' learning and behavior. HLP 16: Use explicit instruction. HLP 20: Provide intensive instruction. HLP 22: Provide positive and constructive feedback to guide students' learning and behavior.

(continued)

TABLE 5-1 (CONTINUED). ALIGNMENT OF INSTRUCTIONAL PRACTICES WITH RECOMMENDED PRACTICES AND HIGH-LEVERAGE PRACTICES (HLPS)

INSTRUCTIONAL PRACTICE	ALIGNED DEC RECOMMENDED PRACTICES	ALIGNED HLPs
Use of SMART IEP goals	TC1: Practitioners representing multiple disciplines and families work together as a team to plan and implement supports and services to meet the unique needs of each child and family.	HLP 5: Interpret and communicate assessment information with stakeholders to collaboratively design and implement educational programs. HLP 8: Provide positive and constructive feedback to guide students' learning and behavior.

DEC = Division for Early Childhood; IEP = Individualized Education Program; SMART = Specific, Measurable, Action oriented, Relevant and realistic, and Time limited.

Data sources: Division for Early Childhood. (2014). DEC recommended practices in early intervention/early childhood special education. 2014. http://www.dec-sped.org/recommendedpractices and McLeskey, J., et al. (2017). *High-leverage practices in special education.* Council for Exceptional Children & CEEDAR Center.

TABLE 5-2. INDIVIDUALS WITH DISABILITIES EDUCATION ACT REQUIREMENT FOR DIFFERENTIATED INSTRUCTION

a (1) Special education means specially designed instruction, at no cost to the parents, to meet the unique needs of a child with a disability, including

(i) Instruction conducted in the classroom, in the home, in hospitals and institutions, and in other setting

b (3) Specially designed instruction means adapting, as appropriate to the needs of an eligible child under this part, the content, methodology, or delivery of instruction

(i) To address the unique needs of the child that result from the child's disability; and

(ii) To ensure access of the child to the general curriculum, so that the child can meet the educational standards within the jurisdiction of the public agency that apply to all children.

Data source: Individuals with Disabilities Education Act (IDEA), Pub. L. No. 108-446, §1401(2), (2004).

TABLE 5-3. PRACTICAL APPLICATIONS OF DIFFERENTIATED INSTRUCTION IN THE EARLY CHILDHOOD CLASSROOM	
IDEAS FOR DIFFERENTIATING CONTENT	• Using books at various reading levels • Incorporating audiobooks • Individualizing learning goals for students • Grouping students by skill level
IDEAS FOR DIFFERENTIATING PROCESS	• Scaffolding instruction • Aligning content with student interests • Using manipulatives • Providing extra time for assignments
IDEAS FOR DIFFERENTIATING PRODUCTS	• Individualizing rubrics • Shortening assignments • Putting assignments on different-colored paper
IDEAS FOR DIFFERENTIATING LEARNING ENVIRONMENT	• Creating classroom routines • Providing flexible seating • Offering a seat near the teacher • Proximity control

Early childhood educators use multiple means of representation to present the learning content to students through various mediums (Glass et al., 2013; Rose & Strangman, 2007). Elementary special education teachers can use a variety of strategies to offer multiple means of representation in their classrooms, including (a) pairing visual cues with verbal instructions, (b) foreign language translation of all written and oral language, (c) hands-on learning activities, (d) think alouds, and (e) modeling (Gauvreau et al., 2019).

Table 5-5 offers a sample teacher instruction section of a lesson plan that has multiple means of representation. This lesson includes oral counting, visual representations, student choice, opportunities for students to use manipulatives to actively engage in mathematics, and technology use.

Finally, teachers may use multiple means of action and expression to allow students the opportunity to show that they have mastered the intended learning outcomes (Center for Applied Special Technologies, 2018; Glass et al., 2013; Meyer & Rose, 2005). Teachers may allow students to demonstrate their knowledge through (a) technology, (b) visual representations, (c) offering options, and (d) hands-on learning activities (Beneke et al., 2019).

A sample assessment a teacher might use with the same lesson is shown in Table 5-6; this assessment uses the UDL principle of multiple means of action and expression. You will notice that students are offered three distinct ways to complete the assignment.

TABLE 5-4. IDEAS FOR INCREASING STUDENT ENGAGEMENT IN THE EARLY ELEMENTARY SPECIAL EDUCATION CLASSROOM

- Greet each student as they enter the classroom each day.
- Be aware of students' likes and interests, and regularly use these in instruction and classroom materials.
- Have a one-on-one conversation with each student regularly.
- Celebrate students' birthdays.
- Incorporate students' interests into lesson planning.
- Ensure that the classroom library includes books that reflect student interests, backgrounds, families, and cultures.
- Offer activities that align with students' interests during free play and recess times.
- Include visuals in the classroom that use a variety of languages and depict children and families from a range of races and ethnicities.
- Ensure that the books in the classroom library reflect the cultural and linguistic diversity present in the classroom.
- Celebrate holidays from various cultures and religious beliefs.
- Ask students and parents to share their culture in meaningful ways.
- Offer opportunities for children to use their knowledge to solve real-world problems.
- Ask students to report whether they understand the lesson.
- Offer choices throughout the day, such as:
  - Where to sit.
  - What color writing utensil to use.
  - Working alone or with a partner.
  - Which math manipulatives to use.

Adapted from Lohmann, M. J., Hovey, K. A., & Gauvreau, A. N. (2018). Using a Universal Design for Learning framework to enhance engagement in the early childhood classroom. *Journal of Special Education Apprenticeship, 7*(2), 1-12.

STANDARDS-BASED LESSON PLANNING

Teachers must ensure that they align all instruction with state learning standards when planning lessons and learning units. The Every Student Succeeds Act mandates standards-based instruction; ensures that all students, including children with disabilities, learn what is expected at each grade level; and reduces the likelihood of student knowledge gaps (National Council on Disability, 2018). The Common Core State Standards (CCSS) were developed in English language arts and math to ensure that students nationwide learn the same concepts and master similar skills. As of fall 2020, 41 states have adopted the CCSS (CCSS Initiative, 2019). States have the option of whether to adopt the CCSS, and those who do generally incorporate the CCSS into their state academic standards; if your state has adopted the CCSS, this will be evident in your state academic standards. States may also be using early learning guidelines or standards to inform planning for preschool and prekindergarten students.

TABLE 5-5. SAMPLE TEACHER INSTRUCTION SECTION OF THE LESSON PLAN

Lesson Objective: First-grade students will add numbers to equal 5 with 85% accuracy.

1. As a class, orally count to 20. While counting, the teacher points to each number on the classroom number line. Students are encouraged to point to each number on the number lines on their desks.

2. The teacher turns on the "Friend of 5 Addition" video for students to view on the classroom board (https://www.youtube.com/watch?v=4vmawwxw_AQ).

3. Students are instructed to go to the math manipulatives shelf to choose their manipulatives. Options include counting teddy bears, beans, several abaci, and iPads (Apple) with a drawing application that allows students to draw and move shapes for counting.

4. Once students have returned to their seats, the teacher turns on the smart board, and the first addition problem (4 + 1) pops up. The teacher asks students to use their manipulatives to set up the math problems on their desks while using manipulatives on the smart board to create a visual representation of the problem.

5. Once all students have created a visual representation of the problem, the teacher demonstrates how to use the manipulatives to solve the problem.

6. The teacher continues putting new problems on the smart board. The students solve the problems, with the teacher asking students to share answers by responding in unison and calling on individual students to describe how they arrived at the answer.

TABLE 5-6. SAMPLE LESSON ASSESSMENT

Each student is given an addition worksheet to complete. Students are provided the following options for completing the worksheet, and all students are encouraged to use both the math manipulatives and the number lines provided on their desks.

- Option 1: Students may put the answers on the worksheet. To put the answers on the worksheet, students may choose to write the answers, use number stamps, or use number stickers.

- Option 2: Students may use the video function on the iPads to record their answers to each question orally. To do so, students will state the problem number and then the answer for each math problem.

- Option 3: Students may use the drawing function on the iPads to record their answers. To use this option, they will need to draw shapes for the numbers being counted and then write the solution to each problem.

When designing standards-based instruction, teachers should note that the standard identifies what knowledge and skills students must master but not how they demonstrate their learning (Rao & Meo, 2016). The lesson plan should include academic standards, including both skills and concepts (Morgan et al., 2014). Teachers can create a two-column table to identify what should be taught (Morgan et al., 2014; Rao & Meo, 2016). The skills a student must master are generally identified with verbs in the standard, whereas the concepts are ideas the student must understand to master the skills (Rao & Meo, 2016). Table 5-7 provides a sample table for a first-grade CCSS math standard.

TABLE 5-7. SAMPLE SKILLS AND CONCEPTS TABLE

CCSS.MATH.CONTENT.1.NBT.A.1

Count to 120, starting at any number less than 120. In this range, read and write numerals and represent a number of objects with a written numeral.

SKILLS	CONCEPTS
Count to 120	Any number less than 120
Read numerals	Represent a number of objects with a numeral
Write numerals	

TABLE 5-8. SAMPLE UNIT AND LESSON OBJECTIVES ALIGNED TO COMMON CORE STATE STANDARDS

Unit Goal: With 90% or more accuracy, first-grade students will independently count both orally and in written format to 120, starting with any number.
Lesson Objective Days 1 and 2: Students will orally rote count to 120 with 90% accuracy.
Lesson Objective Days 3 and 4: Students will write numbers to 120 with 90% accuracy.
Lesson Objective Days 4 and 5: Students will orally count to 120 starting from any number with 90% accuracy.
Lesson Objective Days 5 and 6: Students will write numbers to 120, starting from any number with 90% accuracy.
Lesson Objective Days 6 and 7: Students will orally identify the next number when counting to 120 from various starting points with 95% accuracy.
Lesson Objective Days 8 and 9: Students will fill in missing random numbers on a counting chart to 120 with 95% accuracy.

The vocabulary stated in the academic standard should be used in the lesson objective when teachers use an academic standard to create a unit or lesson objective. A well-written unit or lesson objective will include the behavior the student must exhibit, the minimum criterion (mastery) for that behavior, and the circumstances under which the behavior must occur (Raible et al., 2016). An example of how a teacher might do this in a 2-week unit using the state standard from Table 5-7 can be found in Table 5-8.

Early childhood teachers must use data from both formative and summative assessments to determine the appropriate pacing of lessons and ensure students are learning what is expected. Formative assessments are used during a lesson or unit to provide a teacher with information about students' understanding of the instructional concepts and guide future instruction within the lesson or unit (Klute et al., 2017). Formative assessments may be either formal or informal and often take just a few moments to complete. Table 5-9 offers examples of formative assessment strategies that are effective in the early elementary classroom. Please refer to Chapter 4 for additional assessment information.

TABLE 5-9. FORMATIVE ASSESSMENT STRATEGIES
• Students put thumbs up or down to indicate if they understand.
• Students share two things they don't know about the learning topic.
• Students state what they learned in their own words.
• Students draw a picture of what they learned.
• Students orally answer teacher questions in unison.
• Students write answers on individual whiteboards, and all students show their solutions at the same time.

Although teachers use formative assessments to evaluate learning during the lesson and unit, it is also critical they use summative assessments to ensure that all students achieve the academic standards expected or to determine if additional instruction is necessary. Table 5-9 provides strategies for informal or formative assessments. Summative assessments are given at the conclusion of the lesson or unit and provide data that can be delivered to educational stakeholders and inform educators of class-wide learning (National Foundation for Educational Research, 2019).

EXPLICIT INSTRUCTION

As teachers design standards-based lessons, they must ensure that the lesson includes explicit instruction (EI) for students who need additional, structured teaching. EI is a group of evidence-based teaching strategies that collectively support student learning (Archer & Hughes, 2011; Hughes et al., 2017). Essential strategies of EI include (a) modeling and think alouds, (b) supports and prompts that are systematically removed over time, (c) specific feedback on student responses, and (d) opportunities for students to practice the skill (Hughes et al., 2017). The phrase "I do, we do, you do" is often used to describe EI. The term *gradual release* is used to explain how EI moves from the teacher providing instruction and modeling to the class practicing together and ends with individual practice (Ciullo & Dimino, 2017).

During the "I do" portion of the lesson, teachers provide systematic instruction on the learning material and model for students how to complete the task (Archer & Hughes, 2011). Modeling can occur in three ways: (a) the teacher models the skill for the students, (b) peers or older students model the skill for one another, or (c) the teacher or peers demonstrate the skill via video (Gauvreau et al., 2019). Similar to modeling is the concept of a think aloud. This strategy occurs when a teacher verbally explains their thinking while solving a problem or considering an idea (Morgan & York, 2009).

In his classroom, Mr. Ruiz plans to teach the +1 addition facts, with answers to 10, to his students. For the "I do" section of the lesson, Mr. Ruiz writes the math problems on the classroom whiteboard and then uses stuffed teddy bears as manipulatives to demonstrate how to find the answer. When he answers the question of 3 + 1, Mr. Ruiz puts three teddy bears on the left side of his desk and one teddy bear on the right side. He then says to his students, "Let's find the answer to this math problem. We will put three teddy bears over here plus one teddy bear over here, and then I will count them. One, two, three, four. Four teddy bears. Three plus one equals four. Four teddy bears."

As teachers move to the "we do" portion of the lesson, they ask students to begin working on the skill. At this time, systematic support is necessary for all students, often in the form of scaffolded instruction. A teacher scaffolds instruction when they provide support to help a student and then slowly remove those supports over time (Ciullo & Dimino, 2017).

For the "we do" section of the lesson, Mr. Ruiz gives each student their own set of counting teddy bears while he continues to use the stuffed teddy bears at the front of the classroom. He writes the math problem 2 + 1 = on the whiteboard. Then, he says, "OK. Let's work together to answer this math problem. First, we pick up two teddy bears and put them on one side of our desks. Now, we pick up one teddy bear and put it on the other side of our desk. Has everyone put their teddy bears on their desks? Now, let's count them together. One, two, three. Three teddy bears. Two teddy bears plus one teddy bear equals three teddy bears."

When providing feedback to students, teachers must be specific and give feedback immediately after the student(s) complete the learning task (Archer & Hughes, 2011; Thomas & Sondergeld, 2015). Also, students' feedback should directly relate to the lesson learning objectives (van den Bergh et al., 2013). It should help students understand both their current performance level on the skill and their expected performance (Hattie & Timperley, 2007). Essentially, students need to know promptly if they are learning what they are supposed to be learning. Teachers can offer either oral or visual feedback or a combination of the two (Lingo et al., 2009). Early childhood teachers should provide feedback to help students understand both the areas in which they need improvement and the areas in which they did well (Duhon et al., 2015). In the section of this chapter on Standards-Based Lesson Planning, we noted the need for formative assessment; providing frequent feedback to students offers them an idea of what you have discovered in your formative assessments. Table 5-10 provides examples of feedback statements that a teacher might provide to students on academic and behavior skills in the early elementary classroom. The first two feedback statements in each category identify strengths, and the second two statements identify areas for student improvement.

After completing the "we do" section of the lesson, Mr. Ruiz allows students to practice +1 math problems with his feedback. Mr. Ruiz writes the math problem 5 + 1 on the whiteboard and asks the students to find the answer using their teddy bears and then write the answer on their whiteboards. While students are solving the problem, Mr. Ruiz walks around the classroom and provides feedback to students. He says, "Esther, good job counting your bears. I can hear you counting, and you said the correct answer. Now, can you look at your whiteboard and make sure that you wrote the number you said?"

After explicitly teaching the skill, teachers must provide frequent opportunities for students to practice the skill. When teachers offer students multiple chances to respond and practice the skill and provide explicit feedback on performance, they are more likely to master it (Cuticelli et al., 2016). Teachers should offer students a chance to practice the skill in small groups, with partners, or independently and provide the opportunity to demonstrate mastery of the skill through multiple means of action and expression, as explained in the Differentiated Instruction section of this chapter (see Table 5-3).

EI has proven to be effective for students with disabilities such as autism (Hinton et al., 2016; Root, 2019), so teachers should use EI to ensure high-quality education in all subject areas (Therrien et al., 2017). We recommend planning classroom instruction using the EI "I do, we do, you do" or the gradual release structure. Figure 5-1 provides sample lesson activities that use this model.

TABLE 5-10. SAMPLE FEEDBACK STATEMENTS

BEHAVIOR

- I see that all students are sitting quietly on the rug and are ready for learning. That means we will have time for an extra song during circle time today!
- Thank you, Jose, for raising your hand before speaking.
- Uh oh, class. I hear that you are using unkind words. Please use your kind, respectful words with your classmates.
- Zander, remember to use your walking feet in the hallway.

MATHEMATICS SKILLS

- Asa, you did a great job of counting the numbers to 10. You were loud enough for me to hear you, and you said all of the correct numbers. Good work!
- DeeVann, I see that you put one teddy bear on each dot. Your 1:1 correspondence is really improving. I am so proud of your hard work!
- Charlotte, take a look at your addition again. It is not quite correct.
- Abraham, you are so close on your counting. You missed the number 12. Why don't we count to 20 together?

LANGUAGE ARTS SKILLS

- Abigail, you read all of the words correctly on that page! The word "zebra" can be a little tough, but you got it! Great job!
- Imani, I am so impressed by how neatly you wrote your name! Your handwriting is clear and easy to read. Nice work!
- Esther, let's try that word again. It is a tricky word, and you were close but not quite right.
- Pancho, your answer is close but not quite correct. I think you are mixing up the sounds of the letters "m" and "n." Let's try it again.

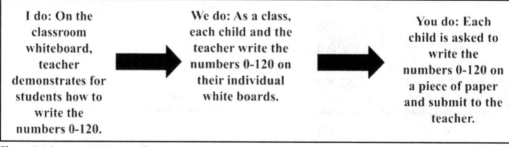

Figure 5-1. Lesson activity using EI.

SMART Individualized Education Program Goals/Objectives

In addition to planning for classroom-wide success, early elementary school teachers must also make plans to ensure each student's success. For students with disabilities, the IEP outlines these individualized plans. In most states, once children with disabilities turn 3 and enter the school system, they are evaluated and, if eligible, are given an IEP instead of an Individualized Family Service Plan (IFSP). However, in some states, children receive special education services through the IFSP until they begin kindergarten. Early intervention teams develop the IFSP to support the needs of children with disabilities and their families between birth and age 3 (Individuals with Disabilities Education Act, 2004). The IEP does not consider family needs like the IFSP did. Instead, the focus of the IEP is on the educational success of the student with disabilities. The IEP contains (a) the present levels of academic achievement and functional performance; (b) a description of the special education services the child requires for success, the date on which those services will start, and the location and frequency of the services; (c) the student's least restrictive environment; (d) an explanation of the extent to which the student will participate in the state and district assessments; and (e) specific and measurable goals for student learning that include information about how the IEP team will measure the student's progress toward those goals (IDEA, 2004).

In the inclusive early elementary school classroom, student learning goals should be directly related to the state academic standards whenever possible and appropriate. This may not be possible for students who are working significantly below grade level (Hedin & DeSpain, 2018). IEP goals must be individualized to the needs of the student (Caruana, 2015) and use the student's present levels of academic achievement and functional performance as a baseline for determining appropriate goals (More & Hart Barnett, 2014). To ensure that IEP goals demonstrate high expectations and that progress can be evaluated, teachers should use the SMART goals acronym (Hedin & DeSpain, 2018). SMART stands for Specific, Measurable, Action oriented, Relevant and realistic, and Time limited (Wright & Wright, 2019). It is critical that IEP goals specifically state student expectations so that all stakeholders (e.g., special and general education teachers, paraprofessionals, and related service providers) have the same understanding of necessary instruction and know what skills to target for instruction and assessment (Jung, 2007). The goal must be measurable to ensure that stakeholders can use data to tell if the student has achieved the goal (More & Hart Barnett, 2014). The goal must use action words to specifically state the behavior that is expected (Wright & Wright, 2019). Also, goals should be relevant to the student and their learning and grade level; this can often be accomplished by connecting IEP goals with state academic standards (Caruana, 2015). IEP teams should write goals with high expectations that are realistic and attainable by the individual student (Wright & Wright, 2019). Finally, the goal needs to state the time period by which it will be accomplished (Jozwik et al., 2018). Table 5-11 provides examples of SMART IEP goals that meet each of these expectations and could be used for early elementary special education students.

Summary

Because classrooms serve an increasingly diverse range of students and families, the need for high-quality instruction is crucial. Many resources inform the effective planning for this instruction (i.e., the Council for Exceptional Children's HLPs, the UDL framework [Center for Applied Special Technologies, 2018], DEC Recommended Practices [DEC, 2014], state standards, and individual state early learning guidelines). Still, the most important aspect of special education is the individualized nature of programming. Goals, learning targets, and instructional strategies will be different for each student depending on their strengths and needs. However, more teachers using UDL principles and creating learning environments that promote the access, participation, and independence of all learners will result in fewer students requiring additional support.

TABLE 5-11. EXAMPLES OF SMART INDIVIDUALIZED EDUCATION PROGRAM (IEP) GOALS

Content Area: Mathematics

SMART IEP Goal: When shown a set of first-grade addition flash cards with 20 or fewer sums, Alejandro will correctly answer 8 out of 10 problems in 2 minutes.

Content Area: Language arts

SMART IEP Goal: When given a second-grade DIBELS reading fluency probe, Asa will read a minimum of 40 words correctly in 1 minute.

SMART = Specific, Measurable, Action oriented, Relevant and realistic, and Time limited.

CHAPTER REVIEW

1. Define differentiated instruction.
2. Name the four ways that teachers may differentiate instruction.
3. What are the three principles of UDL?
4. What law mandates standards-based instruction for all learners?
5. What is the focus on the IEP?
6. What does the acronym SMART stand for?
7. Thinking about the classrooms where you have observed, list differentiation strategies you have witnessed teachers using. Which ones do you believe work? To what extent do you think student needs were being met?
8. Choose one of the following scenarios. List three ways the teacher might differentiate the expectations for students with disabilities.
    a. First-grade students are expected to demonstrate the ability to count to 100 by 1s, 2s, 5s, and 10s.
    b. Second-grade students are expected to orally retell a story they read independently. All key events from the story must be included in the retell, and no teacher prompting is allowed.
    c. Third-grade students are expected to write a three-paragraph paper using correct sentence formation, accurate spelling, and neat handwriting.
9. Offering choices is an evidence-based practice that aligns with the UDL framework. Explain why you believe student motivation and learning are increased when options are offered. Consider how your motivation and learning are impacted when your professor gives choices.
10. Examine your state academic standards and choose one standard. Write a SMART learning goal for an imaginary student that aligns with that standard.
11. Change each of the following goals into SMART learning goals:
    a. Johnny will be able to count to 10.
    b. Zane will read fluently.
    c. Ama will write a paper with no spelling mistakes.
    d. Penelope will count by 5s to 100.
    e. Juanita will accurately answer all of the questions on the +1 math worksheet.

12. Choose one of the following unit goals. For your chosen unit goal, write five daily learning objectives.

    a. First graders will be able to orally articulate the steps in a butterfly's life cycle with 100% accuracy and no prompts.

    b. Second graders will independently be able to identify even and odd numbers to 100 with 95% accuracy.

    c. Third graders will write a nonfiction paragraph that utilizes one reference and has two or fewer spelling or grammatical errors.

RESOURCES

- Archer, A. L., & Hughes, C. A. (2011). *Explicit instruction: Effective and efficient teaching.* Guilford Press.
- Center for Applied Special Technologies. (2018). *Universal Design for Learning guidelines version 2.2.* http://udlguidelines.cast.org
- Colorado Department of Education. (2012). *The standards-based teaching/learning cycle* (2nd ed.). https://www.cde.state.co.us/sites/default/files/documents/communications/download/pdf/standardsbasedteachinglearningcyclepdf.pdf
- Common Core Standards Initiative. (2019). *Read the standards.* http://www.corestandards.org/read-the-standards/
- Gartin, B. C., Murdick, N. L., Perner, D. E., & Imbeau, M. B. (2016). *Differentiating instruction in the inclusive classroom: Strategies for success.* Council for Exceptional Children.
- Gauvreau, A. N., Lohmann, M. J., & Hovey, K. A. (2019). Using a Universal Design for Learning framework to provide multiple means of representation in the early childhood classroom. *Journal of Special Education Apprenticeship, 8*(1), 1-13.
- Gronseth, S. L., & Dalton, E. M. (Eds.). (2020). *Universal access through inclusive instructional design: International perspectives on UDL.* Routledge.
- Hedin, L., & DeSpain, S. (2018). SMART or not?: Writing specific, measurable IEP goals. *Teaching Exceptional Children, 51*(2), 100-110.
- Horn, E. M., Palmer, S. B., Butera, G. D., & Lieber, J. (2016). *Six steps to inclusive preschool curriculum: A UDL-based framework for children's school success.* Brookes Publishing Company.
- IRIS Center. (2019). *Content standards: Connecting standards-based curriculum to instructional planning.* https://iris.peabody.vanderbilt.edu/module/cnm/#content
- IRIS Center. (2019). *Differentiated instruction.* https://iris.peabody.vanderbilt.edu/module/di/#content
- IRIS Center. (2019). *Early childhood environments: Designing effective classrooms.* https://iris.peabody.vanderbilt.edu/module/env/
- IRIS Center. (2019). *Explicit, systematic instruction.* https://iris.peabody.vanderbilt.edu/module/math/cresource/q2/p04/
- IRIS Center. (2019). *IEPs: Developing high-quality individualized education programs.* https://iris.peabody.vanderbilt.edu/module/iep01/#content
- Kennedy, M. J., Peeples, K. N., Romig, J. E., Mathews, H. M., & Rodgers, W. J. (2018). *High-leverage practice #12: Systematically designed instruction towards learning goals.* https://highleveragepractices.org/hlp-12-systematically-design-instruction-toward-specific-learning-goal
- Kennedy, M. J., Peeples, K. N., Romig, J. E., Mathews, H. M., & Rodgers, W. J. (2018). *High-leverage practice #16: Use explicit instruction.* https://highleveragepractices.org/701-2/

- Kennedy, M. J., Peeples, K. N., Romig, J. E., Mathews, H. M., & Rodgers, W. J. (2018). *High-leverage practice #18: Use strategies to promote active student engagement.* https://highleverage-practices.org/701-2-5/

- Lohmann, M. J., Hovey, K. A., & Gauvreau, A. N. (2018). Using a Universal Design for Learning framework to enhance engagement in the early childhood classroom. *Journal of Special Education Apprenticeship, 7*(2), 1-12.

- Murawski, W. W., & Scott, K. L. (Eds.). (2019). *What really works with Universal Design for Learning.* Corwin.

- Novak, K. (2016). *UDL now: A teacher's guide to applying Universal Design for Learning in today's classroom.* CAST Professional Publishing.

- Tomlison, C. A. (2017). *How to differentiate instruction in academically diverse classrooms* (3rd ed.). ASCD.

REFERENCES

Archer, A. L, & Hughes, C. A. (2011). *Explicit instruction: Effective and efficient teaching.* Guilford Press.

Beneke, S., Ostrosky, M. M., & Katz, L. G. (2019). *The Project Approach for ALL learners: A hands-on guide for inclusive early childhood classrooms.* Brookes Publishing Company.

Caruana, V. (2015). Accessing the common core standards for students with learning disabilities: Strategies for writing standards-based IEP goals. *Preventing School Failure, 59*(4), 237-243. https://doi.org/10.1080/1045988X.2014.924088

Center for Applied Special Technologies. (2018). *Universal Design for Learning guidelines version 2.2.* http://udlguidelines. cast.org

Ciullo, S., & Dimino, J. A. (2017). The strategic use of scaffolded instruction in social studies interventions for students with learning disabilities. *Learning Disabilities Research & Practice, 32*(3), 155-165. https://doi.org/10.1111/ldrp.12138

Common Core State Standards Initiative. (2019). *Standards in your state.* http://www.corestandards.org/ standards-in-your-state/

Cuticelli, M., Collier-Meek, M., & Coyne, M. (2016). Increasing the quality of Tier 1 reading instruction: Using performance feedback to increase opportunities to respond during implementation of a core reading program. *Psychology in the Schools, 53*(1), 89-105. https://doi.org/10.1002/pits.21884

Division for Early Childhood. (2014). *DEC recommended practices in early intervention/early childhood special education.* http://www.dec-sped.org/recommendedpractices

Duhon, G. J., House, S., Hastings, K., Poncy, B., & Solomon, B. (2015). Adding immediate feedback to explicit timing: An option for enhancing treatment intensity to improve mathematics fluency. *Journal of Behavioral Education, 24*(1), 74-87. https://doi/10.1007/s10864-014-9203-y

Gartin, B. C., Murdick, N. L., Perner, D. E., & Imbeau, M. B. (2016). *Differentiating instruction in the inclusive classroom: Strategies for success.* Council for Exceptional Children.

Gauvreau, A. N., Lohmann, M. J., & Hovey, K. A. (2019). Using a Universal Design for Learning framework to provide multiple means of representation in the early childhood classroom. *Journal of Special Education Apprenticeship, 8*(1), 1-13.

Glass, D., Meyer, A., & Rose, D. H. (2013). Universal design for learning and the arts. *Harvard Educational Review, 83*(1), 98-119, 266, 270, 272.

Hattie, J., & Timperley, H. (2007). The power of feedback. *Review of Educational Research, 77*, 81-112.

Hedin, L., & DeSpain, S. (2018). SMART or not?: Writing specific, measurable IEP goals. *Teaching Exceptional Children, 51*(2), 100-110.

Hinton, V. M., Flores, M. M., Schweck, K., & Burton, M. E. (2016). The effects of a supplemental explicit counting intervention for preschool children. *Preventing School Failure, 60*(3), 183-193. https://doi.org/10.1080/104598 8X.2015.1065400

Hitchcock, C., Meyer, A., Rose, D., & Jackson, R. (2002). Providing new access to the general curriculum. *Teaching Exceptional Children, 35*(2), 8-17.

Hughes, C. A., Morris, J. R., Therrien, W. J., & Benson, S. K. (2017). Explicit instruction: Historical and contemporary contexts. *Learning Disabilities Research & Practice, 32*(3), 140-148. https://doi.org/10.1111/ldrp.12142

Individuals with Disabilities Education Act. 20 U.S.C. § 1400 (2004).

Jozwik, S. L., Cahill, A., & Sanchez, G. (2018). Collaboratively crafting individualized education program goals for culturally and linguistically diverse students. *Preventing School Failure, 62*(2), 140-148.

Jung, L. A. (2007). Writing SMART objectives and strategies that fit the routine. *Teaching Exceptional Children, 39*(4), 54-58. https://doi.org/10.1177%2F004005990703900406

Klute, M., Apthorp, H., Harlacher, J., & Reale, M. (2017). *Formative assessment and elementary school student academic achievement: A review of the evidence (REL 2017-259)*. Washington, DC: U.S. Department of Education, Institute of Education Sciences, National Center for Education Evaluation and Regional Assistance, Regional Educational Laboratory Central. http://ies.ed.gov/ncee/edlabs

Lingo, A. S., Jolivette, K., & Barton-Arwood, S. M. (2009). Visual and oral feedback to promote appropriate social behavior for a student with emotional and behavioral disorders. *Preventing School Failure, 54*(1), 24-29. https://doi.org/10.3200/PSFL.54.1.24-29

Lohmann, M. J., Hovey, K. A., & Gauvreau, A. N. (2018). Using a Universal Design for Learning framework to enhance engagement in the early childhood classroom. *Journal of Special Education Apprenticeship, 7*(2), 1-12.

Meyer, A., & Rose, D. H. (2005). The future is in the margins: The role of technology and disability in educational reform. In D. H. Rose, A. Meyer & C. Hitchcock (Eds.), *The universally designed classroom: Accessible curriculum and digital technologies* (pp. 13-35). Harvard Education Press.

More, C. M., & Hart Barnett, J. E. (2014). Developing individualized IEP goals in the age of technology: Quality challenges and solutions. *Preventing School Failure, 58*(2), 103-109.

Morgan, J., Brown, N., Hsiao, Y., Howerter, C., Juniel, P., Sedano, L., & Castillo, W. (2014). Unwrapping academic standards to increase the achievement of students with disabilities. *Intervention in School and Clinic, 49*, 131-141.

Morgan, H., & York, K. C. (2009). Examining multiple perspectives with creative think-alouds. *Reading Teacher, 63*, 307- 311.

National Council on Disability. (2018). *IDEA series: Every Student Succeeds Act and students with disabilities.* https://ncd.gov/sites/default/files/NCD_ESSA-SWD_Accessible.pdf

National Foundation for Educational Research. (2019). *An introduction to formative and summative assessment.* https://www.nfer.ac.uk/for-schools/free-resources-advice/assessment-hub/introduction-to-assessment/an-introduction-to-formative-and-summative-assessment/

Raible, J., Bennett, L., & Bastedo, K. (2016). Writing measurable learning objectives to aid successful online course development. *International Journal for the Scholarship of Technology Enhanced Learning, 1*(1), 112-122.

Rao, K., & Meo, G. (2016). Using Universal Design for Learning to design standards-based lessons. *SAGE Open, 6*(4). https://doi.org/10.1177%2F2158244016680688

Root, J. R. (2019). Effects of explicit instruction on acquisition and generalization of mathematical concepts for a student with autism spectrum disorder. *Research in Autism Spectrum Disorders, 57*, 1-6. https://doi.org/10.1016/j.rasd.2018.09.005

Rose, D. H., Gravel, J. W., & Domings, Y. M. (2010). *UDL Unplugged: The role of technology in UDL.* https://www.cast.org/products-services/resources/2012/udl-unplugged-role-technology

Rose, D. H., & Strangman, N. (2007). Universal design for learning: Meeting the challenge of individual learning differences through a neurocognitive perspective. *Universal Access in the Information Society, 5*, 381-391.

Therrien, W. J., Benson, S. K., Hughes, C. A., & Morris, J. R. (2017). Explicit instruction and next generation Science standards aligned classrooms: A fit or a split. *Learning Disabilities Research & Practice, 32*(3), 149-154. https://doi.org/10.1111/ldrp.12137

Thomas, A. F., & Sondergeld, T. (2015). Investigating the impact of feedback instruction: Partnering preservice teachers with middle school students to provide digital, scaffolded feedback. *Journal of the Scholarship of Teaching and Learning, 15*(4), 83-109.

Tomlinson, C. A. (2000). *Differentiation of instruction in the elementary grades.* ERIC Clearinghouse on Elementary and Early Childhood Education Champaign IL. (ERIC Document Reproduction Service No. ED443572).

Tomlinson, C. A. (2017). *How to differentiate instruction in academically diverse classrooms* (3rd ed.). ASCD.

Valiandes, S. (2015). Evaluating the impact of differentiated instruction on literacy and reading in mixed ability classrooms: Quality and equity dimensions of education effectiveness. *Studies in Educational Evaluation, 45*, 17-26. https://doi.org/10.1016/j.stueduc.2015.02.005

van den Bergh, L., Ros, A., & Beijaard, D. (2013). Teacher feedback during active learning: Current practices in primary schools. *British Journal of Educational Psychology, 83*(2), 341-362. https://doi.org/10.1111/j.2044-8279.2012.02073.x

Wright, P., & Wright, P. (2019). *Wrightslaw game plan: SMART IEPs.* https://www.wrightslaw.com/info/iep.goals.plan.htm

Language Development (Prekindergarten to Second Grade)

Sherri K. Prosser, PhD; Kate E. Zimmer, PhD;
Zachary T. Barnes, PhD; and Karin M. Fisher, PhD, CDE

INTRODUCTION

This chapter focuses on children's literacy and language behaviors in prekindergarten to second grade that precede and later evolve into conventional literacy skills. Typical and atypical language development, emergent literacy, how to promote early language development for students with special needs, and considerations for effective classroom practice are covered. We incorporate a case study of a preschool teacher who struggles to find ways to provide a supportive and inclusive environment for a 4-year-old student who is developmentally delayed. The chapter explains and shows connections among (a) evidence-based practices, (b) the Council for Exceptional Children's high-leverage practices, and (c) the Division for Early Childhood Recommended Practices that contribute to language acquisition and skills. Additionally, readers will learn about the role of phonological awareness, pragmatics, semantics, and syntax in promoting language development. We contend that the intentional promotion of early language through carefully designed and implemented lessons based on research is not only possible but also integral in supporting young students with disabilities across all settings. Suggestions for classroom practice include adult–child interactions, play-based activities, peer interventions, and assistive technology devices.

Fisher, K. M., & Zimmer, K. E. (Eds.).
Early Childhood Special Education Programs and Practices (pp. 117-138).
© 2023 SLACK Incorporated.

CHAPTER OBJECTIVES

→ Describe the importance of effective language and emergent literacy instruction.

→ Identify and critically reflect on current trends and issues, terminology, definitions, curriculum, and methods regarding evidence-based language development strategies and developmentally appropriate activities.

→ Analyze the relationship between language development and emergent literacy skills (e.g., print concepts, phonological awareness, and phonemic awareness).

→ Explain the typical and atypical communication patterns and the impact of language development on the academic and social skills of individuals with disabilities.

→ Select evidence-based teaching strategies and interventions that align with the Division for Early Childhood Recommended Practices and the Council for Exceptional Children's high-leverage practices.

KEY TERMS

- **Early Language:** The developing skills young children use to communicate, such as gestures, facial expressions, words, and understanding others.
- **Evidence-Based Practices:** Instructional strategies backed by research that are often content specific but appropriate for use across multiple grade levels.
- **Expressive Language:** How we communicate our wants and needs, including spoken words, gestures, facial expressions, semantics, and syntax.
- **High-Leverage Practices (HLPs):** Critical, proven instructional practices that impact student behavior and achievement that teachers can implement across all content areas, grade levels, and students with varying needs.
- **Phonological Awareness:** The ability to identify, think about, and manipulate sounds in spoken language, such as distinguishing rhyming words or the number of syllables in a word.
- **Pragmatics:** Social communication and how students use language in the context of the speakers (e.g., speaking to adults vs. a baby), intentions (e.g., commands and requests), and rules of discourse (e.g., taking turns in a conversation and using facial expressions).
- **Semantics:** How one understands the meaning and relationships of words and combinations of words. Examples of semantic relationships include categories (e.g., apples and crackers are both types of food), antonyms, and synonyms.
- **Syntax:** The grammatical rules that decide how words are combined and ordered into phrases and sentences. Syntax deficits may manifest in difficulties with word order, verb tense, possessives, and plurals.

CASE STUDY

Mrs. Zing is the lead teacher in an inclusive 4-year-old preschool classroom. Her classroom is colorful and inviting. Beyond the child-sized chairs, furniture, and rug for circle time, her classroom is filled with opportunities that encourage interactive learning activities. She decorated her classroom to reflect this month's theme—under the sea. The fun and magical classroom has blue cellophane hanging from the ceiling to give the illusion of waves, green crepe paper streamers to mimic seaweed, and white balloons attached along strings of fishing line to create bubbles. There is a child-sized pool in the dramatic play center where the children can fish for letters. There are children's storybooks and picture books about fish and other sea creatures in the reading corner. She filled the sensory bin with gel water beads (i.e., vase fillers), plastic ocean animals, small plastic shovels with ridged handles, small beach buckets, and a variety of seashells.

Mrs. Zing smiles as she looks around her classroom and sees how engaged her students are; they are enjoying this month's theme! However, one little boy, Wesley, sits all alone at the reading corner. Wesley currently has a diagnosis of developmentally delayed. He is not presently reaching developmental milestones in the areas of language and communication. Although Mrs. Zing is familiar with characteristics of children with developmental delays and understands that Wesley has more difficulty communicating and interacting socially with his peers, she cannot help but wonder how she can encourage him to interact with his peers and engage more in the daily activities. She has been seeking information from colleagues and websites about creating a more inclusive environment for Wesley.

"Language is power, life, and the instrument of culture. The instrument of domination and liberation."
—*Angela Carter*

Division for Early Childhood Recommended Practices

Of the eight Division for Early Childhood (DEC, 2014) Recommended Practices, the instruction and interaction topics are most relevant to early language development, as noted in Table 6-1. *Instructional practices* are "intentional and systematic strategies to inform what to teach, when to teach, how to evaluate the effects of teaching, and how to support and evaluate the quality of instructional practices implemented by others" (p. 12).

Following the recommended instruction practices to support language development and communication skills, Wesley's teacher could model developmentally appropriate expressive language to comment on nearby children's actions during cleanup time. For example, when Mrs. Zing sees two children cleaning up their station, she could say (in a voice loud enough for others to hear while emphasizing concepts on which the class is focusing) "Ethan is putting the blue crayon inside of the bin labeled 'crayons.'" When Wesley is playing with a train going off the tracks, she can say "Choo choo—oh, no! Crash!" to model words he might want to use.

Interactions or interactional practices that are sensitive and responsive provide a foundation for all learning and support children's language development, cognitive development, and emotional competence (DEC, 2014). Examples of interactional practices include responding to a child's expressions, encouraging a child to initiate or sustain interactions, joining in on the child's actions, and promoting the child's problem-solving behaviors (DEC, 2014).

Following the recommended interaction practices to support language development, Wesley's teacher could incorporate his preferences in collaborative activities to increase his engagement and promote interaction with peers (DEC, 2014). For example, knowing that Wesley likes trains, Mrs. Zing could include a conductor's hat, tickets, travel brochures, and suitcases in the dramatic play area to support the need for both train conductor and passenger roles.

High-Leverage Practices

The instruction strand of high-leverage practices (HLPs) focuses on well-designed and carefully implemented instruction that actively and meaningfully engages all learners (McLeskey et al., 2017).

TABLE 6-1. ALIGNMENT BETWEEN PRACTICES

INSTRUCTIONAL PRACTICE	ALIGNED DEC RECOMMENDED PRACTICES	ALIGNED HLPs
Modeling	INS8: Practitioners use peer-mediated intervention to teach skills and to promote child engagement and learning. INT1: Practitioners promote the child's social-emotional development by observing, interpreting, and responding contingently to the range of the child's emotional expressions. INT2: Practitioners promote the child's social development by encouraging the child to initiate or sustain positive interactions with other children and adults during routines and activities through modeling, teaching, feedback, or other types of guided support. INT5: Practitioners promote the child's problem-solving behavior by observing, interpreting, and scaffolding in response to the child's growing level of autonomy and self-regulation.	HLP 14: Teach cognitive and metacognitive strategies to support learning and independence. HLP 15: Provide scaffolded supports. HLP 16: Use explicit instruction. HLP 18: Use strategies to promote active student engagement.
Naturalistic interventions	E1: Practitioners provide services and supports in natural and inclusive environments during daily routines and activities to promote the child's access to and participation in learning experiences. INS2: Practitioners, with the family, identify skills to target for instruction that help a child become adaptive, competent, socially connected, and engaged and that promote learning in natural and inclusive environments. INS6: Practitioners use systematic instructional strategies with fidelity to teach skills and to promote child engagement and learning. INS13: Practitioners use coaching or consultation strategies with primary caregivers or other adults to facilitate positive adult–child interactions and instruction intentionally designed to promote child learning and development.	HLP 21: Teach students to maintain and generalize new learning across time and settings.

(continued)

TABLE 6-1 (CONTINUED). ALIGNMENT BETWEEN PRACTICES

INSTRUCTIONAL PRACTICE	ALIGNED DEC RECOMMENDED PRACTICES	ALIGNED HLPs
Prompting	INS4: Practitioners plan for and provide the level of support, accommodations, and adaptations needed for the child to access, participate, and learn within and across activities and routines. INS6: Practitioners use systematic instructional strategies with fidelity to teach skills and to promote child engagement and learning. INS10: Practitioners implement the frequency, intensity, and duration of instruction needed to address the child's phase and pace of learning or the level of support needed by the family to achieve the child's outcomes or goals.	HLP 9: Teach social behaviors. HLP 13: Adapt curriculum tasks and materials for specific learning goals.
Assistive technology/ augmentative and alternative communication	E4: Practitioners work with families and other adults to identify each child's needs for assistive technology to promote access to and participation in learning experiences. E5: Practitioners work with families and other adults to acquire or create appropriate assistive technology to promote each child's access to and participation in learning experiences. INS2: Practitioners, with the family, identify skills to target for instruction that help a child become adaptive, competent, socially connected, and engaged and that promote learning in natural and inclusive environments.	HLP 19: Use assistive and instructional technologies.

DEC = Division for Early Childhood; HLPs = high-leverage practices.

Data sources: Division for Early Childhood. (2014). DEC recommended practices in early intervention/early childhood special education. 2014. http://www.dec-sped.org/recommendedpractices and McLeskey, J., et al. (2017). *High-leverage practices in special education*. Council for Exceptional Children & CEEDAR Center.

To support active engagement, Wesley's teacher uses partner-based "barrier games" that teach following directions, listening skills, prepositions, expressive speech, vocabulary, and turn taking; she has many themes to tailor to students' interests. Mrs. Zing uses wait time paired with classroom hand signals for understanding (i.e., thumbs up, thumbs down, and thumbs to the side) to increase participation. Mrs. Zing collaborates with the school-based speech-language pathologist to ensure she uses appropriate interventions, such as thoughtfully choosing students with strong language skills to act as peer models for Wesley during small-group or partner activities. After a classroom observation, the speech-language pathologist suggested that Mrs. Zing's students practice language skills beyond requests and responding "yes/no" by offering multiple choices for an activity.

WHAT IS EARLY LANGUAGE?

Individuals are exposed to language every day in many different ways. For most children, language development follows a natural pattern in which their communication skills expand and become more complex over time. The development of oral language, or communicating using the spoken word, begins at infancy and relies heavily on the experiences and interactions with others. These experiences and interactions help infants and young children learn about the world around them.

Oral language is the foundation for literacy development (Eliason & Jenkins, 2012). Hart and Risley (1995) found that by age 3 there is a 30 million word gap between children from high socioeconomic status (SES) families and children from low SES families. Furthermore, the quantity and richness of language that families and teachers expose young children to correlates with their reading and math achievement by the age of 10. Because of the significant impact that early language has on a child's later academic life, it is essential for early childhood special education (ECSE) teachers to realize the importance of the quality and quantity of spoken words to provide explicit and deliberate practice within their classrooms.

More recent research conducted by Romeo et al. (2018) using functional magnetic resonance imaging showed that regardless of the child's IQ, SES, or number of words spoken to the child by an adult, children who had more conversational turns with adults were significantly more likely to have greater verbal ability. These conversational turns had already been shown to be relevant to language skill development for 2-month-olds to 4-year-olds (Zimmerman et al., 2009), but Romeo et al. (2018) extended these findings to include children up to age 6. This study showed that environmental mechanisms and neural functioning were both underlying factors in the differences between children from lower SES settings and higher SES settings, even though children from higher SES settings had higher language abilities. Romeo et al. urged that conversational turns, along with their inherent opportunities for practice and feedback, be emphasized as a means to develop verbal language. It is not enough to talk *to* children; adults must engage in interactive conversations *with* children (2018).

TYPICAL/ATYPICAL LANGUAGE DEVELOPMENT

The first 3 years of life are when the most intensive period of speech and language development occurs. Therefore, it is critical for young children to be exposed to rich language because their brains are developing and maturing at a rapid rate. Table 6-2 provides a brief overview of normal language development from ages 4 through 8. Although there is a natural progression for the mastery of these skills, the reader should note that there is variability within this timeline.

STAGES OF LANGUAGE ACQUISITION/ ORAL LANGUAGE DEVELOPMENT

Joint attention is when an individual follows others' gaze using eye contact, gesturing to show an object, or getting the attention of people around them (Figure 6-1; Bellon et al., 2000). In its simplest form, joint attention is how humans acquire language because it is a form of preverbal social communication. Young children will often share attention with another adult (usually a caregiver) about a particular object. During this mutual interaction, the adult frequently will label the item, thus exposing the child to language in the context of this interaction (Tomasello & Todd, 1983).

The impact that the adult/child interaction has throughout the day is invaluable. The seminal study by Tomasello and Todd (1983) examined the effects of joint attention and language development. They reported that the amount of time young children interacted with their mothers positively

TABLE 6-2. LANGUAGE MILESTONES FOR AGES 4 THROUGH 8

AGE	LANGUAGE/COMMUNICATION MILESTONES
4	Knows basic rules of grammar Uses correct forms of verbs Sings a song from memory Tells stories Can say first and last name Knows sounds and makes up words Identifies words beginning with same sound Identifies words that rhyme
5	Speaks clearly Tells a simple story using full sentences Uses future tense Says name and address Identifies some or all sounds of letters Knows single sounds and combines into words Understands and combines words to form active sentences
6	Reads simple stories Understands single words have different meanings Begins to understand metaphors and nonliteral language Starts using compound words Understands rules of plurality Speech should be intelligible and socially useful
7	Tells an ordered, connected story Describes relationships between objects and occurrences Knows opposite analogies Reads simple texts Writes the alphabet and many common words
8	Understands what they are reading Writes a simple story Understands jokes and riddles that play on sounds Uses comparison words (e.g., like or as) Uses complex and compound sentences Tells and elaborates on events that occurred in the past Has a full mastery of speech sounds Reads age-appropriate texts Varies rate, speed, and volume of voice Follows fairly complex instructions

Figure 6-1. A child engaged in play-based activity. This image illustrates a child playing with a wooden train track, which would be an opportune time for their teacher to model developmentally appropriate expressive language.

correlated with the child's overall vocabulary. Positive social interactions, such as turn taking, reading a storybook, or playing together with blocks, can increase children's cognitive abilities and communication skills. A lack of joint attention is one of the earliest predictors of autism.

EXPRESSIVE AND RECEPTIVE LANGUAGE

From a young age, children share their thoughts and feelings with others through their words and actions (e.g., crying, smiling, and laughing). In addition to expressing how they feel, young children begin to understand and interrupt others' thoughts and feelings. *Receptive language* is the ability to comprehend the spoken word that one hears or reads (i.e., the input of language). *Expressive language* is the ability to express one's wants and needs through nonverbal (e.g., signs, gestures, facial expressions, and eye contact) or verbal (e.g., speaking, crying, and yelling) communication (i.e., the output of languages). An individual who has difficulty understanding language may have trouble following directions, understanding gestures, identifying objects, or following a story.

Semantics, Pragmatics, and Syntax

Semantics is understanding that words have meaning and the relationship between those words. In young children, semantic development is a gradual process, starting when a child begins to imitate sounds and say their first word. *Pragmatics* refers to how an individual uses language for social communication. For instance, the way one speaks to an adult vs. a baby typically looks and sounds different. How we use language depends on context, intentions (e.g., commands and requests), and discourse rules (e.g., turn taking and facial expressions). In communicative ability, children with autism often need to be explicitly taught the pragmatics of having a conversation, particularly in conversational turn taking and staying on topic, because these skills do not naturally develop like they do for typically developing children. Syntax is based on the grammatical rules that guide how words are joined together in phrases and sentences. Young children may have difficulties with word order, verb tense, possessives, and plurals (e.g., "Her is my friend").

SPEECH AND LANGUAGE DELAYS/DISORDERS

Some children may struggle to understand language (receptive language) or have difficulty with spoken language (expressive language). These delays could impact whether or not a child meets important language milestones. When children have delays in these areas, it may be a sign of a language or speech delay or disorder. Language and speech disorders can exist together or by themselves.

- A *speech disorder* is a condition in which an individual has difficulty forming sounds and/or specific words correctly.
- A *language delay* is identified when an individual's ability to understand or speak develops slower than what is considered the standard range of time.
- *Language disorders* are often developmental, but an illness or brain injury can also cause language disorders.

The reader may find additional information on specific speech and language disorders at the American Speech-Language-Hearing Association (https://www.asha.org/public/speech/disorders/ChildSandL/). As classrooms become more diverse, teachers need to understand the difference between language disorders and linguistic diversity.

LINGUISTIC DIVERSITY

Linguistic diversity can refer to students who are not fluent in English or who do not speak English at home, constituting 20% of K-12 students in the United States (IRIS Center, 2012). Young students who have been identified as *English-language learners*, which is the federal designation, are sometimes referred to as *dual-language learners* or *emergent bilinguals* because they are mastering their native language while acquiring a second language. The term *bilingual* (or *multilingual*) is preferred to keep the focus on the children's strengths instead of on their acquisition of English.

Students generally learn social, or conversational, language in 1 to 2 years, but it takes 5 to 7 years to develop proficiency in academic, or content-specific, language (IRIS Center, 2012); having a disability would inherently lengthen that time frame. The IRIS Center (2012) suggested providing slower and more precise enunciation, multimodal instruction, visual cues or other contextual supports, explicit vocabulary instruction, and corrective feedback to address students' linguistic diversity. Teachers of culturally and linguistically diverse students should also reflect on whether what they think is "developmentally appropriate" reflects the students' families or is based on White, middle-class norms (Thorius et al., 2019).

WHAT IS EMERGENT LITERACY?

Like oral language, the reading process develops over time for beginners (Chall, 1983; Ehri, 1995). Although language development is natural, the act of learning to read is not; teachers must explicitly teach the reading process to beginning readers. There is a link between the development of oral language and the development of one's reading ability. In kindergarten and first grade, one quarter of all students who received speech-language services also received reading services (Gosse et al., 2012). Additionally, the National Early Literacy Panel (NELP, 2008) found a moderately predictive relationship between kindergarten oral language and later decoding ability. *Decoding* refers to applying knowledge of sounds that correspond to letters to pronounce a written word correctly. Because reading develops over time and on a continuum, the term *emergent literacy* focuses on the developmental gains a student makes in early childhood (Whitehurst & Lonigan, 1998). The idea of emergent literacy also comes with an understanding that reading, language, and writing are developing together. The skills used by an emergent reader progress and lead to formal reading and writing.

The earliest stage of the reading process is when teachers introduce the concept of reading. Children initially have to understand the idea and functions of print. The NELP (2008) report defined concepts of print as the basic knowledge of the conventions of print. This means that the reader understands that we read from left to right on a page and that there is a difference between the front and the back of the book. Beginning readers also need to understand the meaning of a book cover, that an author is a person who wrote the text, and that the markings on the page are called *words*. Children can learn print concepts before they even begin to learn the more traditional basic skills of reading. Additionally, understanding these print concepts has a predictive relationship to later reading ability, such as decoding, reading comprehension, and spelling.

As emergent readers engage with day-to-day life interactions and experiences, they are surrounded with environmental print (i.e., the words, symbols, letters, and numbers that we experience in our nonschool daily activities). Preschool children will begin to recognize environmental print, including large billboards, street signs, toy packages, food labels, and restaurant names. Being able to identify environmental print is an essential process in emergent literacy (Adams, 1990). These preschoolers understand that the symbols have meaning behind them. Although many of these emergent readers can correctly "read" the STOP in the stop sign, when you take away the colors and flashiness from environment print, many students cannot read the same word written in a book. Readers at this stage have come to memorize the words with the help of a more proficient reader.

Next, readers begin a formal literacy instruction phase. Readers start to gain *alphabet knowledge*, which is knowing the names and sounds of printed letters. Alphabet knowledge is one of the most critical early literacy skills. The alphabet knowledge skills of prekindergarteners and kindergarteners are highly predictive of later reading ability. In a meta-analysis conducted as part of the NELP (2008), alphabet knowledge had a strong predictive relationship to later decoding and spelling and a moderate relationship to reading comprehension. As readers are developing an understanding of the purpose of books and letter sounds, they are also learning about how sounds play a role in spoken language. This happens through phonological awareness. *Phonological awareness* is when students know they can break up spoken words into parts. This means that students can identify and manipulate spoken sounds (Anthony & Francis, 2005). Phonological awareness is an overarching term that has multiple, separate components. Some of these components include rhyming, alliteration, segmenting, blending, and phonemic awareness. Readers must be able to identify and manipulate sounds independent of the meaning of the word. This means that students can identify and manipulate the spoken words whether they understand what the words mean or not.

Phonemic awareness, a component of phonological awareness, can specifically identify and manipulate phonemes in spoken language (National Institute of Child Health & Human Development, 2000). Instruction in phonemic awareness is key for all students to become proficient readers. Like its definition, instruction in phonemic awareness includes teaching new readers to identify and manipulate phonemes in spoken language (Ehri, 2004). For example, beginning readers need to be able to take the spoken word "bats" and decompose it into /b/ /æ/ /t/ /s/. If you tell a student to replace the b with an h, the student would be using phonemic awareness to reply with the word "hats." Again, these early reading skills are essential for later achievement; phonemic awareness of elementary students is predictive of future word reading ability (Hulme et al., 2012). Chapter 7 provides more in-depth information about emergent readers.

While emergent readers are developing the necessary skills for later reading ability, they are also exploring words and language through writing. *Emergent writing*, also known as *early writing*, is the beginning knowledge that symbols and letters are used to communicate meaning and understanding. As with other emergent skills, early writing is also vital for future reading achievement. A systematic review of emergent writing instruction found that preschool writing instruction improved later reading outcomes, suggesting the importance of using environmental print in preschool play-based activities (Hall et al., 2015). Embedding explicit, authentic writing instruction is also vital for the development of early literacy skills, which includes having students address and send letters and adding writing instruments and paper to create literacy-enhanced play areas (Hall et al., 2015). Chapter 8 provides more in-depth information on early writing instruction.

Teachers cannot consider emergent literacy in isolation. Language, reading, and writing development are interconnected and occur simultaneously. Well-rounded instruction for emergent literacy includes many different parts but taken together could impact students' ability to read for years to come. Even before children begin to read, we must provide a context for them to understand and appreciate language, understand the mechanisms of how sounds are combined, and practice authentic writing instruction. The beauty of education is the ability to instruct in all these areas through various and creative ways. Whitehurst and Lonigan (1998) reported that children's emergent literacy knowledge and skills from their preschool experiences and home life are strongly correlated with their later academic performance.

PROMOTING EARLY LANGUAGE IN EARLY CHILDHOOD SPECIAL EDUCATION

The development of language skills in early childhood sets the groundwork for later skill development in oral language and emergent literacy. Through thoughtful, engaging, and meaningful interactions, an educator can increase a child's early language (Lanter & Watson, 2008; Zimmer, 2017). This can be done through the natural environment and/or manipulating the environmental arrangement throughout the classroom.

Educators must be purposeful in how they set up the classroom environment to support rich language acquisition. Because children learn from their environment, educators can easily incorporate numerous natural learning opportunities through center time; thus, educational centers are encouraged in an early childhood classroom. Although structured, centers create a more naturalistic environment, allowing students with or without disabilities to learn and acquire language in a more relaxed setting. The following evidenced-based strategies can easily be implemented throughout the day through play-based activities and lay the groundwork for promoting early language.

- *Visual supports* are items that teachers use to enhance the communication process when a student has difficulty with receptive or expressive language. The items can be pictures, clip art, drawings, or written words and can be used to show a visual schedule of the school day, steps in a process, or to signify to "wait" or "stop."
- *Incidental teaching* is a strategy that uses principles of applied behavior analysis that follow the child's interest or lead to boost natural engagement. A desired item may be placed out of the child's reach to elicit a response, or the teacher could read the pages of a favorite book and ask the child to name the pictures on each page.
- *Modeling* is when teachers demonstrate language, tasks, or even facial expressions they expect the students to do independently. A teacher could say the word "open" while opening a cabinet or model acting surprised while reading certain parts of a book. When a student is showing signs of distress, a teacher could model the phrase "help."
- *Expanding* refers to increasing a student's language to improve their ability to express their wants and needs, whether vocally or through gestures, signing, visual supports, or a communication device.
- The *mand model approach* refers to teachers using an open-ended question to request (i.e., mand) an expressive language (e.g., verbal or pointing to a picture card) response from a child, such as "Which toy do you want?" If the child responds correctly, they will receive praise and/ or the item requested. If the child does not respond correctly, the teacher will model the correct response.

- *Time delay* involves gradually fading verbal prompts to improve a child's expressive language. A teacher would start by holding out a toy, immediately prompting "truck," and waiting for the student to echo "truck." As the student progresses, the teacher would delay the verbal prompt by 2 seconds and then 4 seconds until the student uses the word unprompted.

Children do not develop language on their own. They build vocabulary with and around others, including parents, guardians, other adults, and peers. Practicing language skills is critical for communication among children and developing foundational knowledge for later literacy learning. For example, the growth of language for preschool children is related to their classmates' language skills (Justice et al., 2011; Mashburn et al., 2009). The positive effect of peers is even more prominent for those with language disabilities. Therefore, it could be beneficial to place students with language disabilities in classrooms with typical peers because typical peers are not negatively influenced by students who have language disabilities (Justice et al., 2011).

ASSISTIVE TECHNOLOGY/AUGMENTATIVE AND ALTERNATIVE COMMUNICATION

Augmentative and alternative communication (AAC) is a type of assistive technology in which educators use an item or equipment to improve the functionality of someone with a disability (Beard et al., 2011). Assistive technology can include electronic devices that change speech to text, pencil grips, specialty keyboards, and AAC devices. For example, a pencil grip can assist a student in gripping the pencil to write. AAC falls under assistive technology, but it is its own specialty related to communication. Researchers address AAC in both the HLPs and DEC Recommended Practices as follows: DEC Recommended Practice E4 (practitioners work with families and other adults to identify each child's needs for assistive technology to promote access to and participate in learning experiences) and HLP 19 (use assistive and instructional technologies).

Unfortunately, not all children will develop foundational language skills at the expected time. These children could have disabilities, such as autism spectrum disorder, Down syndrome, cerebral palsy, or traumatic brain injury (Drager et al., 2010). Depending on the child's language needs, they may require AAC, which is one way someone can communicate without actually talking. There are many types of AAC, and they are wholly dependent on the needs of the child. Some require gesturing, whereas others use an electronic device that speaks on behalf of the child. Inexpensive AAC examples are homemade binders of pictures or symbols or picture exchange communication systems. More costly examples include speech applications on a portable device (e.g., ProLoQuo2Go [AssistiveWare] on an iPad [Apple]) and speech-generating devices (e.g., Dynavox I-Series [Tobii Dynavox]).

For children who are struggling with language acquisition, AAC is itself an intervention. There are many benefits when educators give children the chance to use AAC. In a review on AAC system use, Drager and colleagues (2010) found benefits of AAC interventions in the development of both expressive and receptive language. For example, AAC can positively influence the development of pragmatics and semantics. Additionally, AAC use and the comprehension ability of the communicating individual interact, each demonstrating an impact on the other (e.g., Collins et al., 2019). Most importantly, AAC allows students to express their thoughts, feelings, and needs to those around them.

CONSIDERATIONS FOR PRACTICE

Evidence-based practice is empirical, published research that explains the relationship between practices and outcomes for professionals, families, and, most importantly, children (Raver, 2009). Early childhood special education is based on the following language development evidence-based practices (Odom & Wolery, 2003). These evidence-based practices correlate with the DEC Recommended Practices for families, environment, and instruction. Specifically, they address INS8 (practitioners use peer-mediated intervention to teach skills and promote child engagement and learning).

- Families are the primary nurturing environment (Burris et al., 2019).
- It is essential to strengthening relationships (Lieber et al., 2002). Practitioners should build trusting relationships with families who are sensitive to cultural and socioeconomic differences.
- Children learn through their environment (Dunst et al., 2001). Practitioners create settings that allow for movement to maintain or improve development across domains.
- Teachers promote learning through experiences. They embed systematic instruction to provide contextually relevant learning opportunities.
- Practitioners set goals (Wolery et al., 2002). They implement the duration, frequency, and intensity of instruction needed to achieve those goals as noted in HLP 11 (identify and prioritize long- and short-term learning goals).

Teachers must make sure children are engaged in the activities to implement these evidence-based practices. The following section introduces engagement in the ECSE classroom.

MEASURING STUDENT ENGAGEMENT

Engagement is the amount of time children appropriately spend interacting with their environment and is addressed in HLP 18 (use strategies to promote active student engagement). Quality ECSE programs have a high amount of engagement (Ridley et al., 2000). Indeed, Rock (2004) found that students who are engaged 75% of the time are higher achieving than students who only engage 50% of the time. Unfortunately, students with disabilities are less likely to be engaged than their typical peers (Raver, 2009).

Engagement can be measured by (a) the time the child is appropriately involved with a peer, adults, and learning materials; (b) how long a child participates in a task; (c) the child's decision-making skills while involved in a lesson; and (d) the child's focused attention on the task (Blank & Hertzog, 2003). Teacher behaviors and the characteristics of the activity significantly influence engagement (McCormick et al., 1998). Strategies teachers use to promote engagement include facilitation of learning, direct assistance, positive affect, redirection, proximity control, and lesson preparation (Raver, 2009).

Teachers can improve engagement by structuring their instruction. Even though young children acquire new skills through repetition, relying solely on "drill and practice" seatwork can become tedious. Practitioners need to vary instruction to maintain engagement. Another evidence-based strategy to improve engagement is to use schedules. A schedule could be a picture sequence of what will occur in order for a lesson. Schedules help young children know what is coming next. For example, Mrs. Zing created a schedule for the beginning of the school day. She included pictures of (a) children greeting each other; (b) singing the name song; (c) completing a weather calendar; and (d) discussing what is in the "mystery box," which contains an item related to the week's theme. As the class completes each task, she removes the picture from the schedule and places it in a "completed" folder.

Another evidence-based strategy to increase engagement is the use of scaffolding (e.g., HLP 15 [provide scaffolded supports] and INT5 [practitioners promote the child's problem-solving behavior by observing, interpreting, and scaffolding in response to the child's growing level of autonomy and self-regulation] both address scaffolding). Torgesen (2002) defined scaffolding as adjusting the task, materials, group size, pace, presentation, and teacher support to promote learning. Practitioners should provide direct instruction in steps and allow young children to master each step before moving on to the next step.

For example, Mrs. Zing can increase engagement during play by using the following scaffolded sequence:

1. Asking a child "I wonder what you are going to do with that horse?" This is an example of an indirect verbal command. Indirect verbal commands do not require the child to comply.
2. Mrs. Zing models an action for the young child.
3. Next, Mrs. Zing gives a direct verbal command like "See my horse? Put your horse into the barn like mine."

ECSE teachers can also differentiate to increase the engagement of children with disabilities. Differentiation strategies include adapting materials, providing additional opportunities to respond, peer assistance, and alternative activities.

Focusing on Key Skills in Language Development

Essential skills children need for language development are listening, speaking, reading, and writing. Information on reading is provided in Chapter 7 and writing in Chapter 8. As a result, we focus on listening and speaking in this chapter.

Listening

Listening provides access to learning, especially in early childhood. Ineffective listening makes learning difficult, whereas effective listening requires active cognitive processing, which can be difficult for students with disabilities. Students with speech-language impairments (SLIs) often have difficulty following multistep directions, understanding others' explanations, and gaining information presented by the auditory route, also known as *auditory processing disorders*. Young children need listening competencies to facilitate speaking, reading, and writing. In early childhood classrooms, children need opportunities to develop listening skills to respond in each of the following according to Otto (2002):

- Listening to and comprehending oral instructions/directions in a large-group setting
- Listening to and comprehending explanations of concepts and read alouds
- Listening to peers in play and collaborative group work
- Listening to class discussions
- Listening when engaged in conversations with others

Practitioners can enhance listening comprehension through modeling. For example, Mrs. Zing models listening strategies by focusing on the message children are saying, repeating back what her students tell her, and giving the speaker feedback on her comprehension of what was said. Instead of repeating directions, Mrs. Zing asks a student to repeat the directions.

Speaking

Speaking or speech is talking, which is a way to express language. It involves the muscles of the tongue, lips, jaw, and vocal cords to produce sounds that make up language. By the time children are 4 years old, they should be able to use sentences that give many details, tell stories that stay on topic, communicate easily with other children and adults, say most sounds correctly, use rhyming words, name some letters and numbers, and use adult grammar. Children who cannot meet these milestones are at risk for a speech and/or language impairment.

Some students with SLIs have difficulty retelling stories or providing explanations, selecting and retrieving words, participating in classroom discussions and contributing to conversations, providing background information, indicating how ideas are related to conversations, and talking about events that occurred in the past. The speech of young children with SLIs has the following syntactic characteristics:

- The use of simple and immature sentences
- Little elaboration on noun and verb phrases. Students with SLIs use fewer modifiers, adjectives, prepositional phrases, embedded clauses, and adverbs. For example, instead of saying "Look at the big, round ball," Wesley might say "Look at the ball." Instead of saying "The desk by the window is mine," Wesley might say "That desk is mine." Instead of saying "The video game I received last year is now my brother's," Wesley would say "The video game is now my brother's." Lastly, instead of saying "He runs very quickly," Wesley might say "He runs."
- Young students with SLIs often have difficulty with comparatives (e.g., large/larger) and superlatives (e.g., largest) and advanced prefixes and suffixes like un-, re-, dis-, -ment, and -ness.

Some children with disabilities may not acquire speech at all. They may have limited physical ability to control their muscles or have a hearing impairment. Other children may have disabilities that limit their ability to communicate verbally successfully. For example, children with autism always have a communication disorder. They may not speak at all, which is called *apraxia*, or they may struggle with the social aspects of communication called *pragmatics*.

Using Evidence-Based Practices to Promote Communication

Preschoolers with speech-language disorders are at risk for struggling academically and have difficulty learning to read and write (Schuele, 2004). Exposing young children to literacy activities early on will help facilitate reading later. Teachers and parents may incorporate the following activities into home or classroom settings:

- Phonological awareness activities include sound play, sound blending, and sound manipulation; they are discussed in more detail in Chapter 7.
- When reading a book, ECSE teachers and parents should do the following:
  - Stop periodically and ask questions (i.e., who, what, where, why, and when).
  - Expand the child's descriptions, introduce new words, and recast the child's speech using correct forms.
  - Read the story multiple times and ask the child to retell parts of the story.

To facilitate language skills for children with SLIs, ECSE teachers should incorporate some of the following evidence-based strategies:

- Use simple sentences and questions.
- Use visual cues and simplified shortened directions.
- Ask the student to repeat directions.
- Provide extra wait time to process information and organize thoughts before expecting an answer to a question.
- Provide additional time to complete assignments, homework, and tests.
- Speak clearly and slowly.
- Provide repetition by repeating or reformatting a question or directions.
- Provide cues. For example, Mrs. Zing can provide Wesley with the beginning sound of a word such as "It starts with the sound /r/" or give the word category such as "It is a shape" or "It is like a ball."
- Explicitly explain directions. For example, Mrs. Zing should state the lesson's topic; outline the lesson; write/type important information on the board or smart board; and use pictures, diagrams, and charts to support auditory information.

- Repeat (recast) the student's comments, correcting and adding complexity.
- Ask questions to allow for clarification.
- Explain abstract concepts in greater detail (explicit instruction) and provide examples from the student's life. Use background knowledge to create an association in the student's memory to assist with future retrieval of the concept.
- Provide positive reinforcement to encourage participation in class discussions.
- Explicitly teach classroom rules and expectations and how to ask for help as addressed in HLP 7 (establish a consistent, organized, and respectful learning environment).
- Provide an advanced notice for transitions to a new activity.
- Provide preferential seating to facilitate attention and concentration.

Explicit Instruction

Explicit instruction is also called *direct instruction* and is addressed in HLP 16 (use explicit instruction). It uses precise instructions, structuring, and scaffolding opportunities to practice skills with teacher feedback and then apply and generalize those skills and knowledge across time and situations. Typically, developing children often learn through discovery, trial, error, or incidental learning through indirect knowledge and skills exposure. However, children with disabilities are not as efficient at learning from casual interactions with their environments. As a result, ECSE teachers need to teach those skills directly and systematically. Direct instruction uses instructional time to provide clear instructions and offers multiple practice opportunities.

First, practitioners use assessments (HLP 4 [use multiple sources of information to develop a comprehensive understanding of a student's strengths and need]) to determine skills students lack. For example, if Wesley needs to learn to name and identify a square but has yet to learn it by playing in the block center, Mrs. Zing might use different strategies to teach the skill. She would describe a square as her direct instruction (e.g., "A square has four corners"). She might ask Wesley to identify other blocks of the same shape and then have him match blocks to her representation of a square for guided practice. The teaching session should not last more than 5 to 10 minutes. Mrs. Zing would then allow him to use squares and other blocks to build what he wants. Before moving on to the next activity, Mrs. Zing would ask Wesley to recall the name of the shape he learned, describe it, and identify it to reinforce and maintain the knowledge as her assessment or independent practice. Mrs. Zing ensures learning occurs by providing short, direct instruction during routine activities.

Explicit instruction also involves the following in ECSE classrooms:
- Explain the knowledge or skill to be learned (e.g., direct instruction).
- Model using several different examples (e.g., direct instruction).
- Provide guided practice by giving the students multiple opportunities to practice the skill.
- Provide feedback on performance as instructed in HLP 22 (provide positive and constructive feedback to guide students' learning and behavior).
- Arrange for the student to use the skill independently in many ways to provide for maintenance and generalization as shown in HLP 21 (teach students to maintain and generalize new learning across time and settings).

Fidelity of Implementation

Fidelity of implementation is "the degree to which an intervention is implemented accurately, following the guidelines or restrictions of its developers" (IRIS Center, 2010) and is addressed in INS6 (practitioners use systematic instructional strategies with fidelity to teach skills and to promote child engagement and learning). It is vital that educators not only select evidence-based practices but also implement them as intended. Research has shown that the strategy and/or program is less effective if not implemented as designed (Wilder et al., 2006).

The best way to implement evidence-based practices with fidelity is to attend training and then have an expert coach you on implementing the method and/or program. Research shows that receiving coaching after attending the training is more effective than training without coaching (Joyce & Showers, 2002; Kretlow & Bartholomew, 2010). When training is not available, practitioners should learn the procedures independently by reading the provided materials. Information practitioners should pay close attention to include the following:

- Participants: Make sure your students match the intended participants of the intervention.
- Length of the program: How long (how many days/weeks/months) should you use the intervention?
- Length of each session
- Frequency of sessions or how often
- Needed materials: Make sure you have access to all of the materials required to implement the intervention.

Indeed, INS10 states practitioners implement the frequency, intensity, and duration of instruction needed to address the child's phase and pace of learning or the family's level of support to achieve the child's outcomes or goals. Commercially available programs usually provide their manuals with this information. If the intervention and/or practice you selected does not have a manual, you can create one by reviewing journal articles and books. YouTube videos may also be available to watch about the program or practice. Lastly, collaborate with your colleagues who have successfully implemented the practice and/or program as addressed in HLP 1 (collaborate with professionals to increase student success).

The next step is to prepare to implement the practice and/or program by gathering the needed resources. Resources include materials and equipment as well as time. Once you are prepared, you are ready to implement the program or practice. To execute your practice/program with fidelity, you must adhere to the procedures as intended, follow the program's exposure and/or duration, and deliver it with high quality (e.g., enthusiasm, feedback). It is essential that you do not change the activity and/or program, especially over time.

Progress Monitoring

Teachers use progress to evaluate performance and improvement in response to an intervention. Progress monitoring is addressed in HLP 6 (use student assessment data, analyze instructional practices, and make necessary adjustments that improve student outcomes). They evaluate the intervention's effectiveness and adjust instruction as needed as stressed in INT5 (practitioners promote the child's problem-solving behavior by observing, interpreting, and scaffolding in response to the child's growing level of autonomy and self-regulation). Progress monitoring takes place with individual students, small groups, and even the whole class (IRIS Center, 2005; Stockall et al., 2014). More explicit details on progress monitoring are provided in Chapter 4.

SUMMARY

Children develop language at different rates. Some children do not meet developmental milestones in their language development and need an ECSE teacher's services. This chapter provided an overview of the HLPs and DEC Recommended Practices related to language development and an overview of emergent literacy and promoting language in ECSE. Lastly, we provided evidence-based practices on how to prompt language development in your classrooms.

CHAPTER REVIEW

1. Explain how the various components of language development support the social skills and future academic achievement of students with disabilities.

2. Analyze the relationship between language development and emergent literacy skills (e.g., print concepts, phonological awareness, and phonemic awareness).

3. Compare typical and atypical language development and describe four ways to promote early language in the classroom or home settings.

4. Write a summary of three evidence-based teaching strategies or developmentally appropriate activities that Wesley's teacher could use to support his language development and explain how they align with both the DEC Recommended Practices (www.dec-sped.org/recommend-edpractices) and the Council for Exceptional Children's HLPs (https://highleveragepractices.org/).

5. Read Lemons et al. (2016). Based on a student with whom you work or know, complete the Literacy Instruction and Support Planning Tool on pages 20 to 21. Given the student's abilities and access to literature, create an individualized lesson noting how it supports the student's needs and aligns with both the DEC Recommended Practices (www.dec-sped.org/recom-mendedpractices) and the Council for Exceptional Children's HLPs (https://highleverageprac-tices.org/).

6. Which of the following is NOT a component of expressive language?
   a. Expanding
   b. Pragmatics
   c. Syntax
   d. Semantics

7. Which is an essential process of emergent literacy?
   a. Expressive language
   b. Identification of environmental print
   c. Linguistic diversity
   d. Sustained joint attention

8. Which strategy uses principles of applied behavioral analysis to promote early language development?
   a. Incidental teaching
   b. Mand model
   c. Visual supports
   d. Time delay

RESOURCES

- Additional resources by topic are provided in Table 6-3.
- Council for Exceptional Children. (n.d.). *High-leverage practices in special education: Videos* [Video]. https://highleveragepractices.org/videos/
- Division for Early Childhood. (2016). *DEC Recommended Practices with examples.* http://www.dec-sped.org/recommendedpractices
- Early Childhood Personnel Center. (2018). *Naturalistic instruction e-learning lessons.* http://ecp-cprofessionaldevelopment.org/naturalistic-instruction-e-lesson/

TABLE 6-3. RESOURCES TO ENHANCE LANGUAGE DEVELOPMENT	
High-leverage practices	https://highleveragepractices.org/ https://iris.peabody.vanderbilt.edu/resources/high-leverage-practices/
Joint attention	https://hes-extraordinary.com/joint-attention https://www.speechandlanguagekids.com/establishing-joint-attention-therapy-for-children-who-arent-tuned-in/
Visual supports	https://www.autismspeaks.org/sites/default/files/2018-08/Visual%20Supports%20Tool%20Kit.pdf https://ccids.umaine.edu/resources/visual-supports/ https://www.autismspeaks.org/sites/default/files/2018-08/Visual%20Supports%20Tool%20Kit.pdf
Play based	https://ies.ed.gov/ncee/edlabs/regions/midwest/videos/integrating-play-into-literacy.aspx https://www.asha.org/public/speech/development/activities-to-Encourage-speech-and-Language-Development/
Language related	https://www.cdc.gov/ncbddd/childdevelopment/language-disorders.html https://www.asha.org/PRPSpecificTopic.aspx?folderid=8589935327&section=Treatment https://keystoliteracy.com/blog/fostering-academic-language-development-in-primary-grades/
Teaching online resources	https://ies.ed.gov/ncee/edlabs/regions/midwest/blogs/tips-from-teacher-early-literacy-covid-19.aspx https://nationalp-3center.org/wp-content/uploads/2020/03/PreK-3rd-At-Home_24Mar2020_FINAL.pdf https://www.maine.gov/doe/learning/specialed/covid19/teachers https://www.educatingalllearners.org/

- Educational Activities. (2012, October 2). *Helping parents develop language and literacy at home: Parents as teaching partners DVD* [Video]. https://youtu.be/CleB0AEEq_A
- HLP Videos: https://highleveragepractices.org/videos/
- IDEA Infant and Toddler Coordinators Association. (2019). *Social emotional development as a stepping stone.* https://www.ideainfanttoddler.org/
- IRIS. (2012). *Linguistic diversity.* https://iris.peabody.vanderbilt.edu/module/div/cresource/q2/p04/#content
- IRIS. (2019). *High-leverage practices.* https://iris.peabody.vanderbilt.edu/resources/high-leverage -practices/
- IRIS Module on Evidence-Based Practices: https://iris.peabody.vanderbilt.edu/module/ebp_02/#content
- McDaniel, L. (2013, October 12). *Literacy center in an early childhood special education classroom* [Video]. https://youtu.be/FYluiymtwDU

- McLeskey, J., & Brownell, M. (2015). *High-leverage practices and teacher preparation in special education* (Document No. PR-1). University of Florida, Collaboration for Effective Educator, Development, Accountability, and Reform Center. https://ceedar.education.ufl.edu/wp-content/uploads/2016/05/High-Leverage-Practices-and-Teacher-Preparation-in-Special-Education.pdf
- National Professional Development Center on Autism Spectrum Disorder. (n.d.). *Autism focused intervention resources and modules.* https://afirm.fpg.unc.edu/
- Reading Rockets: https://www.readingrockets.org/article/when-school-closed-resources-keep-kids-learning-home
- Sandall, S. R., Schwartz, I. S., Joseph, G. E., & Gauvreau, A. N. (2019). *Building blocks for teaching preschoolers with special needs* (3rd ed.). Brookes Publishing.
    - See Table 9.1, Strategies for Facilitating Early Literacy Skills Using the Building Blocks Framework, on page 172.
- TTAC Online. (2019). *Video series: High-leverage instructional practices (HLPs).* https://ttaconline.org/resources
- University of Florida Review of Blendable Sounds Video: https://www.youtube.com/watch?v=b78icf-bB7Q
- University of Florida Virtual Teaching Hub: https://education.ufl.edu/ufli/virtual-teaching/main/
- Zero to Three. (2013, June 17). *A window to the world: Promoting early language and literacy development* [Video]. https://youtu.be/zvCzM7SHdsw
- Zimmer, K. (2015). Enhancing interactions with children with autism through storybook reading: A caregiver's guide. *Young Exceptional Children, 20,* 133-144. https://doi.org/10.1177/1096250615593327
- Zimmer, K., Bennett, K. E., & Driver, M. K. (2018). Training caregivers to establish joint attention in children with autism through storybooks. *DADD Online Journal.* http://www.daddcec.com/uploads/2/5/2/0/2520220/updated_dec_doj_2018.pdf

REFERENCES

Adams, M. J. (1990). *Beginning to read: Thinking and learning about print.* MIT Press.

Anthony, J. L., & Francis, D. J. (2005). Development of phonological awareness. *Current Directions in Psychological Science, 14,* 255-259. https://doi.org/10.1111/j.0963-7214.2005.00376.x

Beard, L. A., Carpenter, L. B., & Johnston, L. B. (2011). *Assistive technology: Access for all students* (2nd ed.). Pearson.

Bellon, M. L., Olgetree, B. T., & Harn, W. E. (2000). Repeated storybook reading as a language intervention for children with autism: A case study on the application of scaffolding. *Focus on Autism and Other Developmental Disabilities, 15,* 52-58. https://doi.org/10.1177/108835760001500107

Blank, J., & Hertzog, N. B. (2003). Strengthening task commitment in preschool children: Reflections from an early childhood program. *Young Exceptional Children, 7*(1), 11-20. https://doi.org/10.1177/109625060300700102

Burris, P. W., Phillips, B. M., & Lonigan, C. J. (2019). Examining the relations of the home literacy environments of families of low SES with children's early literacy skills. *Journal of Education for Students Placed at Risk, 24*(2), 154-173. https://doi.org/10.1080/10824669.2019.1602473

Chall, J. (1983). *Stages of reading development.* McGraw-Hill.

Collins, B. C., Browder, D. M., Haughney, K. L., Allison, C., & Fallon, K. (2019). The effects of a computer-aided listening comprehension intervention on the generalized communication of students with autism spectrum disorder and intellectual disability. *Journal of Special Education Technology.* https://doi.org/10.1177/0162643419832976

Division for Early Childhood. (2014). *DEC recommended practices in early intervention/early childhood special education 2014.* http://www.dec-sped.org/recommendedpractices

Drager, K., Light, J., & McNaughton, D. (2010). Effects of AAC interventions on communication and language for young children with complex communication needs. *Journal of Pediatric Rehabilitation Medicine: An Interdisciplinary Approach, 3,* 303-310. https://doi.org/10.3233/PRM-2010-0141

Dunst, C., Bruder, M., Trivette, C., Raab, M., & McLean, M. (2001). Natural learning opportunities for infants, toddlers and preschoolers. *Young Exceptional Children, 4*(3), 18-26. https://doi.org/10.1177/109625060100400303

Ehri, L. C. (1995). Phases of development in learning to read words by sight. *Journal of Research in Reading, 18*(2), 116-125. https://doi.org/10.1111/j.1467-9817.1995.tb00077.x

Ehri, L. C. (2004). Teaching phonemic awareness and phonics: An explanation of the National Reading Panel meta-analyses. In P. McCardle & V. Chhabra (Eds.), *The voice of evidence in reading research* (pp. 153-186). Paul H. Brookes.

Eliason, C., & Jenkins, L. (2012). *A practical guide to early childhood curriculum* (9th ed.). Pearson.

Gosse, C. S., Hoffman, L. M., & Invernizzi, M. (2012). Overlap in speech-language and reading services for kindergartners and first graders. *Language, Speech, and Hearing Services in the Schools, 43*, 66-80. https://doi.org/10.1044/0161-1461(2011/10-0056)

Hall, A. H., Simpson, A., Guo, Y., & Wang, S. (2015). Examining the effects of preschool writing instruction on emergent literacy skills: A systematic review of the literature. *Literacy Research and Instruction, 54*, 115-134. https://doi.org/10.1080/19388071.2014.991883

Hart, B., & Risley, T. R. (1995). *Meaningful differences in the everyday experiences of young American children.* Paul H. Brookes.

Hulme, C., Bowyer-Crane, C., Carroll, J. M., Duff, F. J., & Snowling, M. J. (2012). The causal role of phoneme awareness and letter-sound knowledge in learning to read. *Psychological Science, 23*, 572-577. https://doi.org/10.1080/19388071.2014.991883

IRIS Center. (2005). *Progress monitoring: Reading.* https://iris.peabody.vanderbilt.edu/module/pmr/

IRIS Center. (2010). *Fidelity of implementation: Selecting and implementing evidence-based practices and programs.* https://iris.peabody.vanderbilt.edu/module/fid/

IRIS Center. (2012). *Classroom diversity: An introduction to student differences.* https://iris.peabody.vanderbilt.edu/module/div/

Joyce, B., & Showers, B. (2002). *Student achievement through staff development* (3rd ed). ASCD.

Justice, L. M., Petscher, Y., Schatschneider, C., & Mashburn, A. (2011). Peer effects in preschool classrooms: Is children's language growth associated with their classmates' skills? *Child Development, 82*(6), 1768-1777. https://doi.org/10.1111/j.1467-8624.2011.01665.x

Kretlow, A. G., & Bartholomew, C. C. (2010). Using coaching to improve the fidelity of evidence-based practices: A review of studies. *Teacher Education and Special Education, 33*, 279-299. https://doi.org/10.1177/0888406410371643

Lanter, E., & Watson, L. R. (2008). Promoting literacy in students with ASD: The basics for the SLP. *Language, Speech, and Hearing Services in Schools, 39*(1), 33-43.

Lemons, C. J., Allor, J. H., Al Otaiba, S., & LeJeune, L. M. (2016). Ten research-based tips for enhancing literacy instruction for students with intellectual disability. *Teaching Exceptional Children, 49*, 18-30. https://doi.org/10.1177/0040059916662202

Lieber, J., Wolery, R. A., Horn, E., Tschantz, J., Beckman, P. J., & Hanson, M. J. (2002). Collaborative relationships among adults in inclusive preschool programs. In S. L. Odom, (Ed.), *Widening the circle: Including children with disabilities in preschool programs.* Teachers College Press.

Mashburn, A. J., Justice, L. M., Downer, J. T., & Pianta, R. C. (2009). Peer effects on children's language achievement during pre-kindergarten. *Child Development, 80*(3), 686-702. https://doi.org/10.1111/j.1467-8624.2009.01291.x

McCormick, L., Noonan, M., & Heck, R. (1998). Variables affecting engagement in inclusive preschool classrooms. *Journal of Early Intervention, 21*(2), 160-176. https://doi.org/10.1177/105381519802100208

McLeskey, J., Barringer, M-D., Billingsley, B., Brownell, M., Jackson, D., Kennedy, M., Lewis, T., Maheady, L., Rodriguez, J., Scheeler, M. C., Winn, J., & Ziegler, D. (2017). *High-leverage practices in special education.* Council for Exceptional Children & CEEDAR Center.

National Early Literacy Panel. (2008). *Developing early literacy: Report of the National Early Literacy Panel.* National Institute for Literacy.

National Institute of Child Health & Human Development. (2000). *Report of the National Reading Panel: Teaching children to read: An evidence-based assessment of the scientific research literature on reading and its implications for reading instruction: Reports of the subgroups.* U.S. Government Printing Office.

Odom, S. L., & Wolery, M. (2003). A unified theory of practice in early intervention/early childhood special education: Evidence-based practices. *Journal of Special Education, 37*(3), 164-173. https://doi.org/10.1177/00224669030370030601

Otto, B. (2002). *Language development in early childhood.* Merrill Prentice Hall.

Raver, S. A. (2009). *Early childhood special education - o to 8 years: Strategies for positive outcomes.* Pearson.

Ridley S. M., McWilliam, R. A., & Oates, C. S. (2000). Observed engagement as an indicator of child care program quality. *Early Education and Development, 11*, 133-146. https://doi.org/10.1207/s15566935eed1102_1

Rock, M. L. (2004). Transfiguring it out: Converting disengaged learners to active participants. *Teaching Exceptional Children, 36*(5), 64-72.

Romeo, R. R., Leonard, J. A., Robinson, S. T., West, M. R., Mackey, A. P., Rowe, M. L., & Gabrieli, J. D. E. (2018). Beyond the 30-million-word gap: Children's conversational exposure is associated with language-related brain function. *Psychological Science, 29*(5), 700-710. https://doi.org/10.1177/0956797617742725

Schuele, C. M. (2004). The impact of developmental speech and language impairments on the acquisition of literacy skills. *Mental Retardation and Developmental Disabilities Research Reviews, 10,* 176-183. https://doi.org/10.1177/004005990403600509

Stockall, N., Dennis, L. R., & Reuter, J. A. (2014). Developing a progress monitoring portfolio for children in early childhood special education programs. *Teaching Exceptional Children, 46*(3), 32-40. https://doi.org/10.1177/004005991404600304

Thorius, K. A. K., Moore, T. S., & Coomer, M. N. (2019). We can do better: Critically reframing special education research and practice at the intersections of disability and cultural and linguistic diversity for young children. *Special Education for Young Learners with Disabilities, 34,* 157-171. https://doi.org/10.1108/S0270-401320190000034010

Tomasello, M., & Todd, J. (1983). Joint attention and lexical acquisition style. *First Language, 4*(12), 197-211. https://doi.org/10.1177/014272378300401202

Torgesen, J. K. (2002). The prevention of reading difficulties. *Journal of School Psychology, 40,* 7-26. https://doi.org/10.1016/S0022-4405(01)00092-9

Whitehurst, G. J., & Lonigan, C. J. (1998). Child development and emergent literacy. *Child Development, 69,* 848-872. https://doi.org/10.1111/j.1467-8624.1998.tb06247.x

Wilder, D. A., Chen, L., Atwell, J., Pritchard, J., & Weinstein, P. (2006). Brief functional analysis and treatment of tantrums associated with transitions in preschool children. *Journal of Applied Behavior Analysis, 39,* 103-107. https://doi.org/10.1901/jaba/2006.66-04

Wolery, M., Brashers, M. S., & Neitzel, J. C. (2002). Ecological congruence assessment for classroom activities and routines: Identifying goals and intervention practices in childcare. *Topics in Early Childhood Special Education, 22*(3), 131-142. https://doi.org/10.1177/02711214020220030101

Zimmer, K. (2017). Enhancing interactions with children with autism through storybook reading. *Young Exceptional Children, 20*(3), 133-144. https://doi.org/10.1177/1096250615593327

Zimmerman, F. J., Gilkerson, J., Richards, J. A., Christakis, D. A., Xu, D., Gray, S., & Yapanel, U. (2009). Teaching by listening: The importance of adult-child conversations to language development. *Pediatrics, 124*(1), 342-349. https://doi.org/10.1542/peds.2008-2267

7

Early Childhood Reading

Dena D. Slanda, PhD and Marisa Macy, PhD

INTRODUCTION

Emergent reading is complex—beginning at birth with oral language acquisition and developing over time to include the ability to read text with accuracy and fluency and make meaning of the words on a page. A teacher's ability to understand learning theories and their application to the acquisition of reading skills is critical. This chapter (a) introduces the learning theories that have guided teacher approaches to reading instruction, (b) provides the elements of building literacy knowledge (e.g., print-rich environments, activating background knowledge, and selecting appropriate texts), and (c) establishes the five components of reading (phonemic awareness, phonics, fluency, vocabulary, and reading comprehension) that have guided reading instruction since 2000. Furthermore, this chapter shares each of the models of reading instruction that guide today's reading programs. Finally, this chapter highlights the need for collaboration between teachers, families, and professionals.

Fisher, K. M., & Zimmer, K. E. (Eds.).
Early Childhood Special Education Programs and Practices (pp. 139-160).
© 2023 SLACK Incorporated.

CHAPTER OBJECTIVES

→ Identify theoretical frameworks for developing reading skills, including maturationism, developmentalism, constructivism, social constructivism, and Vygotsky's theory of learning.

→ Select evidence-based teaching strategies and interventions that align with both the Division for Early Childhood Recommended Practices and the Council for Exceptional Children's high-leverage practices.

→ Identify and define the five components of reading as defined by the National Reading Panel, including phonemic awareness, phonics, fluency, vocabulary, and reading comprehension.

→ Evaluate the three reading models guiding reading instruction, and determine which most closely aligns with your philosophy.

→ Explain how a collaborative approach to reading instruction can enhance reading outcomes for children.

KEY TERMS

- **Accuracy:** In reading fluency, teachers determine a student's accuracy by calculating the number of words in a text or passage the student reads correctly.
- **Automaticity:** In reading fluency, automaticity refers to the naturalness of reading. When a child has automaticity, the words come easily, accurately, and quickly (rate). The reader is able to easily express the written word orally (expression).
- **Blends:** A group of consonants where sounds blend together. Blends can be two or three consonants. Examples include br, cr, and str.
- **Digraphs:** A pair of consonants or vowels that together make one distinct sound. Examples of consonant digraphs include ch, ck, ph, and wh. Examples of vowel digraphs include ea, ee, and oa.
- **Diphthongs:** Formed when vowels run together to make one sound. Examples of diphthongs include ai, oi, ou, and ow.
- **Expository Text:** Includes informational text that provides factual information in a structured format.
- **Fluency:** The ability to read text with ease and accuracy. Fluent readers read text at an appropriate rate with expression and automaticity.
- **Graphemes:** A letter or number that represents a sound (phoneme).
- **Homonyms:** Two words that are spelled the same, look the same, and sound the same but have different meanings. Examples include (a) bat, which can be a nocturnal animal or something used to hit a baseball; (b) bright, which can mean smart or filled with light; and (c) ring, which can mean jewelry worn on a finger or the sound made for a doorbell or phone.
- **Homophones:** Words that sound the same but have different spellings and meanings. Examples of homophones include (a) bare and bear, (b) mail and male, and (c) tale and tail.
- **Narrative Text:** Storytelling to relay information, including story elements such as setting, characters, conflict, plot, and resolution.
- **Phonemic Awareness:** A skill in which children are able to hear, identify, and manipulate phonemes (the smallest unit of sound). Children who have phonemic awareness understand the relationship between written words (graphemes) and letter sounds.

- **Phonics:** An instructional approach to reading that emphasizes the relationship between written words and letter sounds. Phonics instruction focuses on systematic principles of written and spoken language. Children are able to apply their knowledge about letter sounds, blends, digraphs, and diphthongs to decode printed words.

- **Rate:** The speed at which students read text measured in words/minute. Students who are fluent are able to decode words quickly and can read more words accurately in a 1-minute time frame. Fluent readers are also able to read with intonation and proper expression.

- **Reading Comprehension:** The ability to listen to or read text and make meaning of the written words. Children are able to understand the explicit or implied message and relate that information to background knowledge.

- **Sight Words:** High-frequency words that typically cannot be sounded out using phonics rules and are words teachers have children commit to memory using various strategies, including flash cards, multisensory approaches, picture-supported methods, computer-based learning methods, and constant rehearsal (Phillips & Feng, 2012). Two comprehensive sight word lists were developed by Dolch (1936) and Fry (1957).

- **Vocabulary:** The words children understand and are able to use in listening, speaking, reading, and writing. Vocabulary is acquired through receptive means, and as children listen, comprehend, and respond to vocabulary, they respond through action or expressive language.

CASE STUDY

Teachers may consider kindergarten a challenging grade level to teach because children begin the year with diverse learning needs and at varied levels in their reading development. Some students enter kindergarten with strong knowledge and skills related to letter–sound relationships, letter identification, and increased vocabularies. However, some students enter kindergarten with limited phonemic awareness and limited vocabularies. This variation in skill levels can make it challenging for teachers to differentiate instruction and meet student needs.

Given this variation, Ms. Brown begins her kindergarten school year getting to know her students. Ms. Brown understands how critical it is to ensure children develop a strong foundation in reading to be successful throughout their schooling years. Through experience, she has developed an understanding of the theoretical frameworks that guide approaches to reading instruction. She uses the theoretical frameworks to design a responsive classroom that meets the individual needs of her students and has created a print-rich environment that fosters early literacy acquisition.

This year, Ms. Brown has a student named Jason who has limited phonemic awareness. Jason's limited phonemic awareness has also impacted his vocabulary knowledge, making it difficult for him to understand the books read to the class. As such, he is often distracted and engages in off-task behaviors to avoid read alouds. Ms. Brown recognizes the distracting behaviors are directly related to academic task avoidance.

What are some strategies you would recommend to Ms. Brown to assist Jason?

"Once you learn to read, you will forever be free . . . "
—*Frederick Douglass*

Emergent Reading in the Early Childhood Years

Reading is a complex skill that develops in early childhood beginning from birth, well in advance of entering formal schooling. Children develop reading skills over time through interactions with their environment and caretakers. Caretakers nurture reading skills initially and then build them through explicit instruction. Socioeconomic and sociocultural differences can impact the development of reading skills. Children who experience difficulties learning to read in the early stages will likely continue to experience difficulty as they progress through formal schooling. In fact, children who enter school with limited reading skills are potentially at risk for identification for special education services (Whitehurst & Lonigan, 2003). Reading is a fundamental skill for all children and is a predictor of academic and career success. Understanding the theoretical underpinnings as they relate to literacy and reading development can assist practitioners with promoting and supporting reading development in their classrooms (Saracho, 2017).

Learning Theories

During the first half of the 19th century, there was a strongly held belief that children needed to mature and gain a sense of self before they could begin formal reading instruction (Crawford, 1995). This theory, known as *maturationism*, assumed that rushing reading instruction would do more harm than good. Within this theory, cognitive development mirrored physical development. Therefore, children could not develop reading skills until they had reached the appropriate age. This approach of reading readiness persisted throughout the first half of the last century and included diagnostic assessments designed to measure a student's "readiness" for reading instruction (Crawford, 1995).

Beginning in the 1960s and 1970s, a newer approach to learning that built on "reading readiness" took hold and was known as *developmentalism* (Durkin, 1966). Developmentalists believed that engaging in prereading could allow children to develop literacy skills; however, if the child lacked the appropriate experiences, their ability to learn would be hindered. Bloom (1964) and Bruner (1960) were developmentalists who believed adults could cultivate experiences to allow children to develop reading and literacy skills.

More student-centered and responsive learning theories related to literacy dominate today's classrooms. The constructivist theory is well grounded in literacy and provides a framework for studying the reading process in children (Spivey, 1989). According to Bruner (1966), the constructivist approach to understanding the reading processes affirms that the child is an active builder of their knowledge through experiences as they navigate the world around them. Closely related to Piaget's research on child development, constructivism concedes that children connect information they already have (i.e., schema) to new information, allowing them to make meaning. Also known as *Bruner's theory*, constructivism includes social and cultural aspects of learning (Sadoski & Paivo, 2013). Classroom application of this theory includes activating prior knowledge, building new knowledge, and scaffolding the process of making connections.

Lev Vygotsky's (1978, 1987) theory of learning extends the social constructivist approach to literacy. Vygotsky's theories influence our understanding of literacy development in part because of their agreement with a social approach to learning. Classroom application of Vygotsky's theories includes the zone of proximal development. Operating within this theory, the classroom teacher would facilitate learning by mediating what the student already knows and connecting it to new knowledge. Specifically related to reading skills, teachers who read aloud or model metacognitive strategies while reading are demonstrating the skills the child should acquire. More recent applications of Vygotsky's theories to literacy include the following principles: (a) learning is mediated through interactions; (b) learning is scaffolded by others in the social environment through a reciprocal process as knowledge is constructed by the active child; (c) learning is inherently social, and language is the primary tool for learning and constructing meaning; and (d) learning is infinite and unbound (Lee & Smagorinsky, 2000).

EARLY CHILDHOOD AND HIGH-LEVERAGE PRACTICES

The Division for Early Childhood (DEC; 2014) of the Council for Exceptional Children released a set of Recommended Practices. These evidence-based DEC Recommended Practices were developed to provide guidance on the most effective ways to improve outcomes for children who have disabilities or are at risk for developmental delays. More importantly, these DEC Recommended Practices provide a framework within which practitioners can provide access in inclusive environments and natural settings while also acknowledging diversity in cultural, linguistic, and ability domains. The DEC Recommended Practices are broken into seven topic areas (assessment, environment, family, instruction, interaction, teaming and collaboration, and transition). The practices are observable, developmentally appropriate, and not disability specific.

Furthermore, in order to implement these practices, teachers use high-leverage practices (HLPs). HLPs reflect a compilation of "frequently used" practices that "have been shown to improve student outcomes" (McLeskey & Brownell, 2015, p. 7) that are organized around four domains: collaboration, assessment, social/emotional/behavioral learning, and instruction. Table 7-1 highlights the DEC Recommended Practices and HLPs that relate to literacy. You will also find references to these practices throughout the chapter.

BUILDING LITERACY KNOWLEDGE

Research over the past 60 years indicates early literacy skills begin to develop well in advance of entering prekindergarten (Neuman, 2004). Chen and de Groot Kim (2014) further affirmed the strong relationship between oral language development and emergent literacy skills. Literacy is built through activities with caretakers in the early development years. This variation in skill development translates to children entering school settings with differences in their abilities. To address this disparity and to foster and develop literacy knowledge, teachers are encouraged to (a) provide print-rich environments, (b) build gaps in background information, and (c) select appropriate texts based on their readability.

FOSTERING PRINT-RICH ENVIRONMENTS

Print-rich environments strengthen a child's curiosity about reading and encourage them to explore their interest in books. When creating a print-rich environment, the classroom teacher must not only consider the literary resources (e.g., books and materials) but also the physical environment (e.g., writing tables, classroom layout, posters and items on the walls, and the variety of symbols found throughout the room) and the psychological environment (e.g., literacy interactions between the teacher and child; Guo et al., 2012). The physical and psychological environment can "communicate the important message that literacy was an integral part of daily activity" (Neuman, 2004, p. 91). The classroom environment and the print included in the environment have a positive effect on literacy. Furthermore, diversity in the environment should reflect the diversity of the classroom. Makin (2003) cautioned that print-rich environments can be rich for some children and poor for children who do not see themselves represented in the environment. Creating print-rich environments aligns with DEC Recommended Practices of providing services and supports in natural and inclusive environments and the HLP of establishing an organized and respectful learning environment.

TABLE 7-1. EARLY CHILDHOOD AND HIGH-LEVERAGE PRACTICES (HLPS) IN LITERACY

DEC RECOMMENDED PRACTICES	HLPs	CLASSROOM APPLICATION EXAMPLE TO BUILD LITERACY
A4: Practitioners conduct assessments that include all areas of development and behavior to learn about the child's strengths, needs, preferences, and interests.	HLP 4: Use multiple sources of information to develop a comprehensive understanding of a student's strengths and needs.	Assess each of the five components of literacy. Develop plans related to the five components.
E1: Practitioners provide services and supports in natural and inclusive environments during daily routines and activities to promote the child's access to and participation in learning experiences.	HLP 7: Establish a consistent, organized, and respectful learning environment.	Foster print-rich environments.
F1: Practitioners build trusting and respectful partnerships with the family through interactions that are sensitive and responsive to cultural, linguistic, and socioeconomic diversity. F7: Practitioners work with the family to identify, access, and use formal and informal resources and supports to achieve family-identified outcomes or goals.	HLP 3: Collaborate with families to support student learning and secure needed services.	Develop relationships with families. Provide information on how to develop literacy in the home through daily reading. Assist with selecting appropriate texts/books.
INS5: Practitioners embed instruction within and across routines, activities, and environments to provide contextually relevant learning opportunities. INS10: Practitioners implement the frequency, intensity, and duration of instruction needed to address the child's phase and pace of learning or the level of support needed by the family to achieve the child's outcomes or goals.	HLP 11: Identify and prioritize long- and short-term learning goals. HLP 12: Systematically design instruction toward a specific learning goal. HLP 15: Provide scaffolded supports. HLP 16: Use explicit instruction. HLP 20: Provide intensive instruction.	Develop plans and measurable goals using assessment data across each of the five components of literacy.
TC1: Practitioners representing multiple disciplines and families work together as a team to plan and implement supports and services to meet the unique needs of each child and family.	HLP 1: Collaborate with professionals to increase student success.	Develop written or oral communication logs with home and professionals.

DEC = Division for Early Childhood.

Data sources: Division for Early Childhood. (2014). DEC recommended practices in early intervention/early childhood special education. 2014. http://www.dec-sped.org/recommendedpractices and McLeskey, J., et al. (2017). *High-leverage practices in special education*. Council for Exceptional Children & CEEDAR Center.

What can Ms. Brown do to foster a print-rich environment in her classroom? To foster a print-rich environment, Ms. Brown can perform the following:

- Create a reading nook in her classroom with flexible seating that is inviting and comfortable.
- Decorate the classroom to increase motivation to read.
- Include reading time in the daily schedule.
- Develop a classroom library that includes books of various genres and books with diverse characters and authors.

What are some ideas you have?

Building Background Knowledge

Background knowledge is essential for reading and listening comprehension and provides a context within which children understand text. Without background knowledge, the text can be challenging for children. Reading comprehension includes the child's ability to construct a mental representation of the text (van den Broek & Helder, 2017), and without background knowledge, creating a mental representation is challenging (Neuman et al., 2014). This can be even more challenging for children with disabilities. Background knowledge supports children with emergent reading skills and may assist them in making meaning of text by allowing them to fill the gaps (Gibson & Moss, 2016).

According to Neuman and colleagues (2014), background knowledge is important for the following reasons:

- Some words have several meanings. Words that are spelled the same, sound the same, and look the same but have one or more meanings are known as *homonyms*. Examples of homonyms include (a) bat, which can be a nocturnal animal or something used to hit a baseball; (b) bright, which can mean smart or filled with light; and (c) ring, which can mean jewelry worn on a finger or the sound made for a doorbell or phone. Additionally, some words sound the same but have different spellings and different meanings. These types of words are known as *homophones*. Examples of homophones include (a) bare and bear, (b) mail and male, and (c) tale and tail. With background knowledge, children are able to apply the correct meaning of the word in the context it is being used.
- Making inferences is dependent on background knowledge. Whether the child is reading or listening, they are actively constructing meaning by making inferences and using previous knowledge to fill missing information in the current text. For example, if a child reads that the grass is wet, they may infer that the sprinklers were on or that it had been raining. Authors sometimes may share in a story that a character has tears in their eyes, and children may infer that the character is upset or hurt.
- Informational text includes content-specific vocabulary and requires the child to apply what they have previously learned to the current text. For example, in a science text, the teacher may want to preteach vocabulary related to the lesson so the child has context for the text.

Before, during, and after reading, classroom teachers can engage in various evidence-based strategies to activate background knowledge. These strategies are particularly critical for children with disabilities who may require additional support to activate prior knowledge. Before reading, classroom teachers can engage children in activities that allow them to think about what they may already know about the topic (Hattan & Dinsmore, 2019). By bringing this knowledge to the forefront, the child is able to relate their prior knowledge to the current text. Furthermore, the child is able to see how the text relates to them personally, which further facilitates their understanding by making the experience more personal. Preteaching keywords and specific vocabulary builds background knowledge for children who may not have familiarity with the topic.

What can Ms. Brown do to build background knowledge in her classroom? To build background knowledge, Ms. Brown can do the following:

- Provide illustrations or visual representations of text.
- Connect what children are reading to their personal lives, previous learning, or experiences.
- Facilitate before, during, and after reading strategies such as predicting, teaching key vocabulary, clarifying words or sentences, and engaging children in questions.

What are some ideas you have?

Selecting Appropriate Text

The readability of a text is guided by its complexity and measured by the percentage of words a child can read correctly (Rasinski, 1999). The complexity of a text depends on the sentence structure, word choice, vocabulary, and presentation (e.g., font size, picture supports, number of words on the page, etc.). There are three levels of readability: independent, instructional, and frustration. According to Gillett and Temple (1986), the following are the criteria for each of the levels. For a text to be considered at the child's independent level, they should be able to read 97% or more of the words in the text with accuracy (fluency). Furthermore, the child should be able to understand what they are reading (comprehension). For a text to be considered at the child's instructional level, they should be able to read the text with 90% to 96% accuracy and understand most of the text. For a text to be considered at the child's frustration level, the child would read less than 90% of the text accurately and would have limited understanding of the text.

A quantitative approach to determining the complexity of a text, or the level of the text, is Lexile scoring. Lexile uses a formula to determine the level of a text, which is assigned a numerical value. Experts assign Lexile scores to books so that teachers and parents know how the book compares with thousands of other books (Hiebert, 2016, 2018). Teachers, parents, and districts use Lexile scores to describe the reading level and ability of a child. Websites such as www.lexile.com provide the ability to match a child with a book at their level. Ensuring the selection of books presented to the reader at their level is critical, especially for new readers, struggling readers, and children with disabilities. Children who attempt to read at their frustration level may develop a distaste for reading and lack motivation for reading. Books should be chosen for their reading levels but also for the following:

- The enjoyment of the child; children who enjoy listening to or reading books will develop a love for reading.
- The interests of the child; children who are provided with the opportunity to listen to or read books that are aligned with their personal interests will want to read more.
- The illustrations; good readers create mental representations to enhance their comprehension of text. Selecting books with high-quality illustrations for early readers and/or children with disabilities allows them to have a mental representation of the text to facilitate their understanding.
- The ability to provide context; when a child is learning about a topic, there are a variety of books and types of text that a child can use to build their knowledge on a topic. Supplemental texts can extend a child's learning and provide background knowledge.

COMPONENTS OF READING INSTRUCTION

In 1997, Congress commissioned the National Institute of Child Health and Human Development and the U.S. Secretary of Education to form the National Reading Panel (NRP). The purpose of the convening of a panel was to determine best practices for improving reading outcomes through research-validated instructional practices. The research conducted was a meta-analysis that included over 100,000 studies of reading instruction since 1966. The thorough review of the literature led to the panel's report in 2000 entitled *Teaching Children to Read: An Evidence-Based Assessment of the*

Scientific Research Literature on Reading and Its Implications for Reading Instruction. The key findings of the report indicated targeted, systematic, and direct skill instruction within five core components of reading could enhance children's success and improve reading outcomes. In response to the report from the NRP, reading programs must include the instructional applications of the five components of literacy to be effective (Copeland et al., 2011). The major components of the reading process include (a) phonemic awareness, (b) phonics, (c) fluency, (d) vocabulary, and (e) comprehension (Copeland et al., 2011; NRP, 2000; Rupley et al., 2009). Table 7-2 provides an overview of each of these components, their characteristics, and strategies teachers can use to develop them.

Phonemic Awareness

Phonemic awareness is a skill in which children are able to hear, identify, and manipulate phonemes (the smallest unit of sound). Children who have phonemic awareness are able to identify individual sounds within words, have a level of awareness of phonemes being associated with written words (graphemes), and understand basic concepts such as print direction (Copeland et al., 2011; Reading Rockets, 2015). Additionally, phonemic awareness includes letter/sound manipulation including blending, segmenting, riming, rhyming, and creating new words.

For children to become proficient readers, they must develop phonemic awareness. When children struggle with phonemic awareness and are not proficient with blending or segmenting words, reading becomes a compilation of sight words, which makes reading a difficult task. Furthermore, phonemic awareness is not only necessary for reading, but also it is a precursor to writing.

Teachers can find fun and engaging methods for incorporating phonemic awareness in their classrooms. Some methods for including phonemic awareness are alliteration, making up nonsense words, singing songs, nursery rhymes, and rhyming. Several authors and children's books incorporate phonemic awareness skill building, such as Bob Books.

Phonics

Phonics extends the association of spoken sounds with letters to printed words (K12 Reader, 2016). Phonics instruction includes teaching children that each grapheme represents a phoneme and that each letter in the alphabet can have multiple sounds (Armbruster & Osborn, 2003). Phonics extends the child's understanding of how sounds make words. According to the International Literacy Association (ILA, 2018), phonics instruction leads to word knowledge, and teachers should use explicit and systematic phonics instruction.

The ILA (2018) further recommended that teachers implement phonics instruction after the child has acquired phonemic awareness. The ability to recognize and produce speech sounds is a requisite for phonics instruction. Letter recognition and letter–sound correspondences are also required skills in order to teach the 26 letters of the alphabet and the 44 phonemes (sounds). Phonics instruction should include analytic and synthetic approaches (ILA, 2018). The analytic approach involves children identifying patterns between words to apply that knowledge to new words (e.g., can/ban) or identifying/segmenting onset and rhyme (e.g., c-an, b-an). The synthetic approach engages the child in blending letter sounds (e.g., c-a-t/cat, b-a-n/ban).

Classroom teachers need to be aware that phonics can be difficult for some children to acquire and master. This can be because sometimes one letter represents more than one sound (e.g., each vowel has a long sound and a short sound) or more than one letter represents the same sound (e.g., c and k). Vowels in the alphabet are represented by 5 letters and 19 phonemes. These differences can be especially challenging for students who have a speech and language impairment, are deaf/hard of hearing, or are English-language learners. English-language learners may have a first language that has different phonemes and graphemes with different rules for language. These differences can make phonics difficult. Classroom teachers can successfully implement phonics instruction by using appropriate texts, building on what students already know, and embedding instruction in meaningful contexts and authentic settings.

TABLE 7-2. OVERVIEW OF READING COMPONENTS, CHARACTERISTICS, AND STRATEGIES

COMPONENT	CHARACTERISTICS	WHAT CLASSROOM TEACHERS NEED TO KNOW	STRATEGIES
Phonemic awareness	Able to hear, identify, and manipulate phonemes Identify individual sounds Letters are associated with words and sounds	Related to ability to blend and segment words Impacts decoding and writing	Alliteration Nonsense words Singing songs/nursery rhymes
Phonics	Association of sounds with letters Letters can have several sounds Extends understanding of how sounds make words	Phonemic awareness is a prerequisite Leads to word knowledge Can be difficult because letters can have more than one sound	Explicit and systematic instructional methods Analytic and synthetic approaches Teach students how to identify word patterns
Fluency	Decoding of written words Measured in accuracy and automaticity Reading rate is measured in correct words/minute Significant component of early literacy	When time is spent decoding words, children will not have the time and cognitive strength to understand what they are reading	Model fluent reading Allow children to hear themselves read Reread same text Build confidence Provide opportunity to read text of interest
Vocabulary	Words children are able to use in listening, speaking, reading, and writing Receptive vs. expressive language	Impacted by environment Directly related to reading comprehension	Explicit instruction Enhanced storybook reading Incidental exposure Embedded instruction
Reading comprehension	Ability to understand text Cognitively demanding Impacts academic outcomes Requires foundational skills in each of the other four components of reading	Requires children recall, infer, and identify causal relationships; generate mental images; and process information Narrative vs. expository text	Assist with creating mental images (graphic organizers) Engage before, during, and after tasks Guided reading and read alouds

Fluency

Fluency refers to the decoding of written words with automaticity and accuracy (Rasinski, 2003; Shanahan, 2006a, 2006b) and is a significant component of early literacy (Algozzine et al., 2009). *Automaticity* refers to the naturalness of the reading, how easily (accuracy) and quickly (rate) the words come to the reader, and how easily they are expressed orally (expression). Fluency indicates the student's reading accuracy and rate, whereas accuracy represents the number of words read correctly (i.e., no misread words). Rate is measured in words/minute. Students who are fluent are able to decode words quickly and can read more words accurately in a 1-minute time frame. Fluent readers are also able to read with intonation and proper expression.

When a student is disfluent, they have difficulty reading words in a passage, spend considerable time decoding multisyllabic words, read at a slow rate, or read without proper expression. Because a considerable amount of the student's energy is spent on reading, the student is likely not able to focus on comprehending what they are reading. Reading fluency and reading comprehension are dependent on one another. If a student struggles with fluency, they will struggle with comprehension. Classroom teachers should assist struggling readers to improve their fluency by (a) modeling fluent reading, (b) providing students the opportunity to listen to themselves read using an audio recording (Rasinski, 2003), (c) encouraging the student to read and reread the same text to build fluency and confidence in reading, and (d) providing the student with the ability to read passages of interest.

Vocabulary

Vocabulary includes words students understand and are able to use in listening, speaking, reading, and eventually writing (Copeland et al., 2011). Students build their vocabulary through receptive means as they are exposed to language. They listen, comprehend, and respond to vocabulary either through receptive action or expressive language. For example, a student who cannot yet speak may hear a parent ask them to retrieve an item from another room and will respond by following the direction. In this instance, they used their receptive vocabulary by receiving the information, understanding the request, and responding accordingly. As students develop, they build their expressive language, gaining the ability to produce language. Vocabulary acquisition is critical because "vocabulary is the building block of language" (Schmitt et al., 2001, p. 55).

In an article entitled "The Early Catastrophe: The 30 Million Word Gap by Age 3," researchers Hart and Risley (2003) conducted a longitudinal study that followed students from a cross section of socioeconomic and sociocultural backgrounds. What they found was vocabulary acquisition begins early in life, and students from more affluent families (higher income and parental education) have larger vocabularies than students from poorer families (lower income and parental education). In fact, in their study, Hart and Risley found the gap in language and vocabulary development was significant by the age of 3; students from affluent families heard 30 million more words than students of poorer families. Given the impact of the environment on vocabulary acquisition, poorer students enter school with a marked disparity in their language development and skills. This is critical because vocabulary development is directly related to reading comprehension. Students with larger vocabularies are able to comprehend text better in comparison to students with limited vocabularies (Juel & Deffes, 2004). "Vocabulary knowledge is one element of oral language that meaningfully contributes to reading and academic success, most notably in later grades" (Loftus-Rattan et al., 2016, p. 392).

To build vocabulary, classroom teachers need to provide rich language experiences for students through multiple means of literacy exposure such as print-rich environments; read alouds; guided reading; and direct, explicit instruction. Classroom teachers can also build vocabulary through play. Evidence-based strategies related to vocabulary development include (a) enhanced storybook reading strategies (Coyne et al., 2007); (b) extended and repeated exposure to targeted words (Penno et al., 2002); (c) incidental exposure through play and storytelling (Loftus-Rattan et al., 2016); and (d) embedded instruction using songs, videos, and pictures.

TABLE 7-3. EXAMPLES OF NARRATIVE AND EXPOSITORY TEXT	
NARRATIVE TEXT	**EXPOSITORY TEXT**
Brave Irene	*African Adventure*
Don't Let the Pigeon Drive the Bus!	*Eating the Alphabet*
Dragons Love Tacos	*Guided Science Readers box set*
Frog on a Log?	*In the Pond*
If You Give a Mouse a Cookie	*Inch by Inch*
No, David!	*National Geographic, Kids! book series*
Pete the Cat	*Pierre the Penguin*
The Day the Crayons Came Home	*Who Would Win? book series*
Where the Wild Things Are	*Who Lives in the Arctic?*

Reading Comprehension

Reading comprehension is the ability of students to listen to or read a passage and understand what they are reading and relate that information to their own knowledge and schema (Armbruster & Osborn, 2003; Palincsar & Brown, 1986). Reading comprehension is a cognitively demanding task and requires the active engagement of the reader. It requires that students have foundational skills in each of the components of reading, especially fluency (decoding) and vocabulary skills. In fact, to comprehend text, it is essential that a reader be able to decode language units and to construct a coherent mental representation of the text (van den Broek & Helder, 2017). Additionally, reading comprehension requires that the reader has the necessary background information to make meaning of text (RAND Reading Study Group, 2002) and the motivation to read.

The significance of reading comprehension on academic outcomes is clear. Students who have difficulty with reading comprehension tend to experience difficulties throughout their K-12 education, and the impact remains as they prepare for postsecondary settings, including college and their career (van den Broek & Helder, 2017). Reading comprehension includes students having the ability to construct meaning, recall events, identify causal relationships, make inferences, generate visual images, and draw conclusions.

To improve reading comprehension, students need to be presented with both narrative and expository text. Narrative text includes short stories and novels. Narrative text can be both fiction and nonfiction. It uses storytelling to relay information and includes story elements such as setting, characters, conflict, plot, and resolution. Expository text differs from narrative text in many ways. Expository text includes informational text that provides factual information in a structured format (e.g., headings, subheadings, etc.). Expository text is written from a tone of authority. Table 7-3 provides a list of age-appropriate examples of narrative and expository text.

To improve reading comprehension, classroom teachers can assist students with creating visual representations of the text. Visual representations of both narrative and expository text are important and can be accomplished through the use of graphic organizers (Figure 7-1), semantic maps (Figure 7-2), or mental maps (Figure 7-3) as well as visualizing strategies such as painting an image (Hall & Strangham, 2002; Kim et al., 2004; see Figures 7-1 through 7-3).

Furthermore, classroom teachers can engage students in metacognitive tasks before, during, and after reading either type of text. These metacognitive tasks include predicting, clarifying, summarizing, and questioning (Palincsar & Brown, 1986). Good readers make predictions before, during, and after reading (Santaro et al., 2008). Teachers can guide the prediction process through read alouds and guided reading by modeling good reading behaviors. An evidence-based strategy that

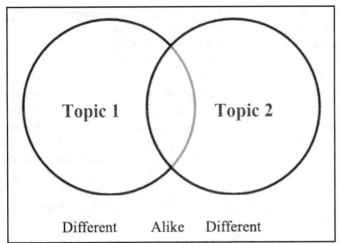

Figure 7-1. An example of a graphic organizer.

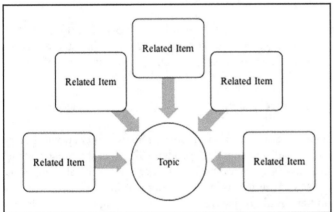

Figure 7-2. An example of a semantic map.

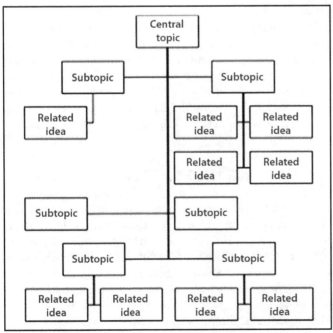

Figure 7-3. An example of a mental map.

assists with the development of metacognitive skills is dialogic reading. *Dialogic reading* is an easy-to-implement strategy in which the teacher and the student engage in a discussion of the story or passage. The reciprocal exchange allows the teacher to scaffold the process of listening and questioning (Quinn et al., 2020; U.S. Department of Education Institute of Education Sciences, What Works Clearinghouse, 2010). Such strategies allow students to enhance their reading comprehension skills.

Students who struggle with reading comprehension may skip words they do not know or choose not to reread sections for clarity. Clarifying strategies such as rereading or reflecting on what was read can also be modeled and scaffolded during read alouds to encourage students to adopt and implement the strategy when they read alone. As students read or are read to, they should be summarizing the text. Summarizing includes finding the main ideas presented during the text and allows both the teacher and the student to check for understanding. Finally, questioning is a strategy that also allows students to make sense of what they are reading. Students clarify and enhance their comprehension of text when they are asked questions during reading or are taught to ask questions internally as they read. Good readers ask questions as they read, which allows them to think more critically about the text and deepen their understanding.

Assessment of Reading Components

Teachers must be able to accurately assess a student's present levels of performance in each of the reading components as well as measure progress as the student develops reading ability in each of the components. Table 7-4 provides assessment resources for each of the components of reading described previously.

Reading Components Are Interdependent

Each of the five reading components (i.e., phonemic awareness, phonics, fluency, vocabulary, and reading comprehension) should be considered as interdependent. Teachers should simultaneously teach the components to students across age spans and grade levels. It is critical to note that students develop each of these five areas concomitantly, and development in one component can positively impact development in another. Similarly, failure to develop a strong foundation in one component can negatively impact development in another. For example, oral language development, which begins at birth, is related to phonological awareness, which research has shown later impacts phonics and reading fluency (Ashby et al., 2013). Additionally, phonological awareness impacts vocabulary skills (Burgess & Lonigan, 1998; Dehaene et al., 2015; Saygin et al., 2013; Wagner et al., 1993), which are strongly related to the ability to comprehend text (Engen & Høien, 2002; Palincsar & Brown, 1986). Likewise, students who can decode words and read with automaticity and accuracy (i.e., fluently) have greater ability to comprehend what they read, making fluency a prerequisite for comprehension (Paige et al., 2015; Rasinski, 2003; Rasinski et al., 2016). To read with proficiency, students must develop a strong foundation during their early childhood years that allows them to "focus their cognitive resources on creating meaning from text" (Paige et al., 2015, p. 103).

MODELS OF READING INSTRUCTION

Reading is a complex process that requires the active engagement of the reader. Now that you have learned more about the five components of reading, you are able to consider the models of learning and how approaches to literacy instruction fit within the three models. It should be noted that best practices for targeted skill instruction are divergent. Each of these models for emergent reading instruction is grounded in research that dates back decades. However, educators have disagreed for decades about how reading should be taught (Saracho, 2017). Experts debate whether or not students should be taught letter–sound correspondences or if they should be taught through memorization of whole words (Ehri et al., 2001). The following sections briefly describe the three models of reading instruction.

TABLE 7-4. ASSESSMENT RESOURCES FOR EACH OF THE COMPONENTS OF READING

COMPONENT OF READING	ASSESSMENT	URL
Phonemic awareness	LAC-3: Lindamood-Auditory Conceptual-ization Test, Third Edition	https://www.proedinc.com/Products/10980/lac3-lindamood-auditory-conceptualization-testthird-edition.aspx
	TOPA-2+: Test of Phonological Awareness, Second Edition	https://www.proedinc.com/Products/11880/topa2-test-of-phonological-awarenesssecond-edition-plus.aspx
	DIBELS: Dynamic Indicators of Basic Early Literacy Skills	https://dibels.uoregon.edu
Phonics	ITBS: Iowa Test of Basic Skills	http://www.mercerpublishing.com/itbs?gclid=CjwKCAjw_uDsBRAMEiwAaFiHa6-NbgbGFxW6Ww0C8JhjcAiZqa8pCqOEUn-zuaEGebVP3DzmE_vG_xoCguUQAvD_BwE
	WJ IV: Woodcock-Johnson IV	https://www.riversideinsights.com/solutions/woodcock-johnson-iv?tab=0&gclid=CjwKCAjw_uDsBRAMEiwAaFiHa36fPeghCC_rZ5UtvF0b6avHUm28LIkqJLivhzz9-srYGDfbE5UrmhoCNZ8QAvD_BwE
	DRS: Diagnostic Reading Scales	http://louis.aph.org/product/Diagnostic-reading-scales-(DRS),34876.aspx
Fluency	GORT-5: Gray Oral Reading Test, Fifth Edition	https://www.wpspublish.com/gort-5-gray-oral-reading-test-fifth-edition?gclid=Cj0KCQjwoebsBRCHARIsAC3JP0IaRHw_pb0awibjfM7k1LNkQgpN-WZ9LynqWAkHLFh7YAYeq9B505QaAvgtEALw_wcB
	DIBELS: Dynamic Indicators of Basic Early Literacy Skills (Oral Reading Fluency and Retell Fluency [ORF])	https://dibels.uoregon.edu
Vocabulary	Ortiz PVAT: Ortiz Picture Vocabulary Acquisition Test	https://www.wspapsych.org/docs/WSPA-MHS-PVAT_Brochure.pdf
	GMRT: Gates-MacGinitie Reading Tests	https://riversideinsights.com/gates_macginitie
Reading comprehension	DAR: Diagnostic Assessment of Reading	https://nrsweb.org/training-ta/ta-tools/assessment/diagnostic-assessments-reading-dar
	DORA: Diagnostic Online Reading Assessment	https://shop.letsgolearn.com/shop/store/product/dora-diagnostic-online-reading-assessment/
	WJ IV: Woodcock-Johnson IV	https://www.riversideinsights.com/solutions/woodcock-johnson-iv?tab=0&gclid=CjwKCAjw_uDsBRAMEiwAaFiHa36fPeghCC_rZ5UtvF0b6avHUm28LIkqJLivhzz9-srYGDfbE5UrmhoCNZ8QAvD_BwE

Part-to-Whole Approach

When the NRP conducted their meta-analysis in 2000, several subgroups were also formed. One of the subgroups conducted a meta-analysis on systematic phonics instruction and the significance of phonics instruction on reading development. Their study indicated phonics instruction allowed students to gain an understanding of the alphabetic system, which provided them with the ability to decode new words (Ehri et al., 2001).

A part-to-whole approach to reading instruction is founded on the idea that students learn to read by first learning letter–sound correspondences and how those sounds fit together to form words. This approach is rooted in phonics and is sometimes referred to as the *phonics* or *linguistic approach*. Teachers who subscribe to this approach to reading instruction believe that students need systematic instruction that includes learning (a) blends (i.e., two letters that blend together but still allow for each letter sound to be heard [e.g., br, dr, fr, pr, sc, st, etc.]), (b) vowel and consonant digraphs (i.e., two letters that make one sound [e.g., ch, ck, ea, ee, ph, oa, wh, etc.]), and (c) diphthongs (i.e., vowels that run together to make one sound [e.g., ai, oi, ou, ow, etc.]). In systematic phonics instruction, phonics elements are taught in a sequential order to beginning readers. Specifically, for students with disabilities or students who struggle to acquire and master reading skills, phonics has been shown to be significantly beneficial (Ehri et al., 2001).

Whole-Part-Whole Language Approach

In the 1960s, reading instruction was known as the *look-say approach* (Chall, 1967; Ehri et al., 2001). In this method, students learn to read words as "wholes" before learning the parts of words. Students practiced and memorized reading words until they had 50 to 100 sight words in their vocabulary (Ehri et al., 2001). Through shared and repeated reading experiences, teachers read books to students as they followed along. During read alouds, teachers focused instruction on rhyming, word endings, and other mechanics of written language including punctuation (DeVries, 2011). Through this approach, teachers may select books for their use of letter sounds or word families. Phonics instruction in this approach may also be systematic and explicit; however, teachers often include phonics instruction after sight words and in the form of invented spelling.

Two of the most comprehensive and well-known sight word lists are by Dolch (1936) and Fry (1957). During the 1930s and 40s, Dr. Edward Dolch created a list of high-frequency words that were used in children's literature during his time. These words remain high-frequency words today. Fry sight words, named after Dr. Edward Fry, were developed in the 1950s, updated in the 1980s, and extended the Dolch sight word lists. They include the 1000 most common sight words found in grades 3 through 9. Common sight words, including Dolch's sight words and Fry's sight words, can be found at www.Sightwords.com. *Sight words* are words that typically cannot be sounded out using phonics rules that teachers have students commit to memory using various strategies, such as flash cards, multisensory approaches, picture-supported methods, computer-based learning methods, and constant rehearsal (Phillips & Feng, 2012). Sight words can be challenging for students with disabilities to commit to memory (Barbetta et al., 1994; Erbey et al., 2017; Kaufman et al., 2011). Teachers need to ensure the strategies they adopt to teach sight words are evidence based and responsive to the individual needs of the student. Some strategies are more effective for some populations of students than others. Knowing the varied approaches (e.g., flash cards, multisensory approaches, picture-supported methods, computer-based learning methods, and constant rehearsal) and providing opportunities for students to practice are critical.

In contrast to the part-to-whole approach to reading instruction, teachers who subscribe to the whole-part-whole approach use stories, books, and texts in lieu of commercially packaged phonics programs (e.g., Letterland [Letterland USA], Lindamood Phoneme Sequencing [Lindamood-Bell], Orton-Gillingham [Orton-Gillingham Academy], Saxon Phonics [Houghton Mifflin Harcourt], and Wilson Reading System [Wilson Language Training]), resources, and worksheets (DeVries, 2011). The whole-part-whole approach to reading instruction is founded on the belief that learning to read is a natural process. Students naturally acquire reading skills as teachers expose them to language and reading skills through meaningful text and authentic reading experiences (Paul & Elder, 2007; Wren, 2001). This approach emphasizes comprehension and appreciation over precision (Wren, 2001).

Comprehensive Approach

For decades, the two instructional reading approaches described earlier dominated the best practice discussion: the bottom-up approach (i.e., the part-to-whole approach) and the top-down approach (i.e., the whole-part-whole approach). The bottom-up approach, which emphasizes phonics instruction, appeals to teachers who believe in the precision of language. Similarly, the top-down approach appeals to teachers who believe students learn best through authentic reading tasks. As the pendulum continues to swing, a new approach to reading instruction has emerged. Experts refer to this approach as the *comprehensive approach* or the *balanced approach*. The comprehensive approach recognizes the benefits of each approach and merges them in an effort to provide a comprehensive approach to reading instruction.

At the turn of the century, Whitehurst and Lonigan (1998, 2003) proposed that children gain literacy knowledge by using two interdependent domains: the outside-in and inside-out domains. For Whitehurst and Lonigan (2003), the outside-in domain represents sources from outside the printed word that support the child's understanding of the print. These outside sources can include vocabulary, background knowledge, and story schemas. The inside-out domain represents sources from the inside that allow the child to make meaning of the print such as the ability to understand the relationship between phonemes and graphemes, including letter knowledge, principles of print, and phonological processing. The researchers argued that "outside-in and inside-out sources of information are both essential to successful reading and are used simultaneously in readers who are reading well" (Whitehurst & Lonigan, 2003, p. 14).

The outside-in and inside-out domains mirror a comprehensive approach to reading instruction that recognizes the strengths of each of the part-to-whole and the whole-part-whole models. The comprehensive approach balances reading instruction through literature-based methods and teaching the mechanics of written language. However, there is no recipe for the perfect balance or an agreement on how much of each approach to incorporate. In a comprehensive or balanced approach, the classroom teacher negotiates the balance and is able to determine how much of each is necessary in response to the individual needs of the students (Nichols, 2009). Some students, including those with disabilities, may benefit from a more prescribed and systematic approach to literacy instruction but should be provided with authentic, embedded approaches to instruction as well.

A COLLABORATIVE APPROACH TO ENHANCING READING OUTCOMES

A collaborative approach to reading instruction can enhance reading outcomes for students, especially students with disabilities. Collaboration with families, educational professionals, and related service personnel not only improves outcomes for students but also (a) increases knowledge and skills for personnel (Schilder et al., 2019), (b) informs and improves programming for students, (c) increases access to related services, and (d) builds relationships with parents. The DEC Recommended Practices emphasize the need for collaboration, and collaboration is supported in federal policies (U.S. Department of Education and U.S. Department of Health and Human Services, 2017).

A child's initial experiences with oral language and printed text are in the home. Parents and families significantly contribute to their child's reading achievement (Sénéchal, 2006). These contributions have positive effects on a child's vocabulary and comprehension in the later years. A longitudinal study focused on parent involvement in literacy experiences found parents who read frequently to their children directly impacted their child's alphabet knowledge and predicted vocabulary in kindergarten. Furthermore, reading to children frequently directly influenced the child's reading fluency abilities and indirectly impacted their child's reading comprehension in fourth grade (Sénéchal, 2006). Moreover, the study indicated that parent reading also influenced spelling and reading for pleasure. Parental influence has been replicated in other studies (e.g., Sénéchal & LeFevre, 2002), and there is a vast amount of literature that supports collaboration with families to improve reading outcomes. Collaborating with families includes teachers providing information on age-appropriate texts, sharing with families resources for building home libraries, and including families in reading progress. This is especially critical for children with disabilities because families may benefit from knowing how to connect home experiences with instructional needs. Oftentimes, parents do not know what strategies or skills to work on at home that would supplement classroom instruction.

The literature also supports the collaboration of classroom teachers with related service personnel to improve reading outcomes. For example, classroom teachers and speech-language pathologists can work collaboratively to address the needs of a student. This relationship can serve as a resource for the classroom teacher. Speech-language pathologists are highly skilled in language acquisition and components of language including phonology, morphology, and the impact on comprehension. Coupling the expertise of the classroom teacher with the expertise of the speech-language pathologist can lead to improved outcomes for the student, especially a student who may be struggling with language or exhibiting early signs of language disorders.

Collaboration has several benefits for classroom teachers who often feel solely responsible for the academic development of a student. Outcomes for children are more effectively addressed by a team rather than through the efforts of one singular person, and this allows for the development of the whole child. Collaboration can encourage problem-solving and is enhanced when multiple perspectives from various experts are included in the conversation. This level of collaboration allows teachers to build their own capacity to address a wide range of needs as students develop their reading skills.

Summary

Theoretical frameworks guide our understanding of the development of reading skills and have evolved over time as our understanding of child development is enhanced with research and learning. We know emergent reading is complex and begins at birth with oral language acquisition. As children develop, they directly and indirectly engage in emergent reading tasks that lay the foundation for their continued growth. Their experiences with print at the early stages in life can have lasting impacts. These impacts are realized as children enter formal education settings with diverse learning experiences, differences in vocabulary and background knowledge, and varied reading abilities.

The meta-analysis conducted by the NRP defined the five components of reading (phonemic awareness, phonics, fluency, vocabulary, and reading comprehension) and has served as a foundational guide for teaching reading since its release in 2000. Although the NRP's report provides a comprehensive understanding and approach to reading development, the debate continues about the most effective way to teach reading. Whether you subscribe to the part-to-whole, whole-part-whole, or comprehensive model for reading instruction, it is clear that teachers can enhance reading instruction through deliberately including evidence-based components in their instruction such as print-rich environments, building background knowledge, and selecting the appropriate text for children. Additionally, reading instruction requires collaboration between teachers, families, and professionals. This collaborative approach has lasting impacts for children's reading abilities.

CHAPTER REVIEW

1. Given the theoretical frameworks for developing reading skills discussed in this chapter, explain how they would impact your approach to reading instruction.

2. List and define the five components of reading as defined by the NRP.

3. What are some ways you can incorporate literacy components and instruction that contribute to literacy knowledge in your classroom?

4. Most classroom teachers identify with one of the three reading models guiding reading instruction presented in this chapter. Which of the three reading models most closely aligns with your philosophy? Explain why you identify with this approach and how it would impact your teaching.

5. What is the collaborative approach to reading instruction, and how can it enhance reading outcomes for children?

6. Which of the following is not a component of reading as defined by the NRP?
   a. Fluency
   b. Decoding
   c. Phonics
   d. Comprehension

7. The belief that engaging in pre-reading skills could allow children to develop literacy skills but their ability would be hindered if they lacked appropriate experiences was held by:
   a. Maturationists
   b. Constructivists
   c. Behaviorists
   d. Developmentalists

8. HLPs include which of the following domains?
   a. Assessment, collaboration, instruction, social/emotional/behavioral learning
   b. Assessment, content, collaboration, instruction
   c. Content, collaboration, social/emotional/behavioral learning, ethics
   d. Ethics, instruction, assessment, collaboration

9. Teachers can foster print-rich environments by considering the:
   a. Literary resources
   b. Psychosocial environment
   c. Physical environment
   d. All of the above

RESOURCES

- Fluency: http://teacher.scholastic.com/resources/fluency/index.html
- Phonemic awareness: https://www.readingrockets.org/article/top-10-resources-phonological-and-phonemic-awareness
- Phonics: https://www.readinga-z.com/phonics/
- Reading comprehension: https://resilienteducator.com/classroom-resources/ten-free-reading-comprehension-exercises-online/
- Vocabulary: https://www.teachthought.com/literacy/21-digital-tools-build-vocabulary/

REFERENCES

Algozzine, B., Marr, M. B., Kavel, R. L., & Dugan, K. K. (2009). Using peer coaches to build oral reading fluency. *Journal of Education for Students Placed at Risk, 14*, 256-270.

Armbruster, B. B., & Osborn, J. (2003). *Put reading first: the research building blocks for teaching children to read* (2nd ed.). U.S. Department of Education, Center for the Improvement of Early Reading, National Institute for Literacy.

Ashby, J., Dix, H., Bontrager, M., Dey, R., & Archer, A. (2013). Phonemic awareness contributes to text reading fluency: Evidence from eye movements. *School Psychology Review, 42*(2), 157.

Barbetta, P. M., Heward, W. L., Bradley, D. M., & Miller, A. D. (1994). Effects of immediate and delayed error correction on the acquisition and maintenance of sight words by students with developmental disabilities. *Journal of Applied Behavior Analysis, 27*(1), 177-178.

Bloom, B. (1964). *Stability and change in human characteristics.* Wiley.

Bruner, J. (1960). *The process of education.* Harvard University Press.

Bruner, J. (1966). *Toward a theory of instruction.* Harvard University Press.

Burgess, S. R., & Lonigan, C. J. (1998). Bidirectional relations of phonological sensitivity and prereading abilities: Evidence from a preschool sample. *Journal of Experimental Child Psychology, 70*(2), 117-141.

Chall, J. S. (1967). *Learning to read: The great debate.* McGraw-Hill.

Chen, J. J., & de Groot Kim, S. (2014). The quality of teachers' interactive conversations with preschool children from low-income families during small-group and large-group activities. *Early Years, 34*(3), 271-288.

Copeland, S. R., Keefe, E. B., Calhoon, A. J., Tanner, W., & Park, S. (2011). Preparing teachers to provide literacy instruction to all students: Faculty experiences and perceptions. *Research and Practice for Persons with Severe Disabilities, 36*(3-4), 126-141.

Coyne, M. D., McCoach, D. B., & Kapp, S. (2007). Vocabulary intervention for kindergarten students: Comparing extended instruction to embedded instruction and incidental exposure. *Learning Disability Quarterly, 30*(2), 74-88.

Crawford, P. A. (1995). Early literacy: Emerging perspectives. *Journal of Research in Childhood Education, 10*(1), 71-86.

Dehaene, S., Cohen, L., Morais, J., & Kolinsky, R. (2015). Illiterate to literate: Behavioural and cerebral changes induced by reading acquisition. *Nature Reviews Neuroscience, 16*(4), 234-244.

DeVries, B. (2011). *Literacy assessment and intervention for classroom teachers.* Taylor & Francis.

Division for Early Childhood. (2014). *DEC Recommended Practices in early intervention/early childhood special education.* https://d4ab05f7-6074-4ec9-998a-232c5d918236.filesusr.com/ugd/95f212_12c3bc4467b5415aa2e76e9fded1ab30.pdf

Dolch, E. W. (1936). A basic sight vocabulary. *The Elementary School Journal, 36*(6), 456-460.

Durkin, D. (1966). The achievement of pre-school readers: Two longitudinal studies. *Reading Research Quarterly, 1*(4), 5-36.

Ehri, L. C., Nunes, S. R., Stahl, S. A., & Willows, D. M. (2001). Systematic phonics instruction helps students learn to read: Evidence from the National Reading Panel's meta-analysis. *Review of Educational Research, 71*(3), 393-447.

Engen, L., & Høien, T. (2002). Phonological skills and reading comprehension. *Reading and Writing, 15*(7-8), 613-631.

Erbey, R., McLaughlin, T. F., Derby, K. M., & Everson, M. (2017). The effects of using flashcards with reading racetrack to teach letter sounds, sight words, and math facts to elementary students with learning disabilities. *International Electronic Journal of Elementary Education, 3*(3), 213-226.

Fry, E. (1957). Developing a word list for remedial reading. *Elementary English, 34*(7), 456-458.

Gibson, S. A., & Moss, B. (2016). *Every young child a reader: Using Marie Clay's key concepts for classroom instruction.* Teachers College Press.

Gillett, J. W., & Temple, C. (1986). *Understanding reading problems* (2nd ed.). Little, Brown and Company.

Guo, Y., Justice, L. M., Kaderavek, J. N., & McGinty, A. (2012). The literacy environment of preschool classrooms: Contributions to children's emergent literacy growth. *Journal of Research in Reading, 35*(3), 308-327.

Hall, T., & Strangman, N. (2002). *Graphic organizers* (pp. 1-8). National Center on Accessing the General Curriculum.

Hart, B., & Risley, T. R. (2003). The early catastrophe: The 30 million word gap by age 3. *American Educator, 27*(1), 4-9.

Hattan, C., & Dinsmore, D. L. (2019). Examining elementary students' purposeful and ancillary prior knowledge activation when reading level texts. *Reading Horizons: A Journal of Literacy and Language Arts, 58*(2), 3.

Hiebert, E. H. (2016). *Multi-level text sets: Leveling the playing field or sidelining struggling readers?* https://franklyfreddy.withknown.com/2016/multi-level-text-sets-leveling-the-playing-field-or-sidelining-struggling

Hiebert, E. H. (2018). *Text complexity systems: A teacher's toolkit.* Text Matters. https://textproject.org/wp-content/uploads/text-matters/tm-5-1-text-complexity-systems/Hiebert-TM-Text-Complexity-Systems.pdf

International Literacy Association. (2018). Explaining phonics instruction: An educator's guide. Literacy Leadership Brief.

Juel, C., & Deffes, R. (2004). Making words stick. *Educational Leadership, 61*(6), 30.

K12 Reader. (2016). *What is phonics?* http://www.k12reader.com/what-is-phonics/

Kaufman, L., McLaughlin, T. F., Derby, K. M., & Waco, T. (2011). Employing Reading Racetracks and DI flashcards with and without cover, copy, and compare and rewards to teach of sight words to three students with learning disabilities in reading. *Educational Research Quarterly, 34*(4), 27-50.

Kim, A. H., Vaughn, S., Wanzek, J., & Wei, S. (2004). Graphic organizers and their effects on the reading comprehension of students with LD: A synthesis of research. *Journal of Learning Disabilities, 37*(2), 105-118.

Lee, C. D., & Smagorinsky, P. (2000). *Vygotskian perspectives on literacy research: Constructing meaning through collaborative inquiry.* Cambridge Press.

Loftus-Rattan, S. M., Mitchell, A. M., & Coyne, M. D. (2016). Direct vocabulary instruction in preschool: A comparison of extended instruction, embedded instruction, and incidental exposure. *The Elementary School Journal, 116*(3), 391-410.

Makin, L. (2003). Creating positive literacy learning environments in early childhood. In N. Hall, J. Larson, & J. Marsh (Eds.), *Handbook of early childhood literacy* (pp. 327-337). Sage.

McLeskey, J., & Brownell, M. (2015). *High-leverage practices and teacher preparation in special education* (Document No. PR-1). University of Florida, Collaboration for Effective Educator, Development, Accountability, and Reform Center. http://ceedar.education.ufl.edu/wp-content/uploads/2016/05/High-Leverage-Practices-and-Teacher-Preparation-in-Special-Education.pdf

National Reading Panel. (2000). *Teaching children to read: An evidence-based assessment of the scientific research literature on reading and its implications for reading instruction; Reports of the subgroups.* https://www.nichd.nih.gov/sites/default/files/publications/pubs/nrp/Documents/report.pdf

Neuman, S. B. (2004). The effect of print-rich classroom environments on early literacy growth. *The Reading Teacher, 58*(1), 89.

Neuman, S. B., Kaefer, T., & Pinkham, A. (2014). Building background knowledge. *The Reading Teacher, 68*(2), 145-148.

Nichols, J. B. (2009). Pendulum swing in reading instruction. *InSight: Rivier Academic Journal, 5*(1), 1-6.

Paige, D., Magpuri-Lavell, T., Rasinski, T., & Rupley, W. (2015). Fluency differences by text genre in proficient and struggling secondary students. *Advances in Literary Study, 3*(4), 102.

Palincsar, A. S., & Brown, A. L. (1986). *Interactive teaching to promote independent learning from text.* The Reading Teacher, 39(8), 771-777.

Paul, R., & Elder, L. (2007). *A critical thinker's guide to educational fads: For parents, educators, and concerned citizens: How to get beyond educational glitz and glitter.* The Foundation for Critical Thinking.

Penno, J. F., Wilkinson, I. A., & Moore, D. W. (2002). Vocabulary acquisition from teacher explanation and repeated listening to stories: Do they overcome the Matthew effect? *Journal of Educational Psychology, 94*(1), 23.

Phillips, W. E., & Feng, J. (2012, October). *Methods for sight word recognition in kindergarten: Traditional flashcard method vs. multisensory approach.* Paper presented at the 2012 Annual Conference of Georgia Educational Research Association, Savannah, GA.

Quinn, E. D., Kaiser, A. P., & Ledford, J. R. (2020). Teaching preschoolers with Down syndrome using augmentative and alternative communication modeling during small group dialogic reading. *American Journal of Speech-language Pathology, 29*(1), 80-100.

RAND Reading Study Group. (2002). *Reading for understanding: Toward an R&D program in reading comprehension.* RAND.

Rasinski, T. V. (1999). Exploring a method for estimating independent, instructional, and frustration reading rates. *Reading Psychology, 20*(1), 61-69.

Rasinski, T. V. (2003). *The fluent reader: Oral reading strategies for building word recognition, fluency, and comprehension.* Scholastic Inc.

Rasinski, T. V., Rupley, W. H., Paige, D. D., & Nichols, W. D. (2016). Alternative text types to improve reading fluency for competent to struggling readers. *International Journal of Instruction, 9*(1), 163-178.

Reading Rockets. (2015). *Phonemic awareness.* http://www.readingrockets.org/reading-topics/phonemic-awareness

Rupley, W. H., Blair, T. R., & Nichols, W. D. (2009). Effective reading instruction for struggling readers: The role of direct/explicit teaching. *Reading & Writing Quarterly, 25*(2-3), 125-138.

Sadoski, M., & Paivio, A. (2013). *Imagery and text: A dual coding theory of reading and writing* (2nd ed.). Routledge.

Santaro, L. E., Chard, D. J., Howard, L., & Baker, S. K. (2008). Making the very most of classroom read-alouds to promote comprehension and vocabulary. *The Reading Teacher, 61*(5), 396-408.

Saracho, O. N. (2017). Literacy and language: New developments in research, theory, and practice. *Early Childhood Development and Care, 187*(3-4), 299-304.

Saygin, Z. M., Norton, E. S., Osher, D. E., Beach, S. D., Cyr, A. B., Ozernov-Palchik, O. Yendiki, A., Fischl, B. Gaab, N., & Gabrieli, J. D. E. (2013). Tracking the roots of reading ability: White matter volume and integrity correlate with phonological awareness in prereading and early-reading kindergarten children. *The Journal of Neuroscience, 33*(33), 13251-13258.

Schilder, D., Curenton, S. M., & Broadstone, M. (2019). Introduction to the special issue on early care and education collaboration. *Early Education and Development, 30*(8), 971-974.

Schmitt, N., Schmitt, D., & Clapham, C. (2001). Developing and exploring the behavior of two new versions of the vocabulary levels test. *Language Testing, 18*(1), 55-88.

Sénéchal, M. (2006). Testing the home literacy model: Parent involvement in kindergarten is differentially related to grade 4 reading comprehension, fluency, spelling, and reading for pleasure. *Scientific Studies of Reading, 10*(1), 59-87.

Sénéchal, M., & LeFevre, J. (2002). Parental involvement in the development of children's reading skill: A 5-year longitudinal study. *Child Development, 73,* 445-460.

Shanahan, T. (2006a). *The national reading report: Practical advice for teachers.* Learning Point Associates.

Shanahan, T. (2006b). Developing fluency in the context of effective literacy instruction. In T. Rasinski, C. Blachowicz, & K. Lems (Eds.), *Fluency instruction: Research-based best Practices* (pp. 21-38). Guildford.

Spivey, N. N. (1989). *Construing constructivism: Reading research in the United States.* Occasional Paper No. 12. Center for the Study of Writing.

U.S. Department of Education Institute of Education Sciences, What Works Clearinghouse. (2010). *Dialogic reading. What Works Clearinghouse intervention report.* ERIC database (ED509373). https://eric.ed.gov/?id=ED509373

U.S. Department of Education and U.S. Department of Health and Human Services. (2017). *PDG progress update.* U.S. Department of Education.

van den Broek, P., & Helder, A. (2017). Cognitive processes in discourse comprehension: Passive processes, reader-initiated processes, and evolving mental representations. *Discourse Processes, 54*(5-6), 360-372.

Vygotsky, L. (1978). Interaction between learning and development. *Readings on the Development of Children, 23*(3), 34-41.

Vygotsky, L. (1987). Zone of proximal development. In M. Cole, V. John-Steiner, S. Scribner, & E. Souberman (Eds.), *Mind in society: The development of higher psychological processes.* Harvard University Press.

Wagner, R. K., Torgesen, J. K., Laughon, P., Simmons, K., & Rashotte, C. A. (1993). Development of young readers' phonological processing abilities. *Journal of Educational Psychology, 85*(1), 83.

Whitehurst, G. J., & Lonigan, C. J. (1998). Child development and emergent literacy. *Child Development, 68,* 848-872.

Whitehurst, G. J., & Lonigan, C. J. (2003). Emergent literacy: Development from prereaders to readers. In S. B. Neuman & D. K. Dickinson (Eds.), *Handbook of early literacy research.* The Guilford Press.

Wren, S. (2001). *What does a balanced literacy approach mean?: Topics in early reading coherence.* Southwest Educational Development Laboratory.

Emergent Writing in the Early Childhood Years

Marisa Macy, PhD and Dena D. Slanda, PhD

INTRODUCTION

Writing is a skill that develops in early childhood (Byington & Kim, 2017; Dennis & Votteler, 2013; Fox & Saracho, 1990). As with other preacademic areas, such as reading, emergent writing skill development does not happen overnight. Writing skills develop slowly and over time. Writing involves other domains, such as fine motor and cognitive development. Professionals must identify instructional targets (Bagnato et al., 2011), especially for emergent writing instruction. The Division for Early Childhood (DEC) of the Council for Exceptional Children contains 13 recommended instruction practices. The DEC (2014) recommended "Practitioners use systematic instructional strategies with fidelity to teach skills and to promote child engagement and learning." High-impact practices for creating opportunities for young children to develop their writing skills with families are a priority. This chapter examines high-impact practices designed to address young children's emergent writing with and without disabilities (DEC Recommended Practice INS6). The objectives of this chapter are to (a) describe positions on teaching writing in the early years, (b) identify theoretical perspectives related to emergent writing, (c) discuss characteristics of emergent writing, and (d) show how to use a linked system approach for supporting early writing development in young children.

Fisher, K. M., & Zimmer, K. E. (Eds.).
Early Childhood Special Education Programs and Practices (pp. 161-178).

CHAPTER OBJECTIVES

➜ Select evidence-based teaching strategies and interventions that align with both the Division for Early Childhood Recommended Practices and the Council for Exceptional Children's high-leverage practices.

➜ Comprehend various positions on teaching writing in the early years to include National Association for the Education of Young Children standards and the Division for Early Childhood Recommended Practices.

➜ Identify theoretical frameworks for emergent writing to include (a) Vygotsky's zone of proximal development and scaffolding, (b) behavioral learning, and (c) the ecological systems theory.

➜ Identify the characteristics of emergent writing.

➜ Synthesize a conceptual model called the *linked system* for emergent writing.

KEY TERMS

- **Activity-Based Intervention:** A research-based instructional practice often used in early childhood with children who have disabilities, are at risk for developing a disability, or have typical development.
- **Assessment:** The initial and ongoing process of gathering information to make decisions.
- **Criterion-Referenced Tool:** Criteria or standards are explained for assessors to rate behavior/skills.
- **Curriculum-Based Assessment:** Creates linkages between program components in which assessment and curriculum are aligned.
- **Developmentally Appropriate Practice:** A set of guiding principles for early childhood curriculum, instruction, and assessment.
- **Linked System:** A systemic approach in which linkages are created across assessment, goals, curriculum and instruction, and evaluation.
- **Norm-Referenced Assessment:** Provides information about a child's developmental status compared with that of their peers.
- **Public Law 99-457:** Public law passed by the 99th Congress; Individuals with Disabilities Education Act amendment in 1986 to the Education of the Handicapped Act that created special education for infants, toddlers, and their families.
- **Screening Assessment:** The process of gathering information to identify children for whom there might be concerns about development.
- **Theory:** Informs our understanding of how children develop.

"Writing is the painting of the voice."
—Voltaire

Writing is a skill that develops in early childhood. As with other preacademic areas, such as reading, emergent writing skill development does not happen overnight. Writing skills develop slowly and over time. John Locke promoted the idea that children are born into this world as a blank slate or *tabula rasa*. The environment and upbringing were entirely influential. Theoretical underpinnings can help put emergent writing in a framework for application (Puranik & Lonigan, 2014).

A theory is "an organized set of proposals about how things operate. It is an attempt to summarize current observations in light of past observations and to predict future ones" (Sroufe et al.,1992,

p. 14). In Chapter 1, an overview of various theories was presented. This chapter returns to that topic and sheds light on how theoretical perspectives are used to inform emergent writing curriculum, instruction, and assessment. In this chapter, we focus on three theories that will help inform our understanding of how children develop in the context of writing.

The child and social environment serve as a foundation for development. In the 1960s, it was a commonly held belief that child development occurred in a unidirectional pattern. During his time, R.Q. Bell (1968) extended the idea that development occurs in a bidirectional way. There is a back and forth that takes place between a baby and their social environment. When a familiar caregiver smiles at a 3-month-old baby, the baby may smile back. The dance that takes place between a child and the caregiver impacts a child's development. Sameroff and Chandler (1975) showed that a transactional model plays a role in the child's social environment, affecting growth and learning. Differentiated stages lead to progressively more complex behavior (Sameroff & Chandler, 1975).

The ecological systems theory (Bronfenbrenner, 1977, 1979, 1986; Bronfenbrenner & Ceci, 1994) considers the many environmental factors that influence a child's development. Urie Bronfenbrenner was a professor at Cornell who noticed the complex interconnections at play with children and their social and contextual environment. Bronfenbrenner's ecological systems theory pushed the envelope even further to show the inter-relatedness of contextual factors that directly or indirectly impact child development. It was groundbreaking because it was the first theory to model early childhood development not as linear (cause-effect process) but rather as the confluence of many different layers of environmental factors (Bronfenbrenner, 1977, 1979). The systems are (a) micro, immediate settings of development; (b) meso, relationships between micro; (c) exo, settings that impact development, but the child does not play a direct role; (d) macro, general organization of the world; and (e) the chronosystem, changes taking place over time. In applying the ecological systems theory, a child develops their writing skills at home with family and at school (microsystem). The sphere of influence expands beyond parent/child to the broader neighborhood community systems. Education laws and taxes to support schools and other influences can indirectly play a part in the child's emergent writing skills development (macrosystem).

The social learning theory (Bandura, 1977, 1985, 1986) is a helpful way to become aware of the roles of familiar adults and peers in a child's development of critical skills. A child may learn how to write from the way the teacher models writing abilities. Writing skills might also be a product of the child learning from peers. For example, a child might be motivated to write their name from watching their friend write "Susan" on the front of an envelope.

Another theorist presented two concepts that we use today to understand emergent writing. The first concept Vygotsky introduced was the zone of proximal development. Lev Vygotsky, a Russian psychologist, believed that children learn through social interactions with others. Vygotsky noted that when children are in the "zone," they are ready to learn. For example, if a teacher were to teach 4-year-old children how to tell time on a clockface, it would probably be labor intensive and tedious for the children. However, if the teacher were to wait until the children were 8 years old, the children would probably be more responsive and learn the content more quickly and easily. When a child is learning to write, understanding where they are developmentally can help identify the zone where learning can best occur (Vygotsky, 1978). To apply the zone of proximal development, adults can embed emergent writing learning opportunities that are neither too hard nor too easy for the child. Learning occurs when the child is functioning in their zone of development.

Scaffolding is the second concept introduced by Vygotsky that is often used in teaching (Quinn et al., 2016; Vygotsky, 1978). To scaffold emergent writing development, the teacher provides learning opportunities that support the child (Quinn et al., 2016). The goal is to fade the adult-directed level of support so the child increases their independence with the skill. Just like a window washer has a scaffold to suspend from the side of a building, the teacher scaffolds instruction for the child.

The previous chapter focused on early literacy, and emergent writing is related to early literacy. Skills in early literacy can predict emergent writing development (Gerde et al., 2012). The current chapter defines what emergent writing is, ways to assess emergent writing, ways to promote emergent writing, and steps to take if a child is struggling with writing.

WHAT IS EMERGENT WRITING?

Emergent writing is when a young child begins to develop the early mechanics of writing (Byington & Kim, 2017). The child becomes aware that they can use a writing utensil to make a mark. Motivation and curiosity stimulate emergent writing (Neumann et al., 2013; Rowe & Neitzel, 2010). Children begin to express themselves in new ways when their writing development emerges. Emergent writing development is essential because it can predict later success in reading (Cabell et al., 2013; National Research Council, 1998). Early writing can also foretell success in language development (Copp et al., 2016).

The development of interest and writing ability is unique for each child (Faugno, 2019). Children develop at their own rate. The mechanics of writing have roots in children's drawings. Parents and professionals observe writing development's emergence with the child holding a writing tool using a three-finger grasp to write or draw. They use the writing utensil to scribble. The child writes using "scribble writing." Drawing and graphic representations are the first building blocks for writing (Wu, 2009). The child writes or draws using straight lines, curved lines, and mixed strokes.

Phonetic writing starts when children use letters from their own name (Both-de Vries & Bus, 2008; Cabell et al., 2009; Drouin & Harmon, 2009). The child copies letters of their first name, and, eventually, they can replicate the letters that make up their full first name (Puranik & Lonigan, 2012). The child writes using developmental spelling and ultimately uses conventional spelling to express themselves in writing (Cabell et al., 2009). Invented spelling is characteristic of young children's alphabetic principles (Ouellette & Sénéchal, 2017). Eventually, children begin to communicate ideas in writing (Dennis & Votteler, 2013; Fox & Saracho, 1990).

CASE STUDY

Adri's preschool teacher, Mr. Galliana, was concerned about her emergent writing development. He administered a curriculum-based assessment (CBA). After reviewing the results, he determined that two goals would be useful for Adri: (a) holding a writing utensil and (b) writing the letters in her name. Mr. Galliana implemented a 6-week intervention from the CBA. He then reassessed with the CBA 2 months later. He found that Adri made significant progress with the fine motor goal of holding a writing utensil, and she had achieved the goal. However, the second goal had not yet been achieved. He continued the intervention and writing curriculum for 6 more weeks. When he reassessed, Mr. Galliana found that Adri met the goal.

LINKED SYSTEM FOR EMERGENT WRITING

A *linked system* is a conceptual framework for aligning with programmatic goals, instruction/intervention, and evaluation (Bagnato et al., 2010; Bricker et al., 2015; Pretti-Frontczak, 2002). Curriculum and instruction are developed to help the child achieve their goals and objectives. Evaluation consists of monitoring the child's progress in meeting their goals (Macy & Hoyt-Gonzales, 2007). At the heart of the linked system is the program goals and philosophy. In early childhood settings, the philosophical approach drives all aspects of the system (Bricker et al., 2015). Program goals show the vision and mission for child development and learning. The linked system framework is shown in Figure 8-1.

Mr. Galliana used a linked system in his approach to support Adri's emergent writing skills. First, Mr. Galliana used an assessment that is aligned with the curriculum he uses in his program.

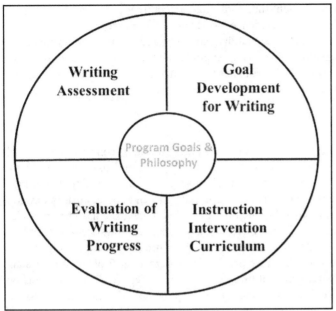

Figure 8-1. A linked system for emergent writing.

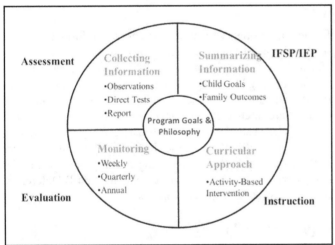

Figure 8-2. Examples of linked system activities for emergent writing.

Second, writing goals were developed for Adri based on the assessment results and tied to interventions and curriculum (Bricker et al., 2015; Macy & Hoyt-Gonzales, 2007; Pretti-Frontczak, 2002). Lastly, Mr. Galliana monitored Adri's progress toward meeting her writing goals when he evaluated her progress on a scheduled basis. He made data-based decisions each step of the way using the linked system, as shown in Figure 8-2.

WHAT ARE WAYS TO ASSESS EMERGENT WRITING?

As discussed in Chapter 4, *assessment* is the initial and ongoing process of gathering information for the purposes of making decisions. Authentic skills should be measured (i.e., real-life environment) and integrated across domains. Multiple measures over time are more accurate and reliable than one-shot assessments (Bagnato et al., 2010). Listen to children talk about their writing and make observations that lead to insights in their development (Roser et al., 2014).

Assessments can be formal; there are published tools that are commercially available (Bagnato et al., 2010). Formal assessments may also be evidence based and have undergone rigorous studies on the psychometric properties to determine their validity, reliability, and/or utility. Assessments can be informal and collections of information gained using unpublished tools and/or materials that are developed through professional expertise. Three types of assessments can be used to collect information about emergent writing: screening, norm-referenced assessment, and CBA.

Screening

Screening is a process used to identify children for whom there might be concerns about development. A screening process is not designed to diagnose a disability. The purpose of screening is to determine whether a child needs additional assessment. Children could be screened to determine if more evaluation is needed to support their emergent writing skills as well as other areas of development and learning. The functions of a screening method are to implement the use of norm-referenced, developmental screening measures. Screening assessment should be nondiscriminatory, have concurrent validity, and be implemented reliably. The following instruments are commonly used for the purposes of screening: (a) American Guidance Service Early Screening Profiles, (b) Ages and Stages Questionnaires, (c) Battelle Developmental Inventory Screening Test, (d) Brigance Preschool Screen and Early Preschool Screen, (e) Denver II, and (f) Developmental Indicators for Assessment of Learning-Revised. Examples of screening instruments are outlined in Table 8-1.

Norm-Referenced Assessment

As noted in Chapter 4, norm-referenced assessments are designed to provide information about a child's developmental status compared with that of their peers. The purposes of norm-referenced assessment are to determine the performance of a norm group. Children could be given a norm-referenced assessment to determine if they are eligible for special educational services in the area of writing as well as other areas of development and learning. Standardized scores are usually used to report outcomes. Norm-referenced tests are often used for screening and diagnostic purposes to separate children whose performance is not consistent with the normative group. The following instruments are commonly used for the purposes of norm-referenced assessment: (a) the Wechsler Preschool and Primary Scale of Intelligence-Revised, (b) the Learning Accomplishment Profile-Diagnostic Standardized Assessment, (c) Bayley Scales of Infant Development, and (d) Differential Ability Scales. Table 8-2 shows examples of norm-referenced assessments.

Curriculum-Based Measurement or Assessment

As noted in Chapter 4, CBA is a form of criterion-referenced measure that creates linkages between program components in which assessment and curriculum are aligned. Criterion-referenced tools are those that contain criteria or standards that are explained for assessors to rate behavior/skills. The purpose of CBA is to link assessment, intervention, and evaluation. The function of CBA is to provide an assessment of skills across developmental domains. Children could be given a CBA to determine where in the curriculum they could enter related to their emergent writing skills as well as other areas of development and learning. Value is added to the program evaluation due to the ongoing nature that is built into the CBA process. We can identify what the child has learned when using a CBA, evaluate the child's progress toward goals and objectives, and measure the impact of the intervention. The following instruments are commonly used for the purposes of CBA: (a) the Assessment, Evaluation, and Programming System for Infants and Children; (b) the Carolina Curriculum for Preschoolers with Special Needs; (c) HELP (Hawaii Early Learning Profile) Strands; and (d) the Transdisciplinary Play-Based Assessment. Examples of CBA are provided in Table 8-3.

We discussed three types of assessment that can be used to gather information about emergent writing. Writing assessment can overlap with multiple domains. For example, assessors can observe how young children use their fine motor skills to operate writing utensils, which may include but are

TABLE 8-1. EXAMPLES OF SELECT SCREENING ASSESSMENTS

TYPE OF SCREENING ASSESSMENT	WITH WHOM IS IT USED?	WHEN IS IT USED?	HOW CAN IT BE USED WITH EMERGENT WRITING?
AGS Early Screening Profiles	Children ages 2 years to 6 years 11 months	It is used to help children who are at risk for developmental problems and/or school failure.	To assess a child's performance in the following domains: cognitive/language, motor, and self-help/social.
Ages & Stages Questionnaires	Children ages 1 to 66 months	It is used to help children who are at risk for developmental problems.	To assess a child's performance in the following five domains: communication, gross motor, fine motor, problem-solving, and personal social.
Battelle Developmental Inventory Screening Test	Children ages birth to 8 years	It is used to help children who are at risk for developmental problems, handicapping conditions, and/or school failure.	To assess a child's performance in the following domains: personal/social, adaptive, motor, communication, and cognition.
Brigance Early Childhood Screens III	Children ages birth to first grade	Three age-specific volumes are used to screen for delays and giftedness.	To screen a child's performance in the following domains: physical development, language development, academic skills/cognitive development, and self-help and social emotional skills.
Denver II	Children ages birth to 6 years	It is used to help children who are at risk for developmental problems, handicapping conditions, and/or school failure.	To assess a child's performance in the following domains: personal/social, fine motor/adaptive, language, and gross motor.
Developmental Indicators for Assessment of Learning-Revised	Children ages 2 years to 5 years 11 months	It is used to measure developmental problems in young children. It was designed to assess a child's performance on various age-appropriate tasks and compares it to the performance of same-age children.	To assess a child's performance in the following domains: motor, concepts, language, and social-emotional.

not limited to pencils, crayons, pens, electronic devices like keyboards, and pads. Another domain that can be observed to learn more about a child's writing is the cognitive domain. For example, assessors can observe how a child solves problems associated with the writing process. Executive functioning involves a person's ability to attend and focus on a task as well as planning ahead, which are skills necessary to the writing process.

TABLE 8-2. EXAMPLES OF SELECT NORM-REFERENCED ASSESSMENTS

TYPE OF NORM-REFERENCED ASSESSMENT	WITH WHOM IS IT USED?	WHEN IS IT USED?	HOW CAN IT BE USED WITH EMERGENT WRITING?
Wechsler Preschool and Primary Scale of Intelligence-Revised	Children ages 3 years to 7 years 3 months	It may be used to determine eligibility, to plan interventions, and/or to document progress.	To provide a full-scale intelligence quotient using two supporting scales of performance and verbal.
Stanford-Binet Intelligence Scale: Fourth Edition	Individuals ages 2 to 23 years	It may be used to determine eligibility, to plan interventions, and/or to document progress.	To assess a child's abilities in verbal reasoning, quantitative reasoning, abstract visual reasoning, and short-term memory.
The Learning Accomplishment Profile-Diagnostic Standardized Assessment	Children ages 30 months to 72 months	When educational decisions concerning placement and developmental profiles are needed.	To assess the following four domains: fine motor, cognitive, language, and gross motor.
Bayley Scales of Infant Development	Children ages 1 through 42 months	It may be used to determine eligibility, to plan interventions, and/or to document progress.	To give a comprehensive developmental assessment: mental, motor, and behavior.
Differential Ability Scale	Children ages 2 years 6 months to 17 years	It may be used to determine eligibility, to plan interventions, and/or to document progress.	To assess cognitive performance for preschool and school age children.

Young children should never be challenged during assessment by separation from their parents or familiar caregivers. Young children should never be challenged by a strange examiner. Formal tests or tools should not be the cornerstone of the assessment of a young child. The assessment information can be used in many ways. One way to use assessment information is to determine emergent writing goals for the child. Once goals have been identified, emergent writing curriculum and instruction follow.

WHAT ARE WAYS TO PROMOTE EMERGENT WRITING?

Emergent writing develops long before a child enters kindergarten (Gerde et al., 2012; Pelatti et al., 2014). One of the best ways to promote emergent writing is to link writing assessment with the curriculum and instruction. In the previous section, CBA was described. The strategy would involve assessing a child's writing development and then implementing a writing curriculum and instruction to support the child's learning and development of writing skills.

The CBA also could be used to monitor the child's progress and development in the area of writing. Take for example a writing skill from the widely used early childhood CBA called the *Assessment*,

TABLE 8-3. EXAMPLES OF SELECT CURRICULUM-BASED ASSESSMENTS

TYPE OF CURRICULUM-BASED ASSESSMENT	WITH WHOM IS IT USED?	WHEN IS IT USED?	HOW CAN IT BE USED WITH EMERGENT WRITING?
The Assessment, Evaluation, and Programming System for Infants and Children	Children ages birth to 6 years	It may be used to provide data for identifying and monitoring goals for the early childhood special education program. An accompanying volume provides a guide to developing intervention activities.	To assess a child's skills in adaptive, cognitive, fine motor, gross motor, social, social communication, early literacy (includes writing), and early math.
The Carolina Curriculum for Preschoolers with Special Needs	Children ages 24 to 60 months	It may be used to provide data for identifying and monitoring goals for the early intervention program.	To assess a child's skills in personal-social, cognition, communication, fine motor, and gross motor.
Hawaii Early Learning Profile (HELP) Strands	Children ages 3 to 6 years	It may be used to provide data for identifying and monitoring goals for the early intervention program. HELP at Home and HELP Activity Guide are available to be used with the strands.	To assess a child's cognitive, language, gross motor, fine motor, social-emotional, and self-help.
The Transdisciplinary Play-Based Assessment	Children ages birth to 6 years	It may be used to provide data for identifying and monitoring goals for the early intervention program. The Transdisciplinary Play-Based Intervention provides curriculum guidelines. A play facilitator interacts with the child.	To assess a child's skills in sensorimotor, emotional and social, communication, and cognitive.

Evaluation, and Programming System for Infants and Children, Third Edition (Bricker et al., 2022) that contains the child skill "writes using developmental spelling." The assessor could perform an initial assessment of this writing skill to determine if the child meets the criterion. The criterion for this skill states "Child prints using recognizable letters or letter approximations that demonstrate understanding of alphabetic principle and represent recognizable phonetic letter–sound associations" (Bricker et al., 2022). Once the assessment is completed, we can determine if the skill is mastered, emerging, or a skill the child is not yet ready to do. Examples from the Assessment, Evaluation, and Programming System for Infants and Children, Third Edition show "After drawing picture of flowers, child writes 'flawrz.' Child draws balloons and writes 'parti' to describe birthday party" (Bricker et al., 2022).

If the child's performance indicates mastery, then we would not need to create goals, provide instruction, or use the curriculum for this writing skill. If the child's performance indicates they are not yet ready for this skill, then we also would not need to create goals, provide instruction, or use the curriculum for this writing skill. However, if it is an emerging skill, then we could create short- or long-term goal(s) to work on this skill with the child. The educator would then create instructional opportunities and use the curriculum from the CBA to address this writing skill with the child. A timeline could be established when instruction would occur. There would be a plan in place when the CBA would be used again to do a progress monitoring check where the follow-up assessment would show if the child has made adequate progress on the skill and whether other decisions should be made based on the data collected from the CBA.

Friedrich Froebel (1782-1852), the father of the kindergarten movement, pioneered early education curriculum in Germany. Froebel promoted value-based child development through structured play activities. Today many early childhood advocates continue to use play as a context for teaching and learning (Bingham et al., 2018). Creating a print-rich environment can help promote emergent reading and writing (Pool & Carter, 2011). The context for emergent writing should be considered. Gerde and colleagues (2015) conducted research on the Writing Resources and Interactions in Teaching Environments and found promise with this evidence-based measure to examine writing practices in early childhood classrooms in the following areas: writing environment, environmental print, teacher modeling writing, teacher scaffolding children's writing, and independent child writing. Environment, routines, and play promote early writing skill development (Zhang & Quinn, 2018). In addition to play, two types of high-impact practices (HIPs) that meet the Division for Early Childhood (DEC) standards in early childhood to promote emergent writing are developmentally appropriate practice (DAP) and activity-based intervention (ABI) (Table 8-4).

Mr. Galliana, a preschool teacher, has a preschool classroom to depict an environment conducive to emergent writing development and other developmental and preacademic skills. He uses DAP philosophy to consider how his class contains curriculum and instructional elements that are individually appropriate, age appropriate, and socially/culturally appropriate for all children. For example, he provides writing opportunities for children that reflect their individual interests, where they are at developmentally, and social and cultural aspects for each student.

Developmentally Appropriate Practice and Emergent Writing

Developmentally Appropriate Practice

The scenario presented earlier shows how a teacher uses DAP to promote emergent writing. The National Association of the Education of Young Children (NAEYC) is the largest professional organization in the United States that serves educators of young children. The NAEYC offers accreditation for early childhood programs that want to meet the high standards that are developed by the organization for young children and their families (Gerde et al., 2018). One of the NAEYC standards is the use of DAP.

DAPs are a set of guiding principles for curriculum, instruction, and assessment (Bredekamp, 1987, 1997; Bredekamp & Copple, 1997; Copple & Bredekamp, 2009). To best understand DAP, it is necessary to understand DAP's underlying theory of constructivism. Constructivism posits that a child should learn from their environment through self-directed play rather than from teacher-directed play. Jean Piaget, a Swiss psychologist, came on the scene in the early part of the 20th century with ideas about how children cognitively function and develop. As discussed in Chapter 1, Piaget

TABLE 8-4. ALIGNMENT OF EMERGENT WRITING INSTRUCTIONAL PRACTICES WITH RECOMMENDED PRACTICES AND HIGH-LEVERAGE PRACTICES (HLPs)

INSTRUCTIONAL PRACTICE	ALIGNED DEC RECOMMENDED PRACTICES	ALIGNED HLPs
Activity-based intervention	INS4: Practitioners plan for and provide the level of support, accommodations, and adaptations needed for the child to access, participate, and learn within and across activities and routines. INS7: Practitioners use explicit feedback and consequences to increase child engagement, play, and skills. INS10: Practitioners implement the frequency, intensity, and duration of instruction needed to address the child's phase and pace of learning or the level of support needed by the family to achieve the child's outcomes or goals. INT5: Practitioners promote the child's problem-solving behavior by observing, interpreting, and scaffolding in response to the child's growing level of autonomy and self-regulation.	HLP 6: Use student assessment data, analyze instructional practices, and make necessary adjustments that improve student outcomes. HLP 8: Provide positive and constructive feedback to guide students' learning and behavior. HLP 13: Adapt curriculum tasks and materials for specific learning goals. HLP 15: Provide scaffolded supports. HLP 18: Use strategies to promote active student engagement. HLP 21: Teach students to maintain and generalize new learning across time and settings. HLP 22: Provide positive and constructive feedback to guide students' learning and behavior.
Developmentally appropriate practice	INS1: Practitioners, with the family, identify each child's strengths, preferences, and interests to engage the child in active learning. INS2: Practitioners, with the family, identify skills to target for instruction that help a child become adaptive, competent, socially connected, and engaged and that promote learning in natural and inclusive environments.	HLP 12: Systematically design instruction toward a specific learning goal. HLP 13: Adapt curriculum tasks and materials for specific learning goals.

DEC = Division for Early Childhood.

Data sources: Division for Early Childhood. (2014). DEC recommended practices in early intervention/early childhood special education. 2014. http://www.dec-sped.org/recommendedpractices and McLeskey, J., et al. (2017). *High-leverage practices in special education.* Council for Exceptional Children & CEEDAR Center.

wrote about the importance of feedback from the environment on the child's development through four levels of cognitive development: sensorimotor, preoperational, concrete operational, and formal operational. Children need to be able to navigate, experience, negotiate, and explore many environments in order to develop cognitive competence. His research and theories became the basis for constructivism. The work of John Dewey expanded on the basis set by Piaget.

John Dewey, an American philosopher and educator, is commonly remembered for his progressive ideas about education. Dewey believed that learning should be relevant and practical to the lives of children. John Dewey emphasized the importance of education nourishing the normally occurring interactions of the child with their environment.

Piaget, Vygotsky, and Dewey established the constructivist ideals that provide the underlying educational theory of DAP. The child constructs their own knowledge and understanding. Constructivism looks at how children learn. When children interact with their environment, they are constructing their own meaningful learning opportunities.

Environment

In DAP classrooms, teachers structure the environment so that children may learn through active exploration and interaction with adults, other children, and materials (Hall et al., 2015). DAPs combine a primary emphasis on child-initiated activities, with a secondary emphasis on active involvement by the teacher. The structure of the physical environment promotes child engagement (Cavallaro et al., 1993). The activity areas are structured to be both flexible and inviting. Children are given access to a variety of materials. Typical materials include but are not limited to fabrics, books, games, sensory materials (e.g., water and sand), blocks, strings/ropes, pulleys, magnifiers, and art supplies. Because learning opportunities are child initiated, many activities are optional and rely on the child's level of interest for participation. Therefore, a child will be more motivated to engage in writing activities if they are interested and supported by the physical and social environment in making choices to write.

Individual, Age, and Social/Cultural Appropriateness

People teaching young children may ask whether emergent writing activities, interactions, and programs are individually appropriate, age appropriate, and socially/culturally appropriate for children. *Individual appropriateness* refers to adaptations being made for the wide range of differences between individual children (Carta, 1995). Young children are different and have unique abilities that vary from child to child. For example, some children are more verbal than others and may master language types of tasks quicker than others.

Age appropriateness means that the learning environment, teaching/interventions, and other elements of the program should be based on what is generally expected of children of various ages and stages (Carta, 1995). The age of the child helps inform expectations for activities that might be motivating for children and achievable (Bredekamp & Copple, 1997). Culture is defined by values, traditions, and beliefs that are shared and passed down from one generation to the next. In order to create programs that are meaningful and supportive, we need to look at children and families within the context of their community and culture (Kostelnik, 1992; Kostelnik et al., 2019).

Adri's preschool teacher, Mr. Galliana, uses ABI to identify functional and generalizable goals for her emergent writing development. He creates embedded learning opportunities in the area of writing throughout the school day to help her during routine and planned activities. Mr. Galliana incorporates a variety of child-centered and teacher-directed activities to create targeted writing interventions that will help Adri meet her goals. For example, Adri has a goal to hold a writing utensil using a three-fingered grasp. Mr. Galliana teaches her to use a tripod when holding a crayon or pencil as well as during other times of the day like mealtimes when self-feeding using a tripod to hold a spoon.

ACTIVITY-BASED INTERVENTION AND EMERGENT WRITING

Activity-Based Intervention

The scenario presented earlier shows how a teacher uses ABI to promote emergent writing. The DEC (2014) contains 13 Recommended Practices for instruction. The sixth and last DEC Recommended Practice states the following: "Practitioners use systematic instructional strategies with fidelity to teach skills and to promote child engagement and learning" (p. 8). Instructional targets are needed to support the development of critical skills in early childhood (Bagnato et al., 2011). An HIP that is aligned with DEC Recommended Practices is ABI (Johnson et al., 2015).

ABI is a research-based instructional practice (Macy, 2019). It is used with children who have atypical development and/or delays (Macy et al., 2006); it can also be used with children who have typical development (Pretti-Frontczak et al., 2003). Emergent writing activities are child directed and transactional. Teachers embed training of child's individual emergent writing goals and objectives in routine or planned activities. Emergent writing instruction can be embedded in content areas like science (Wheatley et al., 2016). The use of logically occurring antecedents and consequences reinforces writing skills. Functional and generalizable emergent writing skills are identified for helping young children develop their writing skills.

WHAT IF A CHILD STRUGGLES WITH EMERGENT WRITING?

Increasingly, children with special needs are participating in the general education and emergent curriculum (Mayer, 2007). To foster inclusion, early childhood teachers are taking on more responsibilities. Some of these legally mandated responsibilities include the development, implementation, and monitoring of Individualized Education Programs (IEPs; Edmiaston et al., 2000). To bridge the gap between early childhood education and early childhood special education, many professionals suggest taking the "best" or "recommended" practices of both and blending them to create educational harmony among the two fields. Our professional community should establish best practices of both (Odom, 1994). The Individuals with Disabilities Education Act described in earlier chapters states that education must be individualized to meet that child's special needs. In practice, this translates into an IEP or an Individualized Family Service Plan, which would be written for emergent writing skills as shown in the Case Study.

The NAEYC and the DEC within the Council for Exceptional Children have collaborated to better understand how developmentally appropriate practice can be individualized for children with disabilities (Carta, 1995; McLean & Odom, 1993). Although they understand that many children are successful in DAP classrooms, they believe that it is imperative for programs to be individualized for children with disabilities. Specialized adaptations, such as in the area of emergent writing, are often required for children with disabilities to be successful in an inclusive DAP classroom (Carta, 1995; Wolery & Bredekamp, 1994). Schools will benefit by training all personnel to work with children with disabilities. This includes training teachers, clerical staff who work in school offices, school nurses, related specialists, administrators, bus drivers, instructional assistants, volunteers, cafeteria workers, school psychologists, and school counselors to meet the needs of all the children who walk through the school doors, especially children with disabilities.

Emergent writing in the early school years is often challenging for children with delays/disabilities (Catts, 1993; Majsterek & Ellenwood, 1995). Children with special needs often do not receive the same types of experiences as their typically developing peers (Marvin, 1994). Investigations have reported that children with disabilities may, for example, receive less exposure to print and have fewer opportunities to interact with adults in literacy activities (Berninger et al., 1999; Koppenhaver et al., 1991; Marvin & Mirenda, 1993).

If a child struggles with emergent writing, there are at least three things to consider. First, intervene during critical developmental years from birth to 6 years old in order to prevent or ameliorate the effects of problems, preventing secondary problems from compounding. Second, provide support and guidance to caregivers/parents to enable them to facilitate their child's emergent writing development. Third, use a linked system to address developmental concerns (Bricker et al., 2015; Macy & Hoyt-Gonzales, 2007; Pretti-Frontczak, 2002).

Digital Learning

Because of COVID-19 and the implementation of digital learning, teachers could use the following resources for an online platform:

- Coffee Chats With Brookes (live and on-demand chats with education professionals and expert authors; https://brookespublishing.com/coffee-chats-brookes/) could be used by professionals to further understand recommended practices and HIPs related to emergent writing and other topics.

- Varsity Tutors (free live classes and camps for children; https://www.varsitytutors.com/) could be used by professionals and/or parents to develop children's emergent writing skills further using virtual and online resources.

- 4H could be used by professionals and/or parents to develop children's emergent writing skills further using virtual and online resources. There is no link associated with this resource because 4H is unique to every community. For example, the extension office of a land grant school (e.g., Penn State University) might be the place to find 4H services, whereas in another community it might be in another agency or office.

- Local public libraries could be used by professionals and/or parents to develop children's emergent writing skills further using virtual and online resources.

Summary

Increasingly, children with special needs in the area of writing are participating in the general education curriculum. To foster inclusion, early childhood teachers are taking on more responsibilities (Bricker, 1995). Some of these legally mandated responsibilities include the development, implementation, and monitoring of IEPs (Edmiaston et al, 2000). To bridge the gap between early childhood education and early childhood special education, many professionals suggest taking the "best" or "recommended" practices of both and blending them to create educational harmony among the two fields. Professional conferences, articles, and books reflect the concept of the "both/and" construct that Bredekamp refers to in the 1997 revision of the DAP. Thinking in early childhood practices is shifting from either/or to both/and. IEP goals and objectives can be embedded into a developmentally appropriate practice model. We can build a coalition by using a DAP framework to address each child's special needs in a mutually responsive and respectful manner.

Children will benefit when teams collaborate and blend the best practices (Gabas et al., 2019). The quote by Voltaire suggests that "Writing is the painting of the voice." When young children's writing skills emerge, they are learning to express themselves in a new way. Parents, professionals, and familiar adults can support children's emergent writing development in the early years that will prepare children for a lifetime of joy with the act of writing (National Center for Family Literacy, 2008).

CHAPTER REVIEW

1. Finish this sentence: Emergent writing is when . . .

2. A conceptual framework for a linked system for writing development may include all but:
   a. Events
   b. Assessment
   c. Goal development
   d. Intervention

3. This person is known for his work showing how many environmental factors influence a child's development:
   a. Friedrich Froebel
   b. Urie Bronfenbrenner
   c. Jean Piaget
   d. Bricker Galliana

4. DAPs are a set of guiding principles for everything EXCEPT:
   a. Holidays
   b. Curriculum
   c. Instruction
   d. Assessment

RESOURCES

- Coffee Chats With Brookes: https://brookespublishing.com/coffee-chats-brookes/
- Varsity Tutors: https://www.varsitytutors.com/

REFERENCES

Bagnato, S. J., McLean, M., Macy, M., & Neisworth, J. (2011). Identifying instructional targets for early childhood via authentic assessment: Alignment of professional standards and practice-based evidence. *Journal of Early Intervention, 33*(4), 243-253.

Bagnato, S. J., Neisworth, J. T., & Pretti-Frontczak, K. (2010). *LINKing authentic assessment and early childhood intervention: Best measures for best practice* (2nd ed.). Brookes.

Bandura, A. (1977). *Social learning theory.* Prentice Hall.

Bandura, A. (1985). A model of causality in social learning theory. In M. Mahoney & A. Freedman (Eds.), *Cognition and therapy.* Plenum Press.

Bandura, A. (1986). *Social foundations of thought and action: A social cognitive theory.* Prentice Hall.

Bell, R. Q. (1968). A reinterpretation of the direction of effects in studies of socialization. *Psychological Review, 75,* 81-91.

Berninger, V. W., Abbot, R. D., Zook, D., Ogier, S., Lemos-Britton, Z., & Brooksher, R. (1999). Early intervention for reading disabilities: Teaching the alphabet principle in a connectionist framework. *Journal of Learning Disabilities, 32*(6), 491-503.

Bingham, G. E., Quinn, M. F., McRoy, K., Zhang, X., & Gerde, H. K. (2018). Integrating writing into the early childhood curriculum: A frame for intentional and meaningful writing experiences. *Early Childhood Education Journal, 46*(6), 601-611.

Both-de Vries, A. C., & Bus, A. G. (2008). Name writing: A first step to phonetic writing? Does the name have a special role in understanding the symbolic function of writing? *Literacy Teaching and Learning, 12*(2), 37-55.

Bredekamp, S. (Ed.). (1987). *Developmentally appropriate practice in early childhood programs serving children from birth through age 8.* National Association of the Education of Young Children.

Bredekamp, S. (1997). NAEYC issues revised position statement on developmentally appropriate practice in early child-hood programs. *Young Children, 52*(2), 34-40.

Bredekamp, S., & Copple, C. (1997). *Developmentally appropriate practice in early childhood programs.* National Association of the Education of Young Children.

Bricker, D. (1995). The challenge of inclusion. *Journal of Early Intervention, 19*, 179-194.

Bricker, D., Dionne, C., Grisham, J., Johnson, J. J., Macy, M., Slentz, K., & Waddell, M. (2022). *Assessment, Evaluation, and Programming System for Infants and Children, Third Edition (AEPS®-3).* Brookes Publishing Co.

Bricker, D., Squires, J., Frantz, R., & Xie, H. (2015). A comprehensive and additive system for child-focused assessment and evaluation in EI/ECSE. *Journal of Intellectual Disability: Diagnosis and Treatment, 3*(4), 187-97.

Bronfenbrenner, U. (1977). Toward an experimental ecology of human development. *American Psychologist, 32*, 513-531.

Bronfenbrenner, U. (1979). *The ecology of human development: Experiments by nature and design.* Harvard University Press.

Bronfenbrenner, U. (1986). Ecology of the family as a context form human development: Research perspectives. *Developmental Psychology, 22*(6), 723-741.

Bronfenbrenner, U., & Ceci, S. J. (1994). Nature-nurture reconceptualized in developmental perspective: A bioecological model. *Psychological Review, 101*(4), 568-586.

Byington, T. A. & Kim, Y. (2017). Promoting preschoolers' emergent writing. *Young Children, 72*(5), 74-82.

Cabell, S .Q., Justice, L. M., Zucker, T. A. & McGinty, A. S. (2009). Emergent name-writing abilities of preschool-age children with language impairment. *Language, Speech, and Hearing Services in Schools, 40*(1), 53-66.

Cabell, S. Q., Tortorelli, L. S., & Gerde, H. K. (2013). How do I write..." Scaffolding preschooler's early writing skills. *The Reading Teacher, 66*(8), 65-659.

Carta, J. J. (1995). Developmentally appropriate practice: A critical analysis as applied to young children with disabilities. *Focus on Exceptional Children, 27*(8), 1-12.

Catts, H. W. (1993). The relationship between speech-language impairments and reading disabilities. *Journal of Speech and Hearing Research, 36*(5), 948-958.

Cavallaro, C. C., Haney, M., & Cabello, B. (1993). Developmentally appropriate strategies for promoting full participation in early childhood settings. *Topics in Early Childhood Special Education, 13*, 293-307.

Copp, S. B., Cabell, S. Q., & Tortorelli, L. S. (2016). See, say, write. *Reading Teacher, 69*(4), 447-451. https://doi.org/10.1002/trtr.1419

Copple, C., & Bredekamp, S. (2009). *Developmentally appropriate practice in early childhood program.* National Association of the Education of Young Children.

Dennis, L. R., & Votteler, N. K. (2013). Preschool teachers and children's emergent writing: Supporting diverse learners. *Early Childhood Education Journal, 41*(6), 439-446.

Division for Early Childhood. (2014). *DEC Recommended Practices in early intervention/early childhood special education.* http://www.dec-sped.org/recommendedpractices

Drouin, M., & Harmon, J. (2009). Name writing and letter knowledge in preschoolers: Incongruities in skills and the usefulness of name writing as a developmental indicator. *Early Childhood Research Quarterly, 24*(3), 263-270.

Edmiaston, R., Dolezal, V., Doolittle, S., Erickson, C., & Merritt, S. (2000). Developing individualized education programs for children in inclusive settings: A developmentally appropriate framework. *Young Children, 55*(4), 36-41.

Faugno, R. S. (2019). Pediatric prewriting stroke developmental stages: Are expectations evolving beyond the child's natural capabilities? *Journal of Occupational Therapy, Schools, & Early Intervention, 12*, 19-39. https://doi.org/10.1080/19411243.2019.1647811

Fox, B., & Saracho, O. (1990). Emergent writing: Young children solving the written language puzzle. *Early Childhood Development & Care, 56*, 81-90.

Gabas, C., Marante, L., & Cabell, S. Q. (2019). Fostering preschoolers' emergent literacy: Recommendations for enhanced literacy experiences and collaborative instruction. *Perspectives of the ASHA Special Interest Group, 4*(1), 167-176. https://doi.org/10.1044/PERS-SIG16-2018-0012

Gerde, H. K., Bingham, G. E., & Pendergast, M. L. (2015). Reliability and validity of the Writing Resources and Interactions in Teaching Environments (WRITE) for preschool classrooms. *Early Childhood Research Quarterly, 31*, 34-46. https://doi.org/10.1016/j.ecresq.2014.12.008

Gerde, H. K., Bingham, G. E., & Wasik, B. A. (2012). Writing in early childhood classrooms: Guidance for best practices. *Early Childhood Education Journal, 40*(6), 351-359.

Gerde, H. K., Skibbe, L. E., Wright, T. S., & Douglas, S. N. (2018). Evaluation of head start curricula for standards-based writing instruction, early childhood education journal. *Early Childhood Education Journal, 47*(1), 97-105.

Hall, A. H., Simpson, A., Guo, Y., & Wang, S. (2015). Examining the effects of preschool writing instruction on emergent literacy skills: A systematic review of the literature. *Literacy Research and Instruction, 54*(2), 115-134.

Johnson, J. J., Rahn, N. L., & Bricker, D. (2015). *An activity-based approach to early intervention* (4th ed.). Brookes.

Koppenhaver, D., Coleman, P., Kalman, S., & Yoder, D. (1991). The implications of emergent literacy research for children with developmental disabilities. *American Journal of Speech and Language Pathology, 1*(1), 33-44.

Kostelnik, M. J. (1992). Myths associated with developmentally appropriate programs. *Young Children, 47*(4), 17-23.

Kostelnik, M. J., Soderman, A. K., Whiren, A. P., & Rupiper, M. L. (2019). *Developmentally appropriate curriculum: Best practices in early childhood education.* Pearson.

Macy, M. (2019). Activity-based intervention to support second language acquisition. *International Journal of Early Childhood Special Education, 11*(1), 43-51.

Macy, M., & Hoyt-Gonzales, K. (2007). A linked system approach to early childhood special education eligibility assessment. *TEACHING Exceptional Children, 39*(3), 40-44.

Macy, M., Sharp, H. L., & Chan, R. J. (2006). Activity-based intervention for young children with autism. *Autism News, 3*(1), 12-14.

Majsterek, D. J., & Ellenwood, A. E. (1995). Phonological awareness and beginning reading: Evaluation of school-based screening procedure. *Journal of Learning Disabilities, 28,* 449-456.

Marvin, C. (1994). Home literacy experiences of preschool children with single and multiple disabilities. *Topics in Early Childhood Special Education, 14*(4), 436. https://doi.org/10.1177/027112149401400405

Marvin, C., & Mirenda, P. (1993). Home literacy experiences of preschoolers enrolled in Head Start and special education programs. *Journal of Early Intervention, 17,* 351-367.

Mayer, K. (2007). Emerging knowledge about emergent writing. *Young Children, 62*(1), 34-41.

McLean, M. E., & Odom, S. L. (1993). Practices for young children with and without disabilities: A comparison of DEC and NAEYC identified practices. *Topics in Early Childhood Special Education, 13*(3), 274-292.

National Center for Family Literacy. (2008). *Developing early literacy: A scientific synthesis of early literacy development and implications for intervention.* Report of the National Early Literacy Panel. National Institute for Literacy.

National Research Council. (1998). *Preventing reading difficulties in young children.* National Academy Press.

Neumann, M. M., Hood, M., & Ford, R. M. (2013). Using environmental print to enhance emergent literacy and print motivation. *Reading and Writing, 26*(5), 771-793.

Odom, S. L. (1994). Developmentally appropriate practice, policies, and use for young children with disabilities and their families. *Journal of Early Intervention, 18,* 346-348.

Ouellette, G., & Sénéchal, M. (2017). Invented spelling in kindergarten as a predictor of reading and spelling in grade 1: A new pathway to literacy, or just the same road, less known? *Developmental Psychology, 53*(1), 77-88.

Pelatti, C. Y., Piasta, S. B., Justice, L. M., & O'Connell, A. (2014). Language- and literacy-learning opportunities in early childhood classrooms: Children's typical experiences and within-classroom variability. *Early Childhood Research Quarterly, 29*(4), 445-456.

Pool, J. L., & Carter, D. R. (2011). Creating print-rich learning centers. *Teaching Young Children, 4*(4), 18-20.

Pretti-Frontczak, K. (2002). Using curriculum-based measures to promote a linked system approach. *Assessment for Effective Intervention, 27*(4), 15-21. https://doi.org/10.1177/073724770202700403

Pretti-Frontczak, K., Barr, D., Macy, M., & Carter, A. (2003). Research and resources related to activity-based intervention, embedded learning opportunities, and routines-based instruction: An annotated bibliography. *Topics in Early Childhood Special Education, 23,* 29-39.

Puranik, C. S., & Lonigan, C. J. (2012). Name-writing proficiency, not length of name, is associated with preschool children's emergent literacy skills. *Early Childhood Research Quarterly, 27*(2), 284-294.

Puranik, C. S., & Lonigan, C. J. (2014). Emergent writing in preschoolers: Preliminary evidence for a theoretical framework. *Reading Research Quarterly, 49*(4), 453-467.

Quinn, M. F., Gerde, H. K., & Bingham, G. E. (2016). Help me where I am: Scaffolding writing in preschool classrooms. *The Reading Teacher, 70*(3), 353-357.

Roser, N., Hoffman, J., Wetzel, M., Price-Dennis, D., Peterson, K., & Chamberlain, K. (2014). Pull up a chair and listen to them write: Preservice teachers learn from beginning writers. *Journal of Early Childhood Teacher Education, 35*(2), 150-167. https://doi.org/10.1080/10901027.2014.905807

Rowe, D. W., & Neitzel, C. (2010). Interest and agency in 2- and 3-year-olds' participation in emergent writing. *Reading Research Quarterly, 45*(2), 169-195.

Sameroff, A. J., & Chandler, M. J. (1975). Reproductive risk and the continuum of caretaking casualty. In F. D. Horowitz, E. M. Hetherington, S. Scarr-Salapatek, & G. M. Siegel (Eds.), *Review of Child Development Research* (Vol. 4, pp. 187-244). University of Chicago Press.

Sroufe, L. A., Cooper, R. G., & DeHart, G. B. (1992). *Child development: Its nature and course.* McGraw Hill.

Vygotsky, L. S. (1978). *Mind in society: The development of higher psychological processes.* Harvard University Press.

Wheatley, B. C., Gerde, H. K., & Cabell, S. Q. (2016). Integrating early writing into science instruction in preschool. *Reading Teacher, 70*(1), 83-92. https://doi.org/10.1002/trtr.1470

Wolery, M., & Bredekamp, S. (1994). Developmentally appropriate practices and young children with disabilities: Contextual issues in the discussion. *Journal of Early Intervention, 18,* 331-341.

Wu, L. Y. (2009). Children's graphical representations and emergent writing: Evidence from children's drawings. *Early Child Development and Care, 179*(1), 69-79.

Zhang, C., & Quinn, M. F. (2018). Promoting early writing skills through morning meeting routines: Guidelines for best practices. *Early Childhood Education Journal, 46*(5), 547-556. https://doi.org/10.1007/s10643-017-0886-2

Early Childhood Mathematics
(Ages 4 to 8)

Lisa A. Finnegan, PhD

INTRODUCTION

This chapter focuses on providing teacher candidates with an understanding of mathematics methods for children 4 to 8 years old. Teacher candidates will connect student learning to mathematical standards, foundational organizations, and pedagogical theorists. This chapter provides a practical approach for assessing students' understanding and knowledge of mathematical concepts and provides an engaging method for instruction that fosters a lifelong curiosity and interest in mathematical concepts. Teacher candidates will explore formal and informal assessments as well as direct instruction and incidental learning opportunities in mathematics activities. Additionally, teacher candidates will identify with the importance of structuring their mathematics instruction with a continuous learning mindset by extending learning into the home environment through collaboration with students' families.

Fisher, K. M., & Zimmer, K. E. (Eds.).
Early Childhood Special Education Programs and Practices (pp. 179-205).
© 2023 SLACK Incorporated.

CHAPTER OBJECTIVES

→ Describe and cultivate evidence-based and effective mathematics instruction strategies, including the practice of direct instruction.

→ Adapt curriculum tasks and materials for specific learning goals.

→ Use multiple sources of information from student work products and student discourse to develop a comprehensive understanding of their strengths and needs.

→ Evaluate student understanding of mathematics knowledge and determine an instructional course of action to scaffold and build understanding.

→ Select evidence-based teaching strategies and interventions that align with Division for Early Childhood Recommended Practices and the Council for Exceptional Children's high-leverage practices.

KEY TERMS

- **Abstract Instruction:** Instruction that uses verbal explanations and discussions to teach concepts.
- **Cardinality:** Counting of a set or collection of objects and naming the total number in the set or collection after counting.
- **Computation:** A mathematical calculation (i.e., addition and subtraction).
- **Concrete Instruction:** Instruction using physical manipulatives to teach concepts.
- **Fractions:** The parts of something whole such as half a cookie but also connecting to the concept of equal parts or sharing.
- **Math Readiness:** Attaining a level of general skills in preparation for formalized mathematics instruction (i.e., early counting concepts, shapes, more, less, big, or small).
- **Measurement:** The size of an object based on how big or small it is to an actual recorded number to identify length, width, weight, etc.
- **Money:** The monetary value given to a number and used to buy goods such as playing store, identifying coins to be used in a vending machine, and so on.
- **Number Place Value:** The numerical value that a digit has based on the position it holds (i.e., counting using a 100s chart, skip counting, and a general sense of number value).
- **Problem-Solving:** Engaged in a task to find a solution using an approach or alternative approaches that may develop new and deeper understandings.
- **Semiconcrete Instruction:** Instruction that uses illustrations and diagrams to teach concepts, also known as *representation*.
- **Shapes:** The outside form of an object, both geometric (circle, square, triangle, etc.) and nongeometric, such as seasonal objects (apples, pumpkins, snowflakes, etc.) and their descriptors (round, flat, corners, etc.).
- **Subitizing:** When a child sees a set amount and "just knows" the number value of the set.
- **Time:** A point of time as measured in days, hours, and minutes and as a concept that an event is coming, such as Thanksgiving, birthdays, and so on.

CASE STUDY 1

Conor is a 4.4-year-old boy who likes dinosaurs and cars. He sits at the table and sorts his gummy fruits. They are a variety of objects (apples, carrots, grapes, and strawberries) and colors. He asks Mr.

Bennett to look at what he did. Conor sorts all of the gummies into similar groups of objects and colors. He names the colors and the objects and tells him why he put things in the groups he did. When Mr. Bennett asks Conor how many fruit snacks he has, Conor begins counting—1, 2, 3, 4, 5, 6, 8, 10, 14, 17, 41, 20. Mr. Bennett assesses Conor's 1:1 number correspondence. He realizes that Conor can count and point up to six objects accurately, but after the number 6 he simply continues to count using numbers he knows. He adds that he knows that this group has two in it, and this other group has three without the need to count them one by one. When asked how old he is, he is unable to respond, but he knows his sister is 3 because she just had a birthday.

CASE STUDY 2

Lilly is in kindergarten. She is 5.6 years old. Lilly is experiencing difficulty counting by 1s, 5s, and 10s. She has had difficulty correctly identifying the numbers and counting objects and connecting the number sign to the number word. Lilly has difficulty with concepts related to amount or size such as more, less, greater, smaller, or largest. Lilly mixes left and right frequently and struggles with naming basic shapes when not reviewed daily. When Lilly was in preschool, she combined the number and letter symbols. Still, she began to recognize the symbols as separate representations as she learned how to recognize and write her name and connect to print in her environment. Lilly says that she does not like mathematics time in school because she isn't good at it.

CASE STUDY 3

Mykia is a student in third grade. She is an avid reader and currently reads above grade level. She is on grade level in mathematics as well and has always learned math concepts eagerly and quickly. Mykia is able to explain how she came up with her answer and will often draw pictures of how she solves a math problem if she is explaining it to a peer. Recently, Mykia has begun struggling to understand adding and subtracting fractions with different denominators. Mykia is able to quickly state the product when multiplying two factors. Because concepts have come relatively easy to her, she has recently started demonstrating some frustration and a feeling of defeat with her newfound challenge. Mykia will start crying or put her head down on her desk and stop working when she does not understand how to approach a problem or gets an answer wrong.

"His teachers said that he was mentally slow, unsociable, and adrift in his foolish dreams."
—*Anonymous quote about Albert Einstein*

Mathematics understanding is logical and sequentially hierarchical in each skill. Students will struggle to compute sums, identify place value, or estimate a sum if they have gaps in knowledge of the prerequisite mathematics skills. Gaps in prerequisite skills may stem from a lack of background or prior knowledge, missing foundational skills, or limited experience with real hands-on meaningful mathematics work and active learning. Instruction that embraces problem-solving rather than drill and practice deepens concept understanding. The National Council of Teachers of Mathematics (NCTM) and the National Association for the Education of Young Children (NAEYC) are two important agencies ensuring the learning process of mathematics for young children is developmentally appropriate and research based while meeting a deepened understanding of mathematical standards. In other words, young children should experience math in ways that are cognitively, physically, socially, and emotionally developmentally appropriate for them (Minetola et al., 2014).

TABLE 9-1. SIX PRINCIPLES FOR SCHOOL MATHEMATICS

Excellence in mathematics education requires equity—high expectations and strong support for all students.
Curriculum is more than a collection of activities; it must be coherent, focused on essential mathematics, and articulated well across the grades.
Teaching requires understanding what students know and need to learn and then challenging and supporting them to learn it well.
Learning mathematics with understanding, actively building new knowledge from experience and previous knowledge.
Assessment should support the learning of essential mathematics and furnish useful information to both teachers and students.
Technology is essential in teaching and learning mathematics; it influences the mathematics taught and enhances students' learning.

Mathematics should be a part of young children's daily learning routine and integrated across curriculum and learning opportunities, such as play, science, and daily routines (Frye et al., 2013). For example, Lilly could count with her teacher while washing her hands. Teachers must know their students in order to enlist their interest and meet their needs, whether as gaps, challenges, or cultural/language differences, based on information attained through screening and progress monitoring. Supporting students in early mathematics learning requires that evidence-based instructional practices be implemented, thereby demonstrating positive outcomes to improve students' understanding of mathematics and potentially engaging their interest. Fundamentally, core mathematics instruction should include instructional design features that are responsive to the needs of every student and contain critical features for at-risk students (Bryant et al., 2008, 2011).

EARLY CHILDHOOD POSITION STATEMENTS IN MATHEMATICS EDUCATION AND DEVELOPMENTALLY APPROPRIATE PRACTICES

The NCTM has outlined principles and standards to improve school mathematics (Table 9-1). The principles reflect guidelines that are fundamental to high-quality mathematics education, whereas the standards are descriptions of what mathematics instruction should enable students to know and do (NCTM, 2002/2010).

The NCTM standards for content identify what students should learn and process and how they should acquire and apply it. Four different grade bands mark the NCTM standards: pre-K through grade 2, grades 3 through 5, grades 6 through 8, and grades 9 through 12 (NCTM, 2002/2010). Content standards and process standards show the connections between what and how.

Content Standards

Numbers and operations center on understanding numbers, developing meanings of operations, and computing fluently. For young children, the focus is on whole numbers (counting), comparing quantities, and developing an understanding of the base 10 number system structure. Numbers and operations taught using a developmental progression provide students with a strong understanding of the foundational concepts that all other concepts build on. For example, students need to understand what a number value means. The number 4 means four objects, which is one more than three, and it comes after the number 3, and it is one less than five and comes before the number 5.

TABLE 9-2. COUNTING OBJECTS		
		How many turtles in all? Circle the turtle that is second in line on the way to the pond.

Developmentally, children need to recognize a set of objects immediately (Frye et al., 2013). Children learn early that they have one nose, mouth, and belly button and two ears, eyes, arms, hands, and feet and that their feet are covered in a pair of socks (two socks) and shoes (two shoes). Once sets of one and two are quickly recognized (subitized), children move on to sets of three, four, and five up to 10, while also connecting to one-to-one correspondence connecting to the final number in the set of objects. Table 9-2 shows a set of four turtles with the last number counted to equal the total number of turtles in the set. If there were seven turtles in the set, seven would be the last number word counted (cardinality), indicating that the set of turtles in that group is seven. As children subitize (i.e., quickly identify how many are in a set of objects) and develop understanding of the cardinality principle (counting on), number and operation sense developmentally progresses toward understanding comparison sets (10 marbles and 8 marbles) of objects and identifying which set is larger and moves onward to continuous counting with a number that comes after any given number (Frye et al., 2013). The use of 5 and 10 frames can assist students with the placement of objects up to 5 and 10 accordingly (see Resources section).

Conor demonstrates a developing number and operation sense by counting on and attaching a number value correspondence to the number of fruit snacks sitting in front of him. Although he is currently only able to count up to 6 with a corresponding object, he quickly identifies sets of objects with one, two, and three without needing to count. By quickly identifying sets with one, two, or three, Conor is demonstrating an ability to subitize a small collection of objects.

Lilly is demonstrating a gap within the learning progression of number and operation sense. She does not yet recognize one object as a set of one immediately but can take the object in her hand and point and count to 1. Lilly will miscount objects greater than one by going back to the objects already counted and recounting them again, adding on but with an incorrect number sequence.

Mykia demonstrates some difficulty in understanding comparing numbers and inefficiently computing a common denominator to add unlike fractions. Even though Mykia is fluent and knowledgeable of her math facts through 12, she is making procedural errors when adding or subtracting two fractions with different denominators. She will learn a strategy to guide her through the process to find the least common denominator to make the fractions equivalent. However, before learning the strategy, she will take a step back to compare two fractions with different denominators using concrete (manipulatives) and semiconcrete (drawings) representations.

To expand on Conor's ability to subitize numbers, Mr. Bennett increases the sets to four, five, etc. until he reaches 10 while also practicing counting on to 100 using a number chart during the morning meeting. He points to a number, and the children say the number and count on to 100 in unison.

Algebra in the early learning years builds on laying the groundwork by using algebraic symbols and procedures. Linking concepts and techniques to the representation of quantitative relations and a style of mathematical thinking for formalizing patterns, functions, and generalizations enhances the learning of algebra. Before students can analyze a pattern mathematically using algebraic symbols and numbers (e.g., 2x + y), they must understand simple repeating patterns (AB, AABB, AAB, etc., as shown later) initially and then more complex patterns in which critical thinking is required to understand what is happening mathematically in the pattern (a number + 2). Children experience

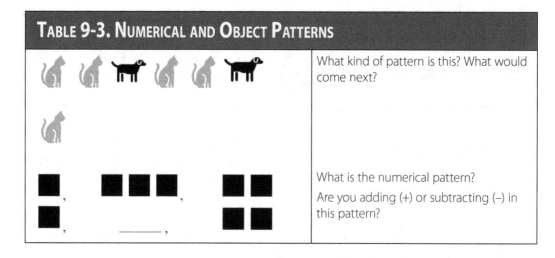

TABLE 9-3. NUMERICAL AND OBJECT PATTERNS	
(cat, cat, dog, cat, cat, dog / cat)	What kind of pattern is this? What would come next?
(numerical object pattern with squares)	What is the numerical pattern? Are you adding (+) or subtracting (–) in this pattern?

patterns in the world around them as they hop across stones laid out on a path and chant "together, apart, together, apart" as their feet land close together on the vertical stone and apart on the horizontal stone pathway or as they recite the colors on a striped shirt they are wearing. Once children can see a pattern and identify it, they are ready to extend patterns, correct an error in a pattern, and lastly create patterns (Frye et al., 2013). Ultimately, children start to expand their algebraic problem-solving in algebra by examining the attributes of objects such as size or color and what is occurring within the pattern (Taylor-Cox, 2003).

Conor rearranges his gummy fruit snacks in a red, orange repeating pattern until he runs out of red and after placing an orange gummy down, he says "Red will go next, but I don't have any more." Mr. Bennett tells Conor he created an AB pattern and gets up from the table and asks Conor to create a pattern that he can draw on the dry-erase board that is different than the one he created.

An example of an assignment for numerical objects and patterns is provided in Table 9-3.

Geometry explores a broader view by calling on students to analyze geometric shapes' characteristics; make mathematical arguments about the geometric relationship; and use visualization, spatial reasoning, and geometric modeling to solve problems. Children begin to understand geometry first by recognizing and naming shapes (Frye et al., 2013). Children see shapes in the world around them through everyday objects (ball, eggs, blocks, etc.) and their environment (buildings, stop signs, yield signs, etc.). Connecting the different attributes of each shape expands geometric understanding until they reach a point where they can combine or separate shapes (Frye et al., 2013).

Because Lilly has difficulty recalling the names and qualities of common shapes such as a circle, square, triangle, and rectangle and she frequently misnames the shapes, she will need small-group or individualized instruction to master the basic level of geometry before she can begin comparing shapes.

Table 9-4 contains some questions to ask to assess students' understanding of a specific shape and can be used to compare two shapes. Students can participate in a shape scavenger hunt in the classroom and even share where they have seen various shapes in their community.

Conor recognizes circles, squares, rectangles, ovals, squares, triangles, and even a hexagon with 100% accuracy. Mr. Bennett has created a center for students to match two-dimensional shapes to three-dimensional shapes, and Conor is currently able to identify and name a cube, cone, and pyramid and

TABLE 9-4. SHAPE EXPLORATION AND IDENTIFICATION	
	What shape is this? How many sides does it have? How many angles does it have? How is it different from a square? Can you draw a line in a square that would make a triangle? Where do we see this shape in our environment? How many triangles can you find posted in our classroom?

TABLE 9-5. MEASURING OBJECTS	
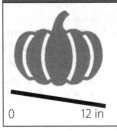	How long is the pumpkin? What unit of measurement was used? If we used our ruler, how many rulers long would it be? If we used a pumpkin seed, how many pumpkin seeds long would it be? What tool would we use to measure how heavy it is?

match it to its two-dimensional shape. He calls the sphere shape a ball because it is a familiar term for a round object for him. Therefore, Mr. Bennett has decided to add marbles, a toy orange, and models of the planets to add to the examples of spherical objects.

Measurement deals with understanding the attributes, units, systems, and processes and applying the techniques, tools, and formulas to determine measures. Children need to make direct comparisons and be familiar with both informal and formal measurement tools. To measure their table, children should first learn to measure using formal measurement tools (e.g., a scale and a ruler) to measure standard units of measurement (inches, feet, cups, ounces, and pounds) along with the vocabulary that connects to measurement concepts such as length, weight, temperature, size, and time (Frye et al., 2013).

Children should measure real objects before moving to abstract concepts on paper. Bringing in a real pumpkin so children can measure how wide it is using their hands provides the concrete learning needed developmentally before moving to an image drawn on paper with a unit of measurement indicating that the object being measured is 12 inches, such as in Table 9-5. Additionally, discussing how students are measuring and the tools they are using to measure with provides an opportunity to use the language associated with this concept in a joint manner so that students understand length in hands or other objects for inches, feet, and yards and pounds for weight.

Mr. Bennett is going to begin a unit on measurement. He decides that he will have children use their hand to find an object in the classroom that is the same length as their hand. He teaches them that they will start at the base of the palm and measure up to the tip of their middle finger. Once they find their object, they return to the table. Mr. Bennett leads the discussion by asking the children what they notice about their objects and the objects of their peers to help students begin to connect to the idea that they may have a different hand size than a peer and ultimately lead to the need to measure using a standard measuring tool. Once students make this connection, Mr. Bennett plans to give student pairs a set of 10 linking chains to find an object in the classroom that would equal 10 chains in length and having pair groups measure all the objects to confirm measurement and connect to a standard measurement value.

TABLE 9-6. GRAPHING AND ANALYZING DATA

 Point to the part that shows the largest slice of pizza? Which part is the smallest part of the pizza? If we cut the pizza into the smallest piece, how many slices would there be? If we cut the pizza into the second largest slice, how many people could eat the pizza? Can more than one person eat the same amount of pizza if the pizza was cut into the largest slice? Why or why not? If we said that the largest area of the circle was people who like cheese pizza only, would that be more or less than 50% of the people who like pizza? How are data related to fractions?

Data analysis is associated with formulating questions and collecting, organizing, and displaying relevant data to answer questions. It emphasizes learning appropriate statistical methods to analyze data, making inferences and predictions based on data, and understanding and using the basic concepts of probability. Children can assist in the collection and be part of the process to organize and represent the data for analysis (Frye et al., 2013). An example of this is a cupcake with each child's birthday month and day displayed on a graph. Children can be taught to place their cupcake at the first spot indicating a value of 1 and count on so that each place indicates one more from the previous number. Class discussion can include which month has the most birthdays, which month has the fewest, which months have no birthday celebrations, and so on. Creating and analyzing data can include activities that provide information about our students (e.g., the number of people in their family, type of home, color of eyes, and pets) and question of the day activities (e.g., analyzing a pizza cut into slices with questions about the size of the slices and how to share them; Table 9-6).

Mr. Bennett incorporates graphs and data analysis from the first day of school. As a class, they have graphed the number of people in their family, their eye color, their birthdays, the types of pets in their home, the types of homes, and daily questions of the day such as what flavor of ice cream they would choose between two different flavors. Mr. Bennett uses these different graphs to discuss the findings but also to add up the total number of responses to equal the total number of students and asking students how many are absent when the count does not equal 20.

Process Standards

Problem-solving is the crux of learning mathematics. Mathematics in the real world is problem-solving; therefore, students need frequent opportunities to tackle and solve complex problems that will require persistent and sustained effort. Students solve problems by applying acquired information to new or different situations. Students may use trial and error, questioning, testing operations, drawing illustrations to represent thinking, and a solution to solve a problem. A significant part of problem-solving entails students reflecting on their thinking during the problem-solving process to apply and adjust their strategies to other problems. Furthermore, building on their thinking is their ability to verbalize their thinking or write their thought processes in a math journal.

Reasoning and proof offer powerful ways of developing and expressing insights about a wide range of phenomena such as patterns, structure, or regularities in both real-world and mathematical situations. Examining if patterns are accidental or if they occur for a reason or making and investigating mathematical conjectures demonstrate reasoning and proof. Children in early mathematics activities develop reasoning skills through purposeful questions, such as why they think something must be true, and involve other students by asking if they think the answer is different than the one given and to explain their thinking. Young children need opportunities to face challenging tasks that

TABLE 9-7. WORD PROBLEM	
Malcolm has 6 more pieces of candy than Jacob. Jacob has 4 less than Salvie. Salvie has 14. How many do Malcolm and Jacob have? Show how you solved the problem using pictures and a written explanation.	Solve the problem. Show your work by representing the numbers into a visual format. The student will need to draw a picture to show what was occurring to find a solution. Write the steps you used to solve the problem. Turn to a partner and tell them what you did to solve this problem in words.

allow them to reason, and their reasoning may not always be mathematically factual (Fonseca, 2018). For example, a child may say that 2 + 2 = 4 because their teacher told them that it did. Developing mathematical arguments and proofs is a formal way of expressing particular reasoning and justification. By exploring phenomena, justifying results, and using mathematical opinions or conclusions (conjectures) in all content areas and with different expectations of sophistication at all grade levels, students should see and expect that mathematics makes sense.

Communication is a way of sharing ideas and clarifying understanding. Through communication, ideas become objects of reflection, refinement, discussion, and amendment. It can be challenging for students to communicate their thinking to others orally or in writing. Students need opportunities to talk to their peers and hear their peers talk about their own mathematical reasoning and proof. By practicing mathematical discourse using probing questions, scaffolding existing knowledge to new concept knowledge, and listening to their peers share their reasoning and proofs, children can learn to be clear, convincing, and precise in their mathematical language use.

Connections integrate mathematical ideas and an understanding of mathematical standards at a more profound and lasting level (i.e., a coherent whole). Mathematical relationships emphasize the inter-relatedness of mathematical concepts; students learn not only mathematics but also about the utility of mathematics.

Representations symbolize the various ways a mathematical concept is shown (e.g., pictures, concrete materials, tables, graphs, number and letter symbols, spreadsheet displays, etc.). The expression of mathematical ideas is fundamental to understanding and using those ideas. When teaching a new concept, instruction should follow a pathway of using concrete instructional materials (manipulatives) to semiconcrete representations of materials (drawn pictures) to abstract (cognitive solution) solutions. Students may revert back to drawing representations with any word problem or creating a representation of what is happening in the word problem in order to demonstrate their understanding of how to solve the word problem. Table 9-7 represents a word problem with a similar task to use representations to show understanding.

Putting the Process Standards Into Action

The NCTM indicates that the principles and standards establish the concept to guide educators for continual improvement in mathematics teaching across all educational systems. In 2010, the NAEYC updated their position statement to affirm that children 3 to 6 years old should receive a high-quality, challenging, and accessible mathematics education. Mathematics education should be engaging and developmentally appropriate while also using research-based practices. The NAEYC (2002/2010) understands there is growing evidence that indicates the early years impact mathematics learning and ability. In the NAEYC/NCTM joint statement (NCTM, 2002/2010), recommendations for teaching mathematics to children 3 to 6 years old build student foundational understanding. Table 9-8 examines the recommendations in more detail.

TABLE 9-8. IDEAS FOR IMPLEMENTING NATIONAL ASSOCIATION FOR THE EDUCATION OF YOUNG CHILDREN/NATIONAL COUNCIL OF TEACHERS OF MATHEMATICS JOINT RECOMMENDATIONS FOR TEACHING MATHEMATICS

RECOMMENDATION	EXAMPLE
1. Enhance children's natural interest in mathematics and their disposition to use it to make sense of their physical and social worlds.	Young children are naturally interested in mathematics. They explore mathematics in play by sorting and classifying objects, comparing quantities, noticing and identifying shapes, and examining patterns. Enhancing children's natural interest in mathematics and their disposition to use math can occur by connecting children to mathematical concepts in nature and play. Children can be shown and create examples of symmetry (insects, leaves, flowers, dolls, toy cars, and blocks), number concepts (tadpoles, hopscotch, toy cars, plastic toy dinosaurs, zoo animals, etc.), measurement (shadows and car ramps), shapes (solar system, bubbles, street signs, and blocks), patterns (animals and LEGO pieces), fractals (trees, fern leaf, coral, and attribution blocks), spirals (shells and pine cones), and tessellations (honeycomb, crystals, coloring books, etc.) in the world around them.  What shapes does the board make on this ladder? How many steps can you climb?
2. Build on children's experience and knowledge, including their family, linguistic, cultural, and community backgrounds; their approaches to learning; and their informal knowledge.	Many children today live in multigenerational homes with grandparents who speak a language other than English. As they learn to count, they may count in Spanish or French creole. Bridging children's experiences and understandings of mathematics from home (prior knowledge) and connecting them to school mathematics requires intentional assessment in knowing what our students know or think they know or believe to understand. Building on children's experience and knowledge of mathematics through family, culture, and community background can occur through examining beadwork, pottery, tools of various indigenous people, graffiti shapes and styles, math tools (e.g., an abacus, arithmetic rope, or French curve), or board games (e.g., Mancala Klappenspiel [Shut the Box], cribbage board, various-sided dice games, etc.), connecting to the mathematics used in jobs of family members of the student. 

(continued)

TABLE 9-8 (CONTINUED). IDEAS FOR IMPLEMENTING NATIONAL ASSOCIATION FOR THE EDUCATION OF YOUNG CHILDREN/NATIONAL COUNCIL OF TEACHERS OF MATHEMATICS JOINT RECOMMENDATIONS FOR TEACHING MATHEMATICS

3. Base mathematics curriculum and teaching practices on knowledge of young children's cognitive, linguistic, physical, and social-emotional development.	Teachers need knowledge of children's cognitive, social-emotional, linguistic, and physical development as they connect to the scope and sequence of mathematics concepts. Young children believe that having eight pennies in a row is more than a dime or that a tall narrow glass filled with chocolate milk is more than the same amount poured into a short wide glass. Teachers need to start where the student's understanding of a concept is and through experiential practice connect to the math vocabulary and provide students with opportunities to refine their knowledge. Although we teach to ensure students master state-provided mathematics standards, student understanding is highly individualized. As part of the mathematics instructional block, small-group instruction can move learning beyond superficial, rote learning. 
4. Use curriculum and teaching practices that strengthen children's problem-solving and reasoning processes and represent, communicate, and connect mathematical ideas.	Problem-solving and reasoning are at the center of mathematics and deepen understanding of mathematical concepts. Problem-solving and logic are taught in an integrated way, not in isolation or for rote learning. They provide children a way to scaffold their knowledge as children reflect and revise their thinking on ways to solve a math problem.  How would you sort these lollipops? What decision did you make to do so? How many lollipops do you have? What are some ways you can group them to help you count more efficiently?
5. Ensure that the curriculum is coherent and compatible with known relationships and sequences of important mathematical ideas.	Mathematics instruction can connect both horizontally (grade-level standards) and vertically (connected to the key or big ideas) in the five content areas. For example, the idea that objects can be compared and contrasted and identified with various attributes or sorted in multiple ways OR the idea that gathering data is purposeful and must be collected and presented with intent and fidelity.

(continued)

Table 9-8 (continued). Ideas for Implementing National Association for the Education of Young Children/National Council of Teachers of Mathematics Joint Recommendations for Teaching Mathematics

6. Provide for children's deep and sustained interaction with key mathematical ideas.	Mathematics instruction should provide a more in-depth understanding of foundational content. The foundational content should focus on number sense and operations, geometry, and measurement with data analysis/probability and algebra woven into daily learning in the early learning years. Teachers can incorporate number sense into simple graphs that focus on the children and their families. How many people are in your family? Do you like chocolate or vanilla ice cream best? Can children share about themselves and learn about each other in these activities? 
7. Integrate mathematics with other activities and other activities with mathematics.	It is not until children enter kindergarten that a scheduled time requirement for learning mathematics typically occurs. Mathematics learning transpires in various learning activities such as circle time and centers in early childhood classrooms. Similarly to weaving foundational mathematics into data analysis/probability and algebra, teachers can weave foundational mathematics content across the curriculum.  How many caterpillars are on this branch? How many caterpillars did we find on all the milkweed plants? How much milkweed do you think the monarch caterpillar eats? What patterns do you notice on the caterpillars' body?
8. Provide ample time, materials, and teacher support for children to engage in play, a context in which they explore and manipulate mathematical ideas with keen interest.	Early education classrooms should resemble learning through some form of play. Counting seashells in the sand table, sorting pine cones and acorns into groups at the nature table, and making a pattern with blocks can all be turned into math learning opportunities. Additional learning opportunities can still be a part of the school day in the primary grades through routine activities, such as lining up (first, second, . . . tenth), lunch (school lunch compared with home lunch, apples on a class wall poster, etc.), and dismissal (car riders, bus riders, after school, or walk/bike), to attending specials (art, physical education, music, library, etc.) to all curriculum (social studies, reading, science, etc.). Mathematics knowledge deepens when students have several opportunities to practice and various ways to demonstrate their understanding. Rotating students through learning centers and introducing mathematics games to reinforce concepts are additional ways for students to practice and deepen their knowledge while adding discourse to share their mathematical thinking.

(continued)

TABLE 9-8 (CONTINUED). IDEAS FOR IMPLEMENTING NATIONAL ASSOCIATION FOR THE EDUCATION OF YOUNG CHILDREN/NATIONAL COUNCIL OF TEACHERS OF MATHEMATICS JOINT RECOMMENDATIONS FOR TEACHING MATHEMATICS

9. Actively introduce mathematical concepts, methods, and language through a range of appropriate experiences and teaching strategies.	Engage students by explaining the learning objective/goal (standard) and the real-world meaningful purpose of the standard. Teach math vocabulary explicitly and demonstrate what the words mean using visuals. Provide learning and multiple opportunities to practice through literature, hands-on activities, games (board games, spinners, dice, etc.), and physical activities with score keeping. Consider a guided instructional approach that provides teachers with a framework to teach the whole group; provide guided instruction; and then move to heterogeneous, flexible small-group differentiated instruction based on specific needs. Mathematics instruction can also use a similar format—whole group (15 to 20 minutes), guided instruction (10 to 15 minutes), and small-group (20 to 25 minutes) instruction/centers. For example, students struggling to count to 5 would work together as one group, students counting up to 20 could be a second group, and students counting beyond 20 could work as a third group. The image below shows a center activity in which students count the number of seeds and match the bite with a number value that equals the seeds counted. 
10. Support children's learning by thoughtfully and continually assessing all children's mathematical knowledge, skills, and strategies.	Assessment is a critical element of all instruction. Assessment should be continuous and ongoing (Finnegan et al., 2019). Teachers use observation, anecdotal records, checklists, probes, error analysis, interviews, and curriculum-based and diagnostic assessments to know what their students know and plan for instruction. No one single source of assessment tells us all that our students know nor should they be used to determine the trajectory of long-term mathematics ability. Assessments must also be equitable and developmentally appropriate for students who are non-native English speakers and children of poverty. Example of anecdotal note: On January 3rd, Lilly counted 10 different sets of objects between the numbers of 1 and 5 with 100% accuracy in a small group.

Data source: National Association for the Education of Young Children (2002).

The Erikson Institute Early Math Collaborative (2021a) uses the concept of "big ideas" in math to map concepts for children 3 to 6 years old to explore key math concepts and "precursor concepts" for children from birth to age 3. Precursor concepts include attributes, comparison, pattern, and change. As you learned in Chapter 6, the years birth to age 3 are a critical time period of language acquisition because the brain is maturing and developing. Mathematic precursor concepts naturally fit into this period of language development. Teachers in early childcare settings build in attributes as they describe the properties and qualities of items (toys, clothing, body parts, objects, food, etc.) they show to the child, simultaneously developing and enhancing language skills. Attributes of objects can then be used for comparison by grouping objects so children begin to recognize object sameness and differences (Erikson Institute Early Math Collaborative, 2021b). These same objects can then be used to build in patterns with the objects (sock, shoe, sock, shoe) but also using patterns through sounds (tapping, clapping, snapping, phonemes) whereby children can begin to make predictions of what will come next. The Erikson Institute Early Math Collaborative (2021b) indicated pattern involves rhythm, sequence, and regularity. Children from birth to age 3 develop routines throughout their day that support the development of sequencing, such as mealtime, bath time, and bedtime routines. Lastly, change is a precursor concept in which infants and toddlers begin to develop an understanding of something becoming different (Erikson Institute Early Math Collaborative, 2021b). The Erikson Institute Early Math Collaborative (2021b) stated this can be either quantitative or qualitative. Understanding a quantitative change can occur when a child eats all of the pieces of the snack after counting how many they started with and counting down as they eat them (separating) or they have put on one shoe and then two (joining); an example of a qualitative change is their clothes or shoes being too small, indicating they have grown but the growth is something they cannot see. Children 4 to 8 years old with disabilities who are still learning these concepts would benefit from these strategies.

Like the precursor concepts, the Erikson Institute Early Math Collaborative (2021a) mapped key mathematical concepts for children ages 3 to 6 that they contend are foundational to lifelong mathematical thinking and can be used to guide teaching and learning. Sets, number sense, counting, operations, pattern, measurement, data analysis, spatial relationships, and shape constitute the "big ideas."

Sets are basic to children's thinking, learning, and our number system (Erikson Institute Early Math Collaborative, 2021a). Sets are a large part of play for children as they collect a group of cars, sticks, or building blocks. Initially, a set may be a mixture of objects or the horse seen on a farm grouped with cats because the child has a cat and all four-legged animals are cats in their world until they begin to connect attributes to the set. The Erikson Institute Early Math Collaborative (2021a) points out that sets or collections as big ideas can be compared and contrasted, can be sorted in different ways, and have attributes that make them sortable into sets.

Number sense is the ability to understand the quantity in a given set and the name that is associated with that amount (Erikson Institute Early Math Collaborative, 2021a). Early on children innately understand some form of number sense in a more abstract way of more or less (e.g., if you gave one child three cookies and another child one cookie or one child a full glass of milk and another child half a glass). The children in this situation would not be able to concretely tell you the number or amount more or less, but they can see that it is more or less. The Erikson Institute Early Math Collaborative (2021a) indicated the big ideas of number sense are small collections of objects that can be intuitively counted or subitized, quantity is an attribute of a set and we use specific names to label that quantity, and numbers are used in many ways.

Counting occurs daily in the lives of young children. A child can be heard counting as they hop across a pattern of concrete stepping stones, repeating one, two as they land on one block and then two in a hopscotch-type pattern; counting their pieces of cereal lined up for their snack; or as they walk up the stairs to their apartment. The Erikson Institute Early Math Collaborative (2021a) pointed out that the big ideas of counting can be used to identify how many are in a collection or set and that there are rules that apply to that set.

Operations focus on what is happening when sets are joined together or a set is separated. Number operations tell a story and are the tools used to answer questions similar to the following: How many are left? How many more? and How many in all? (Erikson Institute Early Math Collaborative, 2021a). The Erikson Institute Early Math Collaborative (2021a) stated it is vital that children learn multiple ways to make sense and solve problems and understand the relationships of the numbers in a number operation problem. Understanding that a quantity (whole) can be decomposed into equal or unequal parts (separated) and the parts can be composed (joined) to equal a whole and that set numerosity attributes can be compared and ordered by more or less than or equal to another set are the big ideas that align to operations (Erikson Institute Early Math Collaborative, 2021a).

Pattern provides children ages 3 to 6 an opportunity to generalize their understanding from one situation to another (Erikson Institute Early Math Collaborative, 2021a). Children begin to recognize the patterns in their life through their daily or weekly routines. The Erikson Institute Early Math Collaborative (2021a) contended that all mathematics is based on pattern and structure including geometric and physical situations. Pattern big ideas are as follows: the same pattern structure can be found in different forms, identification of the rule of a pattern makes it more predictable, and patterns are repeated and growing sequences that are governed by a rule and can be seen in the world and in mathematics (Erikson Institute Early Math Collaborative, 2021a).

Measurement is a mathematical procedure applied in different contexts that produces a quantitative attribute of an object, such as length, width, volume, circumference, radius, temperature, or weight (Erikson Institute Early Math Collaborative, 2021a). The Erikson Institute Early Math Collaborative (2021a) identified measurement big ideas as follows: quantifying a measurement helps us to describe and compare attributes more precisely; all measurement involves a concept of "fair" comparison; and when measuring a single item, it can be measured with different attributes (e.g., length, width, and volume).

Data analysis for children ages 3 to 6 is typically thought of as charts and graphs; however, data analysis can also be about writing a list or writing or talking about what is noticed about a graph (Erikson Institute Early Math Collaborative, 2021a). Data analysis is about collecting information and organizing it in a way that allows children to make comparisons and generalizations about the data set. The big ideas for data analysis are (a) data must be represented in order for it to be interpreted, (b) the collection and organization of data are dependent on the question, (c) it is useful to compare parts of the data and draw conclusions to the whole data set, and (d) the purpose of collecting data is to answer questions that may not have obvious answers (Erikson Institute Early Math Collaborative, 2021a).

Spatial relationships develop in children ages 3 to 6 from birth. As children navigate where an object is and how to grasp it, they are exploring spatial relationships. As children grow, they learn to apply numbers and mathematical terms (parallel or equilateral) to the process of measuring distances and angles as they represent the space and their relational nature of the object within that space. The big ideas for spatial relationships according to the Erikson Institute Early Math Collaborative (2021a) are the following: spatial relationships can be visualized and mentally manipulated, relationships between objects and places can be described with mathematical precision, and our experience impacts the perspective from which we view objects spatially.

Shapes are all around us in the objects that we see. Understanding two- and three-dimensional shapes and their connections assists in the development of understanding their distinct attributes and rules (Erikson Institute Early Math Collaborative, 2021a). Shape big ideas are that shapes can be combined or separated to make new shapes, three-dimensional shapes have a flat-shaped face or side, and the attributes of shapes can be defined and classified (Erikson Institute Early Math Collaborative, 2021a).

The environment, play, teachable moments, projects, curriculum, and intentional teaching are all critical factors in developing mathematical thinking and knowledge in early childhood education (Ginsburg et al., 2008). Play is a rich site for children to compose and decompose numbers (Parks

& Blom, 2014). Based on the work of Ginsburg et al. (2008), students need an environment that includes a variety of materials and equipment to explore, opportunities for intellectual mathematical development through play centers, teacher observation, and feedback that heightens learning. These project-based activities involve asking high-level questions. Students can explore ways to discover answers to mathematical problems using a variety of materials and environments. The Erikson Institute Early Math Collaborative (2021a) provides several learning activities and literature connections for all mathematical big ideas.

ASSESSING MATHEMATICAL KNOWLEDGE AND THINKING

Assessment tells us what our students know and how they think while solving a problem mathematically. Formal assessment is needed to identify specific gaps students may have, whereas informal assessment is needed to determine what students know on a daily basis. Ongoing progress monitoring gives teachers a sense of how students are connecting mathematical concepts together. Observing students while they are solving problems provides teachers with information on students' attitudes and behaviors in a content area that students often describe as challenging or disliked.

Formal Mathematics Assessment

Formal mathematics assessment can provide insight into a child's achievement and identification of mathematics gaps, such as numerical reasoning, computation, and word problems. Further assessment can be given using diagnostic tests after determining an achievement gap exists. The following diagnostic tests are appropriate for students attending pre-K through grade 2.

The Test of Early Mathematics Ability–Third Edition measures the performance of children between the ages of 0 and 3 and 8 and 11 years of age. The test takes approximately 40 minutes to administer and measures both informal and formal concepts and skills. The 72-item assessment focuses on numbering skills, number comparison facility, numeral literacy, mastery of number facts, calculation skills, and understanding concepts. According to the publisher Pro-ed, the Test of Early Mathematics Ability–Third Edition is a norm-referenced measure or a diagnostic instrument to determine specific strengths and weaknesses. It measures progress, evaluates programs, screens for readiness, discovers the baselines for poor school performance in mathematics, identifies gifted students, and guides instruction and remediation.

The KeyMath-3 Diagnostic Assessment is a comprehensive norm-referenced test that measures basic concepts (numeration, algebra, geometry, measurement, and data analysis and probability), operations (mental computation and estimation, written calculation [addition and subtraction], and written computation [multiplication and division]), and applications (foundations of problem-solving and applied problem-solving) for students aged 4.6 to 21.11 years (i.e., grades K-12). Students complete the KeyMath-3 Diagnostic Assessment individually. The 10 subtests take approximately 30 to 90 minutes to administer depending on the student responses. Designed for special education teachers, educational diagnosticians, and mathematics specialists, the KeyMath-3 Diagnostic Assessment identifies specific strengths, weaknesses, and instructional program planning. The KeyMath-3 Diagnostic Assessment assesses the following subtests within each content area: basic concepts (numeration, algebra, geometry, measurement, and data analysis and probability), operations (mental computation and estimation, addition and subtraction, and multiplication and division), and applications (foundations of problem-solving and applied problem-solving), providing a detailed measure of mathematics performance levels that help to determine the instructional scope and sequence. The KeyMath-3 Diagnostic Assessment also has an Essential Resources kit that provides remedial activities (Venn, 2014).

Informal Mathematics Assessment

Informal mathematics assessment gives teachers knowledge of how students are doing day to day and informs our teaching by examining what students do mathematically. Formative assessment in mathematics should be occurring with all children all of the time and in multiple ways. Teachers can "listen in on" and "watch" mathematics discussions and other learning opportunities (centers, recess, and other content area activities) while taking anecdotal notes or recording students' voices as they explain their reasoning used to solve a problem. Observation and data collection allow teachers to gain insight into their students' mathematical thinking and knowledge. Using checklists is a standard method of tracking student learning and can be set up in a way that tracks mathematical skills, knowledge, and behaviors (Minetola et al., 2014) and even connects to the standards. Additionally, completing an error analysis on students' exit tickets, curriculum-based assessment activities, or daily work provides insight into student thinking and their understanding and mastery of skills, processes, and procedures in answering a mathematical problem. Rubrics are great tools that provide guidance on how to meet various mathematical learning objectives when students demonstrate their mathematical understanding while completing a project-based activity or learning center or when linking to state mathematics standards to provide students with guidance on how they are meeting the objective based on evidence.

Additionally, teachers and their students can identify products that demonstrate students' understanding of a mathematical concept and place the product into a portfolio representing their progress (Minetola et al., 2014). Once students receive instruction using a formal curriculum within a school district, the curriculum resources typically contain curriculum-based measurement tools (e.g., worksheets, quizzes, and tests) to assess students' mathematical knowledge and behaviors. Technology tools to practice and determine mathematics understanding are becoming a part of our everyday teaching environment.

MATHEMATICS INSTRUCTION

Mathematics is one of the core curricula taught in schools and is critical. Curriculum design (standards based), teacher beliefs/perceptions, behavior (evidence-based practices), and student engagement impact learners' mathematics achievement. Teachers of mathematics must model knowledge of mathematical concepts, persistence in solving challenging mathematical problems, a positive disposition toward mathematics, and flexibility in the way they teach mathematics concepts and show a personal continuous learning trajectory (Hoffman & Brahier, 2008). Four methods identified as having moderate to strong evidence by the IRIS Center (2010/2017) and further aligned with the Council for Exceptional Children's high-leverage practices (HLPs) are (a) explicit, systematic instruction (HLPs 12 and 16); (b) visual representation (HLP 15); (c) schema instruction (HLP 14); and (4) metacognitive strategies (HLP 14). Table 9-9 provides an overview and classroom examples of the HLPs.

Mathematics vocabulary is "highly decontextualized," meaning mathematics terms are not situated in typical everyday conversations and tend to be "highly formalized" (Dunston & Tyminski, 2013, p. 40). Vocabulary knowledge, in general, is critical to student achievement. For young children, mathematics vocabulary can begin by having students sing along or listen to math-oriented picture books as they develop their language skills. From pre-K through grade 2, students move through a progression of building mathematics language through naming objects and counting, talking about sorting, and identifying patterns to a more formal explicit introduction and then to mathematical terms such as numbers, place value, addition, subtraction, plus, equals, and so on. Trade books or picture books that are math oriented engage learners into a story that connects to mathematical concepts. *The Button Box*, *How Many Snails?*, and *The Doorbell Rang* help to make mathematics come to life through images and examples. Other examples are provided in Table 9-10.

TABLE 9-9. COUNCIL FOR EXCEPTIONAL CHILDREN HIGH-LEVERAGE PRACTICES (HLPs)

HLPs	EXPLANATION	CLASSROOM EXAMPLE
HLP 12: Systematically designed instruction toward a specific learning goal. HLP 16: Use explicit instruction.	Content, skills, and concepts are taught by showing and telling students exactly what to do and think while modeling solving a problem, completing a task, etc. for any new complex skills and concepts. Sequencing concepts and skills that build on each other from foundational knowledge to higher-level concept knowledge; modifications would need to be made based on students' needs and progress through the concepts (McLeskey et al., 2017).	Today we are going to add 0 to a number. Let's count to 10 from 0. Remember 0 means we don't have any. We have nothing. Ready, set, count from 0! 0, 1, 2, 3, 4, 5, 6, 7, 8, 9, 10. Great. You did a great job counting now. Let's see what happens when I add 0 to a number. I need to get bananas at the market. I would like to get 5. If there are 3 bananas in 1 bunch in the bin and there are no more bananas or 0 bananas are left in the bin, how many bananas do I have? Let's write that math sentence out as I place my counters on the table. Count 1, 2, 3; so let's write a 3. Now I want more bananas, so let's make a plus sign (+). When I look in the bin, there are 0 bananas, so now I write a 0. Add by my 3 counters; I put nothing. I put 0 bananas. Let's count the bananas. 1, 2, 3 plus no more equals 3. When I add 0 to 3, the number stays the same; it is 3. I have 3 bananas. Let's do another one. The duck in my neighborhood has some baby ducklings. I saw 5 ducklings walk across the road. I waited in my car to see if any more were going to follow. 0 ducklings followed. Let's count 5 counters for the 5 ducklings I saw. (Continue as above to solve the problem. Solve additional problems until students show readiness to move to guided practice.)
HLP 15: Provide scaffolded supports.	Temporary supports for students to build skills toward independent work completion. Supports can be visual, verbal, or written depending on the needs of the student. As the student gains mastery, the supports are gradually removed or withdrawn (McLeskey et al., 2017). Creating visual representations of a math problem helps students to see the problem without having to use manipulatives. Still, it supports students by providing a way to see what is happening to solve the problem.	We have been using our counters to help us add 0 to a number. Today we are going to draw pictures or visual representations of the matter problems we need to solve. I saw 3 monarch caterpillars on one of my milkweed plants. The other plant had 0 caterpillars. So, let's draw 3 caterpillars. Now let's make our math sentence; 3, and since I want to add the number of caterpillars on my other milkweed plant, I will make the + sign. So, I have 3 +. The number of caterpillars on the other plant equals my total caterpillars. I have 0 caterpillars on the other plant. So, I will draw 0 caterpillars and add a 0 to my math sentence. 3 + 0 =. Let's count the caterpillars I drew. 1, 2, 3. 3 + 0 = 3.

(continued)

TABLE 9-9 (CONTINUED). COUNCIL FOR EXCEPTIONAL CHILDREN HIGH-LEVERAGE PRACTICES (HLPs)		
HLP 14: Teach cognitive and metacognitive strategies to support learning and independence.	Cognitive and metacognitive strategies provide students with a way to check and monitor their understanding and performance. Explicitly teaching the strategies must be part of the process, along with evaluating them for their effectiveness in student outcomes and usage (McLeskey et al., 2017).	Today we will look at keywords that help tell us what we need to do to solve a problem. The first thing we need to do is read the question carefully. "Ms. Olivia saw seven ducklings cross the road. She waited in her car to see if any more ducklings would cross. Two more ducklings crossed. How many ducklings crossed the road?" Now that we have read the problem, we want to ask ourselves "did we understand the question?" If we didn't, we should reread the problem. If we did, we want to find the information that is important to solving the problem. I am going to circle the number words and write the number above them. Seven (7) and two (2). Next, I want to think about what is happening in this problem. What is the question asking me to do? Ms. Olivia saw some ducklings, and then she saw some more. So, we are adding the ducklings together. Let's add $7 + 2$. $7 + 2 = 9$; 9 ducklings in all. Let's check to see if that makes sense; 7 crossed the road, and then 1 is 8, and another is 9. Yes, that makes sense.

Data source: McLeskey, J., et al. (2017). *High-leverage practices in special education.* Council for Exceptional Children & CEEDAR Center.

Mathematical conceptual understanding moves students beyond memorization of a procedure to a deeper understanding of mathematical concepts, operations, and relationships. Although language is still developing for children between the ages of pre-K to grade 2, math discourse should always be a part of mathematics instruction from its inception. Education should move students through a process of understanding from concrete (C) representations to semiconcrete (S) or representational (R) ways to represent their knowledge to an abstract (A) use of numerals. The CRA/CSA instructional sequence is rooted in the work of Bruner and Kenney (1965), who defined learning through the stages of representation (Sealander et al., 2012). Concrete representations of concepts are hands-on use of materials to build foundational understanding, connect to mathematics vocabulary visually and physically, and establish real representations of mathematical problems. They include manipulative objects such as counters, tallies, geoboards, shapes, and so on. Teaching mathematics in a concrete way using manipulative materials provides children with a physical and visual representation of the mathematical concepts and problems they are trying to solve. Concrete experiences should be a part of instruction at every grade level of mathematics instruction when introducing a new concept. Semiconcrete representations or visual representations in mathematics are the diagrams, pictures, and illustrations of manipulatives or other displays (tally marks and so on) that students use to make connections between visual representations and the number sentence they are trying to solve. Visual representations of math problems develop associations between a visual model of the problem and the numerical equation. At the abstract level, students use numerals to solve math problems and apply a set of procedures.

TABLE 9-10. BOOK TITLES WITH CONNECTING ACTIVITY

TITLE AND AUTHOR	STORY SYNOPSIS	MATHEMATICS ACTIVITY
Ten Black Dots by Donald Drews	Different dots are on various objects such as a keyhole (1 dot).	Counting 10 frame
Inch by Inch by Leo Lionni	Inchworm measures other parts of various birds.	Measuring
The Doorbell Rang by Pat Hutchins	A plate full of cookies gets shared by friends that keep ringing the doorbell.	Grouping Division
The Button Box by Margarette S. Reid	A box containing a large variety of buttons gets sorted out into different categories.	Sorting Counting
Each Orange Had 8 Slices: A Counting Book by Paul Giganti Jr.	On the way to different places, there is something seen that has objects with it.	Counting Adding Multiplication Problem-solving
How Many Snails? by Paul Giganti Jr.	A story of how many objects are there with described details.	Counting Sorting
Monster Math by Anne Miranda	Monsters doing a variety of silly things.	Counting Adding by 1s and then 10s
Shapes, Shapes, Shapes by Tana Hoban	Shapes found in things found in a community.	Shapes

Chien et al. (2018) stated that manipulatives take many forms; some are designed specifically for mathematics learning such as base 10 blocks (Dienes blocks), whereas others are found in everyday classroom materials (e.g., dinosaur counters used for sorting size, shape, and color and for counting; calendar patterns; and interlocking cubes). Some can even be found in everyday household materials (i.e., money, paper clips, straws, a deck of cards, and dice). According to Chien and colleagues (2018), teachers suggest providing students with an opportunity to explore manipulatives and share ways they can use them before using them for mathematics learning. This approach allows teachers to guide students to construct uses that mathematically connect and their qualities. Additionally, students should receive several opportunities to work with any one set of manipulatives, and the younger the student, the longer they should be using manipulatives to solve math problems before moving to a semiconcrete and then abstract process (Chien et al., 2018). This would also be true for struggling students or students with special learning needs.

Explicit instruction or explicit, systematic instruction "involves teaching a specific concept or procedure in a highly structured and carefully sequenced manner" (IRIS Center, 2010/2017, p. 4) and is also covered in Chapter 5. Explicit instruction removes the ambiguity that mathematical concepts can have for so many learners, primarily when taught to use a formula to calculate an answer to a problem rather than understand clearly what each part of the formula means and does (Doabler et al., 2012). Three key components characterize direct instructional interactions: "(a) clear and concise teacher demonstrations, (b) frequent opportunities for students to practice what teachers demonstrate, and (c) timely academic feedback from teachers to students related to students' attempts to solve educational problems" (Doabler, 2015, p. 305). Teacher demonstrations are explanations, clarifications, overt demonstrations (procedures), and processes (think alouds) performed in a series of steps to ensure that students know what you want them to know, understand it, and are able to do it (Archer & Hughes, 2010). Practice provides students an opportunity for repeated experiences with the same concept in different ways (Knaus, 2017). Practicing together (teacher with students or students with students) or practicing independently builds student understanding, and when infusing discourse with instruction, student understanding deepens. Practice helps students acquire new knowledge, retain previously learned material, build fluency or automaticity, and connect existing background knowledge with new and more sophisticated content (Pellegrino & Goldman, 1987; Prawat, 1989). Mathematical verbalizations permit students to interact with the teacher and peers around critical mathematics content. Specifically, verbalizing can be viewed as a way to process and practice math content and in this manner becomes a crucial component in supporting the early development of mathematical proficiency. Finally, teachers provide academic feedback to extend learning opportunities and reduce potential misconceptions. In the context of explicit instructional routines, academic feedback is intended to be immediate and directly aligned with the preceding student response. If students identified a number value or procedure in error, the teacher would need to correct the mistake by stating the correct answer. Then, the teacher would ask student responses to correct and verify the solution and their thinking. With that, students receive corrective feedback and an additional opportunity to practice successful problem-solving (Doabler, 2015).

As students move up through the grade levels, they begin to connect a set of rules or procedures to their mathematics solving skills, requiring them to think about what they are doing mathematically. The process of teaching students to think about their mathematical thinking is known as *metacognition*. Metacognitive strategies guide students through planning and evaluating while making modifications as needed, either during or after solving a mathematical problem. The strategy they learn may be a mnemonic (PEMDAS [Parenthesis, Exponents, Multiplication, Division, Addition, Subtraction]) or procedural self-talk (Did I understand the question? What is the operation the problem is asking me to use? Did I write the problem correctly? and Does the answer make sense?).

SUPPORTING STUDENTS WITH DISABILITIES

Some students struggle in mathematics due to gaps in foundational understanding, whereas other students struggle in mathematics due to information processing difficulties. Resources for the delivery of mathematics instruction are often lacking in providing teachers directions for explicit, systematic instruction (Bryant et al., 2008). Supporting students with disabilities and other students at risk for widening their mathematical conceptual understanding gap requires providing explicit instruction at each level of mathematical conceptual understanding—concrete, representational, and abstract. Additional practices of effective instruction for students with disabilities with mathematical deficits are designing instruction to minimize learning challenges; providing a strong conceptual basis for procedural tasks to solve math problems; providing drills and practice; monitoring cumulative, continuous progress; and reinforcing students in their development of self-regulation of engagement and perseverance (Fuchs et al., 2008). Gersten, Beckmann, et al. (2009) and Gersten, Chard, et al. (2009) also identified explicit instruction as a vital instructional practice for students who struggle with mathematics, in addition to sequencing and providing a range of examples to solve as a part of instruction, using visual representations (Jitendra et al., 2016), incorporating student verbalizations of their understanding, devoting 10 minutes each day to build fluent retrieval of basic arithmetic facts, providing ongoing feedback, and monitoring progress. Additionally, Gersten, Chard, et al. (2009) indicated peer-assisted tutoring for students with disabilities or those who may struggle can be considered as an effective strategy, with the exception of students with learning disabilities for which peer tutoring in mathematics has not yet been as effective as it has been in reading.

One approach that can provide support for all learners but is specifically designed for students with special needs is differentiated instruction. *Differentiated instruction* is a systematic approach in planning curriculum and instruction that honors student-centered learning (Tomlinson, 2000,

2017). Tomlinson (2017) stressed that in the process of providing differentiated instruction, teachers must be clear about what students must know (K), understand (U), and be able to do (D), known as *KUDs*, in order for students to grasp new information. In order to address the KUDs, teachers must know their students and their students' present level of performance. Teachers can differentiate what is taught and how students access information (content), how students understand and master the content (process), how they demonstrate their knowledge of the content (product), how to engage students (affect), and how to manage the learning environment (environment; Tomlinson, 2017).

To differentiate the content or how students access the content in mathematics, teachers can use mathematics-oriented concept picture books, videos, blogs, podcasts, models, manipulatives, multicultural resources, or a tiered curriculum or establish a learning goal broken down from the larger learning objective (Adams et al., 2007; Tomlinson, 2017). To differentiate the process or how students master and make the content their own, teachers can provide a choice of concept picture books at varied levels; front-load teaching mathematics terms and academic language; provide mini-lessons, digital mathematics games, or activities; implement whole physical response activities; use diagrams, images, and charts; incorporate physical response activities, collaborative learning, and problem-solving activities with discourse; vary pacing; add manipulatives and materials that meet varied learner levels and interests; and provide flexible seating and grouping (Tomlinson, 2017; Tomlinson & Eidson, 2003). Teachers can differentiate products for students to demonstrate what they know, understand, and are able to do by providing students with rubrics, checklists, or guides explaining the criteria being measured and a choice board of activities to demonstrate their knowledge, such as presentations, projects, peer teaching, demonstrations, a poster, a written assignment, or a student creation choice (Tomlinson, 2017; Tomlinson & Eidson, 2003). As the content, process, and product are differentiated, the affective aspects of learning such as engagement, perseverance, interest, and motivation are met in a caring, nurturing, and supportive differentiated learning environment. Furthermore, mathematical content can be differentiated while also blending in the principles for effective mathematics practice mentioned previously. A shift in teaching mathematics from strictly whole-group instruction followed by independent practice to one that supports students with mathematical difficulties through additional intensive instruction in small groups in between whole-group and independent practice is occurring more frequently as special education research focuses on the impact of multitiered systems of support. Intensive small-group instruction provides additional learning opportunities using research-based practice to fill in gaps and scaffold knowledge. A meta-analysis study evaluating the effects of Tier 2 interventions for students with persistent math difficulties found that students receiving small-group interventions with an intervention model of problem structure instruction had a positive and significant benefit, whereas the intervention model of strategy instruction, although also positive, was not significant (Jitendra et al., 2021).

PROMOTING A LOVE OF LEARNING MATHEMATICS

Using children's literature to teach mathematical concepts lends itself naturally to early childhood mathematics. Young children will listen to the same story read over and over to them. Teachers of prekindergarten through primary school children can capitalize on young children's love for storybooks and use the stories to introduce and enrich mathematical concepts that children are learning (Minetola et al., 2014; Smith, 2013). Furthermore, using storybooks builds language skills, general and academic language, and critical thinking skills as students comprehend a story. Songs that connect to mathematics are equally engaging (e.g., "Feist Sings 1, 2, 3, 4" on Sesame Street YouTube, "The Money Song" by Jack Hartmann Kids Music Channel, "Schoolhouse Rock! Counting by 4s" on KidsTV123 YouTube, and the "Angles Song" or the "Place Value Song for Kids" on MathSongs by the Numberock YouTube Channel). Students in prekindergarten through grade 2 may sing or chant songs as part of their everyday school experience, from academic themes to songs used to transition from learning activity to learning activity and class time to lunchtime. If a song is used in the class to help students learn a concept, teachers should write the song's words or chant on poster paper, teach them to students, and connect them to the concepts. Any idea can be put to a song using a familiar tune. For example, take the song "The Muffin Man" tune and add the following words: "You can add numbers with me, numbers with me, numbers with me; You can add numbers with me; Let's start with 1 + 0."

Exploring mathematics in the world around them should take on a natural element. Children can count and share objects discovered in their natural environment. Pine cones and rocks become manipulatives and opportunities to discuss mathematical concepts such as angles, symmetry, and number value.

Home and school connections are a critical element of student success. According to Minetola and colleagues (2014), a "good connection between home and school provides children with support in what they are learning and extends learning to their world outside the classroom" (p. 10). The world around children beholds a plentitude of mathematical inquiry opportunities, from counting oranges at the grocery store to looking at the symmetry of sticks and rocks. Bringing mathematical language from school to home and community provides families with an opportunity to continue the learning process and extend knowledge into the real world. Teachers can share what concepts and how students learn with their families through a class website or weekly newsletter. Informing families of games such as hide-and-seek where children count to 10 or connecting to objects to build one-to-one correspondence through chores such as setting six dinner plates at the table builds math language and conceptual understanding (Sorkin et al., 2018). Holding mathematics curriculum nights or sending home backpacks with mathematical activities also builds math skills. Understanding students and their families culturally, linguistically, racially, socially, and economically is vital to building relationships with them and collaboratively working with them for their children's success. Sharing math-oriented picture book titles and connecting activities with families promote continuing mathematical conceptual and language knowledge and practice.

SUMMARY

The learning of mathematics begins in early childhood through language-building interactions and play. Early mathematical exploration can impact later mathematics understanding. Using developmentally appropriate research-based mathematics instructional strategies and materials will enhance children's mathematical knowledge from pre-K to second grade. Explicit, systematic instruction; supplemental practice; the use of concrete materials and then visual representations; metacognitive strategies; peer discussion; and connecting to the underlying structure of a problem are effective instructional practices in mathematics (IRIS Center, 2010/2017).

CHAPTER REVIEW

1. What impact has the position statement of NCTM and NAEYC had on teaching mathematics?
2. Name and describe a diagnostic mathematics assessment.
3. How might you assess students at a learning center or other learning activity such as computer station, games, etc.?

4. Linking concepts and techniques to the representation of quantitative relations and a style of mathematical thinking for formalizing patterns, functions, and generalizations enhances the learning of _____?
   a. Number and operation
   b. Reasoning
   c. Algebra
   d. Measuring objects

5. _____ emphasizes learning appropriate statistical methods to analyze data, making inferences and predictions based on data, and understanding and using the basic concepts of probability:
   a. Algebra
   b. Data analysis
   c. Graphing
   d. Geometry

6. Match each NCTM principle label to the correct description.

PRINCIPLE	DESCRIPTION
1) Equity	a) Understanding what students know and need to learn and then challenging and supporting them to learn it well.
2) Curriculum	b) Mathematics with understanding, actively building new knowledge from experience and previous knowledge.
3) Teaching	c) Should support the learning of essential mathematics and furnish useful information to both teachers and students.
4) Learning	d) A collection of activities; it must be coherent, focused on essential mathematics, and articulated well across the grades.
5) Assessment	e) Essential in teaching and learning mathematics; it influences the mathematics taught and enhances students' learning.
6) Technology	f) High expectations and strong support for all students.

7. Use the word bank to connect the process standard term to its description.

Communication	Connections	Problem-solving
Reasoning and proof	Representations	

Mathematics in the real world is (1) _____; therefore, students need frequent opportunities to tackle and solve complex problems that will require persistent and sustained effort. (2)_____ offer powerful ways of developing and expressing insights about a wide range of phenomena such as patterns, structure, or regularities in both real-world and mathematical situations. (3)_____ is a way of sharing ideas and clarifying understanding. (4)_____ integrate mathematical ideas and an understanding of mathematical standards at a more profound and lasting level, a coherent whole. Pictures, concrete materials, tables, graphs, number and letter symbols, spreadsheet displays, etc. are (5)_____ that show the various ways students demonstrate their understanding of ideas mathematically.

RESOURCES

- Erikson Institute Early Math Collaborative: https://earlymath.erikson.edu/
- High-Quality Mathematics Instruction: What Teachers Should Know: https://iris.peabody.vanderbilt.edu/module/math/#content
- National Association for the Education of Young Children Early Childhood Mathematics: Promoting Good Beginnings: https://www.naeyc.org/sites/default/files/globally-shared/downloads/PDFs/resources/position-statements/psmath.pdf
- Parenting the Preschooler: https://fyi.extension.wisc.edu/parentingthepreschooler/learning-and-changing/math-readiness/
- Partnering With Families to Improve Students' Math Skills (K–5): https://education.ohio.gov/getattachment/Topics/Other-Resources/Family-and-Community-Engagement/Framework-for-Building-Partnerships-Among-Schools/Math.pdf.aspx
- Support Math Readiness Through Math Talk: https://www.naeyc.org/our-work/families/support-math-readiness-through-math-talk
  - 5 Frame

  - 10 Frame

  - Number Cards 0-10

0	1	2	3
4	5	6	7
8	9	10	

  - 100s Chart

1	2	3	4	5	6	7	8	9	10
11	12	13	14	15	16	17	18	19	20
21	22	23	24	25	26	27	28	29	30
31	32	33	34	35	36	37	38	39	40
41	42	43	44	45	46	47	48	49	50
51	52	53	54	55	56	57	58	59	60
61	62	63	64	65	66	67	68	69	70
71	72	73	74	75	76	77	78	79	80
81	82	83	84	85	86	87	88	89	90
91	92	93	94	95	96	97	98	99	100

REFERENCES

Adams, C., Pierce, R., & Dixon, F. (2007). *Tiered curriculum project.* https://www.in.gov/doe/students/indiana-academic-standards/tiered-curriculum-project/

Archer, A. L., & Hughes, C. A. (2010). *Explicit instruction— Effective and efficient teaching.* Guilford.

Bruner & Kenney. (1965). *Monographs of society for research in child development* (pp. 1-75). Wiley.

Bryant, B. R., Bryant, D. P., Kethley, C., Kim, S. A., Pool, C., & You-Jin, S. (2008). Preventing mathematics difficulties in the primary grades: The critical features of instruction in textbooks as part of the equation. *Learning Disability Quarterly, 31*(1), 21-35.

Bryant, D. P., Bryant, B. R., Roberts, G., Vaughn, S., Pfannenstiel, K. H., Porterfield, J., & Gersten, R. (2011). Early numeracy intervention program for first-grade students with mathematics difficulties. *Exceptional Children, 78*(1), 7-23.

Chien, J., O'Nan Brownell, J., & Uttal, D. (2018). The use of concrete objects in early mathematics learning. In J. S. McCray, J-Qi Chien, & J. E. Sorkin (Eds.), *Growing Mathematical Minds: Conversations between developmental psychologists and early childhood teachers* (pp. 55-82). Routledge.

Doabler, C. T. (2015). Examining the association between explicit instruction and student mathematics achievement. *The Elementary School Journal, 115*(3), 303- 333.

Doabler, C. T., Strand-Cary, M., Jungjohann, K., Clarke, B., Fien, H., Baker, S., Smolkowski, K., & Chard, D. (2012). Enhancing core mathematics instruction for students at risk for mathematics disabilities. *Teaching Exceptional Children, 44*, 48-57.

Dunston, P. J., & Tyminski, A. M. (2013). What's the big deal about vocabulary? *Mathematics Teaching in Middle School, 19*(1), 39-45.

Erikson Institute Early Math Collaborative. (2021a). *Big ideas of early math.* https://earlymath.erikson.edu/why-early-math-everyday-math/big-ideas-learning-early-mathematics/

Erikson Institute Early Math Collaborative. (2021b). *Precursor concepts.* https://earlymath.erikson.edu/why-early-math-everyday-math/precursor-concepts/

Finnegan, L., Miller, K. M., Randolph, K., & Bielskus-Barone, K. D. (2019). Supporting student knowledge using formative assessment and universal design for learning expression. *The Journal of Special Education Apprenticeship, 8*(2), 1-14. https://scholarworks.lib.csusb.edu/josea/vol8/iss2/7/

Fonseca, L. (2018). Mathematical reasoning and proof schemes in the early years. *Journal of the European Teacher Education Network, 12*, 34-44.

Frye, D., Baroody, A. J., Burchinal, M., Carver, S. M., Jordan, N. C., & McDowell, J. (2013). *Teaching math to young children: A practice guide* (NCEE 2014-4005). National Center for Education Evaluation and Regional Assistance (NCEE), Institute of Education Sciences, U.S. Department of Education. http://whatworks.ed.gov

Fuchs, L. S., Fuchs, D., Powell, S. R., Seethaler, P. M., Cirino, P. T., & Fletcher, J. M. (2008). Intensive intervention for students with mathematics disabilities: Seven principles for effective practice. *Learning Disability Quarterly, 31*(2), 79-82

Gersten, R., Beckmann, S., Clarke, B., Foegen, A., Marsh, L., Star, J. R., & Witzel, B. (2009). *Assisting students struggling with mathematics: Response to intervention (RTI) for elementary and middle schools.* National Center for Education Evaluation and Regional Assistance, Institute of Education Sciences, U.S. Department of Education. https://ies.ed.gov/ncee/wwc/Docs/PracticeGuide/rti_math_pg_042109.pdf

Gersten, R., Chard, D. J., Jayanthi, M., Baker, S. K., Morphy, P., & Flojo, J. (2009). Mathematics instruction for students with learning disabilities: A meta-analysis of instructional components. *Review of Educational Research, 79*(3), 1202-1242.

Ginsburg, H. P. , Lee, J. S., & Boyd, J. S. (2008). Mathematics education for young children: What it is and how to promote it. *Social Report, 22*(1), 3-23.

Hoffman, L., & Brahier, D. (2008). Improving the planning and teaching of mathematics reflecting on research. *Mathematical Teaching in Middle School, 13*(7), 412-417.

IRIS Center. (2010/2017). *High-quality mathematics instruction: What teachers should know.* https://iris.peabody.vanderbilt.edu/module/math/

Jitendra, A. K., Alghamdi, A., Edmunds, R., McKevett, N. M., Mouanoutoua, J., & Roesslein, R. (2021). The effects of tier 2 mathematics interventions for students with mathematical difficulties: A meta-analysis. *Exceptional Children, 87*(3), 307-325.

Jitendra, A. K., Nelson, G., Pulles, S. M., Kiss, A. J., & Houseworth, J. (2016). Is mathematical representation of problems an evidence-based strategy for students with mathematics difficulties? *Exceptional Children, 83*(1), 8-25.

Knaus, M. (2017). Supporting early mathematics learning in early childhood settings. *Australian Journal of Early Childhood, 42*(3), 4-13.

McLeskey, J., Barringer, M-D., Billingsley, B., Brownell, M., Jackson, D., Kennedy, M., Lewis, T., Maheady, L., Rodriguez, J., Scheeler, M. C., Winn, J., & Ziegler, D. (2017, January). *High-leverage practices in special education.* Council for Exceptional Children & CEEDAR Center.

Minetola, J. R., Ziegenfuss, R. G., & Chrisman, J. K. (2014). *Teaching young children mathematics.* Routledge.

National Association for the Education of Young Children. (2002/2010). *Early childhood mathematics: Promoting good beginnings* [Position statement]. https://www.naeyc.org/sites/default/files/globally-shared/downloads/PDFs/resources/position-statements/psmath.pdf

National Council of Teachers of Mathematics. (2002/2010). *Early childhood mathematics: Promoting good beginnings* (NAEYC/NCT Joint Position Statement). Authors.

Parks, A. N., & Blom, D. C. (2014). Helping young children see math in play. *Teaching Children Mathematics, 20*(5), 310-317.

Pellegrino, J. W., & Goldman, S. R. (1987). Information processing and elementary mathematics. *Journal of Learning Disabilities, 20*(1), 23-32, 57.

Prawat, R. S. (1989). Promoting access to knowledge, strategy, and disposition in students: A research synthesis. *Review of Educational Research, 59*(1), 1-41.

Sealander, K. A., Johnson, G. R., Lockwood, A.B., & Medina, C. M. (2012). Concrete-semiconcrete-abstract (CSA) instruction: A decision rule for improving instructional efficacy. *Assessment for Effective Intervention, 38*(1), 53-65.

Smith, S. P. (2013). *Early childhood mathematics* (5th ed.). Pearson Education Inc.

Sorkin, J. E., McCray, J. S., & Levine, S. (2018). Chapter 1 Mathematical language and early math learning. In J. S. McCray, J-Qi Chien & J. E. Sorkin (Eds.), *Growing mathematical minds: Conversations between developmental psychologists and early childhood teachers* (pp. 1- 26). Routledge.

Taylor-Cox, J. (2003). Algebra, in the early years. *Young Children, 58*(1), 14-21.

Tomlinson, C. A. (2000, August). Differentiating of instruction in the elementary grades. *ERIC Digest.* http://files.eric.ed.gov/fulltext/ED443572.pdf

Tomlinson, C. A. (2017). *How to differentiate instruction in academically diverse classrooms* (2nd ed.). ASCD.

Tomlinson, C. A., & Eidson, C. C. (2003). *Differentiation in practice: A resource guide for differentiating curriculum grades k-5.* ASCD.

Venn, J. (2014). *Assessing students with special needs* (5th ed.). Pearson Education Inc.

Teaching Science to Students With Disabilities in Early Childhood Classrooms

Karin M. Fisher, PhD, CDE and Kania A. Greer, EdD

INTRODUCTION

Play and the joy of new experiences often fill early childhood education. It is crucial for educators to develop scientific practices that allow for the joy of play while inspiring a child to develop critical thinking skills. Using two well-established, evidence-based pedagogical practices, the 5E model and play-debrief-replay, this chapter provides early childhood educators with a foundation for taking learning beyond play and into discovery while encouraging a child's development in asking critical questions. Purposeful planning of experiences for early childhood learners requires educators to think beyond a science lesson or activity and consider all learning opportunities. This chapter provides educators with two different lesson plan examples so they have the chance to investigate different modes of planning. Information about the Next Generation Science Standards is provided for educators to implement into their lesson plans. This chapter also provides strategies for educators to differentiate science instruction to meet the needs of all learners. Additionally, we present ideas for specially designed science instruction for students with disabilities. High-leverage practices for all students and students with disabilities and Division for Early Childhood Recommended Practices are provided throughout the chapter to equip early childhood educators with evidence-based practices to meet all students' needs.

Fisher, K. M., & Zimmer, K. E. (Eds.).
Early Childhood Special Education Programs and Practices (pp. 207-232).

CHAPTER OBJECTIVES

→ Explain the play-debrief-replay and the 5E models of instruction.

→ Compare and contrast the differences between conceptual play, exploration of phenomena, and scientific inquiry.

→ Select evidence-based teaching strategies and interventions that align with the Division for Early Childhood Recommended Practices and the Council for Exceptional Children's high-leverage practices.

→ Compare and contrast the Hunter and 5E lesson plan formats.

KEY TERMS

- **Backward Design:** A method of designing an educational curriculum by setting goals before choosing instructional methods and forms of assessment.

- **Differentiation:** Tailoring instruction to meet individual needs. Whether teachers differentiate content, process, products, or the learning environment, ongoing assessment and flexible grouping make this a successful approach to instruction.

- **Early Childhood:** Early childhood education encompasses all forms of education, both formal and informal, provided to young children up to approximately 8 years of age. This education is fundamental to the development of a child and can significantly shape the later years of an individual's life.

- **Facilitate:** To make easier; help bring about.

- **High-Leverage Practices (HLPs):** The fundamentals of teaching. These practices are continuously used and are critical to helping students learn important content. Educators use HLPs across subject areas, grade levels, and contexts.

- **Sciencing:** The act of doing science or SCIENCE! or even using scientific instruments for non-scientific (or non-SCIENCE!ific) purposes.

CASE STUDY

Mrs. Hoofman's kindergarten class includes three students with a language disorder, two with autism, and three with specific learning disabilities. Special educators serve 8 of her 18 students. Like most of the classes at English Estates Elementary School, a majority of her students are at or below the poverty level.

Mrs. Hoofman introduces her unit on rocks by reading If You Find a Rock *by Peggy Christian and presents rocks from her rock collection at the end of the story. Some of the stones in Mrs. Hoofman's collection are ordinary and picked up from her yard, and some she had purchased throughout the years. Mrs. Hoofman allows her students to explore the rocks. The students touch, feel, use handheld magnifying glasses, sort, and play with the stones. During the rocks unit, Mrs. Hoofman sends a letter home to families asking students to bring in rocks from home. Many students participate and are excited to share their gems. After the students explore all of the stones, they fill out a rock report (e.g., what color is my rock, where did I find my rock, and is my rock smooth or rough) and glue them into their science journals.*

Another fun activity Mrs. Hoofman incorporates into this unit is to see if stones float or sink. She selects six rocks, one of them being pumice, and labels them 1 through 6. She makes sure the rocks are of different sizes, shapes, and colors. Mrs. Hoofman asks each child to predict whether or not the rocks will sink or float. She saves the pumice for last, and most children expect it will drop to the bottom. They

Figure 10-1. A young child sorting rocks. There is an empty jar with six piles of small, various rocks. (Holly Michele/Shutterstock.com)

are surprised when it floats. Mrs. Hoofman provides each of the children a piece of pumice to explore and scaffolds questioning that prompts students to discuss the pumice's characteristics, comparing and contrasting them with another rock.

Because Mrs. Hoofman's state standards indicate that kindergartners know how we use stones in everyday life, the class takes a walk around school grounds to look for items made of rocks. Afterward, she shows a PowerPoint (Microsoft) presentation on the different ways people use stones. The children then write or draw the ways people use rocks in their science journals (Figure 10-1).

Mrs. Hoofman knows she needs to differentiate her lessons on rocks for her students with disabilities (SWDs), but she is unsure where to start. She wants to accommodate all of her students and make sure they all meet her science lesson's objective. How can Mrs. Hoofman make sure her eight SWDs know how people use rocks in everyday life?

---

*"Next time someone complains that you have made a mistake,
tell him that may be a good thing.
Because without imperfection,
neither you nor I would exist."*

—Stephen Hawking

Science has always been a part of high-quality early childhood education. In their initial years, science education helps students practice many skills such as communication, collaboration, analytic reasoning, and problem skills. Although many kindergarten through second-grade teachers may have basic knowledge of child development and lesson planning for this age group, it is becoming increasingly necessary to develop strategies that focus on the children's strengths to lay the foundation for scientific inquiry later in life. Regardless of whether children are in a formal preschool educational setting, educators expect them to enter kindergarten with basic knowledge and skills, such as letter recognition and print awareness. Understanding how a child learns and how to use an instructional model in each type of environment will assist early childhood educators with fostering a sense of curiosity while keeping learning at a developmentally appropriate level.

Although children are naturally curious about their world, experts argue that they are not naturally scientific. They need guidance to develop their curiosity into more scientific practice and turn their observations into deeper thinking (Worth, 2010). Worth (2010) argued that for a child to truly develop scientific skills, they must directly interact with the materials. As an example, Worth pointed to dinosaurs (Figure 10-2), a topic often loved by young children. Although dinosaurs are fascinating

Figure 10-2. A young boy playing with a dinosaur. His nose is wrinkled, and his mouth is open like he is roaring. (Unsplash)

to children, there is no opportunity to directly engage with dinosaurs to develop inquiry. However, educators can use dinosaurs to explore animals' adaptations, such as birds and insects, in the child's environment.

In an article addressing science in early childhood classrooms, Worth (2010) proposed four basic ideas for more purposeful development of science teaching in early childhood classrooms:

1. Doing science is a natural part of a child's early learning.
2. Children's curiosity often serves as a catalyst for exploration in work and play.
3. Teachers can build on this curiosity to lay the foundation of inquiry skills.
4. Exploration can help build a child's skills, such as "working with one another . . . motor control . . . and mathematical understanding" (Worth, 2010, p. 1).

These concepts support that play, exploration, and inquiry can serve as a foundational scaffolding for science in early childhood. Table 10-1 provides an overview of play, exploration, and inquiry as they relate to water.

This chapter focuses on two instructional strategies that support early childhood learning: play-debrief-replay and the 5E model. Both approaches encourage inquiry, reinforce a child's natural curiosity, and allow them to engage in what they find interesting. Additionally, the strategies are evidence based and align to high-leverage practices (HLPs) in special education and the Division for Early Childhood (DEC) Recommended Practices.

High-Leverage and Division for Early Childhood Practices

There are HLPs in special education and then additional guidelines for teaching SWDs as well as guidelines for teaching science. All are important, but it can be overwhelming. Many of these practices are used somewhat intuitively by teachers, but taking the time to review them periodically (especially when a lesson does not go well) can help teachers challenge themselves and provide the means to take their teaching from good to stellar. Because of the similarity of many of these practices, Table 10-2 combines these essential practices for teaching science and SWDs in early childhood classrooms. These practices are not all inclusive but include HLPs for SWDs (McLeskey et al., 2017) and DEC Recommended Practices. The authors strongly encourage

TABLE 10-1. EXAMPLES OF THE DIFFERENCES BETWEEN PLAY, EXPLORATION, AND INQUIRY

TOPIC	CONCEPTUAL PLAY	EXPLORATION OF PHENOMENA	SCIENTIFIC INQUIRY
Water	Children explore the substance of water: What does it feel like? How does it move? etc.	Where does water come from? What makes water? What holds water? Mathematical concepts such as full, half, empty, and less can be discussed as well.	How do rivers flow? Where does the water in the ocean come from? How much water is there? Clean water vs. dirty water, etc.
Soil	How can we use different types of soil? Does sand hold together better than dirt? What does soil feel like?	Gardening as a phenomenon: Can plants grow in sand? What kind of soil do we need to grow vegetables? What makes plants grow? Mathematical concepts such as weight, density, and size	Testing which soil is best for seeds to germinate? What happens when there is no moisture in soil?
Shadows	Can you play with your shadow? Where are our shadows? Finger puppet shadows.	When do we see our shadow? Where do they go? Mathematical concepts such as taller, shorter, and height	How are shadows formed? Why don't we see shadows at night? Can anything make a shadow?

teachers to become familiar with the practice domain they feel best suits themselves and their students. Table 10-2 provides a list of the domains (i.e., HLPs and DEC Recommended Practices) and associated practices.

MODELS OF INSTRUCTION IN EARLY CHILDHOOD SCIENCE

Play-Debrief-Replay

Although free play is important, it is equally important to provide SWDs with guided play. Especially in younger children, guided play allows the teacher to better observe and facilitate learning for children. This is after all "why we have educated, expert practitioners—not just to set up and get out of the way—but to observe, interpret, interact, and then change the environment and interactions when that would benefit children" (Clements & Sarama, 2020, para. 4).

During play, children "engage in substantial amounts of foundational [science] skills as they explore patterns, shapes, and spatial relations; compare magnitudes; engineer with various materials; and explore phenomena and concepts" (Clements & Sarama, 2020, para. 6). Using this innate exploration and pairing it with specific tasks can help children to develop habits of mind and engage in scientific thinking. Therefore "combining guided free play with intentional, guided-discovery teaching and promoting play with [science] objects and [science] ideas" (Clements & Sarama, 2020, para. 9) is a powerful classroom technique that provides a rich learning experience for children.

For SWDs, play is an important social and educational part of development. It can also be used as an opportunity for teachers to preassess understanding of ideas and to evaluate learning. Utilizing

TABLE 10-2. HIGH-LEVERAGE PRACTICES (HLPS) AND DIVISION FOR EARLY CHILDHOOD (DEC) DOMAINS AND RECOMMENDED PRACTICES

PRACTICE DOMAINS	PRACTICE
HLP 1	Collaboration with professionals to increase student success. This includes service providers as needed, science professionals, and other teachers. It also includes being the lead in organizing and facilitating meetings with professionals.
HLPs 3, 4, and 5 DEC E4 and 5	Talking with and collaborating with parents and other caregivers to support student learning, identify needs, engage students in active learning, and support the child in becoming competent in all environments. Also, can help teachers understand the students' strengths and needs.
HLP 6 DEC A3, 4, 9, and 10	Utilize ongoing and systematic assessment and assessment data to analyze instructional practices and modify teaching to improve student outcomes. Use assessments not just as a means of gauging student understanding but also as a gauge of your teaching and progress toward objectives.
HLP 7	Teachers should provide a consistent, organized, and respectful learning environment that maximizes learning time and strategically redirects off-task behavior. It also involves setting up norms and routines that are consistent across learning environments.
HLP 8	Teachers should provide explicit oral and written constructive feedback in order to guide learning. Explicit feedback helps students focus attention on specific qualities of their work. Good feedback should be specific, focused on academic work, and support student perceptions of their work. Feedback can be in the form of frequent checks to assess student learning and the current level of understanding.
HLPs 11, 12, and 13 DEC E2	Identify and prioritize short- and long-term goals and systematically design instruction toward those goals that involve multiple means of representation, promote child engagement, and provide instruction in a logical sequence to support the connectedness of learning. Consider Universal Design for Learning to make the learning environment accessible for all students.
HLPs 13, 15, and 18	Adapting the curriculum to meet specific learning goals allows the teacher to support individual students who may be struggling. Teachers can do this by checking for understanding in informal but deliberate ways that provide information to the teacher about a student's level of knowledge acquisition. Utilizing small groups, peer-mediated instruction, and interventions and providing scaffolded supports allow the teacher to customize learning around a topic while meeting specific students' needs.
HLPs 14 and 21	Teaching students to think about their thinking metacognition, draw conclusions based on those thoughts, and back up those thoughts with evidence is the goal of most educators. Using carefully designed questions that can draw out a student's thinking enables students to make sense of new knowledge, support their learning, and direct them toward being independent learners.

(continued)

TABLE 10-2 (CONTINUED). HIGH-LEVERAGE PRACTICES (HLPs) AND DIVISION FOR EARLY CHILDHOOD (DEC) DOMAINS AND RECOMMENDED PRACTICES	
HLPs SWD 16 and 20	Using explicit instruction when students are struggling to understand. Breaking things down into more base parts can help all students grasp more complex material. Also, when given instructions for labs or activities, it is essential to provide self-explanatory step-by-step instructions that allow students to follow along, easily find a step they may have missed, and/or work independently depending on the case.
HLPs 18 and 19	Utilize strategies that you know work, including the use of assistive and instructional technologies that can supplement (not supplant) student learning. At times, teachers rely on technology to take the place of teaching rather than using it as a method to support and reinforce instruction. Care should be taken that your use of technology is in support of your teaching. For SWDs, technology could also help students access the curriculum or provide a distraction-free place to learn. Neither of these two situations removes the teacher from the process, and instruction should consider these students' needs.

SWD = student with disability.

Data sources: Division for Early Childhood. (2014). DEC recommended practices in early intervention/early childhood special education. 2014. http://www.dec-sped.org/recommendedpractices and McLeskey, J., et al. (2017). *High-leverage practices in special education*. Council for Exceptional Children & CEEDAR Center.

play removes the high-stakes pressure of being assessed and allows a child's functional knowledge to become apparent. In addition, it allows for students to learn from peer groups, become familiar with science, and investigate ideas without feeling overwhelmed by academic content.

The play-debrief-replay model was developed in 1988 by Selma Wassermann from Canada. She argued that even at young ages in formalized schooling, educators ask children to learn science by carrying out repeated investigations (Wassermann, 1988). Instead of doing science, students should be *sciencing* (Wassermann, 1988, p. 232), a term she coined to encompass the act of doing science through creative actions. Her model does not require the teacher to have a vast knowledge of various fields of science but instead to be a facilitator of learning through the act of investigation, much like Mrs. Hoofman did in her class when she asked her kindergarten students to investigate rocks.

Play

Most parents and teachers will tell you that children 4 to 8 years old play. They play with water, toys, the environment, and friends (Figure 10-3). Through play, teachers can begin to build curiosity and help students ask questions. Play involves the investigation of toys and manipulating them in ways that may not be based on original intent or design (i.e., throwing a doll in water to see what happens, flipping a car upside down and pushing it along the carpet, and trying to fit square pegs into round holes). Although it may appear the child is not playing "correctly," what if we look at what the child is doing as scientific inquiry? All too often, teachers and parents are quick to correct a child's use of a toy, which hinders growth in questions while the child is investing how their world works. The purpose of play is to "acquire information and concept development" (Wassermann, 1988, p. 233). Allowing children to redesign a toy's original purpose to see what happens facilitates this acquisition and development. While the student plays, the teacher can informally observe the student to understand their strengths and needs. The teacher can then use the information collected in the informal observation to debrief with the student around a scientific standard the state expects the child to meet.

Figure 10-3. A young boy playing with a box of sand, shells, and a sponge. He is holding a wooden hollowed-out square. Next to the box is a dinosaur and a hollowed-out wooden triangle. (Unsplash)

Debrief

Debriefing begins after a child has concluded their play. Teachers ask specifics about what the students did in class to facilitate a conversation. The difficulty in debriefing is to ask reflective, developmentally appropriate questions of the child so they consider what they did and begin to think more deeply about the process.

Mrs. Hoofman teaches the Next Generation Science Standards (NGSS) K-LS1-1 (use observations to describe patterns of what plants and animals [including humans] need to survive). First, she identifies and prioritizes the learning goal (HLPs 11, 12, and 13 and DEC Recommended Practice E2). For this lesson, her learning goal is that the students will explain that plants and animals need water to survive. An example of a conversation might be as follows:

Mrs. Hoofman: "We got to play with/explore water today. Who can tell me about water?"

Students: "It's wet, we drink it, rain is water, plants need water, my dog drinks water, water goes in the bathtub," etc.

Mrs. Hoofman: "Jenny, you are correct; animals and plants do need water. How do you know they need water?"

Jenny: Shrugs.

Mrs. Hoofman: (May ask other students the same question.) Explains why animals and plants need water to grow in developmentally appropriate terms.

A teacher can provide explicit feedback and an evidence-based practice and validate children's theories even if they are not scientifically correct. Educators use feedback to guide student learning to increase motivation, engagement, and independence (McLeskey et al., 2017). Giving feedback to guide student learning (HLP 22) while debriefing is timely, genuine, meaningful, and commensurate with their knowledge acquisition. Developmentally appropriate responses and questioning are vital to building scientific inquiry. Keep questioning focused on the topic, brief, and developmentally appropriate while fostering critical thinking skills. Give children wait time to formulate answers to more challenging questions to begin to apply and understand concepts.

Replay

From debriefing comes replay. Replay happens when the child engages with the same materials again. Often play will be repeated (because it was fun), but new explorations can occur based on the debriefing. Based on teacher questioning, children will test new theories during the debrief. In this way, sciencing becomes a part of their natural play and mimics what scientists do in the laboratory under more formal conditions (they investigate, debrief what they learned, and reinvestigate with new information).

After Mrs. Hoofman explicitly teaches (HLPs 16 and 20) why plants and animals need water to survive by showing and telling students (I do), she provides students additional material in addition to water. She supplies the students with soil, cups, and seeds (to begin observing plant growth). She then allows them to play with the material (we do) and informally observes and questions her students. Sample questions Mrs. Hoofman could ask are as follows:

- *I see you put the water in the cup first; tell me about that.*
- *How much water do you think the seeds need?*
- *Do you think you can give a plant too much water?*
- *What do you think goes in the cup first?*

When given the option to play with the material again, teachers allow students to maintain and generalize (HLPs 14 and 21) what they learned. The natural environment of their play will reinforce the student's learning. While observing the student, the teacher will determine if the student maintained the skills learned in the absence of instruction. Students who appropriately plant the seeds and add water met the objective of the lesson for plants (I do). Students who did not will need scaffolding (HLPs 13, 15, and 18) to conclude that plants and animals need water to survive.

The 5E Model

Bybee and Landes (1990) created the 5E model and based it on the fields of "cognitive psychology, constructivist learning theory and best practices for science teaching" (Duran & Duran, 2004, p. 49). The 5E model consists of five stages of learning: engagement, exploration, explanation, elaboration, and evaluation. It is important to note that even though the creators designed the 5E model in a linear sequence, circling back to an earlier step is often required during one or more phases. Learning is not a straight line and, as such, should be approached as a continuous loop.

The 5E model lends itself to making adaptations for SWDs in the early childhood classroom. In particular, the engagement phase allows SWDs to use manipulatives and come up with ideas before delving into the lesson. In addition, the 5E model works very well with the explicit instruction model (HLPs 16 and 20), which allows for teachers to demonstrate tasks for students during the explanation phase (I do, we do), the elaboration phase (we do), and the evaluation phase (you do).

Stages of the 5E Model

ENGAGEMENT (HIGH-LEVERAGE PRACTICES 13, 15, AND 18)

This phase looks at what a child already knows and is used to spark excitement about future learning (Duran & Duran, 2004; Yoon & Onchwari, 2006). First, a teacher would follow HLP 11, which states teachers need to identify and prioritize learning goals.

For example, if Mrs. Hoofman wanted to continue with NGSS K-LS1-1 (use observations to describe patterns of what plants and animals [including humans] need to survive), she might ask students what they know about the topic. Using a KWL (Know, Want, and Learned) chart, she could ask questions about everyday events such as "What do plants and animals need to survive?" She could ask questions to ascertain what they know; what they want to know; and, eventually, what they learned based on learning outcomes. A typical engagement might be as follows:

Mrs. Hoofman: "Why do we need food?"

Students: "To grow up."

Mrs. Hoofman: "Why do plants need food?"

Mrs. Hoofman takes notes of the children's responses on a whiteboard or flip chart. Once she is satisfied with what students know and what they want to know about why humans need food, she will continue to engage them with a word search.

To accommodate for the diverse learners in her classroom, Mrs. Hoofman could hand out a word search activity with the vocabulary of words for all students to complete in small groups (HLP 17). One of the small groups is her diverse students (culturally and linguistically diverse) and SWDs who she knows will need intensive instruction in the form of preteaching the vocabulary (HLPs 16 and 20). Mrs. Hoofman works with this small group by explicitly teaching (HLPs 16 and 20) the lesson vocabulary to diverse learners while the rest of her students complete the word search independently in small groups. After students have completed their word searches, she brings them back to the whole group, giving instructions for the lesson plan's exploration section.

EXPLORATION

Exploration takes place when the child interacts with the environment, conducts investigations through play, and begins to gather information to support their theories (Duran & Duran, 2004; Yoon & Onchwari, 2006). For this hands-on experience, the teacher acts solely as a facilitator to encourage thinking and curiosity. Exploration often involves active learning.

Mrs. Hoofman will allow the children to explore through a video. She will show a video called "What do Animals Eat?" (https://youtu.be/IRszHiLVmUw).

EXPLANATION

During the explanation phase, teachers guide students to connect the dots and form new explanations of phenomena they have explored (Duran & Duran, 2004; Yoon & Onchwari, 2006). Students have the opportunity to review what they said they knew and what they wanted to learn while teachers engage them in explanations. This is where teachers can use "we do" and work specifically with SWDs to check for understanding. The 5E model lends itself well to the cyclic nature of teaching and allows for a teacher to go back and reillustrate (I do) how to conduct a task as needed.

Mrs. Hoofman encourages her students to think about what living things need to stay alive. She will ask what they and their pets need to stay alive. She will record their answers on an easel or the whiteboard. Next, she will ask why animals eat, what kind of things they eat, and whether they think all living things eat. She will explicitly teach them that animals need to eat for energy, and although plants do not eat, they still need energy. Next, she will facilitate a conversation about where plants receive their life. She will use developmentally appropriate explanations and will not overcomplicate her answers. Even if their answers are not scientifically accurate, she will resist the urge to explain all the fine details fully. She will remember that learning is supposed to be fun. See Table 10-3 for examples of developmentally appropriate explanations.

TABLE 10-3. SCIENTIFICALLY ACCURATE VS. DEVELOPMENTALLY APPROPRIATE EXPLANATIONS

SCIENTIFICALLY ACCURATE ANSWER	DEVELOPMENTALLY APPROPRIATE EXPLANATION
Photosynthesis is the primary means by which plants get their energy. They derive this energy from a sugar called *glucose* ($C_6H_{12}O_6$).	The leaves of a plant absorb sunlight, air, and water.
To make glucose, sunlight is captured in pigments like chlorophyll, the substance that gives leaves their green color.	The sunlight's energy is used to convert the air and water into sugar ("plant food").
The sun's energy is passed through a chain of events that breaks water (H_2O) into oxygen (O_2) and creates a store of energy-rich molecules. These molecules will enter a continuous cycle of events to build glucose out of carbon dioxide (CO_2) from the air.	Sugar is broken down into usable energy when the plant needs energy. Raw sunlight energy is not in a state that can be used by the plant.

During the initial conversation, a student may say that plants get their energy from their roots; even though this is not scientifically accurate, Mrs. Hoofman will resist the urge to explain what plants use roots for at this time. She will probe for more details and be sure to bring the discussion back around to plants and energy.

ELABORATION

During elaboration, teachers expect students to generalize what they learned (HLPs 14 and 21). The student should be able to use another example or setting to explain what they learned to generalize their understanding of the scientific concepts. For example, the video did not discuss plants, but students concluding that both plants and animals need water to survive is an elaboration of the content. Elaboration is when the cyclic nature of the 5E model comes into play. If a child truly does not understand, going back to the beginning and re-asking questions is better than pushing the child into developmentally inappropriate elaborations. The elaboration phase is another opportunity for teachers to engage in "we do" with students.

EVALUATION

Although there may be a summative assessment of learning as a culmination of an experience in a formal educational setting, a review should be happening throughout the process (HLP 6 and DEC Recommended Practices A3, 4, 9, and 10). The assessment consists not only of assessing knowledge of students but also of teachers. We should be evaluating how we are asking questions, what we are doing with the answers, how we are building lessons and learning opportunities around children's interests, and how we are re-engaging students who are struggling with concepts. Evaluation is when teachers promote the "you do" model by giving students the opportunity to show what they learned. For SWDs, evaluation methods may look different than a paper/pencil assessment. Teachers should be encouraged to think about alternative ways that students can express their understanding.

Figure 10-4. Children in a classroom setting. (Unsplash)

Mrs. Hoofman created a summative assessment based on the learning objective of explaining that plants and animals need water to survive. She will conduct this assessment by allowing students to show their learning in multiple ways. Students could choose to draw a picture of what plants and animals need to survive or paste photos colored or cut out of magazines. Students could also choose to verbally explain or complete a worksheet provided by Mrs. Hoofman. She will analyze the data to determine if students were able to understand that both plants and animals need water to survive and reteach as necessary.

Both the play-debrief-replay model and the 5E model use evidence-based strategies, such as conceptual play, exploration of phenomena, and scientific inquiry to design instruction. These approaches allow the teacher to engage children comfortably to enable them to engage in interests while having fun. Teachers can use these techniques with any age group. For early childhood, the brain's development naturally lends itself to thinking about learning for young children in terms of conceptual play and moving toward scientific inquiry as they age and mature. However, they are not linear, and teachers should use the approach that best fits their classroom and topic.

PLANNING FOR SCIENCE WITH YOUNG CHILDREN

Early science instruction promotes educational equity by introducing children to the language of science, the tools for science exploration, and the processes for conducting inquiry-based learning (Figure 10-4). Teachers should support this learning through exposure to science, develop a strong understanding of science concepts, practice science processing skills, and explore questions about their everyday world. Children have a natural curiosity about scientific phenomena that relates to their daily life. Young children often want to know the why and how of many concepts. Teachers should build on this interest and promote confidence in the learning process. This interest and enthusiasm naturally lead to inquiry-based teaching in classrooms. When teachers allow the natural and authentic discussions to drive the investigation, children become engaged in science, process and discuss science with each other, listen and process science into their own words, and make sense of new experiences (Cervini & Veronesi, 2006).

Teachers should plan science learning experiences based on the questions children ask, the ideas and interests they show, and the knowledge and skills they bring to the classroom. Taking advantage of teachable moments takes a high level of pedagogical skills and awareness, and facilitating project-based learning of scientific concepts is challenging. Teachers should provide thought-provoking materials and meaningful real-life activities to diverse learners from different backgrounds and abilities to effectively teach science. However, creating a hands-on experience is not sufficient for teaching science to SWDs. Teachers need to highlight students' strengths (HLP SWD 4), gifts, and talents; assume SWDs are competent; and believe in their capabilities (Falvey, 2005).

Teachers should integrate high-interest, concept-laden subject areas such as science into language, literacy, and mathematics learning to increase student engagement and provide a more natural application of knowledge and skills to real-life tasks. Skills educators need to practice include observation, exploration, inquiry, data collection, reflection, and interpretation and can occur across content areas. Educators should develop planning, learning, and assessment simultaneously (HLP 6 and DEC Recommended Practices A3, 4, 9, and 10). Diverse strategies for authentic learning classroom assessments ensure all learners can show what they can do in various ways. Student demonstrations, representations, presentations, documentation, and samples of work are examples of multiple assessment methods that accommodate diverse learners. Furthermore, formative assessments inform teacher planning and the implementation of meaningful and relevant science experiences. Educators should embed reviews in the learning and assess students while they are learning (HLP 6 and DEC Recommended Practices A3, 4, 9, and 10).

Assessment should help teachers identify conceptual understanding before and after a lesson unit, as discussed in Chapter 3. Evaluations help determine misunderstandings and lead to more effective instruction for generalization and maintenance of the learning (HLPs 14 and 21). After the assessment, students should reflect on their accomplishments and goals. Problem-solving and critical thinking assessments help teachers provide for higher-level thinking skills.

As in backward design planning, beginning with the end in mind allows teachers to think about outcomes first. What teachers want students to know for the year, semester, course, week, and day becomes a way to assess themselves and their students. Knowing where the teacher is going will make sure they are on the right path to get there. Teachers need to write lessons that consider all students to guide their learning. There are almost as many ways to write lesson plans as there are ways to teach. We discuss four approaches: the Hunter model, teaching for knowledge, 5E, and discovery based. These models provide an opportunity for teachers to plan for and teach all students in their classrooms purposefully. Most planning begins with a standard.

Standards

The National Research Council framework provided the basis for the NGSS. Because most states have adopted either the NGSS or developed standards based on National Research Council guidelines, the authors explain the NGSS related to early childhood education.

Next Generation Science Standards

The NGSS are K-12 science content standards designed to give educators the flexibility to design classroom learning experiences. The NGSS were developed by states to improve science education for all students. Experts created the standards to stimulate student interest in science. Within the NGSS are three dimensions to learning science: crosscutting concepts, science and engineering practices, and disciplinary core ideas.

CROSSCUTTING CONCEPTS

Experts designed crosscutting concepts to help students explore connections across the four domains for science. The four domains are physical science, life science, earth and space science, and engineering design. These concepts are explicitly taught (HLPs 16 and 20) to students to help them develop a coherent and scientifically based view of the world around them. These standards set the expectations for what students should know and be able to do. All of the criteria are research based and give teachers the flexibility to design learning experiences to stimulate student interest in science. To learn more about the standards, watch the following video: https://youtu.be/SEc1ENq3FSs.

SCIENCE AND ENGINEERING PRACTICES

Teachers describe science and engineering practices when explaining what scientists do to investigate the natural world and what engineers do to design and build systems. These practices demonstrate and extend on inquiry-based learning. Within these practices, students engage in building, deepening, and applying their knowledge of core ideas and crosscutting concepts.

DISCIPLINARY CORE IDEAS

Disciplinary core ideas are vital ideas that have broad importance within or across multiple sciences or engineering disciplines. The concepts build on each other as students progress through grade levels, and schools group them within the four domains of physical science, life science, earth and space science, and engineering.

Students in elementary school begin to understand the four core ideas (i.e., physical, life, earth, and space sciences) as well as engineering, technology, and applications of science. In early childhood education, students begin recognizing patterns and formulating answers to questions about the world around them. As a result, instructional decisions should include practices that lead to performance expectations within the standards.

Kindergarten as an Example

The performance expectations in kindergarten help students answer questions like "What happens if you push or pull an object harder?" "Where do animals live, and why do they live there?" and "What is the weather like today, and how is it different from yesterday?" Kindergarten students should understand the effects of different strengths or different directions of pushes and pulls on an object's motion to analyze a design. Additionally, teachers expect students to understand what plants and animals need to survive and the relationship between their needs and where they live (refer to the Case Study). Lastly, educators expect kindergarten students to understand patterns and variations in local weather and the purpose of weather forecasting to prepare for and respond to severe weather.

Cross-disciplinary patterns, cause and effect, systems, and system models; the interdependence of science, engineering, and technology; and the influence of engineering, technology, and science on society and the natural world organize concepts for these core ideas. Teachers expect students to demonstrate grade-level proficiency in asking questions; developing and using models; planning and carrying out investigations; analyzing and interpreting data; designing solutions; engaging in argument from evidence; and obtaining, evaluating, and communicating information.

For SWDs and their teachers, demonstrating grade-level knowledge may be a challenge. Students may have more knowledge than what a traditional assessment can show, and it is up to teachers to access that knowledge to obtain a true picture of SWDs' learning. Because kindergarten learning (and indeed all early learning) sets a child on their educational trajectory, it is incumbent on early childhood teachers that they expose students to learning that gives them opportunities to express themselves in alternative ways, gives them options to relearn, and builds students' confidence.

Reading Next Generation Science Standards

Each standard or student performance expectation is listed to support teacher implementation on the following website: https://www.nextgenscience.org/search-standards. Additionally, the NGSS created a video on how to read the standards (https://youtu.be/Q6eoRnrw L-A). On the website, teachers will find quality NGSS units, which provide quality examples of science lessons and units. For instance, the NGSS provides materials for a grade 1 unit on light. The unit can be viewed at the following link: https://www.nextgenscience.org/resources/grade-1-how-does-light-help-me-see-things-and-communicate-others-v11.

Lesson Planning

Lesson planning is the foundation of pedagogy and is also covered in Chapter 5. It is especially important in science, where there is a need for diverse materials for students to explore. We provide two types of lesson planning: the Hunter and the 5E formats. Teachers can think of lessons as a set of procedures for the classroom unit or module. Just like a scientist has formalized processes for experimentation, educators should have formalized plans to deliver content. This way, they can better assess if students reach their objectives.

Hunter Lesson Plan

Although lesson planning has been around in some capacity since the 4th century, the first formalized and widely used lesson plan was developed by Madeline Hunter in the 1970s. The most important part of the lesson plan is the alignment between the standard, objective, and assessment. Alignment ensures students are taught the standard and not a portion or subset of the standard.

The Hunter lesson plan format includes a gradual release of knowledge through explicit instruction (HLPs 16 and 20) based on the standard. We focus on daily science lessons for this text, not a lesson over multiple days or units of numerous activities. The first step for a teacher is to determine the standard students will learn.

The teacher should analyze the standard and create a learning goal (HLPs 11, 12, and 13 and DEC Recommended Practice E2) or an objective based on the standard. When developing the learning goal, teachers prioritize what is most important. Teachers use the standard to make decisions about what to emphasize in their lessons. For SWDs, teachers will also consider students' prior knowledge and Individualized Education Program (IEP) goals to decide what to emphasize. The objective should include the criteria, the learning task, and the level of mastery to be specific and measurable. The verbs in the objective and standard should be similar and based on Bloom's taxonomy or depth of knowledge (see Chapter 1).

Next, teachers should develop an assessment of the objective. The assessment must align with the standard and objective, and the verbs should be similar. After the educator develops the evaluation, they should design the learning tasks. The teacher will then create learning tasks for students based on what students need to know to meet the learning objective and pass the assessment. Learning tasks take the form of teacher and group instruction with help. An example of a Hunter lesson plan for science is provided in Table 10-4.

Teaching for Knowledge

The teaching for knowledge lesson plan format is when instruction consists of the teacher sharing knowledge with the students. To determine if teachers sharing knowledge is appropriate, teachers need to look at their standard, objective, and assessment. Are they based on knowledge or skills? If the standard, objective, and assessment are based on knowledge, then teachers sharing that knowledge in an interactive lecture is appropriate. If the standard, objective, and assessment are based on acquiring a skill, teachers should center the learning tasks around that skill acquisition (e.g., demonstrations and trials).

To better illustrate the difference between knowledge and skill, one should think about teaching yoga vs. the scientific process. Although you could teach yoga through lecture, it would be difficult for learners to follow along without practicing the skill. Therefore, yoga classes are taught through demonstration and practice because it is a skill to be learned. On the other hand, teaching about the scientific process is passing on knowledge to students, and the teacher should interactively share their knowledge.

TABLE 10-4. HUNTER LESSON PLAN EXAMPLE

Name: Teaching Date: mm/dd/yy	Topic: Teaching Time: 00:00-00:00
CURRICULUM STANDARDS	**CENTRAL FOCUS/ESSENTIAL QUESTION**
State Curriculum Standards Use observations to describe patterns of what plants and animals (including humans) need to survive.	What do plants and animals need to survive?

LESSON OBJECTIVE(S) AND KEY KNOWLEDGE AND SKILLS	
Objective: Given different items to explore, the students will compare and contrast items needed to survive by plants and animals and determine if any patterns exist between plants and animals with less than one error.	*List the facts about the topic the student must be taught through direct instruction:* What plants need to survive What animals need to survive *List what the students will do at the end of this lesson:* Students will use observations to describe a pattern of what plants and animals need to survive by comparing and contrasting various items.

ACADEMIC LANGUAGE

Soil, food, nutrients, water, air, sunlight, plants, and animals will be explicitly taught.

ASSESSMENT	
Informal: Check for understanding questions	*Formative/Formal:* Students will complete a Venn diagram of the similarities and differences of different items needed for plants and animals to survive and determine if any patterns exist with less than one error on the Venn diagram.

MATERIALS/RESOURCES/TECHNOLOGY

- Venn diagram
- Video
- Different items animals and plants need to survive (i.e., food, water, and soil)
- Pictures of items plants and animals need to survive (i.e., air, sunlight, and food)
- Coloring worksheets
- Nutrition dictionary worksheet

CLASSROOM MANAGEMENT

Behavior expectations will be reinforced as taught at the beginning of the school year.

TIME CONTINGENCIES

- If I am running out of time, I will continue teaching the lesson tomorrow.
- If I have extra time, students will select a worksheet to color based on food groups.
- Students who finish early will complete a nutrition dictionary worksheet.

(continued)

TABLE 10-4 (CONTINUED). HUNTER LESSON PLAN EXAMPLE

INTRODUCTION

1. Anticipatory set: Ask students what they like to eat.

2. Introduce the essential question: What do plants and animals need to survive?

3. Discuss how you will connect this lesson to previous learning experiences and/or prior knowledge.

INSTRUCTION

Direct Instruction

Show students video "What do Animals Eat" (https://gpb.pbslearningmedia.org/resource/tdc02. sci.life.colt.eat/what-do-animals-eat/)

Discuss Video

- What are some similarities and differences in how the animals shown in the video eat?

- What did you find particularly interesting about how these animals eat?

- Which animal eats most like the way you eat?

Show video "Biome in a Baggie" (https://gpb.pbslearningmedia.org/resource/tdc02.sci.life.stru. baggiezoom/biome-in-a-baggie/)

Discuss Video

What do plants need to survive?

Explain how to determine a pattern. Examples of patterns could include that animals need to take in food, but plants do not; the different kinds of food needed by different types of animals; the requirement of plants to have light; and all living things need water.

Modeling

Introduce a Venn diagram: Label 1 circle with plants, the other with animals. Show students how to complete the Venn diagram with their input. Discuss patterns between plants and animals.

Checking for Understanding

Ask students if they are ready to complete a Venn diagram in small groups.

Guided Practice

Put students in flexible groups of three to four students. Have each group complete another Venn diagram on the similarities and differences between what plants and animals need to survive. Have one person from each group present what their groups came up with and any patterns they noticed.

Checking for Understanding

Ask students if they are ready to complete a Venn diagram independently.

Independent Practice

Students will complete a Venn diagram independently and then underneath it will write what patterns they see between plants and animals.

CLOSURE

1. Summary of the lesson: Today, we learned how to complete a Venn diagram and use it to determine what plants and animals need to survive and describe any patterns we noticed.

2. How will you use the emotional quotient to elicit student articulation of their learning? What do plants and animals need to survive? Do you notice patterns in what they need to survive?

3. Plan for tomorrow.

The Hunter lesson planning model incorporates the gradual release model, which is also known as *I do, we do, you do*. The teacher would either demonstrate (as in modeling a yoga position) or share knowledge (as in a lecture on the scientific process) to the students in the "I do" section of the lesson plan. This is also called *explicit instruction* and is an HLP (16 and 20). In the "we do" section, teachers generally allow students to work in pairs or small groups to either practice the activity (yoga) or interact with the knowledge they learned (scientific process). Examples of interactions with the knowledge could be a practice quiz in a Kahoot, a discussion on the scientific method, or students completing a puzzle with the scientific process steps in small groups.

The last step of the Hunter lesson plan format is the "you do" or independent practice. This could be a formative or summative assessment. During this task, the students work by themselves to show you what they retained from your lesson. In the case of a skill like yoga, the student would demonstrate their skill of the yoga positions back to you. The student would do so without your help or instruction. If the students could not complete the task without your help, they have not mastered it, and the teacher should remediate the missing or incorrect skills. For knowledge like the scientific process, students could show their expertise in various ways, including writing down the steps to the scientific method in a ticket out the door or being given puzzle pieces and asked to put them together by themselves, without help. Just like the yoga example, teachers should remediate students who struggle with completing the task without assistance.

Discovery-Based 5E Lesson Plan

Discovery lesson plans are based on students finding things out for themselves by looking into problems. Students come to their conclusions by asking questions. One model is called the *guided discovery model* in which teachers use examples to guide students to an understanding through involvement, curiosity, and critical thinking. A discovery lesson plan would start with an objective, the standard, materials, accommodations, and procedures or learning tasks. Within the guidelines, teachers will write the preplanning, set induction or anticipatory set, whole-class work, group work, and assessment. An example of a discovery-based lesson plan is 5E.

As mentioned previously, teachers act as facilitators during a 5E lesson. Lesson planning using the 5E model begins with engagement—an HLP (13, 15, and 18). In this section, teachers ask questions to determine what the students already know or think they know about a topic. Your questions should start with "how." The second section is to explore. This is when students decide what makes questions scientifically testable. They will have similar experiences in which to build their understanding of the concept. The third section in the lesson plan is explain. Explain is when students acquire opportunities to connect their background knowledge with current learning and conceptualize the topic's main idea. Explain is when teachers introduce keywords and content to make students' experiences easier to describe. Additionally, teachers explain concepts and address misconceptions. Elaborate comes next on the lesson plan. This is when students apply or extend concepts to new situations, particularly real-world applications. The last section of this lesson plan model is evaluate. This is when students are facilitated by their teacher to review and assess what they have learned and how they learned it. Evaluate can be formative or summative. An example of a 5E science lesson plan is provided in Table 10-5.

TABLE 10-5. 5E LESSON PLAN EXAMPLE

Title: Plant and Animal Survival Needs	Duration: 40 minutes
Learning objective: Given different items to explore, the students will compare and contrast items needed to survive by plants and animals and determine if any patterns exist between plants and animals with less than one error.	Standard: Use observations to describe patterns of what plants and animals (including humans) need to survive.
Materials: Venn diagrams Videos Concrete (water bottles, milk cartons) representative (picture, drawing, or photo) and abstract (written words) of items plants and animals need to survive like: Milk cartons, beans, water bottles, pictures of the sun, pictures of wind blowing, boxes of cereal, various fruits, cups of soil, Venn diagrams, dog food, cat food, etc.	Accommodations: Closed captioning on videos, conscious grouping

PROCEDURES

Large Group

Engage:

- Ask students how plants and animals survive.
- Write ideas on board.

Show students video "What do Animals Eat" (https://gpb.pbslearningmedia.org/resource/tdc02.sci.life.colt.eat/what-do-animals-eat/) and discuss:

- What are some similarities and differences in how the animals shown in the video eat?
- What did you find particularly interesting about how these animals eat?
- Which animal eats most like the way you eat?

Show video "Biome in a Baggie" (https://gpb.pbslearningmedia.org/resource/tdc02.sci.life.stru.baggiezoom/biome-in-a-baggie/) and discuss:

- What do plants need to survive?

Small Groups: 3 to 4 students each

Explore: Students will explore and discuss given items in small groups with each other.

When finished exploring, provide each group a blank Venn diagram and ask them to discuss what they think they should do with it and their items.

(continued)

TABLE 10-5 (CONTINUED). 5E LESSON PLAN EXAMPLE
Explain: Venn diagram: Label one circle with plants, the other with animals.   Explain how to determine a pattern. Examples of patterns could include animals need to take in food, but plants do not; the different kinds of food needed by different types of animals; the requirement of plants to have light; and all living things need water.
Elaborate: Students will return to their seats which have different materials and complete their own Venn diagrams.   Students will provide feedback to a partner on their Venn diagrams and may change it based on that feedback.
Evaluate: Students will place, write, or draw various items on Venn diagrams.   Students will then examine their Venn diagrams and determine if they see a pattern in plants' and animals' needs. They will explain the pattern orally or by writing.   Students have met mastery if they can explain or write: All animals need food to live and grow. They obtain their food from plants or from other animals. Plants need water and light to live and grow.

SPECIALLY DESIGNED INSTRUCTION FOR STUDENTS WITH DISABILITIES

In the Individuals with Disability Education Act (2004), special education is defined as "specially designed instruction, at no cost to parents, to meet the unique needs of a child with a disability" (34 CFR R. § 300.39[a([1]). Lawmakers further define specially designed instruction as the "adapting, as appropriate to the needs of the eligible child . . . the content, methodology, or delivery of instruction" (Individuals with Disability Education Act, 2004). In 2012, the Office of Special Education Programs further stated specially designed instruction is not the same as the delivery of accommodations. If this were the case, SWDs would not need special education. Teachers working with young students may recognize that a child has a disability. In fact, teachers may be the first to notice that a child is struggling or is not developing at the same rate as their peers. Regardless, it is up to the teacher to understand, plan for, and incorporate strategies for teaching SWDs like the child in Figure 10-5. The benefit is many of these strategies work for students without disabilities as well.

Many SWDs have difficulty acquiring information and demonstrating their knowledge in the science content area. In addition to general accommodations (e.g., additional time on assessments and read alouds), SWDs should also have access to various supports specific to science. These supports include science literacy, calculations, audible laboratory equipment, displaying data in multiple formats, making connections, staying on track, games, virtual labs, virtual field trips, and WebQuests (Dieker & Hines, 2014).

Science Literacy

SWDs will likely require extra support decoding and comprehending complex science-related terms and phrases. Vocabulary should be preassessed and explicitly taught before or throughout the unit. An evidence-based practice to help students remember vocabulary is the use of the LINC strategy. In the LINC strategy, teachers perform the following:

Figure 10-5. A child with a disability. (Unsplash)

TABLE 10-6. LINC NOTE CARD EXAMPLE	
FRONT SIDE	**BACK SIDE**
Vocabulary word: Water	Definition: A clear liquid that comes from clouds as rain, forms lakes, streams, and seas.
Reminding word: What	Reminding story: What is rain? Picture:

- List the parts
- Identify a reminding word
- Note a LINCing story
- Create a LINCing picture
- Self-test

This strategy can be used on note cards for the vocabulary word "water," as shown in Table 10-6. Mrs. Hoofman could use a simplified version of this note card for her diverse kindergarten class.

Teachers also can use text-to-speech software with adjustable reading rates, highlighting capabilities, and dictionary and thesaurus features through a free program called Bookshare. Bookshare is available for free for any student with a print disability and can be found at bookshare.org. Text-to-speech software can help students understand unfamiliar science-related terms and concepts.

Figure 10-6. Examples of visual representations of data. (Unsplash)

Calculations

Calculating data is expected in the science content area, including in children 4 to 8 years old. As a result, all students should have access to calculators. However, SWDs who have difficulty transposing numbers could benefit from a talking calculator. Cells in Microsoft Excel or Google Sheets could be preset to compute data in columns and rows quickly. In addition to allowing the use of these accommodations, teachers need to explicitly teach students how to use them (HLPs 16 and 20). Furthermore, teachers should model and scaffold the steps required to use the accommodations so that students can complete their learning tasks successfully and independently.

Audible Laboratory Equipment

SWDs who have trouble comprehending information displayed visually and transpose numbers can benefit from the support of audible laboratory equipment. For example, thermometers and scales that provide verbal measurements can support learners with disabilities. Audible laboratory equipment can also assist students who have difficulty reading units accurately (e.g., kilograms and degrees Celsius).

Displaying Data in Multiple Formats

SWDs often have difficulty understanding science information in standard narrative textbooks. Displaying data in multiple formats assists students in grasping content and connecting the concepts. Teachers can use graphing software designed for children to help create, explore, interpret, and print visual representations of the content (Figure 10-6). Teach SWDs to create tables and charts in Excel and Google Sheets to represent data in various formats to increase their understanding of the data. Like other accommodations, teachers should follow HLPs 16 and 20 and provide explicit instructions on using tables and charts successfully and independently.

Making Connections

Educators can use graphic organizers as teaching and studying tools to demonstrate connections between science concepts and related knowledge. Teachers can use these tools to determine prior knowledge. Explicitly teach students to use graphic organizers (HLPs 16 and 20) as study tools to increase comprehension and ask questions for later inquiry or discussion. Technology-based graphic organizers (Figure 10-7) can support students with text to speech and resources such as a dictionary, thesaurus, and spellchecker.

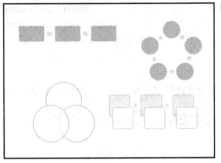

Figure 10-7. Examples of graphic organizers.

Staying on Track

To help SWDs organize reading material, consider teaching them to use highlighting or shading features of electronic texts or word processors. Tables and charts can be color coded. For example, colors could be used for text to determine each phase of the moon. Keywords in the book can be bolded, colored, or enlarged to emphasize the importance. For textbooks, reading guides can be used to help students stay on track while reading. Students can make their own reading guides out of index cards or use a ruler. Teachers can also make them out of color overlays. They are also inexpensive to purchase.

Games

Educators are using learning games to motivate and engage SWDs. Games provide multiple opportunities for learning science content. Examples include Kahoot, Jeopardy, Bingo, Four Corners, and Quizziz.

Virtual Labs

Teachers can use virtual labs as a way to prepare SWDs before they engage in hands-on laboratory work. As a result, they will be more familiar with the concepts and procedures. Virtual labs also provide learning opportunities for SWDs who require repetition to review guidelines multiple times. Teachers can use virtual labs for students with sensory disabilities (i.e., autism spectrum disorder). For example, if the class participates in a dissection and the smell of the formaldehyde bothers some students, allow those students to work in another room in a virtual lab instead of participating in the actual dissection. The National Science Teaching Association provides a list of virtual labs on their website (https://learningcenter.nsta.org/mylibrary/collection.aspx?id=Ft2B7GCI!plus!HM_E).

Virtual Field Trips

Students can explore learning content in new and exciting virtual environments. Virtual field trips can help SWDs visualize the subject matter being applied in the real world. This allows for SWDs to analyze and draw connections between difficult science concepts. Virtual field trips can include museums, science centers, factories, and manufacturing facilities. A list of 25 virtual field trips is provided at https://www.weareteachers.com/best-virtual-field-trips/. Additionally, a free program called Nearpod provides virtual three-dimensional field trips.

WebQuests

WebQuests are a motivational approach to engage SWDs online in science. WebQuests are an inquiry-oriented lesson format in which most or all of the content comes from the internet. Students often work in groups. WebQuests can be short or long term. Short-term WebQuests are completed in one to three class periods and facilitate knowledge acquisition and integration. Long-term

WebQuests can take between 1 week and 1 month to complete. They help students extend and refine knowledge, resulting in analyzing, transforming, and demonstrating an understanding of the content. To learn more about WebQuests, visit http://webquest.org/sdsu/webquestwebquest-es.html.

WRITING SMART INDIVIDUALIZED EDUCATION PROGRAM GOALS FOR EARLY CHILDHOOD SCIENCE EDUCATION

Ensuring that learning for SWDs takes place consistently and with fidelity requires that teachers, parents, and students (where appropriate) work together to develop IEP goals that are SMART (Specific, Measurable, Action oriented, Relevant and realistic, and Time limited). This will help measure the child's progress and ensure the child can access the curriculum at every stage of their education. These goals should be reviewed at least yearly and modified based on input from all stakeholders. Using Mrs. Hoofman as an example, we can look at her unit on water and plants and think about what a child with a disability might need to access that topic.

One of the SWDs in Mrs. Hoofman's class has autism. The student is bright but needs reminders to share materials and work well with others. An appropriate IEP goal for this student would be the following: When working in groups and given hands-on materials, the student will take turns with his peers using the materials for a period of 10 minutes on three out of four observations. The specially designed instruction this student needs based on this IEP goal is on turn taking. The direct instruction should be provided by the student's special education teacher and integrated into science lessons in which Mrs. Hoofman uses hands-on material. The special education teacher would provide direct instruction on turn taking with the student using evidence-based strategies like scripts, video modeling, and embedding choice (Barnett, 2018). The student's special education teacher would also share strategies with Mrs. Hoofman for her to model and use when the specially designed direct instruction is not taking place. The goal is for the student with autism to learn turn taking not only during science lessons in which manipulatives are used more often in small groups but also in all aspects of the student's young life.

SUMMARY

Science instruction for early childhood students often takes place naturally. Teachers are encouraged to take advantage of young students' curiosity and create lessons around that curiosity and student interest. While planning lessons for all students, including SWDs, teachers must understand and use HLPs and DEC Recommended Practices.

Most states have adopted science standards based on the NGSS. It is essential that teachers use their state standards to create lesson objectives. Teachers should design lessons based on teaching a knowledge or a skill. Furthermore, educators should use student strengths, assessment data, learning progression, and benchmarks to decide what is most crucial to emphasize when creating learning goals or objectives (McLeskey et al., 2017). Teachers can use the Hunter or 5E lesson plan formats when planning science lessons based on the students' needs and the content. Educators should use strategies to provide for specially designed science instruction to differentiate instruction for diverse learners.

CHAPTER REVIEW

1. During free play, you notice that many children are playing in the kitchen area. Explain how you could use the play-debrief-replay method to help your students learn about kitchen safety.

2. Using the 5E model, briefly outline a lesson for teaching children about weather patterns including all five areas: engage, explore, explain, elaborate, and evaluate.

3. Compare and contrast the differences between conceptual play, exploration of phenomena, and scientific inquiry.

4. Choose the Hunter or 5E lesson plan model and draft a lesson plan for teaching students about day and night; be sure to explicitly include how you will differentiate for SWDs and culturally and linguistically diverse students.

5. Which of the following are evidence-based teaching strategies that align with the DEC Recommended Practices and the Council for Exceptional Children's HLPs (select all that apply)?
   a. Explicit instruction
   b. Graphic organizers
   c. LINC vocabulary strategy
   d. Clip charts

6. Science education helps students practice which skills?
   a. Communication
   b. Collaboration
   c. Analytic reasoning
   d. All of the above

7. The purpose of play is to:
   a. Acquire information and concept development
   b. Have fun
   c. Collaborate with peers
   d. Develop social skills

RESOURCES

- Next Generation Science Standards: https://www.nextgenscience.org/resources/grade-1-how-does-light-help-me-see-things -and-communicate-others-v11
- Resources to teach science to students with autism: https://autismclassroomresources.com/teaching-science-special-education-classroom/
- Resources to teach science to SWDs from Hoagies: https://www.hoagiesgifted.org/eric/faq/science.html
- Resources to teach science to SWDs from the National Science Teaching Association: https://www.nsta.org/disabilities/
- Virtual field trips: https://www.weareteachers.com/best-virtual-field-trips/
- Virtual labs: https://learningcenter.nsta.org/mylibrary/collection.aspx?id=Ft2B7GCI!plus!HM_ E
- WebQuests: http://webquest.org/sdsu/webquestwebquest-es.html

REFERENCES

Barnett, J. H. (2018). Three evidence-based strategies that support social skills and play among young children with autism spectrum disorders. *Early Childhood Education Journal, 46,* 665-672. https://doi.org/10.1007/s10643-018-0911-0

Bybee, R. W., & Landes, N. M. (1990). Science for life & living: An elementary school science program from biological sciences curriculum study. *The American Biology Teacher, 52*(2), 92-98.

Cervini, L. A., & Veronesi, P. (2006). *The primary classroom: Science, literacy, and inquiry.* NSTA Press.

Clements, D. H., & Sarama, J. (2020, April). *Mythbuster series #4: Children don't need adult guidance in play (or learning).* STEM4EC Blog. https://stem4ec.ning.com/blog/mythbuster-series-4-children-don-t-need-adult-guidance-in-play-or?context=category-Mythbuster

Dieker, L., & Hines, R. (2014). *Strategies for teaching content effectively in the inclusive secondary classroom.* Pearson.

Duran, L. B., & Duran, E. (2004). The 5E instructional model: A learning cycle approach for inquiry-based science teaching. *The Science Education Review, 3*(2), 49-58.

Falvey, M. (2005). *Believe in my child with special needs: Helping children achieve their potential in school.* Paul H. Brookes.

Griffin, R. (2010). *Into the universe with Stephen Hawking.* Darlow Smithson Production Limited.

Individuals With Disabilities Education Act, 20 U.S.C. § 1400 *et seq.* (2004).

McLeskey, J., Barringer, M. D., Billingley, B., Brownell, M., Jackson, D., Kennedy, M., Lewis, T., Maheady, L, Rodriquez, J., Scheeler, M. C., Winn, J., & Ziegler, D. (2017). *High leverage practices in special education.* Council for Exceptional Children & CEEDAR Center.

Office of Special Education Programs. (2012). Dear Ms. Chambers, Specially-designed instruction letter. https://sites.ed.gov/idea/files/idea/policy/speced/guid/idea/memosdcltrs/11-026517r-ma-chambers-definitions-5-4-12.pdf

Wassermann, S. (1988). Play-debrief-replay: An instructional model for science. *Childhood Education, 64*(4), 232-234.

Worth, K. (2010). *Science in early childhood classrooms: content and process.* University of Illinois. http://www.predskolci.rs/HTML/Literatura/Science%20in%20Early%20Childhood%20Classrooms.pdf

Yoon, J., & Onchwari, J. A. (2006). Teaching young children science: Three key points. *Early Childhood Education Journal, 33*(6), 419-423.

Social Studies in Prekindergarten to Second-Grade Classrooms

Stacy Delacruz, EdD and Raynice Jean-Sigur, PhD

INTRODUCTION

The foundation of an early childhood classroom lies in forming relationships with others, building community, engaging with others, and contributing to the group. All of these skills are embedded naturally in the social studies curriculum. This chapter begins with a presentation of a case study demonstrating how to differentiate instruction for all learners while focusing on the social studies curriculum. A developmental approach to teaching social studies in early childhood classrooms is discussed. This discussion highlights evidence-based instruction in special education within social studies. Social studies strands from kindergarten through fifth grade are introduced, along with suggestions for teachers to consider when developing lesson plans and preparing to teach social studies. Evidence-based practices and high-leverage practices align with these suggestions. Ten themes addressed for pre-K through 12th-grade social studies instruction are shared. The authors also include a book list for the social studies classroom and virtual resources.

Fisher, K. M., & Zimmer, K. E. (Eds.).
Early Childhood Special Education Programs and Practices (pp. 233-255).

CHAPTER OBJECTIVES

→ State the relationship between social studies and child development and compare the various strands of social studies in early childhood education.

→ Identify the social studies concepts and how they are related to teaching diverse early learners.

→ Develop differentiated supports for a social studies unit or lesson.

→ Use evidence-based teaching strategies that align with the Division for Early Childhood Recommended Practices and the Council for Exceptional Children's high-leverage practices.

→ Select evidence-based teaching strategies and interventions that align with both the Division for Early Childhood Recommended Practices and the Council for Exceptional Children's high-leverage practices.

KEY TERMS

- **Anthropology:** The study of cultures and the development of societies.
- **Citizenship:** The act of participating and becoming members of a community and country. People can have multiple citizenships.
- **Civic Ideals:** An understanding of civic ideals and practices is critical to full participation in society and is an essential component of education for citizenship. This theme enables students to learn about the rights and responsibilities of citizens of a democracy and to appreciate the importance of active citizenship. These themes typically appear in units or courses dealing with civics; history; political science; cultural anthropology; and fields such as global studies, law-related education, and the humanities in schools.
- **Civics:** The study of the rights and duties of citizenship.
- **Consumers:** People who buy goods and services to satisfy their wants.
- **Culture:** The customary beliefs, social forms, and material traits of a racial, religious, or social group.
- **Democracy:** A system of government in which rule is by the people, either as a direct democracy in which the people make their laws or as a representative democracy (i.e., a republic) in which laws are made by the people's representatives.
- **Economics:** The careful use of money, resources, and means of production.
- **Geography:** The study of places and humans in relation to their environments.
- **Global Connections:** The realities of global interdependence require an understanding of the increasingly important and diverse global connections among world societies. This theme prepares students to study issues arising from globalization. It typically appears in units or courses dealing with geography, culture, economics, history, political science, government, and technology.
- **Patriotism:** Loving, honoring, and/or sacrificing for our country.
- **Pride:** Someone feeling happy or satisfied with one's achievements or the accomplishments of someone close to them.
- **Producers:** People who combine resources to make goods and services.
- **Realia:** Objects and material from everyday life, especially when used as teaching aids.
- **Self-Identity:** An individual's ability to recognize one's traits such as body image, voice, physical characteristics, and likes and dislikes about others around them.
- **Self-Regulation:** The ability to manage one's emotions and behaviors.

- **Social Studies:** The integrated study of the social sciences and humanities to promote civic competence. Within the school program, social studies provides a coordinated, systematic study drawing on such disciplines as anthropology, archaeology, economics, geography, history, law, philosophy, political science, psychology, religion, and sociology, as well as appropriate content from the humanities, mathematics, and natural sciences.
- **Socialization:** A growing awareness of social norms and customs.
- **Tiered Instruction:** A method that varies the level of assignments so all students have a chance to find success and make progress.

CASE STUDY

Mr. Gibbs teaches the social skill of listening to his second-grade students during their study of economics. First, he focuses on increasing appropriate behaviors by adopting an instructional approach in which he explicitly teaches and models the social skills of listening. He puts toys and other household ads out and asks students to cut and paste a picture of something they would spend their money on vs. something they would save for. The class then sits at circle time and shares their spending and saving choices. He models to students how whenever a friend is sharing, they should give the friend their attention and listen while the child shares. He reiterates the steps of listening with his students by making an anchor chart and reviewing the steps. Mr. Gibbs then offers students multiple opportunities to practice listening throughout the school day. He provides them specific, positive feedback, such as "I like the way Aubree was paying attention to me and she was quiet when I was speaking." Establishing and maintaining a consistent, organized, and respectful learning environment are critical for success.

"Our goal as educators is to treat diversity as the norm, not the exception. Therefore, an effective approach to diversity is to represent it in the daily lives of people."
—Ann S. Epstein

PREKINDERGARTEN TO SECOND-GRADE SOCIAL STUDIES DEVELOPMENT

When reviewing the concept of social studies for early learners, it is essential to understand the relationship between social studies and social-emotional development. This high-leverage practice is vital during the first weeks and months of school because early learners establish relationships with peers and adults and learn to be part of a classroom community. Both social studies and social-emotional development are related because they focus on the inter-relationship and interaction of others and the environment. Social studies learning begins with social-emotional development for very young children because the child's learning about interaction and others begins with self and self-identity. Learning social studies for young children is a developmental process in which children learn about themselves and how they relate to others and the world. Young children exhibit many developmental traits that demonstrate that they are ready for social studies and have been learning social studies principles since birth. Mindes (2005) stated that young children begin their social studies learning from birth. They begin to realize they are a part of a family and explore the surroundings around them. Table 11-1 provides a visual representation of this developmental approach and its relation to subjects and social studies topics. Educators must acknowledge and focus on the development of social studies to engage and help build social studies concepts in children.

TABLE 11-1. DEVELOPMENTAL APPROACH TO SOCIAL STUDIES

DEVELOPMENTAL RANGE OF CHILD	SOCIAL STUDIES CONCEPT	QUESTIONS THE CHILD MAY ASK OR EXPERIENCE	SOCIAL STUDIES CONCEPT
Birth and beginning of development bonding with caregivers	Focus on self-identity	Who am I, all about me, how do I fit in the world?	Culture/ anthropology Geography
Early development and gaining independence	Self-regulation	What are my feelings and emotions? How do I express myself? How do I regulate my emotions? What are the rules that I know and the rules that are around me? How can I express my independence and the right to grow and learn? What is happening in the present? How does that relate to what has happened to me in the past? What will happen next?	Culture/ anthropology Geography Civics/ government History
Early development and exploration	Self as a part of the world	What am I learning about the world around me? What do I know about my world? What do I know about my family and friends and the people who are important to me? What are the social cues that I am learning? What are the spoken and unspoken social rules around me? How do I fit into the world around me and the world that I am discovering? What are the responsibilities? How do I accomplish those responsibilities? What is happening in the present? How does that relate to what has happened to me in the past? What will happen next? What is growing in my world? How did it look in the past? Now? What will it look like in the future?	Culture/ anthropology Geography Civics/ government History
Early development and exploration	Focus on self as a part of a group	What are friends? How do I make friends? How do I learn to work with others? How do I communicate with others so that my rights are valued and respected? What have we done in the past? What do we do now? What can we do in the future?	Culture/ anthropology Geography Civics/ government History

(continued)

TABLE 11-1 (CONTINUED). DEVELOPMENTAL APPROACH TO SOCIAL STUDIES			
Middle development and productive citizen	Focus on self as a part of a group and community	How do I understand others and the rules of another group, culture, or society? How do I work together for a common goal? How do I take on duties and responsibilities that will make me a productive person? What can we build or make as a group to share or produce for others?	Culture/ anthropology Geography Civics/ government History Economics

The topics of history, geography, civics, economics, anthropology, and government are thought of as learning about social studies and social relationships. For preschool and prekindergarten children, learning to be part of a group, a community, and the world in which they exist is a part of the learning process. All children learn at different rates with different abilities. Some children, including children with disabilities, may still be developing self-identity and self-regulation. *Self-regulation* is the process of children learning about their feelings and emotions and how to manage them effectively. Educators can teach the skills of managing emotions in the classroom. Teachers must understand that all children develop differently and recognize the variability in instructional planning. Additional information about this topic is provided in Chapter 3.

An essential factor to consider when teaching social studies and child development is the child's social development. Theorists such as Erik Erikson acknowledged that young children between 3 and 6 years of age are learning social roles and finding purpose. Early in a child's social development, the child begins to wonder about the safety and the surrounding world. As the child develops, the child starts to question the world, find purpose, and contribute to the world; asking the questions of "why" or "how" are common during this time. Even if the child cannot verbalize these questions, the teacher must know that this natural curiosity is typical during the early learning years (Krishnan, 2011). Some children who have limited language ability may express this questioning and interest through exploration and play. The actions displayed may include exploring relationships with friends and others or figuring out who they are through play, such as making faces in front of a mirror. In Figure 11-1, the little girl is exploring self through play and looking at herself in a mirror.

Children also may take phrases and instructions literally at this age, misinterpret how they are taught, and may own this as a part of their social behavior or self-concept. An example of this may include teachers asking 4-year-old students to write a letter to a friend, and they may write an alphabet letter such as "T." Teachers may need to use visual cues and examples to demonstrate what they are teaching.

Krishnan (2011) cautioned adults to be careful when phrasing directions or guiding children in this stage. They may interpret the negative response or critical guidance as being an awful person or "unacceptable" in the eyes of the teacher or peers. For example, some children, including those with cognitive processing issues, may not fully understand and respond incorrectly to directions such as "Can you stop doing this?" This question may get a response of "yes" or "no" from the child. Teachers need to be specific, clear, and precise in their instructions with a positive tone (e.g., "Gianna, please tell us two things that you like about the picture. You may tell us one thing if you only can think of one thing at this time.").

A significant aspect to consider when addressing social studies at this young age is to focus on teaching these topics in a developmental manner. A few developmental theorists would argue that some social studies topics, such as history, economics, civics, government, and anthropology, may be too abstract for young children to process and may not be of interest to this age group. Child development knowledge and the understanding of young children are important considerations when teaching social studies, such as culture, civics, self-identity, geography, economics, and history.

Figure 11-1. A girl in front of a mirror. The little girl is exploring self through play and looking at herself in a mirror.

Culture

All children have a culture and bring culture to the learning environment. Children can learn about other cultures as well. Providing activities that help children identify their culture while building on their strengths is essential (Derman-Sparks & Edwards, 2010). Teaching children about their similarities and differences and appreciating these concepts are a part of social studies instruction. Children should have opportunities to learn ways to address bias and respect themselves, their peers, and others. Many children, even at young ages, experience bias, including children with disabilities.

Teachers need to be sensitive to children and families who may not be aware of their culture. Guided questions and discussions with families may assist in this process; including families in the teaching of this topic is critical. Kuh and colleagues (2016) provided a framework for educators to include antibias and cultural awareness practices. Children can find different ways of engaging through making cultural songs, stories, books, role plays, artwork, and videos with family members. Children and family members can choose how they wish to express their culture and share it with the class through various means, such as show-and-tell. The child in Figure 11-2 is expressing her Mexican culture by wearing a costume and makeup for the Day of the Dead.

Time, Continuity, and Change

The concept of time may be difficult for very young learners. It may be difficult for some children to understand sequencing; order; and the terms past, present, and future or yesterday, today, and tomorrow. Social studies lessons involving time and historical events may be limited to the self-view of the child (what happened yesterday only or in the last activity). Providing visual cues such as a timeline or checklist of what happened in order may help instruction. Visual timers and auditory cues such as a bell or familiar song may help trigger children to know when change is happening or the time has stopped.

Playing turn-taking games also helps with understanding the concept of time, continuity, and change. Children can learn what is next when they must pass a ball to other classmates. Teachers can guide by asking who had the ball first or before (past), who has it now (present), and who will have it next (future). Including families and the home learning environment is another way to support learning about time, continuity, and change. Teachers can ask parents and grandparents or other family members to tell stories about their past and discuss and share these stories at home. Children can gather pictures of the past and bring them to class to share.

Figure 11-2. Child dressed up for Mexican holiday—Day of the Dead. (Yuganov Konstantin/Shutterstock.com)

PEOPLE, PLACES, AND THE ENVIRONMENT

Field trips to other places in the community and inviting guest speakers to class help students learn about their community and the people in them. Technology can also help with this process by videoconferencing with a guest speaker or conducting a virtual trip to a new place. Students can summarize their participation in this lesson by participating in a scavenger hunt with words and pictures, making artwork or a scrapbook of the field trip, or creating a song about the experience. Again, families can be connected in this process by sharing their stories as guest speakers, going to field trip sites, or starting discussions with their children about their community and people in them.

Historical Understanding

Special education teachers follow a strategic, reflective, recursive process and use their content and pedagogical knowledge using high-leverage practices to deliver effective instruction. Elementary classroom instruction includes specific social studies topics. Historical understandings encompass one of these topics. History has been a long-standing staple in the social studies curriculum in the United States. In 1916, schools started to integrate history, geography, and political science into the early childhood curriculum (Mindes, 2005). Research in early childhood classrooms has shown that children 3 to 5 years old have "some awareness of time, can recognize different interpretations of stories, and are capable of deductive reasoning in informal situations" (Skjaeveland, 2017, p. 10). Additional research conducted in Switzerland found that most 4- to 4.5-year-old children in their study gained knowledge of both historical facts and concepts.

Beginning in pre-K, children start to make sense of historical concepts. Student historical understanding includes an awareness of national and cultural holidays, American symbols, historical figures and their contributions, and cultures of the past. To help them develop historical understandings and concepts of time, teachers can reiterate how all students were once babies and are now bigger boys and girls. "Statements such as these about changes in their own life histories reveal a consciousness about change and an awareness of a connection between the past and the present" (Skjaeveland, 2017, p. 18). Although students may not have an abstract or metric concept of time yet, they can still learn that "time is embedded in experiences and lived experiences" (Lippitz, 1983, p. 175). As teachers provide instruction about national and cultural holidays, they can build on what children already know. For instance, teachers can survey parents to determine celebrated cultural holidays in their families. Teachers may build on the results of the survey to teach students about national holidays. National holidays that early childhood students should know include Christmas,

Columbus Day, Independence Day, Labor Day, Martin Luther King Jr. Day, Memorial Day, New Year's Day, Presidents' Day, Thanksgiving, and Veterans Day. National holidays provide a connection to American symbols. It is important to remember to model community building and move away from the tourist focus of teaching holidays and celebrations so that children learn how diversity and social studies can come from them and their families in their communities.

Teachers might relate July 4th, a national holiday, to the American flag as a symbol of the United States. We honor our flag and show allegiance to our country by reciting the Pledge of Allegiance so students can participate in this hands-on activity by holding the flag or leading the pledge. Early childhood teachers need to note that there may be children who, because of beliefs, choose not to participate in certain celebrations or civic events. This behavior is not necessarily a lack of good citizenship. Families can help engage children in activities that involve citizenship. Two questions to ask families are (a) In what ways do you help your child learn about the country or community in which they dwell? and (b) What are some ways that you may celebrate or participate in community activities?

The National Council for the Social Studies (NCSS) developed a position statement regarding early childhood in the social studies context. The NCSS (2019) asserted that "curricular and instructional decisions embrace diversity and social justice while intentionally contesting bias and inequity" (p. 19). Early childhood classrooms should celebrate children's cultures and languages and should foster inclusion and equity. Another critical piece is teachers' efforts to intentionally embed diverse languages, materials, and experiences into classroom practices (Durden et al., 2015). The Division for Early Childhood (DEC) of the Council for Exceptional Children discusses the topic area of instruction for early childhood educators. One instructional practice DEC details is that practitioners embed instruction within and across routines, activities, and environments to provide contextually relevant learning opportunities (INS5). As you embed the act of reciting the pledge, instruction can take place. Additional American symbols taught in early childhood classrooms may include the national anthem, the bald eagle, the Statue of Liberty, the Lincoln Memorial, the Washington Monument, and the White House. Generally speaking, storytelling along with physical and bodily experiences such as dramatic play or role-playing are ways to teach history in early childhood classrooms. Storytelling led by family and community members can help students gain historical knowledge. Scholars have emphasized the impact that stories have on learning about children's pasts (Durden et al., 2015; Farmer & Heeley, 2004).

Geographic Understanding

Two main subfields compose the geography discipline: human geography and physical geography. The National Geographic Society (2019) described *human geography* as studying the distribution of networks of people and cultures on the Earth's surface. In contrast, *physical geography* is learning about the Earth's seasons, climate, atmosphere, soil, streams, landforms, and oceans. "Through interactions with the environment and with each other, children develop geo-literacy skills, become empowered, and see themselves as capable social beings" (Brillante & Mankiw, 2015, p. 3).

Geographic understanding standards in the elementary curriculum include differentiating land and water features on simple maps and globes; describing how historical figures were influenced by their time and place; identifying and locating cities, counties, states, countries, and continents on a map or globe; finding and comparing major topographical features and defining how these features affect the Earth's surface; and describing how physical systems affect human systems. Central to an early childhood curriculum, play-based modalities enact inquiry. Through structured and free play, children's understanding of geography can develop. For example, students can use molding clay to form mountains, valleys, oceans, and forests. A Play-Doh (Hasbro) mountain constructed by children is shown in Figure 11-3.

Figure 11-3. A Play-Doh mountain.

Geography plays a crucial role in helping students develop awareness between people and the environment. This awareness provides students with a sense of place, an essential part of cognitive, social, and emotional development (Brillante & Mankiw, 2015). A sense of place can also equate to a sense of belonging among young learners. Brilliante and Mankiw (2015) asserted that "many geography-related investigations and curriculum ideas for young children begin with children's relationships with people and places" (p. 5). For example, during snack time, children might converse about where their home is and about other students' homes in the classroom. It is about building a sense of community, developing respect, and learning about each other in the classroom to build inclusion and equity. To expand students' geographic awareness, teachers can invite parents and friends to mail postcards from different states and countries to the classroom. These can be hung up on a classroom map to document where each postcard comes from in the world.

Government/Civic Understanding

In early childhood classrooms, learning about the rights and duties of being a citizen helps learners gain social competence and civics education. Kemple (2017) wrote learners need to "experience real-life personal situations in which concepts such as fairness, the common good, and the rule of law, come into play, and practice the requisite social skills" (p. 628). These concepts need to be embedded into their world before they can "identify and exercise the rights and responsibilities of citizens" (NCSS, 2010, p. 90). According to the DEC Recommended Practices (2014), Interaction Goal 4 emphasizes that educators "promote the child's cognitive development by observing, interpreting, and responding intentionally to the child's exploration, play, and social activity by joining in and expanding on the child's focus, actions, and intent" (p. 14). This type of interaction helps to promote civics education. The early childhood standards in government and civic understanding include demonstrating an understanding of good citizenship, describing examples of positive character traits exhibited by good citizens (e.g., honesty, patriotism, courtesy, respect, pride, and self-control), defining the concept of government and the need for rules and laws, and identifying elected officials (e.g., president, governor, and mayor). Overall, the standards' intent is for students to demonstrate an understanding of what it means to be a good citizen.

Economic Understanding

The teaching of economic understanding is a core component of the social studies education curriculum. Kindergarten through fifth-grade students are interested in and capable of learning about economic concepts, such as production, consumption, and decision making; yet, these ideas are often not taught to younger students (Parker & Beck, 2017). Casey and Casey (2019) stated that this lack of instruction might be due to the lack of quality resources available to early childhood teachers. These researchers asserted that opportunities to engage in economic thinking are a part of early learning instruction. Kiddynomics, an economics curriculum for young learners, was developed by researchers, the Federal Reserve Bank of St. Louis (2019), and other educators. This free, online resource introduces students to basic personal finance and economic concepts. For example, the Social Studies Georgia Standards of Excellence emphasize that students in early childhood classrooms should describe the work people do and explain that people earn income by working. Students can explain the use of money to purchase goods and the ability to make choices because they cannot have everything they want.

Recommendations for Teachers, Social Studies, and Child Development

There are several suggestions for teachers to consider when developing lesson plans and preparing to teach social studies. Table 11-2 provides examples of suggestions based on the DEC and special education high-leverage practices.

Differentiated Instruction in Social Studies

Effective teachers adapt instruction to meet the needs of individual learners. Differentiating instruction in social studies aims to help all students experience success regardless of their learning needs. As teachers consider differentiation, they decide curriculum adaptation, instructional design, and instructional tools to implement. As Chick and Hong (2012) wrote, the second goal of differentiation in social studies is "for students to experience a democratic classroom where the responsibility for learning is shared" (p. 112).

Early childhood educators must differentiate. Students with disabilities are included in the regular education setting for social studies instruction. However, social studies might not be taught due to time constraints or other curriculum initiatives. Thus, integrating children's literature with social studies allows students to "critique, analyze from multiple perspectives, and springboard into a discussion of complex issues" (Shea, 2010, p. 35). Table 11-3 contains a list of social studies picture books with various social studies strands.

An example of a differentiated activity in social studies is known as *RAFTing*. When students complete RAFTs, they have choices in what they produce. The R stands for the Role the student takes on, the A the Audience, the F the Format, and the T the Topic. For example, to integrate learning about Martin Luther King and provide students with multiple perspectives on a topic, a second-grade teacher may do a RAFT (Table 11-4). Students can select which RAFT prompt they would like to complete, or the teacher may assign a RAFT prompt to different subgroups of learners.

Chick and Hong (2015) discussed tiered learning experiences as another option for differentiated instruction. For example, teachers might divide students into subgroups (e.g., green group = struggling learners, blue group = on–grade-level learners, and yellow group = advanced learners) and provide different ways for students to demonstrate their knowledge.

TABLE 11-2. LESSON PLAN SUGGESTIONS

EDUCATIONAL BEST PRACTICES	DEC RECOMMENDED BEST PRACTICES	SPECIAL EDUCATION HLPs
Set the tone of the learning environment that all children are a part of the learning environment and belong.	E1: Practitioners provide services and supports in natural and inclusive environments during daily routines and activities to promote the child's access to and participation in learning experiences.	HLP 7: Establish a consistent, organized, and respectful learning environment.
Include songs, pictures, and books that support diversity and reflect differences in ethnicity, age, ability, family composition, language, gender, belief, culture, and race.	F1: Practitioners build trusting and respectful partnerships with the family through interactions that are sensitive and responsive to cultural, linguistic, and socioeconomic diversity.	HLP 3: Collaborate with families to support student learning and secure needed services. HLP 18: Use strategies to promote active student engagement.
Provide teaching opportunities that allow children to learn about their feelings and emotions. Consult with families and other caregivers about identifying emotional cues and how to help children express and effectively share their emotions.	INS13: Practitioners use coaching or consultation strategies with primary caregivers or other adults to facilitate positive adult–child interactions and instruction intentionally designed to promote child learning and development.	HLP 18: Use strategies to promote active student engagement.
Allow each child to have a role or job in the class.	INS6: Practitioners use systematic instructional strategies with fidelity to teach skills and to promote child engagement and learning.	HLP 7: Establish a consistent, organized, and respectful learning environment.
Guide children in developing classroom rules.	INS7: Practitioners use explicit feedback and consequences to increase child engagement, play, and skills.	HLP 7: Establish a consistent, organized, and respectful learning environment.

(continued)

TABLE 11-2 (CONTINUED). LESSON PLAN SUGGESTIONS

EDUCATIONAL BEST PRACTICES	DEC RECOMMENDED BEST PRACTICES	SPECIAL EDUCATION HLPs
In addition to classroom rules, begin to build some classroom rituals and routines. Many teachers practice the concept of daily routines. A classroom ritual is a practice that makes the classroom routine meaningful to the teacher, children, other caregivers, and families. A classroom ritual involves children and other adults in the children's lives and is thoughtful and intentional. An example of a classroom ritual is a "Welcome Song" when new children and families arrive.	INS5: Practitioners embed instruction within and across routines, activities, and environments to provide contextually relevant learning opportunities.	HLP 3: Collaborate with families to support student learning and secure needed services. HLP 7: Establish a consistent, organized, and respectful learning environment.
Arrange opportunities for all children to work together with different groups.	E2: Practitioners consider Universal Design for Learning principles to create accessible environments.	HLP 17: Use flexible grouping.
Inform and invite families into the learning process and have them participate in instruction as much as possible.	INS2: Practitioners, with the family, identify skills to target for instruction that help a child become adaptive, competent, socially connected, and engaged and that promote learning in natural and inclusive environments.	HLP 3: Collaborate with families to support student learning and secure needed services.
Give children choices. Guide them in making choices that will be beneficial to self as well as the group. For example, ask a child if they would like to sing the "ABC Song" or the "Good Morning Song." Do not overwhelm them with too many choices, but notice and record some common preferences and allow for these.	INS6: Practitioners use systematic instructional strategies with fidelity to teach skills and to promote child engagement and learning.	HLP 15: Provide scaffolded supports.
Communicate with children in healthy ways. It is vital to avoid negatively stating phrases. For example, instead of saying, "Don't run in the class!" state what can be done. "Do use your feet for walking so you will not trip and hurt yourself." As stated earlier, children learn about the world around them and need explanations when learning about self, rules, and the world around them.	INS7: Practitioners use explicit feedback and consequences to increase child engagement, play, and skills.	HLP 8: Provide positive and constructive feedback to guide students' learning and behavior.

Data sources: Division for Early Childhood. (2014). DEC recommended practices in early intervention/early childhood special education. 2014. http://www.dec-sped.org/recommendedpractices and McLeskey, J., et al. (2017). *High-leverage practices in special education*. Council for Exceptional Children & CEEDAR Center.

TABLE 11-3. SOCIAL STUDIES PICTURE BOOKS

SOCIAL STUDIES CONCEPT	BOOK TITLE	DESCRIPTION
Geography (1-2)	*A World of Wonders: Geographic Travels in Verse and Rhyme* by J. Patrick Lewis	This book highlights a collection of travel verses and examines explorers, cities, and facts worldwide.
Geography (pre-K–1)	*Signs in My Neighborhood* by Shelly Lyons	In this book, children are introduced to people in the community and signs around the neighborhood.
Geography (pre-K–1)	*This Is My Neighborhood* (Cloverleaf Books-Where I Live) by Lisa Bullard	Help Malik find his dog Buddy as they search the different businesses and places in his neighborhood.
Geography (K-2)	*Magic Treehouse* Series by Mary Pope Osborne	Join Jack and Annie on travels throughout the world.
Geography (K-2)	*Me on the Map* by Joan Sweeney	A playful introduction to maps.
Historical (pre-K)	*This Little Trailblazer: A Girl Power Primer* by Joan Holub	A board book that discusses influential women who changed history.
Historical (K-4)	*Little Leaders: Bold Women in Black History* by Vashti Harrison	Meet 40 trailblazing women who broke barriers of race and gender to pave the way for future generations.
Historical (pre-K)	*This Little Explorer: A Pioneer Prime* by Joan Holub	Learn all about the most influential explorers who searched the world far and wide in this engaging and colorful board book perfect for pioneers in training.
Economics (1-2)	*Let's Chat About Economics!: Basic Principles Through Everyday Scenarios* by Michelle Balconi	This book identifies and illustrates basic economic principles through familiar scenarios.
Economics (1-2)	*The Berenstain Bears' Trouble With Money* by Stan and Jan Berenstain	Brother and Sister Bear open up a lemonade stand to earn money for their wants and needs.
Economics (pre-K–1)	*Little Critter: Just Saving My Money* (My First I Can Read) by Mercer Mayer	Little Critter wants to save money for a new skateboard, but he realizes it is hard to do.
Economics (pre-K–1)	*Lily Learns about Wants and Needs* (Cloverleaf Books-Money Basics) by Lisa Bullard	Lily learns about wants and needs and goes around town with her dad to decide what she should save for.
Government (pre-K–2)	*U.S. Symbols* (First Step Nonfiction-Government) by Ann-Marie Kishel	An introduction to symbols in the United States.

(continued)

TABLE 11-3 (CONTINUED). SOCIAL STUDIES PICTURE BOOKS

Government (pre-K–K)	*This Little President: A Presidential Primer* by Joan Holub	Learn all about the U.S. presidents with this fun and colorful board book perfect for leaders in training!
Citizenship (pre-K–2)	*We Live Here Too! Kids Talk About Good Citizenship* by Nancy Loewen	This nonfiction text introduces children to scenarios that show good citizenship.
Citizenship (pre-K–2)	*I Can Follow the Rules (Myself)* by Molly Smith	Eva discovers classrooms have rules for a reason.
Social-emotional (pre-K–2)	*But Why Can't I? A Book About Rules (Our Emotions and Behavior)* by Sue Graves	Jenny, the babysitter, shows Noah how to follow the rules and explains why they keep us safe.
Social-emotional (pre-K–2)	*MySELF Theme: I Get Along With Others* by multiple authors	Help children build social and emotional intelligence through shared reading and engaging texts that prompt discussions about real-world experiences.

TABLE 11-4. TIERED LEARNING EXPERIENCE WORK CARDS

GREEN GROUP	BLUE GROUP	YELLOW GROUP
1. Draw a picture of a community helper. 2. The teacher will help you take a photograph of your picture. 3. Then record yourself explaining how that community helper helps the community using a PowerPoint or Google slide.	1. Select one of the five pictures related to community helpers. 2. Glue the picture on a sheet of paper. 3. Caption the picture so that your caption relates to how the community helper helps the community.	1. List a community helper you want to learn more about. 2. Next, create three questions you would like to ask the community helper related to how they help the community. 3. Share your questions on our classroom social media page or via our classroom email.

The activity work cards contain objectives for the social studies lesson. Students can work in groups to complete their cards, or they can work individually. Teachers might assign students to groups based on ability level; however, they may also encourage students to choose their work card. It was also recommended by Hong and Chick (2012) that "students are permitted, and even encouraged, to move in and out of groups based on their needs or strengths on a particular day or during a specific lesson" (p. 116).

Meeting the Learning Needs of Diverse Children in Inclusive Prekindergarten Through Second-Grade Classrooms

Recommendations for teaching children in inclusive classrooms include the Universal Design for Learning (UDL) framework. The principles of UDL are multiple means of representation, multiple means of engagement, and multiple means of expression (Meyer et al., 2014). Educators embed UDL into instruction and ensure all students' inclusion in the instruction process. Teachers do more than adjust or adapt the curriculum to meet the needs of particular students. With the utilization of UDL, all children are a part of the learning group in the planning, implementation, and assessment process of instruction.

Some examples of multiple means of representation for social studies instruction include the use of charts; pictures; graphs; and I Know, I Think I Know, I Wonder charts to help introduce, organize, and summarize social studies information in different ways. Children can make three-dimensional symbols and objects that represent important social studies concepts, such as peace symbols, their country or state flag, and a flag to represent them and their families. Teachers can also incorporate technology and have children make a cultural or social studies infographic using poster maker software, PowerPoint (Microsoft), or Google Docs. An infographic is a method for children and teachers to show information about current facts, data, polling results, and the child's culture using technology. Current facts, data, culture, and polling results can be put into the infographic along with supporting pictures or illustrations. Pictures of historical persons can be presented along with a discussion. Teachers should make sure that the pictures are accurate and are reflective of the historical figure.

Examples of multiple means of engagement may involve introducing videos with movement and songs related to social studies topics, such as citizenship, historical holidays, and facts to help students. Children can dress up as community helpers and discuss the role that these people have in their communities. Students can also use puppets to demonstrate good citizenship and model friendship. In addition, teachers and children can highlight or circle words that may be new or difficult or may have multiple meanings and put them on display on a chart with different colors or on index cards during the lesson so that they can be discussed further.

Teachers can provide diverse means of expression to share responses to social studies activities. Children can use their bodies to express ideas by nodding their heads or holding up one finger for yes or two fingers for no. Anchor charts, which demonstrate the concepts being taught (e.g., the difference between a good and a service), could be made, and children could point to the correct responses. Audio recordings of responses from students can also be recorded so that children can state their answers. Teachers can also allow for group responses in which the group decides and one student shares the response for the whole group. Sticky notes can be given to students so that they can write or draw their ideas.

Preplanning Strategies for Social Studies and Diverse Learners

There are recommended steps that teachers can take before instruction to help build community and maximize the inclusion of children in the learning process. Several recommendations have been provided for teachers at the preplanning, planning, and instructional levels. One recommendation is getting to know the students, families, and the surrounding community. This can be done by reviewing students' files and Individualized Education Programs (IEPs) and surveying and interviewing the families for interests, likes, dislikes, child/family preferences, and culture knowledge. Teachers can also learn more about the community of the families and children and how it connects to the school community. Teachers may investigate local field trips, community helpers, and parent/faith-based/social groups that may be able to engage with the learning environment and become a part of the instruction. Based on the information gathered, teachers can form their instructional plan.

PLANNING FOR SOCIAL STUDIES INSTRUCTION AND DIVERSE LEARNERS

Social studies instructional planning involves teachers' focus on building healthy self-identity, learning about self and others, learning about friendships, building a sense of community, and learning about self and the world. For some classrooms, children with disabilities are purposefully excluded from the classroom community or expected to interact with an adult educator or caregiver. It is important for the teacher to promote the sense of community as a part of the social studies curriculum and instruction. Teachers can build community within the classroom by arranging desks and tables for group work and discussion and setting up workstations or learning centers where children can participate in learning projects. Teachers can also consider spaces for large- and small-group activities as well as individual time when a child may want to work independently by their choice or if the child wants to take a break from group work. The planning process continues from the preplanning steps and curriculum web development to additional information gathering about the students in the class.

Children in the class can create an "All About Me" book to share who they are. Teachers can continue to know and learn about the children in the learning environment through this activity and note information about the child's culture, family life, and the community surrounding the child.

Observation is another approach that works in planning for social studies instruction. Throughout the day, teachers can "look and listen" for children's likes and dislikes and note these. Children may not be able to or want to verbalize what they like or dislike but may demonstrate their preferences by playing with certain toys more than other toys; holding on to specific toys or objects throughout the day; moving, rocking, swaying, singing, or dancing to a favorite song; or repeating certain activities because they are engaging and fun to the child. Teachers should note these preferences and use them during the instructional process.

Other resources that are helpful in planning include obtaining graphic organizers and three-dimensional instructional tools that are related to the social studies lesson, such as maps, globes, flags, and so on. It has been suggested that teachers build a scaffolding tool kit with items in order to support social studies learners (e.g., file folders, graphic aids, and sentence starters).

Teachers should also get to know the school resources to support social studies. For example, identify who in the school can help with the social studies lesson; community helpers in school, parent groups, a social worker, or a nurse may be added to the curriculum web. A guest list of potential speakers and class helpers can be developed after the teacher identifies potential school and community resources. Teachers should also read and review their lesson plans for multiple-meaning words or new vocabulary and topics that may be challenging for some students with disabilities. For example, a lesson that may be taught is the difference between a good and a service. Some children may not grasp the concept of the term *good* as it relates to a product and may connect it to behavior. Teachers will want to highlight or note multiple meanings of words and provide ways to clarify. Children should know that the word good has two different meanings in this lesson. Teachers should begin with how students view the term good in their world and how it will be used in the lesson. Adding three-dimensional examples of a good would also be helpful during instruction.

INSTRUCTIONAL APPROACHES AND CURRICULUM MODIFICATIONS

Sandall et al. (2015) shared a model that uses the building block approach to curriculum modification in early childhood education. This approach supports the maximum participation of all young children in the learning environment. There are eight recommended strategies within this model that can be incorporated into social studies instruction. They include environmental support, material support, activity simplification, child preferences, specialized equipment, adult support, peer support, and invisible support.

Environmental support involves adjusting the teaching and learning areas to help children succeed in instruction. An example of environmental support during instruction is to place maps, graphics, globes, flags, and visual pictures at the eye level of all children in the class including children in wheelchairs so that all children may be able to interact with these instructional resources.

Material support includes adjusting instructional materials so the child can participate in the activities without help as much as possible. Teachers can use this approach by attaching popsicle sticks or potato chip bag clips to help children turn pages in books. Teachers may also use a baking sheet as a work mat for children who may need a work space to help hold items on their tables or desks.

Teachers may use an I Know, I Think I Know, I Wonder chart to help children organize and process social studies information. For some children, this chart may be modified so that the child feels successful. For example, a child may think they know or may be familiar with a social studies fact. The teacher may only request a response for the I Think I Know section of the chart or may only request the I Think I Know and I Wonder sections of the chart. This is one example of how activity simplification can be used during instruction. Children asked to develop an "All About Me" book about self, family, and community can develop a book that only includes self and/or family and then later focus on community.

Child preferences are those activities that engage the child in instruction by providing choices based on the child's likes or favorites. For example, when teaching community helpers, a teacher may ask a child to select their favorite community helper to draw out of a limited choice of helpers. Children could have choices regarding a workstation, learning center, or a social studies project. If a teacher is discussing community heroes, a teacher may start off the lesson about a child's favorite superhero to get the child engaged in the learning process.

Some children with IEPs may require specialized equipment to assist them in the instructional process. Special equipment may include but is not limited to low- and high-tech assistive technology, wheelchairs, walkers, and ball chairs. Special equipment can be purchased as well as teacher made. Clipboards are a good example of equipment that can hold papers, maps, graphs, and pictures steady while children use these materials during instruction.

Many teachers are familiar with adult support and instructing children with IEPs. A teacher, parent, paraprofessional, therapist, or classroom helper can assist with instruction through modeling, demonstration, providing support, or any other activity in which the adult in the classroom provides intervention for the student who needs assistance. Teachers should use other forms of support as well so that the teacher does not feel overwhelmed, continues to build relationships with peers, and helps children feel successful during instruction.

Peer support and invisible support, also recommended by Sandall et al. (2015), provide ways for teachers to modify instruction so that children who need assistance can feel successful and a part of the classroom community. *Peer support* is the process of allowing peers and/or siblings to help with completing learning tasks. An example of using peer support would be for a teacher to partner a child who may have difficulty developing a map of their neighborhood with a child who may live in the same neighborhood so that they can build this structure together. Group discussions and responses from peer groups about social studies topics are another example of peer support.

Invisible support involves preplanning and intentionally setting up the learning activity so that success occurs naturally with the child based on what the teacher knows about the child and their environment. Invisible support can occur when a child is participating in a play and must memorize lines but has difficulty memorizing lines or long phrases. The teacher can assign a role to the child where they can repeat lines in the play to help with memorization. If a child is having difficulty identifying community helpers and their roles, let the child state community helpers they are most familiar with as they engage in school activities, such as the school nurse, other teachers, the school custodian, the crossing guard, the bus driver, and the cook. The child can state the roles that these individuals do to help the community based on what the child observes on a daily basis.

When teaching social studies, 10 common themes emerge (Wilson and Papadonis, 2006). These themes include (a) culture; (b) time, continuity, and change; (c) people, places, and the environment; (d) identity and individual development; (e) individuals, groups, and institutions; (f) power, authority, and governance; (g) production, distribution, and consumption; (h) science, technology, and society; (i) global connections; and (j) civic ideas and practices (Wilson & Papadonis, 2006, p. vii-viii). Teaching to these 10 social studies concepts in an inclusive learning environment requires the teacher to focus on the following:

- The development of the child (e.g., Is the child learning about self-identity and development and/or learning about self as a part of a group? How does the child view self and the surrounding world?)
- The strengths that each child brings to the learning environment (e.g., What are the strengths the child has, and what areas of strength does the child bring to the group and the classroom?)
- The variety of ways to teach and engage children in social studies lessons (e.g., How can I get the child/children engaged in social studies lessons through a variety of ways? What are the various ways children can express what they are learning and what they know about social studies?)

Knowing these areas and building on these will provide a diverse and inclusive teaching environment for pre-K through second-grade students.

Individual Development and Identity

Social studies and social-emotional development are related, as mentioned earlier in this chapter. Teachers have the opportunity to build children's self-esteem and self-image through social studies lessons. Examples that may allow for this instruction include arranging lessons in which children can state something positive about themselves, their families, and their classmates. Helping children read books about their and others' identities in and out of the classroom helps build knowledge of self and others.

There are several children's books that support this concept. *It's Okay to be Different* by Todd Parr is a children's book that helps children see that their uniqueness and different attributes are sufficient and celebrated. Children also learn that having different abilities is a part of the learning process, and including others who are different from us is positive and valuable. *I Can Change the World* by Jennifer Dewing is another example of a children's book that emphasizes self-identity and roles in which young children can contribute to the world around them. Teachers can read this book to the class and facilitate a discussion of the various ways children can contribute to their community or world based on the children's strengths and interests.

Figure 11-4. Two sisters working together on a family project.

INDIVIDUALS, GROUPS, AND INSTITUTIONS

Social studies allows young children to learn more about the roles others play in their world and the world around them. Teachers can help in this process by inviting guest speakers and taking children to places of interest as a part of their learning. *Project-based learning* (PBL) is an instructional approach that allows all children to learn about their world. According to Larmer (2018), PBL is an instructional approach that is not a trend but rather an educational practice grounded in research. This approach contains seven recommended components, including a stimulating question, opportunities for student research based in real-world activities, student options, and critique with reflection, as well as opportunities for sharing with a broad out-of-classroom audience. Teachers can begin with asking essential questions throughout the project work. Sample questions could be "What jobs do people have in my community and what do they do?" or "What was it like to be a child when your parents or caregivers were your age?" Children are encouraged to work together in groups. Teachers can assist children by assigning roles based on the children's strengths and interests. All children should have a part or task in the project regardless of ability differences. Because of their ability, some children may not be able to complete the same tasks simultaneously or at the same rate. Some children should be allowed to complete some of the tasks or work with partners to complete the assignment. Nevertheless, all children should feel successful in this work. Teachers can encourage families to participate in this project. Figure 11-4 displays two sisters working together on a family project.

PRODUCTION, DISTRIBUTION, AND CONSTRUCTION

The making, distribution, and construction of products and services are things that young children can learn through social studies. Teachers can plan activities in which children learn about the production, consumption, and distribution of goods and services in their neighborhoods and communities. Teachers can use various means of representation in teaching this theme. Examples may include field trips to local stores or farms, role-playing product making, and shopping. It is important to note that all children should have a role.

Learning centers can be created where students can explore goods and services. At one center, students could make pretend cupcakes, which are goods they can pretend to sell to other classmates. Another center could allow students to pretend to be a nurse or doctor, which provides a service to other classmates.

SCIENCE, TECHNOLOGY, AND SOCIETY

There is a relationship between science, technology, and social studies. Children can learn about the environment, biology, chemistry, and other scientific concepts through social studies. An example of this relationship is asking children to discuss what will happen to the community when we recycle. Children can use PBL to determine how the weather, biological creatures, water, and air are affected by recycling. Children can learn scientific concepts such as developing a hypothesis, observation, and experimentation.

There are several ways of including technology into social studies instruction. The use of the smart board is an example. Teachers can find different photos of artwork from various places around the world and project it on the smart board. Children can analyze the artwork for details, common themes, items, and topics. Technology includes virtual field trips to different places and computer games that focus on social studies. Technology is a tool that can assist children included in the social studies instruction when typical instructional practices will not allow some children to participate fully. The use of assistive technology is a helpful way for children to share in group work, communicate with each other, and retain information. Teachers should use technology as a tool to assist the child in the learning process and not replace the child's participation in learning.

GLOBAL CONNECTIONS

Global connections in early childhood education are very important elements of social studies instruction. Young children are global citizens and a part of a larger world community. Children in early childhood and elementary settings are introduced to global concepts such as citizenship, respect for the earth, and cultural awareness of others. Bell et al. (2015) provided several recommendations for helping young children learn about global concepts. Young children can learn about the world, others, and cultures through literature and technology. Bell and colleagues (2015) provided the following six components for early childhood educators to use: perspective consciousness or viewing from other's perspectives, cross-cultural awareness or understanding the culture of others, state-of-the-planet awareness or respecting the earth, system connectedness or understanding how one's culture connects to others, awareness and utilization of technology, and options for participation or attendance in global activities. Some examples of activities include lessons about recycling, virtual field trips to other countries, and dance and book readings from different cultures and countries. Inviting families from other countries to classrooms (face to face or virtually) as guest speakers is another way that children can learn about system connectedness and global awareness.

Teachers need to know how to include and incorporate global connections in their teaching. Jean-Sigur and colleagues (2016) emphasized the importance of global instruction to young children and provided recommendations on how to instruct teacher candidates so that they can teach these principles to the young children in their classrooms. These recommendations align with Bell et al.'s six components for teaching global concepts to young children (Bell et al., 2015) and provide opportunities for children to reflect and participate in their own culture and awareness as global citizens.

CIVIC IDEAS AND PRACTICES

Social studies provides an opportunity for teachers to help children learn about their government and what they can do to participate in a democratic society. Young children can participate in voting activities and a mock election. Some elections may begin with favorite foods, music, topics to study, or class rewards. Children will learn about the voting process, counting, and the importance of having a role in their learning environment.

A mock election with fictitious candidates can also occur. As children get older, they may want to run for office in the classroom or school. They should be encouraged but not be forced to run in an election. This action gives children choices and a basic understanding of their rights.

Children can also participate as a group in the process of governing their classrooms. All children should be included. They should participate in developing the class rules and determining options for consequences. The teacher can help facilitate positive and meaningful ways of governing the classroom by discussing classroom procedures and how children can help in this process.

CHAPTER REVIEW

1. Compare and contrast the various social studies strands of understanding that pre-K through second-grade students need to know. Which strands could you embed into the daily lives of students?

2. Discuss the relationship between social studies and child development. What are the factors to consider when preparing social studies lessons with young children?

3. List ways of including social studies in inclusive classrooms. State how UDL may be used in social studies instruction. Discuss how teachers can differentiate instruction to meet children's learning needs and goals in their classes.

4. What types of differentiated activities or supports could you embed within your own social studies lessons?

5. List five themes that occur in teaching social studies. Discuss how teachers can teach these themes in an inclusive teaching environment.

6. Teachers have the opportunity to build children's _____ and _____ through social studies lessons. An example is having a student share something positive about a peer.
   a. Economic understandings, geographic understandings
   b. Diversity, equity
   c. Self-esteem, self-image
   d. Perceptions, biases

7. PBL stands for:
   a. Public building lessons
   b. Problems before learning
   c. Perspectives by learning
   d. Project-based learning

8. Which of the following considerations should be made when addressing social studies concepts with young learners?
   a. Teach the topics in a developmental manner
   b. Do not teach young learners history, economics, civics, and government topics
   c. Provide critical guidance
   d. Teachers should not use visual cues or examples to demonstrate what they are teaching

9. The integrated study of the social sciences and humanities to promote civic competence is known as:
   a. UDL
   b. Social studies
   c. DEC
   d. Culture

RESOURCES

Postcard Exchange

- You are invited to participate in an opportunity to teach your students about collaboration and make connections with other states. Your class will send one postcard to each of the 49 states, excluding your own. In return, you will receive postcards from 49 classrooms around the country: https://www.facebook.com/groups/PCEpostcardexchange

Geographic Understandings Resources

- https://www.kids-world-travel-guide.com/geography-for-kids.html
- National Geographic Kids: https://www.natgeokids.com/uk/category/discover/geography/

Economic Understandings Resources

- Kiddynomics: https://www.stlouisfed.org/education/kiddynomics-an-economics-curriculum-for-young-learners
- Financial Literacy for Kids: https://www.incharge.org/financial-literacy/resources-for-teachers/financial-literacy-for-kids/

Government/Civics Understanding Resources

- U.S. Government for Kids: https://www.ducksters.com/history/us_government.php
- We the Civics Kids: https://constitutioncenter.org/learn/educational-resources/we-the-civics-kids

REFERENCES

Bell, D., Jean-Sigur, R., & Kim, Y. (2015). Going global in early childhood education. *Childhood Education, 91*(2), 90-100.

Brillante, P., & Mankiw, S. (2015). A sense of place: Human geography in the early childhood classroom. *Young Children, 70*(3), 16-23.

Casey, E. M., & Casey, J. H. (2019). Building democratic citizenship competencies in K-5 economics through analysis of popular culture. *Social Studies Research and Practice, 14*(1), 136-149.

Chick, K. A., & Hong, B. S. S. (2012). Differentiated instruction in elementary social studies: Where do teachers begin? *Social Studies Research & Practice, 7*(2), 112-121.

Derman-Sparks, L., & Edwards, J. O. (2010). *Anti-bias education for young children and ourselves.* National Association for the Education of Young Children.

Division for Early Childhood. (2014). *Recommended Practices.* https://www.dec-sped.org/dec-recommended-practices

Durden, T. R., Escalante, E., & Blitch, K. (2015). Start with us! Culturally relevant pedagogy in the preschool classroom. *Early Childhood Education Journal, 43*(3), 223-232.

Epstein, A. S. (2012). *Social studies.* HighScope Press.

Farmer, A., & Heeley, A. (2004). Moving between fantasy and reality: Sustained, shared thinking about the past. In H. Cooper (Ed.), *Exploring time and place through play: Foundation stage-key stage one* (pp. 52-64). David Fulton.

Federal Reserve Bank of St. Louis. (2019). *Kiddynomics: An economics curriculum for young learners.* https://www.stlouisfed.org/education/kiddynomics-an-economics-curriculum-for-young-learners

Jean-Sigur, R., Bell, D., & Kim, Y. (2016). Building global awareness in early childhood teacher preparation programs. *Childhood Education, 92*(1), 3-9. Kemple, K. M. (2017). Social studies, social competence and citizenship in childhood education: Developmental principles guide appropriate practice. *Early Childhood Education, 45*, 621-627.

Krishnan, M. (2011). *The seeds of self-esteem: Initiative vs. guilt.* Inner Space. http://innerspacetherapy.in/parenting/initiative-versus-guilt-2/

Kuh, L. P., LeeKeenan, D., Given, H, & Beneke, M. R. (2016). Moving beyond anti-bias activities: Supporting the development of anti-bias practices. *Young Children, 71*(1), 58-65.

Larmer, J. (2018). Project-based learning in social studies. *Social Education, 82*(1), 20-23.

Lippitz, W. (1983). *The child's understanding of time.* Routledge.

Meyer, A., Rose, D. H., & Gordon, D. (2014). *Universal design for learning: Theory and practice.* CAST Professional Publishing.

Mindes, G. (2005). *Social studies in today's early childhood curricula.* Young Children on the Web. http://ocw.umb.edu/early-education-development/eec-preschool-learning-standards-and-guidelines/social-science-readings/Social%20Studies%20in%20Early%20Childhood%20Curricula.pdf/at_download/file.pdf

National Council for the Social Studies. (2010). *National curriculum standards for social studies: A framework for teaching, learning, and assessment.* National Council for the Social Studies.

National Council for the Social Studies. (2019). *Early childhood in the social studies context.* https://www.socialstudies.org/early-childhood-social-studies-context

National Geographic Society. (2019). *What is geography?* https://www.nationalgeographic.org/education/what-is-geography/

Parker, W., & Beck, T. (2017). *Social studies in elementary education.* Pearson.

Sandall, S. R., Schwartz, I. S., Joseph, G. E., Gauvreau, A. N., & Hemmeter, M. L. (2015). *Building blocks for teaching preschoolers with special needs.* Brookes Publishing.

Shea, P. (2010). Eliciting picture books responses up and down the grade level ladder, and back and forth across the curriculum. *New England Reading Association Journal, 46*(1), 31-37, 110.

Skjaeveland, Y. (2017). Learning history in early childhood: Teaching methods and children's understanding. *Contemporary Issues in Early Childhood, 18*(1), 8-22.

Wilson, W., & Papadonis, J. (2006). *Differentiated instruction for social studies: Instructions and activities for the diverse classroom.* Walch.

Social-Emotional Learning
for Young Children

Marla J. Lohmann, PhD; Kania A. Greer, EdD; and Marisa Macy, PhD

INTRODUCTION

High-quality classroom instruction requires early childhood special educators to consider the needs of the "whole child" through a focus on all developmental domains, including academic, social-emotional, physical, and psychological development. When teachers support social-emotional learning (SEL) of young children, children are more successful both inside and outside the classroom. Teaching SEL skills involves a combination of structured and unstructured instruction, an understanding of how trauma impacts children's development, and a collaborative approach with the families of young children. This chapter provides teachers with practical strategies for supporting SEL development in the early childhood classroom.

Fisher, K. M., & Zimmer, K. E. (Eds.).
Early Childhood Special Education Programs and Practices (pp. 257-268).

CHAPTER OBJECTIVES

→ Define the term *social-emotional learning*.

→ Plan collaboration with stakeholders, including families, to create high-quality social-emotional learning experiences for young children.

→ Design social-emotional instruction that is culturally relevant and developmentally appropriate for young children.

→ Select evidence-based teaching strategies and interventions for social-emotional learning that align with the Division for Early Childhood Recommended Practices and the Council for Exceptional Children's high-leverage practices.

KEY TERMS

- **Adverse Childhood Experiences:** Traumatic events that occur during childhood.
- **Culturally Relevant Instruction:** A teacher uses students' cultural strengths and experiences to empower and support learning in all developmental domains.
- **Embedded Learning Opportunity:** A naturalistic teaching strategy that can be mapped onto the child's natural environment.
- **Social-Emotional Learning:** The ability to understand emotions of self and others, regulating and expressing emotions, having a positive self-concept, setting appropriate personal goals, making good decisions, and establishing appropriate relationships with peers and adults.

CASE STUDY

Mrs. Huang is a kindergarten teacher with 23 students, seven of whom have an Individualized Education Program. Two of the students have a disability of emotional disturbance, so Mrs. Huang has provided explicit instruction and feedback on managing emotions for those two students. As the school year has progressed, Mrs. Huang has noticed that several other students in her classroom also struggle to manage their emotions and build positive and appropriate relationships with classmates. She is contemplating teaching social-emotional skills to all students in her classroom.

As early childhood special educators, we are concerned about meeting the needs of the "whole child," which entails viewing classroom instruction as more than just teaching academics and acknowledges the role that social-emotional, physical, and psychological development have on children's learning (Darling-Hammond & Cook-Harvey, 2018). Secure attachments and positive relationships impact brain development for young children (Darling-Hammond & Cook-Harvey, 2018), and daily experiences, both inside and outside the school setting, impact children's abilities to feel safe and secure in the classroom (Ho & Funk, 2018). A child's sense of security and safety in the classroom can be impacted by their emotions, relationships, and experiences (Darling-Hammond & Cook-Harvey, 2018). In addition, children's social-emotional competence correlates with their academic success (Darling-Hammond & Cook-Harvey, 2018; Zins et al., 2007). Jones and Kahn (2018) stated that "many social, emotional, and cognitive capacities are processed in the same parts of the brain" (p. 2), indicating that directly addressing children's social-emotional learning (SEL) needs will have a positive impact on their ability to learn in the classroom. Researchers define SEL as (a) the ability to understand emotions of self and others (Denham et al., 2012), (b) regulating and expressing emotions (Denham et al., 2012; Rakap et al., 2018; Weissberg, 2019), (c) having a positive self-concept (Ng & Bull, 2018), (d) setting appropriate personal goals (Weissberg, 2019), (e) making good decisions (Denham et al., 2012; Ng & Bull, 2018; Weissberg, 2019), and (f) establishing appropriate relationships with peers and adults (Denham et al., 2012; Ng & Bull, 2018; Rakap et al., 2018; Weissberg, 2019). Because of the importance of SEL for young children, instruction in this area is a critical component of a high-quality early childhood special education classroom. Consequently, institutes of higher education must prepare teachers of young children to support their students in gaining SEL skills.

In Chapter 4, the authors introduced evidence-based classroom management skills, including the use of Positive Behavior Interventions and Supports (PBIS). Social-emotional instruction is an integral part of ensuring success for all learners, and it should be considered part of Tier 1 PBIS at either the classroom- or school-wide level. All young children need instruction on how to (a) manage emotions, (b) meet personal goals, (c) make decisions, (d) build relationships, and (e) interact with others (Collaborative for Academic, Social, and Emotional Learning [CASEL], 2021). In addition, some young children will need additional support to gain SEL skills through Tier 2 and 3 PBIS interventions.

Instruction on SEL skills aligns with the Division for Early Childhood Recommended Practices (Division for Early Childhood, 2014) and the Council for Exceptional Children/Collaboration for Effective Educator Development, Accountability, and Reform Center's high-leverage practices (HLPs). Specifically, Division for Early Childhood Recommended Practices A4, E3, F4, INS2, INT1, and INT2 as well as HLPs 7 and 9 align with social-emotional instruction in the early childhood classroom. Figure 12-1 offers a list of each of these practices, and their connection to SEL is noted throughout the chapter.

CASEL (2020) developed a framework for supporting children in developing SEL skills. Within this framework, there are four key settings in which children gain SEL skills: (a) classroom, (b) school, (c) family/caregiver, and (d) community. On their website, listed in the Resources section of this chapter, CASEL visually presents the framework in a wheel that demonstrates how the settings overlap and work together to support student growth. As early childhood special educators, we are directly responsible for ensuring that the first two settings, the classroom and school, are designed in a manner that best facilitates student growth and development in social-emotional competencies.

TRAUMA AND SOCIAL-EMOTIONAL LEARNING

Many children have traumatic experiences in today's classrooms, also known as *adverse childhood experiences* (ACEs) (Centers for Disease Control and Prevention, 2022), and traumatic events can occur at any age. Commonly experienced ACEs include experiencing or witnessing acts of violence, family members with substance abuse problems, and parental separation or divorce (Centers for Disease Control and Prevention, 2022). More than 1 in 10 children have experienced three or more ACEs by the time they complete kindergarten (Jiminez et al., 2017). For children who have experienced ACEs, SEL is even more critical. Consequently, teachers must ensure that all SEL instruction is trauma informed (Jagers et al., 2018; Pawlo et al., 2019), and children who have experienced trauma may require additional or more intense SEL instruction than their peers (Pawlo et al., 2019). In many cases, SEL skill deficits, such as defiance or issues with boundaries in relationships, are a result of the trauma a child has experienced (Cook et al., 2005; Pawlo et al., 2019). When early childhood educators create a trauma-aware classroom, they are meeting the Division for Early Childhood Recommended Practices of INT1 and INT2 as well as HLP 7.

Early childhood special educators can address the impacts of ACEs through SEL skill instruction that occurs within a positive school climate. A positive school climate occurs when students feel connected and safe in the school setting (Hamlin, 2020). Educators can generate this environment when they create and follow predictable routines and expectations because this helps young children feel safe in the school setting (Pawlo et al., 2019). As the authors discussed in Chapter 4, PBIS can be an effective way to improve the school climate for children and other stakeholders (Bradshaw et al.,

Recommended Practices & High Leverage Practices that Align with Teaching SEL Skills

Division for Early Childhood Recommended Practices

A3: Practitioners use assessment materials and strategies appropriate for the child's age and level of development and accommodate the child's sensory, physical, communication, cultural, linguistic, social, and emotional characteristics.

A4: Practitioners conduct assessments that include all areas of development and behavior to learn about the child's strengths, needs, preferences, and interests.

E3: Practitioners work with the family and other adults to modify and adapt the physical, social, and temporal environments to promote each child's access to and participation in learning experiences.

F4: Practitioners and the family work together to create outcomes or goals, develop individualized plans, and implement practices that address the family's priorities and concerns and the child's strengths and needs.

INS2: Practitioners, with the family, identify skills to target for instruction that help a child become adaptive, competent, socially connected, and engaged and that promote learning in natural and inclusive environments.

INT1: Practitioners promote the child's social-emotional development by observing, interpreting, and responding contingently to the range of the child's emotional expressions.

INT 2: Practitioners promote the child's social development by encouraging the child to initiate or sustain positive interactions with other children and adults during routines and activities through modeling, teaching, feedback, or other types of guided support.

High Leverage Practices

HLP 7: Establish a consistent, organized, and respectful learning environment.

HLP 9: Teach social behaviors.

Figure 12-1. DEC Recommended Practices and HLPs that align with teaching SEL skills. (Data sources: Division for Early Childhood. [2014]. *DEC Recommended Practices in early intervention/early childhood special education 2014.* http://www.decsped.org/recommendedpractices and McLeskey, J., Barringer, M.-D., Billingsley, B., Brownell, M., Jackson, D., Kennedy, M., Lewis, T., Maheady, L., Rodriguez, J., Scheeler, M. C., Winn, J., & Ziegler, D. [2017]. *High-leverage practices in special education.* Council for Exceptional Children & CEEDAR Center.)

2009). In addition, when adults demonstrate emotional stability through their actions and behaviors, young children see how emotions can be managed appropriately and feel safe in school (Pawlo et al., 2019).

HOW TO TEACH SOCIAL-EMOTIONAL LEARNING

SEL should occur in both structured and unstructured ways. Similar to how we teach academics, teachers should provide structured lessons to teach critical social-emotional skills. In the early childhood classroom, these lessons may occur during circle time or other whole-class instructional times. Additionally, it is often necessary to offer social-emotional instruction through small-group instruction for students who need additional support. When teachers provide lessons on social-emotional skills, they should structure lessons like all high-quality lessons. Lessons on SEL should include (a) a lesson introduction, (b) instructional input, (c) student participation and practice of the skill, (d) assessment of student learning, (e) feedback on student performance, (f) a lesson wrap-up, and (g) teacher reflection after the lesson (IRIS Center, 2004). These instructional steps align with the evidence-based strategy of explicit instruction for all learners (Archer & Hughes, 2011), which is HLP 16. Pawlo et al. (2019) emphasized the importance of repeated practice with explicit feedback for learning SEL skills. Ideas for activities that early childhood special educators can use in SEL lessons include (a) using stories to discuss feelings, (b) making faces to show emotions, (c) role-playing

TABLE 12-1. CHILDREN'S BOOKS FOR TEACHING SOCIAL-EMOTIONAL LEARNING (SEL) SKILLS

BOOK TITLE	AUTHOR	SEL SKILLS
There Might Be Lobsters	Carolyn Crimi	Responding to fear
Anita and the Dragons	Hanna Carmona	Responding to fear
The Book of Mistakes	Corinna Luyken	Learning from mistakes
The Dot	Peter H. Reynolds	Learning from mistakes
Rulers of the Playground	Joseph Kuefler	Friendship
Stick and Stone	Beth Ferry	Friendship
Argyle Fox	Marie Letourneau	Responding to challenges
Nadia: The Girl Who Couldn't Sit Still	Karlin Gray	Responding to challenges/persistence
The Smile Shop	Satoshi Kitamura	Showing kindness to others
Pass It On	Sophy Henn	Showing kindness to others
Evelyn Del Ray Is Moving Away	Meg Medina	Responding to sadness
The Memory String	Eve Bunting	Responding to grief
When Sophie Gets Angry—Really, Really Angry	Molly Bang	Responding to anger
David Gets in Trouble	David Shannon	Self-control
The Secret Life of the Red Fox	Laurence Pringle	Helping others

scenarios of challenging situations, and (d) discussing how children can request assistance and support from adults in managing their own emotions and needs (CASEL, 2015). Table 12-1 offers a list of children's books that can be used in SEL lessons. Intentional instruction on SEL skills aligns with DEC Recommended Practices A3, E3, INS2, INT1, and INT3 as well as HLPs 7 and 9.

Teachers may choose to create their own SEL lessons, or they may use a commercial SEL curriculum. The following are some curriculums that are endorsed by the Center for Early Childhood Mental Health Consultation (n.d.): (a) Al's Pals; (b) The Incredible Years; (c) Preschool PATHS; (d) Second Step; (e) Social Skills in Pictures, Stories, and Songs; and (f) Preschool I Can Problem Solve.

Teachers should integrate SEL into all aspects of the day in early childhood classrooms. Although it is essential to include specific lessons on social-emotional skills, educators should also include instruction and support during play and other instructional times. Unstructured times, such as centers, recess, and snack times, offer teachers an ideal opportunity to support SEL in natural settings. It is important that teachers consider these unstructured times as instructional opportunities and not an opportunity to catch up on lesson planning or paperwork. During unstructured times, teachers should walk around the room/learning space, listen to students talk, and offer guidance in interactions as necessary. Figure 12-2 offers an example of an interaction that might occur during recess. You will notice that the children refer to a story the class has previously read during a social-emotional lesson. The specific book referenced is *The Secret Life of the Red Fox* by Laurence Pringle. In the scenario, the teacher identifies the problem but asks the students to use the skills he has taught during SEL lessons to solve the issue. If they could not solve it on their own, Mr. Sanchez would have reminded them of the book and offered potential solutions. He may also select to model for the students how to work through the situation. Modeling is an evidence-based instructional strategy in which a teacher demonstrates how to complete a specific skill (Lopez et al., 2017).

Scenario: SEL Guidance During Recess

Avni and Zaire are playing together in the sandbox. They are working together to build a sandcastle. A few minutes later, Penelope joins them and Mr. Sanchez immediately hears a disagreement ensue, so he walks over to the sandbox to find out what is happening. When he arrives at the sandbox, Mr. Sanchez hears Avni yell, "that is not what we are doing!" Mr. Sanchez asks the children what is happening. Avni tells him that Penelope wants to put a moat around the sandcastle, but she and Zaire had already decided not to do that before Penelope arrived. Mr. Sanchez asks the children to sit in a circle with him. Then, he asks the children, "what does it mean to work as a team? What should it look like when we are working together to accomplish a goal?" Zaire says, "it means that we listen to everyone's ideas and nobody is in charge. It's like that story we read about the foxes who had to work together to take care of their family." Penelope chimed in, "yeah! That's right. They had to help each other and neither fox was always in charge." Mr. Sanchez responds by saying, "You are correct! Working together means that everyone gets a say. How can you three work as a team to build this sandcastle and consider everyone's ideas?" Avni says, "I think we can take turns choosing something to add to the sandcastle. Penelope, we can add a moat if you want." Zaire shakes his head to indicate that he agrees. Mr. Sanchez says, "great job, children! I am proud of you for choosing to be a team and work together! I cannot wait to see the sandcastle when you are done!" Then, Mr. Sanchez left the children to play while he walked around to check on the other students.

Figure 12-2. Scenario: SEL guidance during recess.

Opportunities for SEL instruction also occur during academic instruction. For some children, academic expectations may lead to frustration and elicit a variety of emotions, especially when the expectations are challenging. Institutes of higher education should prepare early childhood special educators to support social-emotional development in academics. Teachers must address student social-emotional needs during academic instruction because social-emotional competence impacts their academic success (Zins et al., 2007). Within the academic context, social-emotional skills that are frequently required for success include (a) emotional regulation, (b) self-control, (c) problem-solving, (d) setting goals, and (e) working toward achieving those goals (Zins et al., 2007). One way that early childhood special educators can teach SEL skills in academics is by sharing how they manage each of these skills in the context of their own lives. Figure 12-3 offers an example scenario of Ms. Smith sharing with her second-grade students how she manages frustration.

CASEL (2015) also recommended various additional strategies for embedding SEL instruction in unstructured activities and academic lessons in the early childhood classroom. They recommended that teachers (a) use developmentally appropriate vocabulary when discussing emotions, (b) acknowledge the physical and emotional cues that indicate children's emotions, (c) talk about their feelings and how they can appropriately respond to those feelings, and (d) encourage children to reflect on their feelings and responses to those feelings.

Collaboration With Families

Although teachers can set the groundwork for SEL in their classrooms, they cannot do it alone; effective instruction in all areas requires a team approach. Families are essential in the delivery of specialized services provided under the Individuals with Disabilities Education Act. Parents, siblings, grandparents, familiar caregivers, and others play a significant role in a child's social-emotional development. Children benefit when effective partnerships occur between home and school. One way to create mutually beneficial collaborations with a child's family is to share resources with families.

Scenario: SEL Modeling During Academics

Ms. Smith is a teacher in an inclusive second-grade classroom and is currently teaching a lesson on addition to 100. She has noticed that a few of the students in her classroom struggle with the concept and become frustrated. One student has his head on his desk and refuses to work, and another student is crying. Ms. Smith decides to stop the lesson for a few minutes to share a story with her students. She says, "Class, please raise your hand if adding to 100 is a little bit hard for you." About half of the students in the class raise their hands. Ms. Smith says, "Did you know that some things are hard for me, too? Everyone has things that are hard for them to do sometimes. Would you like for me to tell you about something that is hard for me?" The students nod and Ms. Smith continues with a story: "Just like you, I go to school and am learning. I am taking a class called Statistics, which is a kind of math. It is really hard for me, and sometimes, I get frustrated. In fact, I was working on my homework last night, and it was so hard that I wanted to quit. So, what do you think I did?" One student yells out, "I think you quit," and another student says, "I think you kept trying." Ms. Smith says, "Those are both good guesses. Would you like to know what I did?" After the students nod, she says, "I knew that when I get frustrated, it can be hard for me to focus and be successful, so I took a short break. I closed my eyes and took 10 deep breaths. Then I looked at the homework to find out what exactly was making me upset. After figuring that out, I sent an email to my teacher to ask for help. And, do you know what? My teacher was happy to help me; teachers love to help when we ask. Would you all like to try my strategy?" The students nod and follow as Ms. Smith walks them through the steps of closing their eyes, taking deep breaths, and asking for help.

Figure 12-3. Scenario: SEL modeling during academics. (Data sources: Division for Early Childhood. [2014]. *DEC Recommended Practices in early intervention/early childhood special education 2014.* http://www.decsped.org/recommendedpractices and McLeskey, J., Barringer, M.-D., Billingsley, B., Brownell, M., Jackson, D., Kennedy, M., Lewis, T., Maheady, L., Rodriguez, J., Scheeler, M. C., Winn, J., & Ziegler, D. [2017]. *High-leverage practices in special education.* Council for Exceptional Children & CEEDAR Center.)

Parents and familiar caregivers can obtain tools to facilitate social-emotional development in their children (Woods et al., 2004; Wright & Kaiser, 2017). When early childhood educators team with families, they meet the expectations for DEC Recommended Practices E3, F4, and INS2.

Professionals support family members by sharing ways that a child's learning and growth are enhanced at home. Families can create embedded learning opportunities (ELOs) to support their child's social-emotional development (Friedman & Woods, 2015; Macy & Bricker, 2007). ELOs are a naturalistic teaching strategy that can be mapped onto the child's natural environment (Snyder et al., 2015).

Planned Embedded Learning Opportunities

Families can create planned activities to address their child's social and emotional development throughout the day, week, and special events (Bagnato et al., 2011; Horn et al., 2001; Johnson et al., 2016). They should consider a specific sequence for intentionally designed planned activities for ways that can promote the child's development of social skills.

Adults consider when and how planned activities will be used (Johnson & McDonnell, 2004). For example, there might be a specific time or special event when the ELO will be optimal for the child, such as a birthday party. Maybe the child has a goal to initiate social interactions with others. The parent can plan to have their child greet people as they arrive for the birthday party. They can use opportunities for social learning during planned activities that build on the child's strengths (e.g., maybe the family enjoys doing crafts together). The parents could design a planned activity that considers a project the child and family enjoy and implement social interactions during the craft activity that addresses the child's social and emotional goals.

Routine Embedded Learning Opportunities

Families can also create routine activities to address the child's social and emotional development throughout the day, week, and special events (Daugherty et al., 2001; Macy & Bricker, 2007). Routines are familiar to the child and family and occur with consistency, frequency, and predictability. When opportunities arise naturally, that is another time when families can implement ELOs.

ELOs within daily routines take advantage of what the family is already doing to support child development and then add intentional interactions that promote social skill development (Noh et al., 2009; Pretti-Frontczak & Bricker, 2001). Adults can create ELOs when following the child's lead during routines (e.g., the child might be interested in making bubbles while washing hands). The adult can embed opportunities for addressing the child's social-emotional goals during the routine. Maybe the child has a goal of taking turns, which the adult can use to share a bar of soap with a sibling.

Adults can embed planned and routine activities into the natural context of a child's daily life. Parents and professionals can collaborate to implement ELOs and then evaluate the overall effectiveness. Ongoing opportunities to address SEL at home, school, and in the community are beneficial for children and families (Horn et al., 2000; Pretti-Frontczak et al., 2003).

CULTURAL RELEVANCE

In addition to being a collaborative process with families, instruction on SEL skills must be culturally relevant and responsive to the unique needs of the child and family. Culturally relevant instruction occurs when a teacher uses students' cultural strengths and experiences to empower and support learning in all developmental domains (Rajagopal, 2011). Children from diverse backgrounds are more likely to have experienced ACEs before entering the school system (Roberts et al., 2012), so creating a culturally responsive classroom is critical. Instruction on SEL skills helps all students access educators who respect and value unique differences in the classroom (CASEL, 2015).

In addition, a focus on cultural relevance in SEL instruction can address issues of privilege and discrimination that occur in some settings (Jagers et al., 2018). Some affluent districts and teachers working in them may not feel it is necessary to address culture directly (Jara, 2020), but cultural relevance should be considered in all classrooms and for all learners. Within SEL instruction, teachers must ensure that they are selecting curriculums and unbiased activities and that they are teaching skills appropriate for the cultures and communities in which children live.

SUMMARY

Young children require instruction designed to address their development in all domains, including their SEL. Institutes of higher education must prepare early childhood educators to support children's SEL development through structured and unstructured classroom lessons. Because there is a correlation between experiencing trauma and the need for additional SEL support, teachers must be prepared to use trauma-informed practices in SEL instruction. Finally, SEL instruction is most effective when implemented in collaboration with families and other education stakeholders.

CHAPTER REVIEW

1. Provide a definition for the term *social-emotional learning* and list at least three competencies that fall under SEL skills.
2. Explain why it is important to consider children's ACEs when designing SEL instruction. In what ways are trauma and social-emotional competence correlated?
3. Design and share a step-by-step plan for collaborating with families to provide SEL skills instruction.
4. Using what you have learned about SEL skills instruction, create a lesson plan that you might use to support this learning in your classroom.
5. Ideas for activities that early childhood special educators can use in SEL lessons include:
    a. Using stories to discuss feelings
    b. Making faces to show emotions
    c. Role-playing scenarios of challenging situations
    d. All of the above
6. True or False: When teachers create and follow predictable routines and expectations, this helps young children feel safe in the school setting.
7. What are the four key settings where children gain SEL skills?
    a. Classroom, school, bus, family/caregiver
    b. School, bus, family/caregiver, community
    c. Community, school, classroom, restaurants
    d. Family/caregiver, school, community, classroom
8. A child's sense of security and safety in the classroom can be impacted by their:
    a. Upbringing, relationships, and experiences
    b. Emotions, upbringing, and experiences
    c. Relationships, emotions, and experiences
    d. Emotions, relationships, and upbringing

9. All young children need instruction on how to:
   a. Manage emotions
   b. Meet personal goals
   c. Make decisions
   d. All of the above

10. More than ___ in 10 children have experienced ___ or more ACEs by the time they complete kindergarten.

Resources

- American Institutes for Research: https://www.air.org/topic/education/social-and-emotional-learning
- CASEL: https://casel.org
- Center for Social and Emotional Foundations for Early Learning: http://csefel.vanderbilt.edu
- Center for Social and Emotional Foundations for Early Learning, *What Works Brief*: http://csefel.vanderbilt.edu/resources/wwb/wwb9.html
- Erikson Institute: https://www.erikson.edu/professional-development/sel-initiative/
- Harvard Graduate School of Education Family Engagement and SEL: https://www.gse.harvard.edu/news/uk/18/07/family-engagement-and-sel
- Ho, J., & Funk, S. (2018). Promoting young children's social and emotional health. *Young Children, 73*(1), 73-79. https://www.naeyc.org/resources/pubs/yc/mar2018/promoting-social-and-emotional-health
- IRIS Early Childhood Behavior Management: http://www.iris.peabody.vanderbilt.edu/wp-content/uploads/pdf_case_studies/ics_behaviormgmt.pdf
- National Association for the Education of Young Children Building Environments That Encourage Positive Behavior: https://www.naeyc.org/resources/pubs/yc/mar2016/building-environments-encourage-positive-behavior-preschool#:~:text=Warm%2C%20responsive%20relationships%20build%20a,likelihood%20of%20using%20appropriate%20behavior
- National Center for Healthy Safe Children: https://healthysafechildren.org/topics/1-promoting-early-childhood-social-and-emotional-learning-and-development
- National Center for Pyramid Model Interventions: https://challengingbehavior.cbcs.usf.edu/
- PBS Learning Media: https://rmpbs.pbslearningmedia.org/subjects/preschool/social-and-emotional-development/
- Second Step: https://www.secondstep.org/social-emotional-learning
- Understood.org, What Is Social-Emotional Learning: https://www.understood.org/en/learning-thinking-differences/treatments-approaches/educational-strategies/social-emotional-learning-what-you-need-to-know
- Zero to Three: https://www.zerotothree.org/resources/series/developing-social-emotional-skills

REFERENCES

Archer, A. L., & Hughes, C. A. (2011). *Explicit instruction: Effective and efficient teaching.* The Guilford Press.

Bagnato, S. J., McLean, M., Macy, M., & Neisworth, J. (2011). Identifying instructional targets for early childhood via authentic assessment: Alignment of professional standards and practice-based evidence. *Journal of Early Intervention, 33*(4), 243-253.

Bradshaw, C. P., Koth, C. W., Thornton, L. A., & Leaf, P. J. (2009). Altering school climate through school-wide positive behavioral interventions and supports: Findings from a group-randomized effectiveness trial. *Prevention Science, 10,* 100. https://doi.org/10.1007/s11121-008-0114-9

Center for Early Childhood Mental Health Consultation. (n.d.). *Finding social-emotional curricula.* https://www.ecmhc.org/tools/curricula.html#list

Centers for Disease Control and Prevention. (2022). *What are adverse childhood experiences.* https://www.cdc.gov/violenceprevention/aces/fastfact.html

Collaborative for Academic, Social, and Emotional Learning. (2015). *Sample teaching activities to support core competencies of social and emotional learning.* https://www.casel.org/wp-content/uploads/2017/08/Sample-Teaching-Activities-to-Support-Core-Competencies-8-20-17.pdf

Collaborative for Academic, Social, and Emotional Learning. (2020). *CASEL's SEL framework.* https://casel.org/wp-content/uploads/2020/12/CASEL-SEL-Framework-11.2020.pdf

Collaborative for Academic, Social, and Emotional Learning. (2021). *What is SEL?* https://casel.org/what-is-sel/

Cook A., Spinazzola J., Ford J., Lanktree C., Blaustein M., Cloitre M., DeRosa, R., Hubbard, R., Kagan, R., Liautaud, J., Mallah, K., Olafson, E., & van der Kolk, B. (2005). Complex trauma in children and adolescents. *Psychiatric Annals, 35,* 390-398.

Darling-Hammond, L., & Cook-Harvey, C. M. (2018). *Educating the whole child: Improving school climate to support student success.* Learning Policy Institute.

Daugherty, S., Grisham-Brown, J., & Hemmeter, M. L. (2001). The effects of embedded skill instruction on the acquisition of target and non-target skills in preschoolers with developmental delays. *Topics in Early Childhood Special Education, 21*(4), 213-221.

Denham, S. A., Bassett, H., Mincic, M., Kalb, S., Way, E., Wyatt, T., & Segal, Y. (2012). Social-emotional learning profiles of preschoolers' early school success: A person-centered approach. *Learning and Individual Differences, 22*(2), 178-189. https://doi.org/10.1016/j.lindif.2011.05.001

Division for Early Childhood. (2014). *DEC Recommended Practices in early intervention/early childhood special education 2014.* http://www.decsped.org/recommendedpractices

Friedman, M., & Woods, J. (2015). Coaching teachers to support child communication across daily routines in early head start classrooms. *Infants & Young Children: An Interdisciplinary Journal of Early Childhood Intervention, 28*(4), 308-322.

Hamlin, D. (2020). Can a positive school climate promote student attendance?: Evidence from New York City. *American Educational Research Journal, 58*(2), 315-342. https://doi.org/10.3102%2F0002831220924037

Ho, J., & Funk, S. (2018). Promoting young children's social and emotional health. *Young Children, 73*(1), 73-79.

Horn, E., Lieber, J., Li, S. M., Sandall, S., & Schwartz, I. (2000). Supporting young children's IEP goals in inclusive settings through embedded learning opportunities. *Topics in Early Childhood Special Education, 20,* 208-223.

Horn, E., Lieber, J., Sandall, S., & Schwartz, I. (2001). Embedded learning opportunities as an instructional strategy for supporting children's learning in inclusive programs. In M. Ostrosky & S. Sandall (Eds.), *Teaching strategies: What to do to support young children's development* (DEC Monograph No. 3; pp 59-70). Sopris West Educational Services.

IRIS Center. (2004). *Content standards: Connecting standards-based curriculum to instructional planning.* https://iris.peabody.vanderbilt.edu/module/cnm-5/

Jagers, R. J., Rivas-Drake, D., & Borowski, T. (2018). *Equity & social and emotional learning: A cultural analysis. measuring SEL.* Report from Establishing Practical Social-Emotional Competence Assessment Work Group. https://measuringsel.casel.org/wp-content/uploads/2018/11/Frameworks-Equity.pdf

Jara, S. (2020). *Social and emotional learning & culturally responsive and sustaining teaching & the impact on student experiences* (Doctoral dissertation, California State University).

Jiminez, M. E., Wade, R., Schwartz-Soicher, O., Lin, Y., & Reichman, N. E. (2017). Adverse childhood experiences and ADHD diagnosis at age 9 years in a national urban sample. *Academic Pediatrics, 17*(4), 356-361. https://doi.org/10.1016/j.acap.2016.12.009

Johnson, C. R. B., & Losardo, A., & Botts, D. C., & Coleman, T. J. (2016). Use of parent-mediated activity-based intervention to promote joint attention and enhance social communication in a toddler with autism: An exploratory pilot study. *Journal of Communication Disorders, Deaf Studies, and Hearing Aids, 4*(1), 1-6. https://doi.org/10.4172/2375-4427.1000150

Johnson, J. W., & McDonnell, J. (2004). An exploratory study of the implementation of embedded instruction by general educators with students with developmental disabilities. *Education & Treatment of Children, 27*(1), 46-63.

Jones, S. M., & Kahn, J. (2018). The evidence base for how learning happens: A consensus on social, emotional, and academic development. *American Educator, 41*(4), 16-21, 42-43.

Lopez, P., Torrance, M., Rijlaarsdam, G., & Fidalgo, R. (2017). Effects of direct instruction and strategy modeling on upper-primary students' writing development. *Frontiers in Psychology, 8*, 1054. https://doi.org/10.3389/fpsyg.2017.01054.

Macy, M., & Bricker, D. (2007). Embedding individualized social goals into routine activities in inclusive early childhood classrooms. *Early Child Development and Care, 177*(2), 107-120.

Ng, S. W., & Bull, R. (2018). Facilitating social-emotional learning in kindergarten classrooms: Situational factors and teachers' strategies. *International Journal of Early Childhood, 50*, 335-352. https://doi.org/10.1007/s13158-018-0225-9

Noh, J., Allen, D., & Squires, J. (2009). Use of embedded learning opportunities within daily routines by early intervention/early childhood special education teachers. *International Journal of Special Education, 24*, 1-10.

Pawlo, E., Lorenzo, A., Eichert, B., & Eliaz, M. J. (2019). All SEL should be trauma-informed. *Phi Delta Kappan, 101*(3), 37-41.

Pretti-Frontczak, K. L., Barr, D., Macy, M., & Carter, A. (2003). Research and resources related to activity-based intervention, embedded learning opportunities, and routines-based instruction: An annotated bibliography. *Topics in Early Childhood Special Education, 23*, 29-39.

Pretti-Frontczak, K. L., & Bricker, D. D. (2001). Use of the embedding strategy by early childhood education and early childhood special education teachers. *Infant and Toddler Intervention: The Transdisciplinary Journal, 11*(2), 111-128.

Rajagopal, K. (2011). *Create success: Unlocking the potential of urban students*. ASCD.

Rakap, S., Balikci, S., Kalkan, S., & Aydin, B. (2018). Preschool teachers' use of strategies to support social-emotional competence in young children. *International Journal of Early Childhood Special Education, 10*(1), 11-25.

Roberts, A. L., Gilman, S. E., Breslau, J., Breslau, N., & Koenen, K. C. (2012). Race/ethnic differences in exposure to traumatic events, development of post-traumatic stress disorder, and treatment-seeking for post-traumatic stress disorder in the United States. *Psychological Medicine, 41*(1), 71-83.

Snyder, P. A., Rakap, S., Hemmeter, M. L., McLaughlin, T. W., Sandall, S., & McLean, M. E. (2015). Naturalistic instructional approaches in early learning. *Journal of Early Intervention, 37*(1), 69-97.

Weissberg, R. P. (2019). Promoting the social and emotional learning of millions of school children. *Perspectives on Psychological Science, 14*(1), 65-69. https://doi.org/10.1177%2F1745691618817756

Woods, J., Kashinath, S., & Goldstein, H. (2004). Effects of embedding caregiver-implemented teaching strategies in daily routines on children's communication outcomes. *Journal of Early Intervention, 26*, 175-193.

Wright, C. A., & Kaiser, A. P. (2017). Teaching parents enhanced milieu teaching with words and signs using the teach-model-coach-review model. *Topics in Early Childhood Special Education, 36*(4), 192-204.

Zins, J. E., Bloodworth, M. R., Weissberg, R. P., & Walberg, H. J. (2007). The scientific base linking social and emotional learning to school success. *Journal of Educational and Psychological Consultation, 17*(2&3), 191-210. https://doi.org/10.1080/1047441070141345

Conclusion

Kate E. Zimmer, PhD and Karin M. Fisher, PhD, CDE

Thank you for embarking on this academic journey with us! During this collaborative effort, we met with each author to discuss how this textbook could engage and empower educators. This textbook can be used as a resource to reference often throughout your teaching career. We created a textbook that intertwines the framework of inclusive early childhood practices with research-based strategies. This text is unique because it illustrates evidence-based practices and procedures through captivating vignettes, many of which were based on real-life teaching experiences and events.

The authors were purposeful in promoting the importance of high-leverage practices, evidence-based practice, and culturally sustaining pedagogy throughout the textbook. These components are backed by research and are critical to helping young children learn essential content and become a part of an inclusive environment. In addition, we aligned this work with the Division for Early Childhood Recommended Practices, skills, and competencies because the Division for Early Childhood promotes practices that support families and enhance the development of young children who have or are at risk of developmental delays and/or disabilities.

We believe each chapter brings something new and exciting to the table. Educators are lifelong learners, constantly seeking out information to elevate their teaching. This textbook intends to help pre- and in-service teachers develop, build, and add to their "teaching tool kit"—a set of robust, research-based instructional strategies to enhance student outcomes. Although this textbook is thorough, the reader can easily add engaging techniques for effective teaching to their tool kits.

The authors throughout this book are also committed to being lifelong learners. One of the ways we do this is through joining a professional organization and attending conferences. Thus, we recommend that all educators find an organization to learn, ask questions, and share ideas with other educational professionals who can relate to your everyday realities, triumphs, and challenges. The following are some of our recommendations:

Fisher, K. M., & Zimmer, K. E. (Eds.).
Early Childhood Special Education Programs and Practices (pp. 269-270).
© 2023 SLACK Incorporated.

- Council for Exceptional Children: https://exceptionalchildren.org/
- Division for Early Childhood: https://www.dec-sped.org/
- National Association for the Education of Young Children: https://www.naeyc.org/
- National Head Start Association: https://www.nhsa.org/

We hope that you now have the confidence, knowledge, and skills to begin to incorporate and deliver evidence-based instruction in your classrooms. Embedding these practices throughout your instructional day will increase academic and behavioral outcomes for young children with disabilities.

When teachers create an inclusive and engaging classroom for young children with or without disabilities, research shows it improves the learning outcomes for everyone. It adds diversity and strength to the classroom. Young children learn empathy, friendship, acceptance, and the importance of high expectations. Everyone wins.

Glossary

Abstract Instruction: Instruction that uses verbal explanations and discussions to teach concepts.

Accommodations: Services or supports that allow a student to access the general education curriculum without changing the content or reducing the expectations/requirements.

Accuracy: In reading fluency, accuracy refers to the number of words in a text or passage that are read correctly.

Activity-Based Intervention: A research-based instructional practice often used in early childhood with children who have disabilities, are at risk for developing a disability, or have development that is atypical.

Adverse Childhood Experiences: Traumatic events that occur during childhood.

Anecdotal Observations: A narrative description of an observed event or incident.

Anthropology: The study of cultures and the development of societies.

Applied Behavioral Analysis: A type of therapy that focuses on improving specific behaviors, such as social skills, communication, reading, and academics, as well as adaptive learning skills, such as fine motor dexterity, hygiene, grooming, domestic capabilities, punctuality, and job competence.

Assessment: The initial and ongoing process of gathering information for the purposes of making decisions.

Automaticity: In reading fluency, automaticity refers to the naturalness of reading. When a child has automaticity, the words come easily, accurately, and quickly (rate). The reader is able to easily express the written word orally (expression).

Backward Design: Backward design is a method of designing an educational curriculum by setting goals before choosing instructional methods and forms of assessment.

Behaviorism: The theory or doctrine that human or animal psychology can be accurately studied only through the examination and analysis of objectively observable and quantifiable behavioral events in contrast to subjective mental states.

Fisher, K. M., & Zimmer, K. E. (Eds.).
Early Childhood Special Education Programs and Practices (pp. 271-277).

Blends: A group of consonants whose sounds blend together. Blends can be two or three consonants. Examples include br, cr, and str.

Cardinality: Counting of a set or collection of objects and naming the total number in the set or collection after counting.

Citizenship: The act of participating and becoming members of a community and country. People can have multiple citizenships.

Civic Ideals: An understanding of civic ideals and practices is critical to full participation in society and is an essential component of education for citizenship. This theme enables students to learn about the rights and responsibilities of citizens of a democracy and to appreciate the importance of active citizenship. In schools, these themes typically appear in units or courses dealing with civics; history; political science; cultural anthropology; and fields such as global studies, law-related education, and the humanities.

Civics: The study of the rights and duties of citizenship.

Classical Conditioning: A learning process that occurs when two stimuli are repeatedly paired; a response that is at first elicited by the second stimulus is eventually elicited by the first stimulus alone.

Cognitive Development: Attempts to understand, explain, organize, manipulate, construct, and predict the world around them.

Common Core State Standards: A set of academic standards adopted in most U.S. states that outlines the learning goals in English and mathematics for students at each grade level, from kindergarten through 12th grade, with the objective of teaching the same educational essentials to all students throughout the country.

Computation: A mathematical calculation (i.e., addition and subtraction).

Concrete Instruction: Instruction using physical manipulatives to teach concepts.

Consumers: Consumers are people who buy goods and services to satisfy their wants.

Criterion-Referenced Tool: Criteria or standards are explained for assessors to rate behavior/skills.

Critical Culturally Sustaining/Revitalizing Pedagogy (CSRP): McCarty and Lee (2014) highlighted the importance of maintaining and reviving Native American students' unique traditions, including their language, history, culture, and distinct living styles. This pedagogy is named CSRP.

Culturally Relevant Instruction: A teacher uses students' cultural strengths and experiences to empower and support learning in all developmental domains.

Culturally Relevant Pedagogy (CRP): Ladson-Billings (1995) is the first scholar who systematically explored CRP with a focus on academic success, cultural competence, and sociopolitical consciousness of African American/Black students.

Culturally Relevant Pedagogy 2.0 (CRP 2.0): CRP 2.0 is an update of CRP by Ladson-Billings (2015), who extended the scope and meaning of her initial CRP to remix the latest innovations of current cultural theories, research, and practices.

Culturally Responsive Teaching (CRT): Gay (2000/2002) proposed CRT to include five essential components for preparing teachers who work with culturally and linguistically diverse students: (a) a cultural diversity knowledge base, (b) culturally relevant curricula, (c) cultural caring and a learning community, (d) cross-cultural communications, and (e) multiculturalism and cultural congruity.

Culturally Sustaining Pedagogy (CSP): Paris (2012) emphasized education must help foster and support linguistic, literature, and cultural pluralism of students who have been marginalized by systemic inequalities. He named this approach CSP.

Culture: The customary beliefs, social forms, and material traits of a racial, religious, or social group.

Curriculum-Based Assessment: Creates linkages between program components where assessment and curriculum are aligned.

Curriculum-Based Measurement: An assessment used to directly assess and monitor a student's academic skills.

Data-Based Individualization: A research-based approach to help teachers plan instructional programs that accelerate the growth of students with and without disabilities.

Democracy: A system of government in which rule is by the people, either as a direct democracy in which the people make their own laws or as a representative democracy (i.e., a republic) in which laws are made by the people's representatives.

Developmentally Appropriate Practice: A set of guiding principles for early childhood curriculum, instruction, and assessment.

Dexterity: Skill or adroitness in using the hands or body; agility.

Differentiated Instruction: Occurs when teachers individualize instruction and support for specific students, providing extra help or information, or change the environment in a way that will help the student learn or participate independently.

Differentiation: Differentiation means tailoring instruction to meet individual needs. Whether teachers differentiate content, process, products, or the learning environment, the use of ongoing assessment and flexible grouping makes this a successful approach to instruction.

Digraphs: A pair of consonants or vowels that together make one distinct sound. Examples of consonant digraphs include ch, ck, ph, and wh. Examples of vowel digraphs include ea, ee, and oa.

Diphthongs: Formed when vowels that run together to make one sound. Examples of diphthongs include ai, oi, ou, and ow.

Early Childhood: Early childhood education encompasses all forms of education, both formal and informal, provided to young children up to approximately 8 years of age. This education is fundamental to the development of a child and can significantly shape the later years of an individual's life.

Early Language: The developing skills young children use to communicate, such as gestures, facial expressions, words, and understanding others.

Economics: The careful use of money, resources, and means of production.

Egocentric Speech: The act of a child talking to themselves, usually through an event or activity.

Eligibility: The comprehensive evaluation process once a child is referred for special education to qualify for services under the Individuals with Disabilities Education Act.

Embedded Learning Opportunity: A naturalistic teaching strategy that can be mapped onto the child's natural environment.

Emergent Writing: The ability to listen to a text, interpret the vocabulary, derive sentences using that vocabulary, and be able to discuss the interpretation of the text.

Erogenous Zone: An area of the body that is sensitive to stimulation, such as touch.

Evidence-Based Practices: Instructional strategies backed by research that are often content specific but appropriate for use across multiple grade levels.

Explicit Instruction: A group of evidence-based teaching strategies that collectively support student learning; strategies include modeling and think alouds, supports and prompts that are systematically removed over time, specific feedback on student responses, and opportunities for students to practice the skill.

Expository Text: Includes informational text that provides factual information in a structured format.

Expressive Language: How we communicate our wants and needs including spoken words, gestures, facial expressions, semantics, and syntax.

Facilitate: To make easier; help bring about.

Fidelity: Strict observance of procedure or intervention with adherence to a predetermined, specified process.

Fine Motor Skills: Fine motor skills generally refer to the small movements of the hands, wrists, fingers, feet, toes, lips, and tongue.

Fluency: The ability to read text with ease and accuracy. Fluent readers read text at an appropriate rate with expression and automaticity.

Formative Assessment: Used during a lesson or unit to provide a teacher with information about students' understanding of the instructional concepts and guide future instruction within the lesson or unit (Klute et al., 2017).

Fractions: The parts of something whole such as half a cookie but also connecting to the concept of equal parts or sharing.

Geography: The study of places and humans in relation to their environments.

Global Connections: The realities of global interdependence require an understanding of the increasingly important and diverse global connections among world societies. This theme prepares students to study issues arising from globalization. It typically appears in units or courses dealing with geography, culture, economics, history, political science, government, and technology.

Graphemes: A letter or number that represents a sound (phoneme).

Gross Motor Skills: Physical skills that require whole-body movement and involve core-stabilizing muscles of the body to perform everyday functions.

High-Leverage Practices (HLPs): Grounded in theory and research, the Council for Exceptional Children and the Collaboration for Effective Educator Development, Accountability, and Reform Center compiled 22 effective practices that have been shown to make a positive impact on students with disabilities. Five of the HLPs have a strong focus on working with culturally and linguistically diverse students and their families (McLeskey et al., 2017).

Critical, proven instructional practices that impact student behavior and achievement that teachers can implement across all content areas, grade levels, and students with varying needs.

The fundamentals of teaching. These practices are continuously used and are critical to helping students learn important content. Educators use HLPs across subject areas, grade levels, and contexts.

Homonyms: Two words that are spelled the same, look the same, and sound the same but have different meanings. Examples include (a) bat, which can be a nocturnal animal or something used to hit a baseball; (b) bright, which can mean smart or filled with light; and (c) ring, which can mean jewelry worn on a finger or the sound made for a doorbell or phone.

Homophones: Words that sound the same but have different spellings and meanings. Examples of homophones include (a) bare and bear, (b) mail and male, and (c) tale and tail.

Inappropriate Behavior: Behavior that does not provide adequate or appropriate adjustment to the environment or situation.

Individualized Education Program (IEP): The educational program identifies an individual's strengths and areas of need, specific disability, present levels of performance, accommodations and modifications, assessment considerations, a continuum of service delivery, least restrictive environment, behavior intervention plans, and transition plans (as appropriate). Assessment is an integral part to all aspects of IEP development and implementation.

Interwoven: To intermingle or combine as if by weaving.

Linked System: A systemic approach in which linkages are created across assessment, goals, curriculum and instruction, and evaluation.

Literacy Development: The ongoing development of skills needed to successfully communicate through written communication.

Math Readiness: Attaining a level of general skills in preparation for formalized mathematics instruction (i.e., early counting concepts, shapes, more, less, big, or small).

Measurement: The size of an object based on how big or small it is to an actual recorded number to identify length, width, weight, and so on.

Metacognitive Strategies: Methods used to help students understand the way they learn; in other words, it means processes designed for students to "think" about their "thinking."

Modifications: Adaptations that alter the level of difficulty and/or actual content as a part of specially designed instruction and assessment.

Money: Monetary value given to a number and used to buy goods such as in playing store, identifying coins to be used in a vending machine, and so on.

Narrative Text: Storytelling to relay information including story elements such as setting, characters, conflict, plot, and resolution.

Norm-Referenced Assessment: Provides information about a child's developmental status compared with that of their peers.

Number Place Value: The numerical value that a digit has based on the position it holds (i.e., counting using a 100s chart, skip counting, and a general sense of number value).

Operant Conditioning: A type of associative learning process through which the strength of a behavior is modified by reinforcement or punishment.

Oral Comprehension: The ability to listen to a text, interpret the vocabulary, derive sentences using that vocabulary, and be able to discuss the interpretation of the text.

Patriotism: Loving, honoring, and or/sacrificing for our country.

Phonemic Awareness: Phonemic awareness is a skill in which children are able to hear, identify, and manipulate phonemes (the smallest unit of sound). Children who have phonemic awareness understand the relationship between written words (graphemes) and letter sounds.

Phonics: An instructional approach to reading that emphasizes the relationship between written words and letter sounds. Phonics instruction focuses on systematic principles of written and spoken language. Children are able to apply their knowledge about letter sounds, blends, digraphs, and diphthongs to decode printed words.

Phonological Awareness: The ability to identify, think about, and manipulate sounds in spoken language, such as distinguishing rhyming words or the number of syllables in a word.

Public Law 99-457: Public law passed by the 99th Congress; Individuals with Disabilities Education Act amendment in 1986 to the Education of the Handicapped Act that created special education for infants, toddlers, and their families.

Planned Ignoring: A consequence used to decrease inappropriate behavior whereby the child's targeted behavior is deliberately and intentionally ignored.

Positive Behavior Interventions and Supports: A proactive approach that schools use to improve school safety and promote positive behavior.

Pragmatics: Social communication and how students use language in the context of the speakers (e.g., speaking to adults vs. a baby), intentions (e.g., commands and requests), and rules of discourse (e.g., taking turns in a conversation and using facial expressions).

Preverbal Child: A child who has not yet acquired or demonstrated verbal language.

Pride: Someone feeling happy or satisfied about one's own achievements or the achievements of someone close to them.

Print Awareness: The ability to understand the overall rules and functions of written language.

Problem-Solving: Engaged in a task to find a solution using an approach or alternative approaches that may develop new and deeper understandings.

Producers: Producers are people who combine resources to make goods and services.

Progress Monitoring: Assessment measures administered frequently to provide data over a set period of time on current instruction and intervention. Progress monitoring data provide an indicator of a student's performance in relation to an intervention or instruction. These data help provide feedback on the current intervention, which can be used to adjust various components, such as dosage or rate of reinforcement.

Proprioceptive Sense: Controls the self-awareness of our body's position and degree of movement.

Proximal Development: The distance between the actual developmental level as determined by independent problem-solving and the level of potential development as determined through problem-solving under adult guidance or in collaboration with more capable peers.

Psychoanalytic: A systematic structure of theories concerning the relation of conscious and unconscious psychological processes.

Punishments: A change in a human's or animal's surroundings that, occurring after a given behavior or response, reduces the likelihood of that behavior occurring again in the future.

Rate: Measured in words/minute. Students who are fluent are able to decode words quickly and can read more words accurately in a 1-minute time frame. Fluent readers are also able to read with intonation and proper expression.

Reading Comprehension: The ability to listen to or read text and make meaning of the written words. Children are able to understand the explicit or implied message and relate that information to background knowledge.

Realia: Objects and material from everyday life, especially when used as teaching aids.

Reinforcement: The process of encouraging or establishing a belief or pattern of behavior, especially by encouragement or reward.

Representational Thinking: The ability to represent objects in one's thoughts with symbols such as words.

Reward: An appetitive stimulus given to a human or some other animal to alter its behavior.

Scaffolding Instruction: A process through which a teacher adds support for students in order to enhance learning and aid in the mastery of tasks.

Schedule of Reinforcement: A predetermined schedule of reinforcement with a set duration or a number of correct responses occurring between reinforcement.

School Readiness: School readiness is foundational across early childhood systems and programs. It means children are ready for school, families are ready to support their children's learning, and schools are ready for children.

Sciencing: Sciencing is the act of doing science or SCIENCE! or even using scientific instruments for nonscientific (or non-SCIENCE!ific) purposes.

Screening Assessment: A process of gathering information to identify children when there might be concerns about development.

Self-Identity: An individual's ability to recognize one's own personal traits such as body image, voice, physical characteristics, and likes and dislikes in relation to others around them.

Self-Regulation: The ability to manage one's emotions and behaviors.

Semantics: How one understands the meaning and relationships of words and combinations of words. Examples of semantic relationships include categories (e.g., apples and crackers are both types of food), antonyms, and synonyms.

Semiconcrete Instruction: Instruction that uses illustrations and diagrams to teach concepts, also known as *representation*.

Shapes: The outside form of an object, both geometric (circle, square, triangle, etc.) and nongeometric, such as seasonal objects (apples, pumpkins, snowflakes, etc.) and their descriptors (round, flat, corners, etc.).

Sight Words: High-frequency words that typically cannot be sounded out using phonics rules and are words teachers have children commit to memory using various strategies, including flash cards, multisensory approaches, picture-supported methods, computer-based learning methods, and constant rehearsal (Phillips & Feng, 2012). Two comprehensive sight word lists were developed by Dolch (1936) and Fry (1957).

SMART (Specific, Measurable, Action oriented, Relevant and realistic, and Time limited) Individualized Education Program (IEP) Goals: SMART IEP goals that specifically state what is expected of the student so that all stakeholders have the same understanding of necessary instruction and know what skills to target for instruction and assessment.

Social-Emotional Learning: The ability to understand emotions of self and others, regulating and expressing emotions, having a positive self-concept, setting appropriate personal goals, making good decisions, and establishing appropriate relationships with peers and adults.

Social Learning Theory: Explains human behavior in terms of continuous reciprocal interaction between cognitive, behavioral, and environmental influences.

Social Studies: The integrated study of the social sciences and humanities to promote civic competence. Within the school program, social studies provides coordinated, systematic study drawing on such disciplines as anthropology, archaeology, economics, geography, history, law, philosophy, political science, psychology, religion, and sociology, as well as appropriate content from the humanities, mathematics, and natural sciences.

Socialization: A growing awareness of social norms and customs.

Sociocultural Theory: Ties different language frameworks together by allowing the students to learn via their social interactions.

Socioemotional: A psychological theory that human personality is developed through a repeating series of crises and resolutions.

Standardized Assessment: This assessment follows standard administration procedures for all children using the same sequence, testing and scoring methods, and materials.

Stimuli: Any object or event that elicits a sensory or behavioral response in an organism.

Subitizing: When a child sees a set amount and "just knows" the number value of the set.

Summative Assessment: This is given at the conclusion of the lesson or unit and provides data that can be delivered to educational stakeholders and inform educators of class-wide learning.

Syntax: The grammatical rules that decide how words are combined and ordered into phrases and sentences. Syntax deficits may manifest in difficulties with word order, verb tense, possessives, and plurals.

Theory: Informs our understanding about how children develop.

Theory of Mind: The ability to distinguish between their point of view and the point of view of others.

Tiered Instruction: A method that varies the level of assignments so all students have a chance to find success and make progress.

Time: A point of time as measured in days, hours, and minutes but also as a concept that an event is coming such as Thanksgiving, birthdays, and so on.

Universal Design for Learning: A systematic framework for supporting the learning needs of all children in the classroom through the use of multiple means of (a) engagement, (b) representation, and (c) action and expression.

Vestibular Sense: Our sense of balance.

Vocabulary: The words children understand and are able to use in listening, speaking, reading, and writing. Vocabulary is acquired through receptive means, and as children listen, comprehend, and respond to vocabulary, they respond through action or expressive language.

FINANCIAL DISCLOSURES

Dr. Zachary T. Barnes has no financial or proprietary interest in the materials presented herein.

Dr. Gliset Colón has no financial or proprietary interest in the materials presented herein.

Dr. Stacy Delacruz has no financial or proprietary interest in the materials presented herein.

Dr. Kathy Ralabate Doody has no financial or proprietary interest in the materials presented herein.

Dr. Melissa K. Driver has no financial or proprietary interest in the materials presented herein.

Dr. Lisa A. Finnegan has no financial or proprietary interest in the materials presented herein.

Dr. Karin M. Fisher has no financial or proprietary interest in the materials presented herein.

Dr. Ariane N. Gauvreau has no financial or proprietary interest in the materials presented herein.

Dr. Kania A. Greer has no financial or proprietary interest in the materials presented herein.

Dr. Katrina A. Hovey has no financial or proprietary interest in the materials presented herein.

Christie H. Ingram has no financial or proprietary interest in the materials presented herein.

Dr. Raynice Jean-Sigur has no financial or proprietary interest in the materials presented herein.

Dr. Nai-Cheng Kuo has no financial or proprietary interest in the materials presented herein.

Dr. Marla J. Lohmann has no financial or proprietary interest in the materials presented herein.

Dr. Marisa Macy has no financial or proprietary interest in the materials presented herein.

Dr. Sherri K. Prosser has no financial or proprietary interest in the materials presented herein.

Dr. Dena D. Slanda has no financial or proprietary interest in the materials presented herein.

Dr. Kate E. Zimmer has no financial or proprietary interest in the materials presented herein.

INDEX

abstract instruction, **180**

accommodations, **42, 271**

accuracy, **271**

accuracy in reading, **140**

activity-based intervention, **271**

activity-based writing intervention, **162**, 173

adverse childhood experiences, **271**

alternative communication, 128

anecdotal observations, **70, 271**

anthropology, **234, 271**

applied behavioral analysis, **2, 271**

appropriate text, selecting, 146

assessing mathematical knowledge/thinking,
    194-195

assessment, **271**

assessment of reading components, 152

assessment of writing, **162**

assessments, 41-68

    accommodations, **42**

    case study, 43-44

    collaboration, 45-54

    cultural considerations, 44-45

    curriculum-based measurement, **42**

    data-based individualization, **42**, 62-63

    eligibility, **42**

    formative assessment, **42**

    guidelines, 54-62

    individualized education program (IEP), **42**

    to inform instruction, 59-62

    linguistic considerations, 44-45

    modifications, **42**

    norm-referenced assessment, **42**

    progress monitoring, **42**, 62-63

    purpose of, 44

    special education eligibility, 47-54

    standardized assessment, **42**

    summative assessment, **42**

assistive technology, 128

audible laboratory equipment, 228

augmentative communication, 128

automaticity, **271**

automaticity in reading, **140**

backward design, **208, 271**

behavior, as form of communication, 79-80

behavior/instructional strategies, function of

    MEATS acronym, 78-79

    sensory inputs, 79

behavioral analysis, **2**

behavioral expectations, 73-74

behavioral supports, 69-98

behaviorism, **2**, 4-6, **271**

    theory of child development, 4-6

blends, **272**

blends in reading, **140**

calculations, 228

cardinality in mathematics, **180, 272**

citizenship, **234, 272**

civic ideals, **234, 272**

civic ideas, practices, 252-253

civics, **234, 272**

classical conditioning, **2, 272**

cognitive development, **2, 272**

cognitive development theory, 6-7

    child development, 6-7

cognitive knowledge, developmental domain,
    11-14

collaboration, 45-54

collaborative approach, 155-156

common core state standards, **100, 272**

communication, behavior as form of, 79-80

components of reading instruction, 146-152

    assessment of reading components, 152

    fluency, 149

    phonemic awareness, 147

    phonics, 147-148

    reading components are interdependent, 152

    reading comprehension, 150-152

    vocabulary, 149-150

comprehensive approach, model of reading in-
    struction, 155

computation, **180, 272**

conceptual domain, **272**

concrete instruction, **180, 272**

consequences, teaching replacement behaviors,
    82-83

construction, 251
consumers, **234, 272**
core state standards, **100**
criterion, **272**
criterion-referenced tool, **272**
critical culturally sustaining/revitalizing pedagogy, **24**, 26-27, **272**
cultural considerations, 44-45
cultural relevance, 264-265
    behavior management, 74-76
cultural sensitivity, 29-30
    assessment high-leverage practices, 30
    collaboration high-leverage practices, 30
    instruction high-leverage practices, 30
    social/emotional/behavioral high-leverage practices, 30
culturally relevant instruction, **272**
culturally relevant pedagogy, 23-40
    case studies, 24-25
    critical culturally sustaining/revitalizing pedagogy, **24**, 26-27
    cultural sensitivity, 29-30
        assessment high-leverage practices, 30
        collaboration high-leverage practices, 30
        instruction high-leverage practices, 30
        social/emotional/behavioral high-leverage practices, 30
    culturally relevant pedagogy, 25
        high-leverage practices, alignment of, 29-34
    culturally relevant pedagogy 2.0, **24**, 27
    culturally relevant pedagogy, **24**
    culturally responsive teaching, **24**, 26
    culturally sustaining pedagogy, **24**, 26
    expectations, sustaining, 32-33
        assessment high-leverage practices, 32
        collaboration high-leverage practices, 32
        instruction high-leverage practices, 33
    framework, 34-35
    high-leverage practices, **24**, 27-29
        alignment of, 29-34
    inclusive setting, 33-34
        assessment high-leverage practices, 33-34
        collaboration high-leverage practices, 33-34
        instruction high-leverage practices, 34
        social/emotional/behavioral high-leverage practices, 33-34
    respect, demonstrating, 31-32
        assessment high-leverage practices, 31
        collaboration high-leverage practices, 31
        instruction high-leverage practices, 32
        social/emotional/behavioral high-leverage practices, 32

trust, establishing, 30-31
    instruction high-leverage practices, 31
    social/emotional/behavioral high-leverage practices, 31
culturally relevant pedagogy 2.0, **24**, 27, **272**
culturally relevant pedagogy, **24**, **272**
culturally responsive teaching, **24**, 26, **272**
culturally sustaining pedagogy, **24**, 26, **272**
culture, **234**, 238, **272**
curriculum-based assessment, **273**
curriculum-based measurement, **42, 273**
curriculum-based measurement/assessment, 166-168

data-based individualization, **42**, 62-63, **273**
data collection, monitoring student progress through, 84-85
debrief, 214
delays/disorders, 125
delays/disorders in language development, 125
democracy, **234, 273**
development, early childhood, 1-22
    applied behavioral analysis, **2**
    behaviorism, **2**
    classical conditioning, **2**
    cognitive development, **2**
    developmental domains, 8-18
        cognitive knowledge, 11-14
        general knowledge, 11-14
        language, 9-11
        learning approaches, 14-17
        literacy, 9-11
        mathematics skills, 11-13
        motor development, 17-18
        physical well-being, 17-18
        scientific skills, 13-14
        socioemotional, 18
    dexterity, **2**
    egocentric speech, **2**
    emergent writing, **2**
    erogenous zone, **2**
    fine motor skills, **2**
    gross motor skills, **2**
    literacy development, **2**
    metacognitive strategies, **2**
    operant conditioning, **2**
    oral comprehension, **2**
    positive behavior interventions and supports, **2**
    print awareness, **2**
    proximal development, **2**
    psychoanalytic, **2**
    punishments, **2**
    reinforcement, **3**

representational thinking, **3**
reward, **3**
scaffolding instruction, **3**
school readiness, **3**
social learning theory, **3**
socioemotional, **3**
special education, 18-19
stimuli, **3**
theories of child development, 3-8
   behaviorism, 4-6
   cognitive development theory, 6-7
   psychoanalytic theory, 3-4
   psychosocial development theory, 4
   social learning theory, 7-8
   sociocultural theory, 8
theory of mind, **3**
developmental domains, 8-18
   cognitive knowledge, 11-14
   general knowledge, 11-14
   language, 9-11
   learning approaches, 14-17
   literacy, 9-11
   mathematics skills, 11-13
   motor development, 17-18
   physical well-being, 17-18
   scientific skills, 13-14
   socioemotional, 18
developmentally appropriate practice, 170-172,
   273
   environment, 172
   individual, age, 172
dexterity, **2, 273**
differentiated instruction, **100**, 101, 242-246, **273**
differentiation, **208, 273**
digital learning, 174
digraphs, **273**
diphthongs, **140, 273**
disabilities, students with, teaching mathematics
   to, 199-200
discrete trial training, 82-83
displaying data in multiple formats, 228
division for early childhood recommended practices, 119

5E mathematics model, stages of, 215-218
   elaboration, 217
   engagement (high-leverage practices 13, 15,
      and 18), 215-216
   evaluation, 217-218
   explanation, 216-217
   exploration, 216
5E model, 215-218
early childhood, **208, 273**

early childhood development. *See* development,
   early childhood
early language, **118, 273**
   defining, 122
early language promotion, in childhood special
   education, 127-128
economic understanding, 242
economics, **234, 273**
egocentric speech, **2, 273**
eligibility, **42, 273**
embedded learning opportunity, **273**
emergent literacy, defining, 125-127
emergent reading in early childhood years, 142
emergent writing, **2**, 161-178, **273**
   activity-based intervention, **162**
   assessment, **162**
   case study, 164
   criterion-referenced tool, **162**
   curriculum-based assessment, **162**
   developmentally appropriate practice, **162**
      social/cultural appropriateness, 172
   emergent writing, defining, 164
   linked system, **162**
   linked system for emergent writing, 164-165
   norm-referenced assessment, **162**
   Public Law 99-457, **162**
   screening assessment, **162**
   theory, **162**
environment, 239-242
erogenous zone, **2, 273**
evidence-based practices, **118, 273**
   to promote communication, 131-132
      explicit instruction, 132
expectations, sustaining, 32-33
   assessment high-leverage practices, 32
   collaboration high-leverage practices, 32
   instruction high-leverage practices, 33
explicit instruction, **100**, 108-110, **273**
expository text, **140, 273**
expressive language, **118, 273**
expressive/receptive language, 124
   pragmatics, and syntax, 124
   semantics, pragmatics, and syntax, 124
   syntax, 124

facilitate, **208, 273**
families, collaboration with, 262-264
family involvement, 88
fidelity, **70, 274**
fidelity of implementation, 132-133
fine motor skills, **2, 274**
fluency, **140**, 149, **274**
formal mathematics assessment, 194
formative assessment, **42, 274**

fractions, **180, 274**
framework, 34-35
function of behavior/instructional strategies, 77-79

games, 229
general knowledge, developmental domain, 11-14
generative knowledge, **274**
geographic understanding, 240-241
geography, **234, 274**
global connections, **234**, 252, **274**
government/civic understanding, 241
graphemes, **140, 274**
gross motor skills, **2, 274**
guidelines, 54-62

high-leverage and division for early childhood practices, 210-211
high-leverage practices, **24**, 27-29, **118**, 119-121, 143, **208, 274**
historical understanding, 239-240
homonyms, **140, 274**
homophones, **140, 274**

inappropriate behavior, **70, 274**
inclusive setting, 33-34
    assessment high-leverage practices, 33-34
    collaboration high-leverage practices, 33-34
    instruction high-leverage practices, 34
    social/emotional/behavioral high-leverage practices, 33-34
individual development, identity, 250-251
individualization, data-based, 62-63
individualized education program (IEP), **42, 274**
informal mathematics assessment, 195
institutions, 251
instruction high-leverage practices, 31
instruction of mathematics, 195-199
instructional approaches, 249-250
intervention supports, 73
interwoven, **70, 274**
involvement of family, 88

key skills in, 130-131
    listening, 130
    speaking, 130-131
kindergarten as example, 220

language, developmental domain, 9-11
language development, 117-138
    alternative communication, 128
    assistive technology, 128
    augmentative communication, 128
    case study, 118-119
    considerations for practice, 129
    delays/disorders, 125
    division for early childhood recommended practices, 119
    early language, **118**
        defining, 122
    early language promotion, in childhood special education, 127-128
    emergent literacy, defining, 125-127
    evidence-based practices, **118**
        to promote communication, 131-132
            explicit instruction, 132
    expressive language, **118**
    expressive/receptive language, 124
        pragmatics, and syntax, 124
        semantics, pragmatics, and syntax, 124
        syntax, 124
    fidelity of implementation, 132-133
    high-leverage practices, **118**, 119-121
    key skills in, 130-131
        listening, 130
        speaking, 130-131
    linguistic diversity, 125
    monitoring progress, 133
    phonological awareness, **118**
    pragmatics, **118**
    progress monitoring, 133
    semantics, **118**
    stages of language acquisition/oral language development, 122-123
    student engagement, measuring, 129-133
    syntax, **118**
    typical/atypical language development, 122
learning approaches, developmental domains, 14-17
learning theories, 142-143
lesson planning, 221-226
    discovery-based 5E lesson plan, 224-226
    Hunter lesson plan, 221
    standards-based, 105-108
    teaching for knowledge, 221-224
linguistic considerations, 44-45
linguistic considerations in assessments, 44-45
linguistic diversity, 125
linked system, **274**
literacy, developmental domain, 9-11
literacy development, **2, 274**
literacy knowledge, 143

making connections, 228-229
maladaptive, **274**
math readiness, **180, 274**

mathematics, 179-206, **180**
    abstract instruction, **180**
    assessing mathematical knowledge/thinking, 194-195
    cardinality, **180**
    case studies, 180-182
    computation, **180**
    concrete instruction, **180**
    5E model, stages of, 215-218
        elaboration, 217
        engagement (high-leverage practices 13, 15, and 18), 215-216
        evaluation, 217-218
        explanation, 216-217
        exploration, 216
    formal mathematics assessment, 194
    fractions, **180**
    informal mathematics assessment, 195
    lesson planning
        discovery-based 5E lesson plan, 224-226
        Hunter lesson plan, 221
        teaching for knowledge, 221-224
    math readiness, **180**
    mathematics instruction, 195-199
    measurement, **180**
    money, **180**
    next generation science standards
        crosscutting concepts, 219
        disciplinary core ideas, 220
        science and engineering practices, 220
    number place value, **180**
    position statements, 182-194
    problem-solving, **180**
    promoting love of learning mathematics, 200-201
    semiconcrete instruction, **180**
    shapes, **180**
    students with disabilities, 199-200
    subitizing, **180**
    time, **180**
mathematics instruction, 195-199
mathematics skills, developmental domain, 11-13
measurement, **180, 274**
MEATS acronym, function of behavior/instructional strategies, 78-79
meeting learning needs, 247
metacognitive strategies, **2, 275**
modeling, 83-84
models of instruction in early childhood science, 211-218
models of reading instruction, 152-155
    comprehensive approach, 155
    part-to-whole approach, 154
    whole-part-whole language approach, 154-155

modifications, **42, 275**
money, **180, 275**
monitoring progress, 62-63, 133
motor development, developmental domain, 17-18

narrative text, **140, 275**
next generation science standards, 219-220
    crosscutting concepts, 219
    disciplinary core ideas, 220
    science and engineering practices, 220
norm-referenced assessment, **42,** 166, **275**
number place value, **180, 275**

operant conditioning, **2, 275**
oral comprehension, **2, 275**

part-to-whole approach, model of reading instruction, 154
patriotism, **234, 275**
phonemic awareness, **140,** 147, **275**
phonics, **141,** 147-148, **275**
phonological awareness, 118, 275
physical well-being developmental domain, 17-18
planned embedded learning opportunities, 264
planned ignoring, 70, 81-82, 275
planning, 248
planning for science with young children, 218-226
play, 213-214
play-debrief-replay, 211-215
position statements, teaching mathematics, 182-194
positive behavior intervention and supports, **2,** 73, **275**
positive behavioral supports, 69-98, **70,** 74
    anecdotal observations, **70**
    behavioral expectations, 73-74
    case study 1, 70-71
    case study 2, 71-72
    communication, behavior as form of, 79-80
    consequences, teaching replacement behaviors, 82-83
    cultural relevance, behavior management, 74-76
    data collection, monitoring student progress through, 84-85
    discrete trial training, 82-83
    family involvement, 88
    fidelity, **70**
    function of behavior/instructional strategies, 77-79
        MEATS acronym to formulate hypothesis, 78-79
        sensory inputs, 79

inappropriate behavior, **70**
interwoven, **70**
modeling, 83-84
planned ignoring, **70**, 81-82
positive behavior intervention and supports, 73
preverbal child, **70**
proprioceptive sense, 70
punishing consequences, 81-82
reinforcing consequences, 80-81
schedule of reinforcement, **70**
social-emotional learning, 85-88
socially appropriate replacement behaviors, 83
    cautions, 83
sociocultural theory, **70**, 77
theories of behavior, 77
vestibular sense, **70**
pragmatics, **118, 275**
    and syntax, expressive/receptive language, 124
prekindergarten to second-grade social studies development, 235-238
preplanning strategies, 247-248
preverbal, **275**
preverbal child, **70, 275**
pride, **234, 275**
print awareness, **2, 275**
print-rich environments, 143-146
problem-solving, **180, 275**
procedural knowledge, **275**
producers, **234, 275**
progress monitoring, **42**, 62-63, 133, **275**
promoting emergent writing, 168-170
promoting love of learning mathematics, 200-201
proprioceptive sense, **70, 276**
proximal development, **2, 276**
psychoanalytic, **2, 276**
psychoanalytic theory, 3-4
    child development, 3-4
psychoanalytic theory of child development, 3-4
psychosocial development theory, 4
    child development, 4
punishing consequences, 81-82
punishments, **2, 276**

rate of reading, **141**
reading, 139-160, **140**
    accuracy, 140
    appropriate text, selecting, 146
    automaticity, 140
    background knowledge, 145-146
    blends, 140
    case study, 141
    collaborative approach, 155-156

components of reading instruction, 146-152
    assessment of reading components, 152
    fluency, 149
    phonemic awareness, 147
    phonics, 147-148
    reading components are interdependent, 152
    reading comprehension, 150-152
    vocabulary, 149-150
digraphs, **140**
diphthongs, **140**
emergent reading in early childhood years, 142
expository text, **140**
fluency, **140**
graphemes, **140**
high-leverage practices, 143
homonyms, **140**
homophones, **140**
learning theories, 142-143
literacy knowledge, 143
models of reading instruction, 152-155
    comprehensive approach, 155
    part-to-whole approach, 154
    whole-part-whole language approach, 154-155
narrative text, **140**
phonemic awareness, **140**
phonics, **141**
print-rich environments, 143-146
rate, **141**
reading comprehension, **141**
sight words, **141**
vocabulary, **141**
reading components are interdependent, 152
reading comprehension, **141**, 150-152, **276**
reading next generation science standards, 220
realia, **234, 276**
reinforcement, **3, 276**
reinforcing consequences, 80-81
replacement behaviors, socially appropriate, 83
    cautions, 83
replay, 215
representational thinking, **3, 276**
respect, demonstrating, 31-32
    assessment high-leverage practices, 31
    collaboration high-leverage practices, 31
    instruction high-leverage practices, 32
    social/emotional/behavioral high-leverage practices, 32
reward, **3, 276**
routine embedded learning opportunities, 264

scaffolding instruction, **3, 276**
schedule of reinforcement, **70, 276**
school readiness, **3, 276**
science, teaching to students with disabilities,
     207-232
science literacy, 226-228
sciencing, **208, 276**
scientific skill developmental domain, 13-14
screening, 166
screening assessment, **276**
self-identity, **234, 276**
self-regulation, **234, 276**
semantics, **118, 276**
     pragmatics, and syntax, expressive/receptive
          language, 124
semiconcrete instruction, **180, 276**
seminal learning theory, **276**
sensory inputs, 79
shapes, **180, 276**
sight words, **141, 276**
SMART individualized education program goals/
     objectives, 111
SMART (specific, measurable, action oriented,
     relevant and realistic and time limited) indi-
     vidualized education program (IEP), **277**
     goals, **100**
social/emotional/behavioral high-leverage prac-
     tices, 31
social-emotional learning, 85-88, 257-268, **258,**
     269-270, **277**
     adverse childhood experiences, **258**
     case study, 258-259
     cultural relevance, 264-265
     culturally relevant instruction, **258**
     embedded learning opportunity, **258**
     families, collaboration with, 262-264
     planned embedded learning opportunities,
          264
     routine embedded learning opportunities,
          264
     social-emotional learning, **258**
     teaching, 260-262
     trauma, 259-260
social learning theory, **3,** 7-8, **277**
social learning theory of child development, 7-8
social studies, **234, 277**
     anthropology, **234**
     case study, 235
     citizenship, **234**
     civic ideals, **234**
     civic ideas, practices, 252-253
     civics, **234**
     construction, 251
consumers, **234**
culture, **234,** 238
democracy, **234**
differentiated instruction, 242-246
economic understanding, 242
economics, **234**
environment, 239-242
geographic understanding, 240-241
geography, **234**
global connections, **234,** 252
government/civic understanding, 241
historical understanding, 239-240
individual development, identity, 250-251
institutions, 251
instructional approaches, 249-250
meeting learning needs, 247
patriotism, **234**
planning, 248
prekindergarten to second-grade social stud-
     ies development, 235-238
preplanning strategies, 247-248
pride, **234**
producers, **234**
realia, **234**
recommendations, 242
self-identity, **234**
self-regulation, **234**
social studies, **234**
socialization, **234**
society, 252
tiered instruction, **234**
time, 238-239
socialization, **234, 277**
socially appropriate replacement behaviors, 83
     cautions, 83
society, 252
sociocultural theory, 8, **70,** 77, **277**
sociocultural theory of child development, 8
socioemotional, **3, 277**
socioemotional developmental domain, 18
special education, 18-19
special education eligibility, 47-54
stages of language acquisition/oral language devel-
     opment, 122-123
standardized assessment, **42, 277**
standards, 219-220
standards-based lesson planning, 105-108
state standards, **100**
staying on track, 229
stimuli, **3, 277**
struggles with writing, 173-174
student engagement, measuring, 129-133
students with disabilities, 199-200

specially designed instruction for, 226-230
teaching of, 199-200
subitizing, **180, 277**
success, planning for, 99-116
summative assessment, **42, 277**
syntax, **118, 277**
expressive/receptive language, 124

theories of behavior, 77
theories of child development, 3-8
behaviorism, 4-6
cognitive development theory, 6-7
psychoanalytic theory, 3-4
psychosocial development theory, 4
social learning theory, 7-8
sociocultural theory, 8
theory, **277**
theory of mind, **3, 277**
tiered instruction, **234**
time, **180**, 238-239, **277**
trauma, 259-260
trust, establishing, 30-31
instruction high-leverage practices, 31
social/emotional/behavioral high-leverage
practices, 31
typical/atypical language development, 122

Universal Design for Learning, **100**, 101-105, **277**

vestibular sense, **70, 277**
virtual field trips, 229

virtual labs, 229
vocabulary, **141**, 149-150, **277**

WebQuests, 229-230
whole-part-whole language approach, model of
reading instruction, 154-155
writing, 161-178, **162**, 165-168, 173
activity-based intervention, **162**, 173
assessment, **162**
case study, 164
criterion-referenced tool, **162**
curriculum-based assessment, **162**
curriculum-based measurement/assessment,
166-168
developmentally appropriate practice, **162**,
170-172
environment, 172
individual, age, 172
digital learning, 174
emergent writing, defining, 164
linked system, **162**
linked system for emergent writing, 164-165
norm-referenced assessment, **162**, 166
promoting emergent writing, 168-170
Public Law 99-457, **162**
screening, 166
screening assessment, **162**
struggles with, 173-174
theory, **162**
writing SMART individualized education program, 230

CPSIA information can be obtained
at www.ICGtesting.com
Printed in the USA
JSHW030806190822
29504JS00004B/8

9 781630 917029